The Legislative Process in Canada

The Need For Reform

edited by
William A.W. Neilson
and
James C. MacPherson

Proceedings of a Conference held
at the University of Victoria
and sponsored by the
Institute for Research on Public Policy
and the
Faculty of Law, University of Victoria
March 31-April 1, 1978

Institute for Research on Public Policy/Institut de recherches politiques

Distributed by
Butterworth & Co. (Canada) Ltd.
Toronto

ISBN 0 920380 11 5

Legal Deposit Fourth Quarter
Bibliothèque nationale du Québec

Institute for Research on Public Policy/Institut de recherches politiques
3535, chemin Queen Mary, Bureau 514
Montréal, Québec H3V 1H8

Typesetting by Tri-Graphic Printing (Ottawa) Ltd.

Preface

All good conferences are memorable; and because this was an exceptional conference, it provided many extraordinary moments including: Robert Stanfield's impassioned argument that in trying to do everything for everybody, government has become so over-burdened that our parliamentary system is failing, and indeed may not be salvable, because it is no longer possible for our system of government to be both efficient and parliamentary; Arthur Tremblay's poignant plea that there must be a public ground swell for constitutional reform so that the people of Quebec will have a real 'third option' between the 'status quo' and 'souveraineté association' when they go to polls in the Quebec referendum; and the late John MacKintosh, ebullient, optimistic and humorous, who refused to accept the thesis that parliamentary government was doomed and unmanageable and whose summation was the highlight of the conference as he suggested ways in which parliamentary government could be made to work.

But, as the papers in this monograph attest, the conference was much more; and as such, these papers are recommended for study to anyone concerned about the future of parliamentary government. I am confident that those who read them will find them both evocative and instructive.

It is important to note also that this is the first of four monographs on the governmental process which will be published by the Institute during the next two years. Each will be the product of a conference. The subjects to be debated and the location of each conference are:

— *The Legislative Process* (with the Faculty of Law) University of Victoria. March 31 — April 1, 1978;

— *Methods and Forums for the Public Evaluation of Government Spending* (with the School of Public Administration) Carleton University. October 19-21, 1978;

— *Methods for Citizen Input into Public Policy Making* (with the Government Studies Program) Dalhousie University. April 4-6, 1979;

— *La décentralisation aura-t-elle lieu?* (with the Policy Analysis Program) Laval University. October 4-6, 1979.

Michael J.L. Kirby
President
November 1978

Préface

Toute conférence de qualité est marquante, et celle-ci ayant été exceptionnelle, nous y avons vécu des moments passionnants. Robert Stanfield, par exemple, a soutenu avec ferveur la thèse selon laquelle à tenter de tout faire pour tous, le gouvernement se retrouve tellement surchargé que notre système parlementaire est agonisant et peut-être irrécupérable: notre appareil gouvernemental est désormais incapable de fonctionner de manière et efficace, et parlementaire. Arthur Tremblay, à son tour, a souligné avec conviction la nécessité d'un mouvement collectif en faveur de la réforme constitutionnelle, de façon que s'offre à la population du Québec une "troisième voie" valable, entre le "statu quo" et la "souveraineté-association", lorsqu'elle votera au moment du référendum. Signalons enfin feu John Mackintosh, enthousiaste, optimiste et plein de verve, qui, rejetant la thèse qui veut que le gouvernement parlementaire soit condamné et ingouvernable, a suggéré, en conclusion, des façons de le remettre sur pied, intervention qui fut le point saillant de la conférence.

Cependant, comme en témoignent les divers articles de cette monographie, la conférence recèle bien davantage; et c'est pourquoi nous recommandons la lecture de ces articles à quiconque s'intéresse à l'avenir du gouvernement parlementaire. Je crois fermement que ceux qui les liront les jugeront évocateurs autant qu'enrichissants.

Il est important de noter, en outre, que cet ouvrage est la première de quatre monographies qui traiteront du processus gouvernemental et seront publiées par l'Institut au cours des deux prochaines années. Chacune de ces monographies sera le bilan d'une conférence. Voici donc les sujets de discussion et les endroits où se dérouleront ces conférences.

- *Le processus législatif,* avec la Faculté de Droit de l'Université de Victoria, du 31 mars au 1er avril 1978;
- *Méthodes et tribunes appropriées à l'évaluation collective des dépenses publiques,* avec l'École d'administration publique de l'université Carleton, du 19 au 21 octobre 1978;
- *Modes d'intervention du citoyen dans l'élaboration des politiques,* avec le *Government Studies Program* de l'université Dalhousie, du 4 au 6 avril 1979;
- *La décentralisation aura-t-elle lieu?,* avec le Programme d'analyse des politiques de l'université Laval, du 4 au 6 octobre 1979.

Michael J.L. Kirby
Président
Novembre 1978

Table of Contents

NOTES ON CONTRIBUTORS

Catherine BERGMAN
National radio correspondent for Société Radio-Canada, Ottawa, since 1977; similar position for CBC International Services, Ottawa, 1975-77; Head, CBC Newsroom (French), Vancouver, 1971-75.

Ronald M. BURNS
Chairman, Advisory Committee to the B.C. Cabinet Committee on Confederation, 1977- ; Director, Executive Development Training Programme, University of Victoria, 1976- ; Director, Institute of Intergovernmental Relations and Professor of Political Studies, Queen's University, 1965-75; Deputy Provincial Treasurer, Secretary of Treasury Board and Chairman, Manitoba Housing Commission, Province of Manitoba, 1959-65; Director, Federal-Provincial Relations Division, Department of Finance, Ottawa, 1954-59; Assistant Deputy Minister of Finance, British Columbia, 1946-54.

William H.R. CHARLES
Professor, Faculty of Law, Dalhousie University, Halifax, N.S., since 1969 and a member of the Faculty since 1960; Visiting Professor, University of Victoria, 1975-76; Member, Nova Scotia Law Reform Advisory Commission; Past Member of Uniform Law Conference of Canada; Member, Advisory Academic Panel, Canada Council, 1974-78.

Ronald I. CHEFFINS
Professor, Faculty of Law, University of Victoria, since 1974; Professor and first Chairman of the Department of Political Science, University of Victoria, 1965-73; member of the Faculty of Law, McGill University, 1957-65; author of *The Constitutional Process in Canada* and a number of journal articles on constitutional law.

Johanna den HERTOG
Director of Research and Legislation, British Columbia Federation of Labour 1977- ; Ombudswoman, Vancouver Status of Women, 1975-76; initial organizer and director, Rape Relief, Vancouver, 1973-75.

Richard F. DOLE, Jr.
Professor, Bates College of Law, University of Houston; formerly Professor of Law, University of Iowa; Member, National Conference of Commissioners on Uniform State Laws; author of a number of journal articles and monographs, particularly on the development and improvement of model state legislation.

C.E.S. FRANKS
Professor, Department of Political Studies, Queen's University, Kingston, Ontario, and a member of the Department since 1967; Founding Chairman, Canadian Study of Parliament Group; prior to 1967, Clerk Assistant of the Legislative Assembly of Saskatchewan; extensive writings on Canadian government and parliamentary practices.

John A. FRASER
Progressive Conservative Member of Parliament for Vancouver South since 1972; presently Labour Critic; served on the House Standing Committees on Fishing & Forestry, Labour, Manpower and Immigration, and Natural Resources; law practice, Vancouver, until 1972, including a Director of the Vancouver Legal Aid Society and Past Chairman of the Environmental Law Subsection, Canadian Bar Association.

Gordon F. GIBSON
Member of the Legislative Assembly of British Columbia for North Vancouver-Capilano since 1974; elected Leader of the Liberal Party in B.C. in 1975; former businessman, newspaper columnist, radio commentator; previously Executive Assistant to the Prime Minister and special or executive assistant to federal Ministers of Northern Affairs and Natural Resources, Indian Affairs and Northern Development.

Richard GUAY
Member of the National Assembly of Quebec for Taschereau since 1976; Parliamentary Assistant to the Minister of Communications.

John A. HOLTBY
First Clerk Assistant, Ontario Legislative Assembly since 1974, a member of the Clerk's Office since 1970.

Bruce HUTCHISON
Editorial Director, *Vancouver Sun;* author of a number of significant books including *The Unknown Country, The Incredible Canadian, The Struggle for the Border, Mr. Prime Minister* and most recently, *The Far Side of the Street.*

The Honourable Lou HYNDMAN
Minister of Federal and Intergovernmental Affairs, Alberta, since April 1975; Member of the Legislative Assembly for Edmonton Glenora since 1967; Opposition Party Whip, 1967-71; Minister of Education, 1971-75; Government House Leader, 1971-   ; Chairman of Cabinet Social Planning Committee and Legislative Review Committee, also member of Energy Committee and Priorities, Finance and Co-ordination Committee; law practice, Edmonton, 1960-71.

The Honourable Mr. Justice Douglas LAMBERT
Court of Appeal of British Columbia; Chairman, Law Reform Commission of British Columbia, January-June 1978, and Commissioner, 1976-78; Commissioner, Uniform Law Conference of Canada, 1974-78; Chairman, Legislation Committee (1972-74) and Statute Revision Committee (1975-78), B.C. Branch, Canadian Bar Association; Special Lecturer, Faculty of Law, University of Victoria, 1978- ; law practice, Vancouver 1969-77; Advisory Counsel, Department of Justice, Ottawa, 1959-64.

Donald C. MACDONALD
Member of the Provincial Parliament of Ontario for York South since 1955; elected Ontario CCF Leader in 1953; first leader of the Ontario New Democratic Party, 1961-70; NDP Federal President, 1971-75; Chairman of the Select Committee on Hydro and member of the Standing Committee on Procedural Affairs; editor, *Government of Politics of Ontario* (1975); part-time lecturer in Political Science, Atkinson College, York University.

Flora MACDONALD
Member of Parliament (Progressive Conservative) for Kingston and The Islands since 1972; appointed P.C. Spokesman for Federal-Provincial Relations in April, 1976; Executive Director, Committee for an Independent Canada, 1971; National Secretary, P.C. Association of Canada, 1966-69; Administrative Officer and Tutor, Queen's University, Department of Political Studies, 1966-72.

John P. MACKINTOSH (deceased July 30, 1978)
Labour Member of Parliament for Berwick and East Lothian; Professor and Head, Department of Politics, University of Edinburgh, 1977-78; elected Fellow of Royal Historical Society, 1973; author of several books including *The British Cabinet, The Devolution of Power,* and *The Government and Politics of Britain;* political columnist of *The Scotsman* and *The Times;* Chairman of the Hansard Society for Parliamentary Government, 1974-78; Joint Editor of the *Political Quarterly,* 1975-78.

James C. MacPHERSON
Assistant Professor, Faculty of Law, University of Victoria since July 1976; Assistant Chairman, National Conference on the Legislative Process, March 31-April 1, 1978; Consultant on Constitutional Matters to the Government of British Columbia, 1977-78; Consultant on Constitutional Matters to the Task Force on Canadian Unity (Pepin-Robarts Commission), 1978.

Alasdair J. McKICHAN
President since 1975 of the Retail Council of Canada; from 1971 to 1975, associated with the T. Eaton Company in Toronto as Vice-President of

Consumer and Corporate Affairs; General Manager of Retail Council of Canada, 1963-71; Secretary and General Counsel to North-West Line Elevators Association, Winnipeg, 1960-62; in law practice in Winnipeg, 1958-60.

William A.W. NEILSON
Professor, Faculty of Law, University of Victoria, since January 1977; Chairman, National Conference on the Legislative Process, March 31-April 1, 1978; Professor, Osgoode Hall Law School of York University, 1966-73; Deputy Minister, Department of Consumer Services, Government of British Columbia, 1973-76; Director, Interprovincial Staff Group, Western Premiers' Task Force on Constitutional Trends, 1976-77; Senior Advisor, B.C. Cabinet Committee on Anti-Inflation Programs, 1976- ; Member, Corporate and Financial Services Commission, 1977- .

Pierre O'NEIL
Director of Television News Société Radio-Canada, Montreal, since 1977; Director of the Centre des Sciences et Techniques de l'Information at Dakar University, Senegal, 1975-77; Press Secretary to the Prime Minister of Canada, 1973-75; Assistant News Director La Presse, Montreal, 1972-73; Information Director, Secretary of State, Ottawa, 1971-72; Ottawa Bureau Chief of La Presse, 1969-71; federal political correspondent for Le Devoir in Ottawa, 1967-69 and previously National Assembly of Quebec Bureau Chief for La Presse.

Samuel C. PATTERSON
Professor, Department of Political Science, University of Iowa, since 1967, and a member of the Department since 1961; Visiting Professor, University of Essex, 1969-70; Editor, American Journal of Political Science, 1970-73; Editorial Board, British Journal of Political Science, 1975- ; books include The Legislative Process in the United States (with M.E. Jewell), Comparative Legislative Behaviour (co-editor), Comparing Legislatures (co-author) and the forthcoming A More Perfect Union (with R. Davidson and R.B. Ripley); author of numerous journal articles and several monographs in the areas of legislative process, comparative politics and legislative behaviour.

John M. REID
Member of Parliament for Kenora-Rainy River since 1965, elected as Liberal-Labour Member and sits with the Liberal Party; Member of the Standing Committees on Procedure and Organization and Regulations and Statutory Instruments; Chairman of the Standing Committee on Broadcasting, 1968-72; Parliamentary Secretary to the President of the Privy Council, 1972-75.

Andrew J. ROMAN
Executive Director/General Counsel for the Public Interest Advocacy Centre, Ottawa, an organization providing a range of advocacy services to citizens' groups, since 1976; previously associated with the Consumers' Association of Canada as General Counsel (Regulated Industries Program).

Norman J. RUFF
Assistant Professor, Department of Political Science, University of Victoria, since 1973; Director, Province of British Columbia Executive Development Training Programme, 1974-76; Commissioner, Commission of Inquiry on Employer-Employee Relations in the Public Service of B.C., 1972.

Frances RUSSELL
Political Columnist, *Winnipeg Tribune,* 1977-   ; previously with the *Vancouver Sun* (Victoria Bureau) in 1975-77, *Winnipeg Free Press* in 1973-75, *Winnipeg Tribune* in 1971-72 and *Globe & Mail* (Ottawa and Queen's Park) and United Press International (Ottawa).

Donald V. SMILEY
Professor of Political Science, York University, Toronto; Fellow of Royal Society of Canada, 1974; Editor, *Canadian Public Administration,* 1974-   ; President, Canadian Political Science Association, 1968-69; Adviser to Royal Commission on Bilingualism and Biculturalism, 1963-68; author of numerous papers and several books and monographs, including *Conditional Grants and Canadian Federalism, Constitutional Adaptation and Canadian Federalism since 1945* and *Canada in Question, Federalism in the Seventies.*

William T. STANBURY
Associate Professor and Chairman, Policy Analysis Division, Faculty of Commerce and Business Administration, University of British Columbia; Director, Regulation and Government Intervention Program, Institute for Research on Public Policy, Montreal; Director, Regulation Reference, Economic Council of Canada, Ottawa; author of a number of journal articles including several recent studies of Canadian competition policy including *Business Interests and the Reform of Canadian Competition Policy, 1971-1975* (1977).

The Honourable Robert L. STANFIELD
Member of Parliament for Halifax since 1968; Leader of the Progressive Conservative Party of Canada, 1967-76; Privy Council, 1967; first elected as Member of the Legislature of Nova Scotia in 1949, returned in 1953; Premier of Nova Scotia, 1956-67; Queen's Counsel, 1950; law practice, Halifax, 1945-56.

Geoffrey STEVENS

Associate Editor, *Globe & Mail,* Ottawa; with the *Globe & Mail* in Ottawa since 1973 as political columnist; *Time Magazine,* Ottawa, 1970-73; *Globe & Mail,* Queen's Park Bureau Chief, 1969-70; other postings beginning in 1962 with *Globe & Mail* in Toronto, Ottawa and Paris; author of *Stanfield* (1973).

Paul G. THOMAS

Assistant Professor and Head of the Department of Political Studies, University of Manitoba, Winnipeg; associated with the Department since 1972; works in progress include a book, *On Parliament Hill: Studies in Legislative Process.*

Arthur TREMBLAY

Professor, National School of Public Administration, University of Quebec; Deputy Minister of Intergovernmental Affairs, Quebec, 1971-77; Deputy Minister of Education, 1964-69; Director-General, Planning and Development Office, Quebec, 1969-71; Officer of the Order of Canada, 1976; Fellow of the Royal Society of Canada, 1959.

Walter D. YOUNG

Professor and Chairman of the Department of Political Science, University of Victoria since 1973; University of British Columbia, 1964-73; author of *The Anatomy of a Party, the CCF 1932-61* and a number of journal articles and reviews concentrating on provincial and federal affairs.

Chapter One

Executive Summary: An Overview of the Papers

by
*W.A.W. Neilson**

and

*J.C. MacPherson***

Drawing upon his extensive political experience at both the provincial and national levels, **Robert Stanfield** opens **Chapter 2** by reminding us that any assessment of our parliamentary system must take into account the public's expectations of government and the pervasive influence of the electronic media. He asserts ''that we are asking parliamentary responsible government to operate in conditions and to perfrom roles that were not anticipated'' for it. The choice for Canadians, according to Mr. Stanfield, is ''between all-pervasive government and parliamentary responsible government . . . we cannot have both.''

Mr. Stanfield sees some merit in the argument that Parliament suffers from ''the tyranny of the executive and the vested interests of the dominant parties,'' but ''above all,'' he holds firmly to the view

> that parliamentary responsible government is not fitted for what it is being asked to do: that both the government and the Parliament are overloaded to the point that we have poor government; and Parliament cannot cope with government.

In support of his overload thesis, Mr. Stanfield cites the variety of impossible duties and responsibilities placed on ministers and members and the growing gap between democratically elected people and the bureaucracy. The overriding remedy must be the pursuit of ''the goals and values of our society . . . without overloading our democracy.'' This first requires our understanding that procedural and related reforms are not enough to clear the impasse; ''[w]e have run up against the limits of human capacity to be both efficient and parliamentary.''

---

* Professor of Law, University of Victoria.
** Assistant Professor of Law, University of Victoria.

The choice posed by Mr. Stanfield prompted an interesting range of responses from his commentators. **Gordon Gibson,** a Member of the British Columbia legislature at the time of writing, is prepared to accept Mr. Stanfield's prescription but only "as long as we retain our straightjacket of the British parliamentary system." Significant success in reducing governmental responsibilities "to the point where Parliament can control [the government] is one that is simply not going to happen."

The correct answer, says Mr. Gibson, is to practise radical surgery on our parliamentary institutions. His priorities would include a greater readiness to employ such instruments of 'direct democracy' as initiatives and referenda. On the 'indirect' side, he favours "a semi-separation" of the executive and legislative branches to ensure a strong connection for purposes of policy integration while allowing for a release of Cabinet's "iron grip on Parliament" by granting the executive an assured tenure. Fixed terms between elections, a proper committee system and electoral reform leaning towards proportional representation are among Mr. Gibson's proposals. His suggestions have taken on a wider significance in view of his announcement in September that he would henceforth pursue them in the federal political arena.

The next comment by **Richard Guay,** a government Member of the Quebec National Assembly, concentrates on a number of measures recently instituted or proposed in that forum to enhance the role of its members. Success in this direction, he believes, will bring about a process of proper accountability by the executive and the bureaucracy to the legislative branch without which we run the grave risk of having a closed system of government more intent on cover-up and self-protection than the rule of law.

Picking up on Mr. Stanfield's 'overload' thesis, Mr. Guay concludes his comment by analysing the overlap and duplication of services offered to (and paid by) residents of Quebec by the federal and Quebec governments. He extends this variation on a theme by arguing that

> [b]eyond the new powers that the government of Quebec may take over from the government of Canada, the ultimate solution resides in the decentralization of these same powers throughout the territory of Quebec in favour of local and regional institutions.

A very different slant on the balance sheet offered by Mr. Stanfield comes from Professor **Ronald Cheffins** from the Faculty of Law at the University of Victoria. He explores the extent to which constitutional considerations are a constraint on "experimentation in legislative functioning." Based on a careful analysis of the *British North America Act* and constitutional practice, Professor Cheffins concludes that "[t]he constitution remains incredibly flexible in this area" and that "[t]he problem once again is a question of political motivation and political will."

The conduct of federal-provincial relations in a parliamentary system is discussed in **Chapter 3.** Professor **Donald Smiley** of York University contributes the major paper to the discussion and he wastes little time in declaring that "the characteristic role of the Parliament of Canada and of the provincial legislatures in federal-provincial relations is to discuss actions which have been already taken." The reality of "executive federalism" is further emphasized in the growing propensity of "governments bypassing their respective legislatures in announcing future policies" of significance to relations between them. An intricate, and at times impenetrable, executive-bureaucratic network has established itself to manage intergovernmental relations leaving the legislators out in the cold and "frustrated in any efforts to find out what is going on and to exercise a modicum of surveillance or control over these activities." This process, Professor Smiley hastens to remind us, is "being carried on within the context of a struggle for the survival of the federation itself."

After analysing earlier attempts to reform our constitution, Smiley argues that the current attempts must go beyond the question of the distribution of powers to the more effective representation of our deeply felt "territorial particularisms" in the institutions of the central government; otherwise, he fears that our overriding need for an effective national government will fall before the provincial governments' claim to "the almost exclusive franchise to represent attitudes and interests that are territorially bounded." The electoral system for the House of Commons must be changed to allow for more balanced regional and provincial representation. Rejecting proportional representation, Professor Smiley would prefer the addition of one hundred "provincial" M.P.'s to the Commons "chosen by ranking in each province those candidates who had received the highest proportion of popular votes to the winning candidates." In addition, he is convinced in the area of relations between the political executive and Parliament that "we should move in the direction of the American congressional model." His reasons for being skeptical about the chances for significant reform of the Senate deserve careful study.

It will not be surprising to learn that the first commentator, The Honourable **Lou Hyndman**, Alberta's Minister of Federal and Intergovernmental Affairs, disputes Smiley's contention that

> . . . the current disposition to deal with our discontents by enhancing the power of the provinces without reforms in the institutions of the central government can lead only to unfortunate results.

Mr. Hyndman's preference is to call for "a fundamental change in attitude on the part of . . . the bureaucracy of the central government in Ottawa." His goal is a power relationship in which "the federal government and each provincial government are balanced and complementary." He takes issue with the 'parliamentary bypass' lament of Professor Smiley, citing his own responsibilities to the Alberta House whose members regularly debate that province's relations with the federal and other governments.

Mr. Hyndman's general preference for the status quo is not shared by his fellow commentators. Professor **Norman Ruff** of the University of Victoria detects further evidence of Parliament's declining involvement in federal-provincial relations and exhibits little appetite for this trend notwithstanding Mr. Hyndman's observations. He offers his own version of a proposal to add 'provincial' M.P.'s to the Commons while acknowledging that the public and the politicians are very cool to any ideas for electoral reform "even in the face of such sensible proposals."

Ronald M. Burns observes that the benefits normally accruing to "the melding of legislative and executive responsibilities in the parliamentary system" may suffer diminishing returns in a federal system. Too often, he argues, there is an

> inevitable tendency for the most routine processes to become politicized with the involvement of the executive in almost every aspect of government at both national and regional levels.

The net result is the sad eclipse of the legislator. Some possible solutions are canvassed and Professor Burns contributes some carefully phrased and persuasive thoughts on possible reforms of the Senate substantially influenced by the West German experience. His comments strike a helpful balance to the emphasis placed by Professor Smiley on electoral reform for the Commons.

In the penultimate comment, **Arthur Tremblay** of Quebec City indicates his serious concern with the pace of constitutional reform given the reality of the forthcoming referendum in Quebec. Good faith in the rest of Canada may be in abundant supply, he concedes hopefully, but there is an urgent need to reach a national consensus on the distribution of legislative powers. This priority must rank ahead of any reform of the institutions of the central government for two reasons. First, there is little support in Quebec for the thesis of executive federalism insofar as it applies to the handling of intergovernmental relations in Quebec in the past decade or more. The National Assembly, in Mr. Tremblay's experience, has been very much involved in the practice and scrutiny of federalism because "the people of Quebec have always felt that their own destiny as a community was at stake in those relations." More importantly, there must be a public groundswell for new constitutional arrangements in order that the people of Quebec will have "a real and significant 'third option' between the status quo and 'souveraineté-association'" when they go to the Quebec referendum.

Miss **Flora MacDonald's** remarks, on the other hand, tend to reinforce Professor Smiley's emphasis on the need to provide for more effective regional representation at the federal level. Undeterred, however, by his caveats concerning the selling of Senate reform, Miss MacDonald recommends turning the Senate into a House of the Provinces with a majority of the members being appointed by the provincial governments. The result, she feels, "while not replacing the myriad of federal-provincial negotiations, . . . would substantially integrate this process into Parliament itself." Miss MacDonald is firmly in support of other measures to strengthen the role of individual M.P.'s but clearly her primary focus is on those reforms necessary "to change Ottawa from being a *central* government to being a truly *federal* government."

Two months following the conference, the latest package of proposed constitutional changes was released by the Prime Minister. One of the striking features of Bill C-60 is the emphasis placed on reforming central institutions so as to ensure a greater and more formal provincial voice in the formulation of national policy in areas of substantial importance to the provinces. But the reform of central institutions is not House of Commons-directed as Professor Smiley would wish; rather, the proposals centre on Senate reform and, in so doing, adopt many of the premises and themes invoked by Professor Burns and Flora MacDonald. Indeed, one of the fascinating themes emerging from a number of advocates of constitutional reform — the Government of Canada (Bill C-60), the Canadian Bar Association (Report released in August 1978), the Government of Ontario (Report prepared by Advisory Committee) and the Government of British Columbia (see Premier Bennett's submission to the Task Force on Canadian Unity) to name but a few — is the great emphasis being attached to Senate reform as a major vehicle for solving some of the perceived problems in the operation of our national democratic institutions. Whether fundamental reform of an essentially undemocratic and, up to this time, irrelevant component of our national lawmaking system coupled with a virtual ignoring of Commons reform is either logical or useful remains to be seen. Fortunately, at the conference there were articulate advocates for both types of reform. A reading and critical comparison of the remarks of such thoughtful analysts as Smiley, Burns and MacDonald cannot but help serve as a valuable theoretical framework against which to evaluate the mound of constitutional reform proposals presently piling up on our desks.

The sympathetic references to the American system of the constitutional separation of powers by several of the speakers give a special relevance to the remarks prepared by Professor **Samuel Patterson** of the University of Iowa in **Chapter 4.** At the outset, he notes that the separation has created an environment "in which the independence of the legislature from the executive could flourish." In contrast to the weight of opinion concerning the Canadian legislative process, Patterson concludes that:

> Congress has proved to be highly autonomous, adaptive to changes in its political environment, very open to public scrutiny, and highly permeable to the representation of a wide variety of interests and constituencies.

The significance of Congress as a legislative body is contrasted to the general situation "in which lawmaking has in most countries fallen heavily into the hands of the executives."

Three aspects of the "semi-sovereign" Congress are reviewed. In the first, Dr. Patterson analyses the electoral system, notes the high rate of election return for incumbents and cites "evidence that political party identification accounts for a declining proportion of the congressional election vote." The significant increase in resources made available to representatives and senators to service their constituencies helps to reinforce the influence of the incumbent (assisted in some cases by the absence of clear accountability for the problems attributed to others, including the President). The sheer quantum of these resources boggles the parochial mind (e.g., House members are authorized to hire up to eighteen staff; Senators' staff allowances range up to $844,608). Between one-third and one-half of these staff have been assigned to service the constituency in the district or state involved.

The second topic chosen by Professor Patterson concerns changes in the organizational mechanics of Congress — in the committee structure, the party leadership, and the staff. While some Canadian observers are calling for a stronger committee system for legislators to check Cabinet power, congressional leaders are trying to bring their burgeoning committee system under control by cutting back the number of subcommittees, concentrating legislative responsibilities in fewer committees and by creating *ad hoc* structures to consider major presidential policy initiatives (e.g., energy) that would otherwise "cut across the dispersive power structure of subcommittee governments." On the support side, congressional staffs have increased markedly in recent years, both in members' offices and in serving the large committee network — the latter development has prompted an increasing concern that the congressional bureaucracy of staff aides now controls policy decisions "by virtue of their tenure and expertise."

In the third part of his paper, Professor Patterson analyses the growing role assumed by Congress in reviewing the activities and policies of the executive branch, particularly since Watergate. This "oversight" activity includes a larger degree of control over the federal budget.

The American perspective offered by Dr. Patterson will yield the reader immediate rewards in better understanding the uniqueness of the legislative process in their Congress and the care with which one must approach suggestions for the importation of institutional reforms from other countries.

John Reid, a Member of Parliament since 1965, takes on the challenging topic of "The Backbencher and the Discharge of Legislative Responsibilities" in **Chapter 5**. The paper's general tone, certainly at first reading, is satisfaction with the present system as it controls and shapes the role of the individual legislator, a view less that enthusiastically picked up by his commentators.

Part of his apparent contentment may be explained by Mr. Reid's emphasis on the *opportunities* for legislative initiatives (broadly defined) by individual M.P.'s, as opposed to the overall, measurable impact of their efforts. Thus, Mr. Reid reviews the occasions on which private members may take the lead in educating others on the need for particular reforms, in presenting private members' bills, in presenting resolutions to the House, in contributing to House debates, and in pursuing their committee responsibilities. Only a small minority of M.P.'s take their legislative duties seriously, argues Mr. Reid, for the work frequently is far from the spotlight, requires a detailed comprehension of House rules and is very time-consuming.

"The most important constraint on the role of the private member," observes Mr. Reid, "is his party affiliation." The pressure to toe the party line and to present "as uniform a position as possible on a wide variety of issues" has been increased by the advent of televised proceedings. Party discipline is "necessary . . . for the functioning of the House" although there is a closing hint that many backbenchers are unpersuaded by the comprehensive nature of the "constraints imposed by party" as they continue to open up the legislative process to individual initiatives.

John Fraser, Conservative Member for Vancouver South, disputes the significance of the several legislative opportunities cited by the principal speaker. In his comment, Mr. Fraser characterizes them as "very limited." In referring to committee work, for example, he argues that the opposition backbencher really must depend upon a minority government situation to make any headway for only then do "the government members needing the support of some of the opposition, develop an amazing propensity to deal."

In general terms, the legislative "responsibility of the opposition member, if really opposed to [a government bill], is to try to stop it." Mr. Fraser accepts the adversary nature of the system although he appears to sense the downside of the drawing battle lines in an unthinking and arbitrary manner. Hence, the suggestion to re-examine the committee system by "removing the party lines to a considerable degree in committee" thereby allowing "a competent government member" (and opposition member(s) also?) to "view the bill in a much more objective manner." He would also support the provision of independent staff resources to the committees. Mr. Fraser supports the view "that party discipline often goes beyond necessity" and strikes a plaintive note in observing that "[t]he Cabinet and the bureaucracy really run the show and all too often the backbencher ends up as an onlooker, just waiting for the division bells to ring."

The former leader of the Ontario New Democratic Party and Member of the Ontario Legislative Assembly for York South since 1955, **Donald C. MacDonald**, contributes the second comment on Mr. Reid's paper. He sharply criticizes the state of affairs by which the Cabinet has assumed the exclusive prerogative for initiating legislation "with the private member reduced to little more than an objector or a rubber-stamp supporter." The current Ontario experiments for increasing the potential success of private members' bills offer some hope although "the prospect of even this small measure of progress surviving is unlikely, should the government regain a majority."

Standing committees do provide an opportunity for backbencher involvement but their "organization and operation . . . have been the bane of parliamentary life." Select committees (which meet only when the House is not in session) too frequently have been devices to provide busywork for the backbenchers of a big majority government. Their ultimate success depends "very much on the quality of the staff of the committee."

For Professor **Paul Thomas** of the University of Manitoba, the Reid paper conveyed an unreal air of optimism and failed to answer "the other available accounts of a backbencher's existence [which] reveal a strong sense of frustration, bordering on futility . . . " He regrets the failure of Mr. Reid "to discuss the impediments to a creative legislative role by backbenchers." On the other hand, he acknowledges, John Reid's paper "draws our attention to [the] neglected, private dimensions of the legislative process" and "the importance of the representation process working through M.P.'s."

Professor Thomas then offers some very perceptive views on strengthening the Commons to oversee the administration. The earlier comments by Dr. Patterson in reference to the oversight powers of Congress come to mind. Thomas argues persuasively that the Commons should recognize

> its limited capacity to shape the content of legislation and concentrate more upon the scrutiny of legislative performance and the transmission of popular demands to the Cabinet and the bureaucracy. . . .

Future reforms should strengthen the surveillance function of the members; and,

> [b]y increasing its supervisory activities, the Commons could aslo increase its opportunities for participation in lawmaking since it would be better informed about the nature of government operations.

Professor Thomas offers some detailed comments on specific points raised by Mr. Reid and concludes that private members "are frustrated by their incapacity to affect policy." A number of suggested reforms are offered. Together the suggestions constitute a checklist of substantial changes in parliamentary procedure, many of which would increase the power and influence of the individual legislator. Professor Thomas' enthusiasm for these suggested future changes, however, is tempered by his prognosis that reform

> will be incremental in character, both because of a desire by governments not to foster changes which would upset the existing political balance to their detriment and because of the difficulty of forecasting all the consequences of any change.

Most of the papers delivered at the Conference analysed various internal aspects of the legislative process — legislative drafting, the conduct of federal/provincial relations, parliamentary procedure, the purposes and performance of Parliament and the future of parliamentary democracy. But two papers focused on the influence of institutions and activities external to the mainstream of the legislative process and tried to assess the responsibilities of those institutions in their dealings with actors involved in the legislative process.

The principal paper in **Chapter 6**, Professor **William Stanbury's** "Lobbying and Interest Group Representation," is a serious attempt to provide a comprehensive analytical framework for the study of interest group representation in Canada. Because lobbying is so widespread in Canada, such an undertaking is of great value.

Two of the strong features of Professor Stanbury's paper are his description of the breadth of lobbying activity in Canada today and his dispelling of some of the conventional myths about lobbying and lobbyists. Although the term 'lobbying' probably originated in Great Britain, where private citizens would talk to their members of Parliament in the lobbies of the House of Commons, the standard Canadian stereotype of the lobbyist is probably based on his conception of the American lobbyist — the fat man with a big cigar, a big car and a big bankroll. Professor Stanbury correctly points out that there is no single model of lobbyist or of lobbying activity. Lobbyists appear in various settings — associations permanently on guard for their clients, special individuals hired for special assignments and *ad hoc* groups who mount campaigns for particular legislative battles — and they conduct their activities in many different fashions.

Professor Stanbury's basic starting point is that lobbying is a reality and that, on the merits, it is a legitimate part of the democratic process. Lobbying meshes with the pluralist ideal of democratic theory in that it provides a vehicle for the articulation of citizen interests and for assessing the relative weight or merit of those interests. In addition, the growth in size and complexity of modern government requires that there be an effective flow of information between the governors and the governed. Lobbying is one means of structuring that flow.

Following this generally complimentary assessment of the theoretical role of lobbying in a democratic society, Professor Stanbury explores in detail three aspects of lobbying activity — lobbying targets, vehicles for lobbying and the timing of lobbying activity. His conclusions on these aspects are that effective Canadian lobbyists (a) deal primarily with Cabinet ministers and senior civil servants, (b) use subtle, low-key and informal approaches (Stanbury describes "the opaque character of the communications between lobbyists and their ministerial and civil service targets"), and (c) commence their lobbying activity as early as possible (the ideal lobbyist is one who plants his own legislative seed with a senior policy maker, not one who merely reacts, however effectively, to seeds planted by other sources). In painting this picture of the effective Canadian lobbyist, Professor Stanbury makes a number of interesting comparisons between Canadian and American lobbyists and lobbying practice. For example, American lobbying appears to be much more open and aggressive and the targets of American lobbyists are quite different (legislators) than those of their Canadian counterparts (Cabinet ministers, civil servants).

Professor Stanbury's paper did not escape unscathed at the conference. Drawing upon her experience as a lobbyist on behalf of labour and women's interests, **Johanna den Hertog** disagreed with Professor Stanbury's assessment of the beneficial consequences of lobbying in Canadian society. She argues that lobbying, as presently conducted in Canada, fails to break down class differences by providing all citizens with a means to articulate their interests and by providing legislators with a vehicle for the assessment of the relative merits of the competing interests. On the contrary, den Hertog contends that many groups lack access to the lobbying process and that other groups lack expertise in utilizing that process. Consequently, those with easy access to, and expertise in, the lobbying process, namely, the corporate community, are able to use that process to perpetuate class differences in Canada. Lobbying as a useful component of the pluralist ideal is a myth — rather, as it is presently conducted in Canada, it is a denial of that ideal.

Andrew Roman, the Executive Director and General Counsel of the Public Interest Advocacy Centre in Ottawa, also disagrees with some of Professor Stanbury's conclusions. For example, he suggests that although many academic writers have posited that effective lobbyists try to deal primarily with senior policy makers such as Cabinet ministers and high-level civil servants, in actual fact the most successful lobbyists in Ottawa are those who start at the bottom of the policy-making process. In his view, the most effective lobbyists are "so discrete, so secretive that you have probably never heard of them," or are not thought of as lobbyists (law firms and lawyers) and ply their trade in other uniforms. The astute lobbyist, contends Roman, knows where and when to pierce the "seamless web" of the federal government which "is not a machine which can be run, but a series of discrete, random events: a happening" which is "beyond the effective control of anyone at any particular point in time." Mr. Roman's remarks conclude with an analysis of the problems faced by public interest groups in their mounting any lobbying activity, ending with a reference to the case of competition legislation discussed earlier in considerable depth by Professor Stanbury.

The third commentator, **Alasdair McKichan**, is President of the Retail Council of Canada and in this most senior of appointed capacities in the Council, he acts as the representative of a wide range of retail-oriented enterprises in their dealings with governments and legislators across the nation. Mr. McKichan systematically reviews the common characteristics of the more successful lobby groups (in which he includes labour, contrary to Ms. den Hertog's comments) and rejects the argument that size, wealth and experience are guarantees of lobbying success. He is persuaded by the pluralist rationale posed by Professor Stanbury, not only in theory but also in practice. Far from accepting the cases raised by the principal speaker (competition, patent law revision, and consumer credit reform) as illustrative of the force of the business lobby, however, McKichan argues that each measure "could have been equally well chosen as examples of the ineffectiveness of the business lobby." His comments then deal with two very constructive topics — the strategies followed by successful practitioners of lobbying and some suggestions for governmental action to facilitate better public input to the legislative process. It is interesting to notice the correlation between many of his recommendations and a number of the reforms advocated in Chapter 5 (The Backbencher) and Chapter 8 (Procedural Reform).

The second paper dealing with an institution and an activity somewhat removed from the mainstream of the legislative process was delivered by **Geoffrey Stevens**, Ottawa political columnist for the *Globe & Mail*. In spite of the traditional journalistic inclination to "eschew introspection," Stevens presents a thoughtful paper entitled, "The Influence and Responsibilities of the Media" in **Chapter 7.** Stevens argues that the influence and visibility of the media in this post-Watergate era of journalism mean that "the need for self-examination and self-criticism has never been greater." In a thorough and lucid paper, Stevens provides this examination and criticism of his profession. He does not flinch from the unhappy conclusions to which he is drawn: "The fact remains that the media stand indicted for superficiality, for concentrating on trivia and ignoring substance, for focusing on the drama and losing sight of the serious functioning and equally serious malfunctioning of the process."

Concerning media influence, Stevens contends that the media is not particularly influential once legislation has been introduced in Parliament. Rather, the media exercises an effective prior influence on government policy through the opinions expressed in editiorial pages and political columns and through the selection of issues for news coverage and the slant given to news reports.

Stevens feels that these latter two areas — news selection and method of coverage — present the major problems of media responsibility. Stevens grapples with the problems of definition and of theory posed by the words 'media responsibility'. Responsibility for what — for honesty, fairness, candor, comprehensiveness? Responsibility to whom — oneself, editors, publishers, readers? In the end, Stevens says, a journalist's responsibility is twofold: he has a duty to become as well acquainted as possible with the issues about which he writes and he has a duty to be "as objective as humanly possible" in the selection of items to be reported and on the actual coverage of those items.

Professor **Walter Young** in the first comment is critical of several explanations offered by Stevens for the incompetence of the press. He then offers the perhaps controversial suggestion that concentration of newspaper ownership is not the bogeyman it is often portrayed to be. At a time when the "besetting sin of the newspaper business" is its "fascination with trivia and the deeply imbedded belief in the importance of the parochial over the provincial or national," Young argues that the theoretical benefits of the concentration of media ownership — news coverage of greater breadth and depth — are not being maximized. The mediocre state of the fourth estate, he contends, is borne out in its surrender to the political executive's "judicious use of press releases and leaks." As a captive of political manipulation, "the press has surrendered much of its freedom, and in so doing has forsaken its once signal role as the fourth estate. Given the condition of the third estate, that is a sad circumstance indeed."

In the following comment, the veteran author and political commentator, Mr. **Bruce Hutchison**, reminds us and his colleagues that the media must lift its sights above the hurly-burly of the transient issues of the day and occasionally focus on the larger issues that will face mankind in the future. He concludes: "Hence the final responsibility of the media is to prepare the public for a future very different from the present and, I would suspect, much less comfortable."

Mr. Stevens' definition of media responsibility in terms of objectivity is a theme that recurs in the comments made by the other journalists who participated in the panel discussion which followed his paper at the conference. In addition, the commentators make a number of other valuable points. **Catherine Bergman** discusses the difficulties of the French-language press in the midst of an overwhelming English-speaking media. She agrees with Stevens that the real power of the press is a power of selection, but then continues, "but the francophone press does not have that power. For example, the front page of the *Globe & Mail* determines not only the line-up of the CBC news, and the front pages of many English-Canadian newspapers; it influences the line-up of the French news as well." This type of situation leads Bergman to speculate that "there is no media at the present time to reflect exclusively the Quebec view of things, let alone a Quebec view of things Canadian."

Pierre O'Neil worries about the remoteness of reporters — and politicians — from the concerns of ordinary citizens and suggests that this remoteness means that the media have very little influence — on either politicians or their audience.

Frances Russell of the *Winnipeg Tribune,* with experience in Ottawa and several provincial capitals, concentrates on the impact of polarized politics on the quest for objectivity. The political journalist, she stresses, must acquire and protect "the ability to stand aside personally and assess both sides critically and to avoid partisan identification." Put into practice, that professional ideal has a measurable and beneficial impact on the politicians, the legislative process and the public. But in the polarized political climates found in such provinces as British Columbia and Manitoba, Russell argues, the serious political commentator is in for "a shattering experience" for "[l]ike nature abhors a vacuum, polarity abhors objectivity. It will label you, willy-nilly." She exhorts the media to withstand these pressures and to be "a voice for moderation and common sense against . . . the 'true believers'." Judged against the prevailing tone of the preceding comments, Ms. Russell's plea seems destined for a disappointing fate which should be a matter of serious concern to all Canadians.

In **Chapter 8** we are introduced to the daily operations of our parliamentary system and its inability to handle the public's business. In a thoughtful and detailed paper, Professor **C.E.S. Franks** of Queen's University analyses both the theoretical reasons for, and the actual results of, the procedural reforms that have been made in the federal legislative system, particularly in the last decade.

Although parliamentary reform is not a subject matter that often grabs public attention or even provokes much serious academic analysis — Professor Franks modestly states that "doubtless to many people, worrying about parliamentary procedure is something like arguing over wine lists on the Titanic" — it is certainly wrong to equate this lack of visibility and current interest with lack of importance. The House of Commons is still the most visible and most important lawmaking body in the country, and therefore deserves careful expert and citizen appraisal.

Two striking facts concerning the House of Commons are emerging in the latter half of this decade — and both are worthy of analysis. First, the actual productivity of the House of Commons has decreased in recent years. One of the interesting highlights of the Trudeau years has been the large number of pieces of important legislation that have died on the Order Paper at the end of a legislative session. Yet in a number of provinces, British Columbia included, the productivity of the provincial assemblies has increased noticeably. In order to achieve this result, many of the provinces have rationalized and greatly streamlined their rather rudimentary legislative systems. For example, British Columbia has established a Cabinet committee system (relatively successful) and a legislative committee system (much less successful). What is interesting about these innovations is that they are primarily based on the federal Cabinet and legislative committee systems developed so carefully by Prime Minister Trudeau. Yet, in spite of the parallel structures, the results in the two systems have been markedly different. Federal creation of a streamlined committee structure has not contributed to parliamentary passage of an increased volume of legislation; yet provincial adaptation of that structure has had precisely that result. Although there are undoubtedly certain extraneous factors which may assist in explaining this anomaly (for example, much of the legislation enacted by the British Columbia legislature in its productive 1977 session was of a minor or "housekeeping" nature), there are undoubtedly some significant insights to be gained from a careful comparative study of the operation of the federal and provincial legislative processes in the last decade.

The other important fact relating to the House of Commons is how little attention is being focused on Commons reform in the current national unity debate. It is now conventional wisdom that the stage for discussion of our national crisis is not the House of Commons — rather the real stage is a combination of the federal/provincial conference and the mass media, particularly television. But not only is the House of Commons not providing a *forum* for national debate; in addition it is not a *subject matter* of that debate. In this latter respect, the contrast between the Commons and the Senate is striking. Almost every important national politician — the Prime Minister, Joe Clark, Flora MacDonald, Premier Bennett, Premier Davis through the medium of his Advisory Committee — has emphasized major Senate reform as an important component of necessary constitutional reform. Indeed some politicians appear to regard Senate reform as the single most important area of constitutional reform. In a sense this collective national passion (Henri Bourassa once said that Senate reform, "comes periodically like other forms of epidemics and current fevers") over a reformed Senate is incongruous. We devote great intellectual energy to the branch of our national lawmaking system that has played only a very minor role in our history and, at the same time, almost completely ignore the institution which in reality is — and should be — the lifeblood of our democratic process.

Professor Frank's paper is a useful antidote to this current national preoccupation with Senate reform. He recognizes that the House of Commons is the lawmaking fulcrum in Canada and that the quantity and quality of our national laws will depend largely on whether or not the Commons is operating effectively. He sets out to examine this issue and presents many useful insights — on two levels. First, his analysis of the actual operation of the Commons, and in particular of the reformed legislative committee system, is both detailed and enlightening. Secondly, building on this analysis, Professor Franks is able to make a number of useful observations concerning the probable directions the Commons will take in future years (for example, he concludes that, "one of the biggest dangers to Parliament over the next few years will, I suspect, be its being put into the shade as federal-provincial relations, and possibly the working out of a new constitution, take the lime-light"). And finally, Professor Franks makes a number of specific suggestions for improving the parliamentary process. These proposals are imaginative and, in places, controversial (for example, Professor Franks suggests that the Standing Committee on Public Accounts should meet *in camera*) and form a fine conclusion to one of the most thorough and helpful analyses of the House of Commons in recent years.

In the following comment, **John Holtby** calls upon his experience as First Clerk Assistant to the Ontario Legislative Assembly to provide a provincial perspective. He offers a very useful and incisive analysis of the recent procedural change in Ontario designed to enhance the role of the private member and then explores the reforms felt necessary for proper parliamentary scrutiny of public expenditures. His suggestions carry a good deal of practical sense, particularly in respect of those applying to committee membership, staff resources and initial workload. In turn, he would support measures to increase the number of House debates devoted to the analysis of departmental policy and to place a regular obligation on the House to go on tour within its territorial jurisdiction.

Mr. Holtby joins issue with those views of Professor Franks that he feels amount to expediting "the government's work by cutting back on the abilities of members of the House to scrutinize the government's stewardship." A close reading of the comment suggests a core concern with the suitability of the parliamentary system to a modern society. "Would it be useful," the question is posed, "to consider a separation of the executive and legislative branches, keeping in place the Question Period?"

Chapter 9 features a paper delivered by Professor **W.H. Charles** of Dalhousie University, a long-time student of the legislative process and one of the pioneers in the teaching of a course in Legislation in Canadian law schools. Professor Charles' paper is entitled "Public Policy and Legislative Drafting" and in it he seeks to answer the question: does a legislative drafter have any creative role to play in the formulation of legislative policy or is he a mere technician who simply gives effect to policy set by legislators or civil servants?

A great merit of Professor Charles' paper is the significant empirical research he undertook in order to answer the question posed above. Professor Charles sent a detailed questionnaire to twenty leading Canadian legislative counsel and received full responses from most of them. Consequently Professor Charles' paper gives us perhaps the first clear picture of the actual role and influence of legislative drafters in Canada.

A number of useful (and perhaps surprising) insights emerge from the Charles' paper. For example, it appears that the policy-making role of legislative counsel is in inverse proportion to the size and extent of development of the drafting branch of the government. Those drafters who exercise a substantial creative input into policy formulation appear to come from the smaller provinces with smaller government bureaucracies.

A second highly valuable portion of Professor Charles' paper is his discussion of the role of legislative drafters in the preparation of subordinate legislation. Two points emerge from this discussion. First, regulations are usually drafted by officials in the line department responsible for the administration of the enabling legislation. Secondly, it appears that the policy-making role of the drafter is substantial. In Professor Charles' words:

> Quite clearly, the expectation is that the draftsman will have a significant role to play in developing the substantive content of the regulations, much more than is the case with the drafting of statutes. . . . Considering the great quantity of subordinate legislation that is enacted annually, the contribution of draftsmen to the policy contained thereon could be very substantial.

If one makes the not unreasonable assumption that departmental officials who draft regualtions are not as proficient as professional drafters employed in legislative counsel offices, an interesting picture emerges: the role of professional drafters in policy making is perhaps substantially less than the policy-making role of non-expert drafters.

Notwithstanding this possible source of concern, Professor Charles concludes that the Canadian legislative counsel performs a key role as the architect of statutory schemes, as the writer or composer of language that must accurately reflect the policy chosen and as the "unofficial watchdog and protector of individual rights." Whatever their individual influence on policy matters of broader import, the legislative drafters, in his view, have withstood any tendency to abuse their office because of their "well-developed sense of personal and professional integrity."

In the first comment, **J. Douglas Lambert** loses little time in declaring that "[a]dvising on matters of law is only one area of the competence of legislative counsel." He contends that a broader policy-making (advice-giving) role is legitimate. He draws an interesting comparison between the private lawyer (who is expected to give advice as well as perform technical legal functions) and the legislative drafter (who, many would contend, should be denied the former function) and concludes that the training and expertise of many legislative drafters equip them to fulfill the dual functions of his private practice counterpart. However, just as in private practice, the lawyer-adviser must avoid straying into areas of policy for which he does not have any particular expertise. Similarly, legislative counsel/drafters must maintain and guard their position of independence vis-à-vis their client (Attorney General or legislative Assembly). This means that they actively advise their client without identifying themselves with the proponents. Their advice ultimately must rest on "the objectivity and judgment which can only come from a detachment from the consequences flowing from the alternative solutions to the problem."

An American perspective is provided by Professor **Richard Dole, Jr.**, of the University of Houston. A substantial number of legislative drafters in the United States are not lawyers and this situation obtains whether their product is draft legislation or regulations. Their involvement in the early development of legislative proposals is very limited, partly due to the dispersal of initiating power in the congressional system and also because of a stronger willingness to leave the issue of constitutionality of statutes to the courts. Although the professional bill drafter in the United States enjoys less involvement in policy development than many of his or her Canadian counterparts, Professor Dole remains firmly of the view that the practice of their art inherently carries substantial power and responsibility. Indeed, he calls for clear guidelines to allow the use of "objective legislative history as an extrinsic aid to statutory construction regardless of the facial ambiguity of statutory text." He believes this to be necessary because the "legislative branch of government is too important for the effectuation of its policies [as reviewed by the courts] to depend upon the words selected by a professional bill drafter."

Several interesting questions raised by members of the audience are answered in the final part of **Chapter 9**. The entire session was chaired by G. Alan Higenbottam, Legislative Counsel for British Columbia whose death this past summer is mourned by legislative drafters and his many friends across Canada.

In **Chapter 10,** the late **John Mackintosh**, then Member of Parliament (Berwick & East Lothian) and Head of the Department of Politics at the University of Edinburgh delivers in his own eloquent and witty manner some very independent opinions on "The Future of Representative Parliamentary Democracy." An influential and independent backbencher and a scholar of international reputation, Dr. Mackintosh deftly weaves together the observations of preceding contributors and offers some wide-ranging and thought-provoking observations on the basic requirements for improving the parliamentary system. The shock of his unexpected death on July 30th, 1978, saddened countless numbers of admirers and friends and released a torrent of tributes from both sides of the Atlantic. For those who had the privilege of talking with and listening to him at the conference, his passing took on a special and very personal meaning for he was a "combative and witty" speaker, "lively and challenging with the gift of establishing easy human relationships" (*The Times,* July 31, 1978) and readily described by his peers "as one of the five or six great orators of his generation" (The *Scotsman,* July 31, 1978). His performance on the closing evening of a very busy conference whose every session had attracted his close interest confirmed and magnified the sincerity of these tributes to a most extraordinary individual. His passing deals a serious blow to the efforts in both the United Kingdom and Canada to rebuff the trend toward executive government.

In his remarks, Dr. Mackintosh expresses some practical doubts about Mr. Stanfield's overload thesis while agreeing that "we simply must produce a theory of the mixed economy which, without engaging in senseless curtailments of government activity, clearly draws the line at those aspects of private rights and economic activity which are not suitable for the state to regulate." Without a chart "for legitimate government activity," we will always be reacting "to non-ending demands for action which in turn lead to political promises that set unattainable goals leading to a cumulative discrediting of the whole system."

Within this realm of 'attainable politics', Dr. Mackintosh argues, the Commons and the legislative assemblies must re-emerge as the forums for debating and shaping the major decisions in public affairs. He alludes to the possibilities of electoral reform to better represent "power blocs," regional considerations and the like as part of the prescription, with particular reference to the second chamber. He clearly favours greater freedom (and political responsibility) for the backbencher, aptly noting that the available means are much more in evidence than "the political will of the government and the people concerned." The answer, he is convinced, rests in an effective committee system in which members are expected to perform an investigatory function and to hold public bodies and officials responsible for their policies and their expenditures. In his words, this would be accepted "as legitimate activity for legislators in a parliamentary system [ranking] ahead of a reactive and automatic ethos of supporting your party" and proof of a broader responsibility toward your constituents "that within the task of supporting your party, there is this sub-task . . . of criticism and control."

The absence of political will noted earlier is made worse by the growing confusion between direct and representative democratic institutions. After excluding those referenda concerning the entrenchment of specific clauses in written constitutions, Dr. Mackintosh outlines his opposition to any other attempts to run the nation's affairs by questionnaire. In this part, he employs some of his own home-grown examples to great advantage to press his point. His remarks are published as Messrs. Lang and Trudeau declare a new affection for the paraphernalia of 'direct democracy'. Dr. Mackintosh clearly fears a further weakening of a gravely weak representative system should the support for "Yes-No" balloting take root. Complex choices involving the allocation of scarce resources cannot be boiled down "to a set-off between red buttons and blue buttons."

What is needed instead is truly representative parliamentary democracy in which the legislators are accountable for their actions, in which party support is not an ethical straightjacket and in which parties stand or fall on their performances measured against their carefully articulated electoral programs. Representative government, Dr. Mackintosh believes, is "*not* a poor alternative to direct democracy, but *the proper* way of conducting democracy in any modern society."

In further support of the need for an activist legislature, Dr. Mackintosh argues that executive or Cabinet government really becomes anonymous government dominated by unelected civil servants. This trend has further widened the gap between government and the general population and threatens to undermine the consensual base so vital to a functioning democracy.

Dr. Mackintosh clearly touched many nerve ends in his remarks which in turn led to a spirited question and answer period.

Chapitre un

Abrégé: Revue des articles

par:
W.A.W. Neilson *

et

J.C. MacPherson **

Se fondant sur une vaste expérience politique, tant à l'échelle provinciale que nationale, **Robert Stanfield** introduit le **Chapitre 2** en nous rappelant que toute évaluation de notre système parlementaire doit tenir compte de ce que le public attend du gouvernement, ainsi que de l'influence profonde qu'exercent les organes d'information électroniques. Il affirme ''que nous nous attendons à ce qu'un gouvernement responsable vis-à-vis du Parlement agisse dans des conditions et joue un rôle qui n'étaient pas prévus'' pour lui. Selon M. Stanfield, le choix offert aux Canadiens se situe ''entre un gouvernement qui s'insinue partout et un gouvernement responsable vis-à-vis du Parlement . . . nous ne pouvons avoir les deux''.

M. Stanfield admet que le Parlement souffre effectivement de ''la tyrannie de l'exécutif et des intérêts acquis par les partis dominants'', mais ''par-dessus tout'', il croit fermement

> qu'un gouvernement responsable vis-à-vis du Parlement n'est pas apte à ce qu'on attend de lui; que le gouvernement et le Parlement sont tellement surchargés qu'ils en sont inefficaces; et que le Parlement est incapable de fair face aux exigences du gouvernement.

A l'appui de sa thèse de la ''surcharge'', M. Stanfield énumère la variété de tâches et de responsabilités invraisemblables qui incombent aux ministres et aux parlementaires, ainsi que le fossé qui s'élargit entre les personnes démocratiquement élues et la bureaucratie. Le principal remède doit être la recherche ''des objectifs et des valeurs de notre société . . . sans que soit surchargée notre démocratie''. Par conséquent, il nous faut d'abord comprendre que la réforme des procédures et les réformes connexes ne suffisent pas à nous sortir de cette

---

* Professeur de droit, Université de Victoria.
** Professeur adjoint de droit, Université de Victoria.

impasse; ''nous atteignons les limites des facultés humaines lorsqu'il s'agit d'être en même temps efficace et parlementaire''.

Le choix proposé par M. Stanfield a provoqué une série intéressante de réactions de la part de ses commentateurs. **Gordon Gibson**, actuellement membre de l'Assemblée législative de Colombie-Britannique, est prêt à accepter l'ordonnance de M. Stanfield mais seulement ''tant que nous conserverons la camisole de force imposée par le système parlementaire britannique''; il ne faut pas s'attendre à ce que l'on réduise les responsabilités gouvernementales à tel point que le Parlement puisse contrôler le gouvernement.

La meilleure solution, déclare M. Gibson, consiste à trancher dans le vif de nos institutions parlementaires. Selon lui, une des priorités serait d'utiliser plus volontiers certaines méthodes de ''démocratie directe'', comme le droit d'initiative et les référendums. Du côté ''indirect'', il préfère ''une se-mi-séparation'' des secteurs exécutif et législatif, en vue d'assurer un lien solide pour l'intégration de politiques, tout en permettant le relâchement de la ''poigne d'acier'' du Cabinet sur le Parlement en accordant à l'exécutif une stabilité garantie. Entre autres, M. Gibson suggère des termes fixes entre les élections, un système effectif de comités et des réformes électorales portant sur la représentation proportionnelle. Ses suggestions ont pris une importance d'autant plus grande qu'il annonçait en septembre qu'à l'avenir, il y donnerait suite à l'échelle de la politique fédérale.

Le commentaire suivant est de **Richard Guay**, membre de l'Assemblée nationale du Québec, et porte sur diverses mesures récemment instituées ou proposées dans le cadre de ce forum en vue d'élargir le rôle des parlementaires. Selon M. Guay, le succès de ces mesures parlementaires entraînera un processus rendant, à juste titre, l'exécutif et la bureaucratie comptables devant le corps législatif, ce sans quoi nous courons le risque sérieux d'avoir un système gouvernemental fermé, plus intéressé par la dissimulation et l'autoprotection que par le respect de la loi.

Se référant à la thèse de la surcharge de M. Stanfield, M. Guay conclut ses commentaires par l'analyse du chevauchement et de la duplication des services offerts aux résidents du Québec, à leurs frais, par les gouvernements fédéral et provincial. Il poursuit ainsi cette variation sur un thème:

> Au-delà des nouveaux pouvoirs que le gouvernement du Québec prendra éventuellement en charge au lieu du gouvernement fédéral, la solution ultime se situe dans la décentralisation de ces mêmes pouvoirs dans tout le territoire du Québec en faveur des institutions locales et régionales.

Après avoir analysé les tentatives précédentes en vue de réformer notre Constitution, Smiley déclare que les efforts actuels doivent porter, au-delà de la question de la distribution des pouvoirs, sur la représentation plus efficace de nos ''particularités territoriales'' en ce qui concerne les institutions du gouvernement central, particularités dont nous avons profondément conscience; autrement, il craint que notre besoin primordial d'être dirigés par un gouvernement national efficace s'effondre devant la revendication des gouvernements provinciaux du ''droit presque exclusif d'être les porte-parole des attitudes et les défenseurs des intérêts strictement territoriaux''. Le système électoral pour la Chambre des communes doit changer afin de permettre une représentation régionale et provinciale plus équilibrée. Rejetant la représentation proportionnelle, M. Smiley préférerait l'adjonction de cent membres ''provinciaux'' aux Communes, ''choisis en classant dans chaque province les candidats ayant reçu la plus grande proportion du vote populaire parmi les élus''. De plus, il est convaincu que dans le domaine des relations entre l'exécutif politique et le Parlement, ''nous devrions nous orienter vers le modèle du Congrès américain''. Les raisons pour lesquelles il est sceptique en ce qui concerne les chances de réformes importantes du Sénat méritent d'être étudiées à fond.

Il n'est pas surprenant que le premier commentateur, l'honorable **Lou Hyndman**, Ministre des Affaires fédérales et intergouvernementales de l'Alberta, conteste l'affirmation suivante de Smiley:

> . . . les mesures actuelles pour faire face à notre mécontentement en élargissant le pouvoir des provinces, sans réformer les institutions du gouvernement central, ne peuvent mener qu'à des résultats négatifs.

Monsieur Hyndman préfère pour sa part réclamer ''un changement fondamental de l'attitude de . . . la bureaucratie du gouvernement central à Ottawa''. Il a pour objectif une relation des pouvoirs dans le cadre de laquelle ''le gouvernement fédéral et chacun des gouvernements provinciaux s'équilibrent et se complètent''. Il conteste l'affliction de M. Smiley relative au fait que le gouvernement passe outre au Parlement et mentionne ses propres responsabilités vis-à-vis de la Chambre de l'Alberta, dont les membres délibèrent régulièrement sur les relations de la province avec les gouvernements, fédéral et autres.

La préférence de M. Hyndman pour le statu quo n'est pas partagée par les autres commentateurs. Le professeur **Norman Ruff**, de l'Université de Victoria, discerne d'autres preuves du déclin de l'engagement du Parlement en matière de relations fédérales-provinciales et, malgré les observations de M. Hyndman, montre peu d'intérêt pour cette tendance. Il offre sa propre version d'une proposition recommandant l'adjonction de membres ''provinciaux'' aux Communes, tout en reconnaissant que le public et les hommes politiques sont très froids à toute idée de réforme électorale ''même lorsqu'il s'agit de propositions aussi judicieuses''.

Ronald M. Burns observe que les bénéfices qui résultent normalement ''de l'introduction des responsabilités législatives et exécutives dans le système parlementaire'' peuvent diminuer au sein d'un système fédéral. Trop souvent, signale-t-il, il y a une

> tendance inévitable à rendre politiques les procédures les plus routinières lorsque l'exécutif s'engage dans presque tous les aspects de gouvernement à l'échelle nationale aussi bien que provinciale.

La triste éclipse du législateur: voilà le résultat net. On sollicite des solutions applicables, et M. Burns avance prudemment quelques idées persuasives concernant des réformes possibles du Sénat, considérablement influencées par l'expérience de l'Allemagne de l'Ouest. Ses commentaires viennent à point pour contrebalancer l'accent mis par M. Smiley sur la réforme électorale des Communes.

Dans l'avant-dernier commentaire, **Arthur Tremblay**, de la Ville de Québec, souligne l'importanee qu'il attache au rythme de la réforme constitutionnelle, compte tenu de l'approche d'un référendum au Québec. Il reconnaît avec confiance que le reste du Canada est sans doute rempli de bonne foi, mais qu'il y a un besoin urgent d'arriver à l'unanimité nationale en ce qui concerne la distribution des pouvoirs législatifs. Cette priorité doit prendre le pas sur toute réforme des institutions du gouvernement central, et ce pour deux raisons. Il se trouve peu de partisans, au Québec, du concept de fédéralisme exécutif, dans la mesure où celui-ci s'applique à la gestion des relations intergouvernementales au Québec ces dix dernières années ou plus. A en juger par l'expérience de M. Tremblay, l'Assemblée nationale s'est engagée très sérieusement dans le maniement ainsi que dans l'examen rigoureux du fédéralisme car ''la population québécoise a toujours estimé que son propre destin en tant que collectivité était en jeu dans le cadre de ces relations''. Plus important encore, il doit y avoir un vaste mouvement public en faveur de nouvelles dispositions constitutionnelles, afin que la population du Québec ait ''une troisième option'', effective et pertinente, entre le statu quo et la ''souveraineté-association'', lorsqu'on lui présentera le référendum.

Par contre, les remarques de mademoiselle **Flora MacDonald** tendent à renforcer la position de M. Smiley sur la nécessité de garantir une représentation régionale plus efficace à l'échelle fédérale. Nullement découragée, cependant, par son opposition à la réforme sénatoriale, Mlle MacDonald recommande la transformation du Sénat en Chambre des provinces dont la majorité des membres seraient nommés par les gouvernements provinciaux. Le résultat, estime-t-elle, ''même s'il ne se substituait pas aux myriades de négociations fédérales-provinciales, . . . intégrerait solidement ce processus dans le Parlement même''. Mlle MacDonald soutient fermement diverses autres mesures en vue de renforcer le rôle des membres individuels du Parlement; mais, de toute évidence, elle donne priorité aux réformes nécessaires ''pour transformer Ottawa en gouvernement réellement *fédéral,* et non plus *central* ''.

Deux mois après la conférence, le dernier groupe de propositions de changements constitutionnels fut rendu public par le Premier ministre. L'un des traits saillants du projet de loi C-60 est l'insistance avec laquelle il mise sur la réforme des institutions centrales pour mieux renforcer et structurer la voix provinciale dans la formulation de la politique nationale pour les domaines de grande importance au regard des provinces. Cependant, la réforme des institutions centrales ne porte pas sur la Chambre des communes, comme le souhaiterait M. Smiley; les propositions sont plutôt aiguillées sur la réforme du

Sénat et adoptent ainsi plusieurs des prémisses et des thèmes invoqués par M. Burns et Mlle Flora MacDonald. En fait, l'une des idées particulièrement intéressantes que privilégient plusieurs défenseurs de la réforme constitutionnelle — le Gouvernement du Canada (projet de loi C-60), l'Association du barreau canadien (rapport publié en août 1978), le Gouvernement de l'Ontario (rapport préparé par le Comité consultatif) et le Gouvernement de la Colombie-Britannique (voir le plaidoyer du Premier ministre Bennett devant la Commission sur l'unité canadienne), pour n'en nommer que quelques-uns — est la grande importance accordée à la réforme du Sénat, susceptible, mieux que tout autre procédé, de résoudre certains des problèmes éprouvés dans la gestion de nos institutions démocratiques nationales. Reste à savoir si la réforme fondamentale d'un élément essentiellement non démocratique et, jusqu'à maintenant, non pertinent de notre système législatif national, jointe à l'ignorance virtuelle d'une réforme des Communes, est soit logique, soit utile. Par bonheur, les deux types de réforme ont trouvé de fermes défenseurs lors de la conférence. La lecture et la comparaison critique des remarques d'analystes aussi avertis que Smiley, Burns et MacDonald ne peuvent que contribuer à dresser un cadre théorique valable grâce auquel pourront être évaluées les innombrables propositions de réforme constitutionnelle qui s'amoncellent actuellement sur nos bureaux.

Plusieurs conférenciers ont manifesté leur penchant pour le système américain de séparation des pouvoirs, ce qui a donné une valeur toute spéciale aux remarques livrées par le professeur **Samuel Patterson,** de l'Université d'Iowa, au **Chapitre 4.** D'entrée de jeu, il note que cette séparation de pouvoirs a créé un milieu ''favorable à l'indépendance de la législature par rapport à l'exécutif''. Par opposition au poids de l'opinion en ce qui a trait au processus législatif canadien, Patterson conclut:

> Le Congrès n'a plus à prouver sa grande autonomie, ni sa capacité d'adaptation aux changements de son environnement politique; il est très ouvert à un examen minutieux par le public et tout à fait disposé à laisser s'exprimer et à écouter les électeurs et les intérêts les plus variés.

Par son importance en tant que corps législatif, le Congrès américain se distingue, ''puisque dans la plupart des pays, la responsabilité de l'élaboration des lois est en grande partie tombée aux mains des dirigeants''.

M. Patterson passe en revue trois aspects du Congrès ''semi-souverain''. En premier lieu, il analyse le système électoral, note le taux élevé de votes lors de l'élection de titulaires et déclare que ''l'identification à un parti politique s'est avérée responsable d'une perte de votes au Congrès''. L'augmentation substantielle des ressources mises à la disposition des représentants et des sénateurs pour soutenir leur circonscription renforce l'influence de l'élu (qui est aidé, dans certains cas, du fait qu'il n'est pas tenu responsable des problèmes attribués à d'autres, y compris au Président). Le volume de ces ressources dépasse l'imagination (par exemple, les membres de la Chambre peuvent engager jusqu'à dix-huit employés; les allocations sénatoriales destinées au personnel s'élèvent jusqu'à \$844 608). Entre un tiers et la moitié de ces employés sont affectés au service d'une circonscription située dans le district ou l'Etat en question.

M. Patterson a choisi comme deuxième thème les changements dans les mécanismes d'organisation du Congrès — dans la structure des comités, la direction du parti et le personnel. Bien que certains observateurs canadiens réclament un système de comités plus puissant qui permettrait aux législateurs de contrôler le pouvoir du Cabinet, les dirigeants du Congrès essayent de prendre en main leur système bourgeonnant de comités, en réduisant le nombre de sous-comités, en concentrant chez un plus petit nombre de comités les responsabilités législatives et en créant des groupes *ad hoc* destinés à étudier les principales initiatives présidentielles (l'énergie, par exemple) qui, sinon, "iraient à l'encontre de la structure de dispersion du pouvoir des gouvernements par sous-comités". Du côté positif, le personnel du Congrès a considérablement augmenté ces dernières années, aussi bien dans les bureaux des membres que dans le cadre de l'important réseau de comités. Ce dernier développement amène, en fait, de plus en plus de gens à s'inquiéter du contrôle qu'exerce aujourd'hui la bureaucratie du Congrès sur les décisions politiques "en vertu de l'ancienneté et de l'expérience de ses membres".

Dans la troisième partie de son article, M. Patterson étudie le rôle croissant que joue le Congrès en ce qui concerne la revue des activités et des politiques de l'exécutif, surtout depuis Watergate. Cette "surveillance" comprend également un contrôle plus étroit du budget fédéral.

La perspective américaine présentée par M. Patterson permettra au lecteur de mieux comprendre le caractère unique du processus législatif du Congrès américain et la prudence avec laquelle il faut aborder toute suggestion visant à importer des réformes institutionnelles d'autres pays.

Au **Chapitre 5**, John Reid, membre du Parlement depuis 1965, s'attaque à une question épineuse: "The Backbencher and the Discharge of Legislative Responsibilities".* D'après le ton général de l'article, du moins à la première lecture, il semble satisfait du système actuel, dans la mesure où celui-ci contrôle et façonne le rôle du législateur individuel; mais ses commentateurs sont loin de partager ce point de vue.

Son apparente satisfaction peut s'expliquer en partie par l'importance que M. Reid attache aux *occasions* qui sont offertes aux membres individuels du Parlement de prendre des initiatives législatives (définies en termes génTraux) par opposition à l'impact global mesurable de leurs efforts. C'est ainsi que M. Reid passe en revue les occasions qu'ont eues de simples députés de prendre l'initiative de démontrer la nécessité d'instaurer certaines réformes particulières, de présenter des projets de loi qu'ils avaient élaborés, de présenter des propositions, de participer aux débats de la Chambre et de faire leur travail en

---

* Le député de l'arrière-plan et l'exercice des responsabilités législatives.

comités. Seule une petite minorité des membres du Parlement prennent au sérieux leurs devoirs législatifs, déclare M. Reid, car leurs activités se situent souvent loin du centre d'attention; elles exigent une compréhension approfondie des règlements de la Chambre et elles demandent beaucoup de temps.

''La contrainte la plus importante du rôle du simple député, ajoute M. Reid, est son affiliation au parti.'' La pression qui l'oblige à suivre la politique du parti et à présenter ''une position aussi uniforme que possible à l'égard d'un grand nombre de questions'' s'est accentuée depuis que les débats sont télévisés. La discipline du parti est ''nécessaire . . . au fonctionnement de la Chambre'', bien qu'en fin de compte, on ait l'impression qu'un grand nombre de députés sans portefeuille ne sont pas convaincus que les ''contraintes imposées par le parti'' doivent être respectées en tout temps et en tout lieu, puisqu'ils continuent à prendre des initiatives individuelles dans le cadre du processus législatif.

John Fraser, membre conservateur de Vancouver Sud, conteste l'importance des nombreuses occasions législatives énumérées par le conférencier principal. Au cours de ses commentaires, M. Fraser les décrit comme étant ''très limitées''. Il parle, par exemple, des activités des comités et maintient que le simple député de l'opposition ne peut faire un progrès quelconque que dans une situation où le gouvernement est minoritaire, car c'est le seul cas où ''les membres du gouvernement, qui ont besoin de l'appui de quelques membres de l'opposition, font preuve d'une étonnante tendance à négocier''.

En gros, la ''responsabilité [législative] d'un membre de l'opposition réellement hostile [à un projet de loi du gouvernement] est d'essayer de l'arrêter''. M. Fraser accepte la nature du système qui favorise les antagonismes, bien qu'il semble avoir conscience du côté négatif d'affrontements menés de façon irréfléchie et arbitraire. Par conséquent, il suggère de revoir le système des comités ''en levant la majorité des directives des partis pendant les débats en comités'', afin de permettre à ''un membre compétent du gouvernement'' (et peut-être à un ou des membre(s) de l'opposition) ''d'étudier le projet de loi de façon plus objective''. Il serait également en faveur de pourvoir les comités de ressources indépendantes en personnel. M. Fraser soutient le point de vue selon lequel ''la discipline du parti dépasse souvent les exigences'' et il se plaint du fait que ''le Cabinet et la bureaucratie dirigent réellement tout ce qui se passe et bien trop souvent, le député de l'arrière-plan finit par être un simple spectateur, attendant que sonne le timbre qui appelle les députés au vote''.

L'ancien chef du Nouveau parti démocratique de l'Ontario, député de York Sud à l'Assemblée législative de l'Ontario depuis 1955, monsieur **Donald C. MacDonald**, livre le deuxième commentaire relativement à l'article de M. Reid. Il critique énergiquement les circonstances qui ont permis au Cabinet de s'octroyer la prérogative exclusive de présenter des lois, ''le simple député étant pratiquement réduit à s'objecter ou opiner du bonnet''. Les expériences actuelles en Ontario, destinées à valoriser éventuellement les projets de loi des simples parlementaires, offrent toutefois une lueur d'espoir, bien que ''la perspective d'arriver même à un progrès aussi minime n'ait que peu de chances s'il advenait que le gouvernement récupère la majorité''.

Les comités permanents donnent effectivement au simple député l'occasion d'agir mais ''leur organisation et leur fonctionnement . . . constituent la bête noire de la vie parlementaire''. Certains comités sélectionnés (qui ne se réunissent que lorsque la Chambre ne siège pas) sont trop souvent des instruments destinés à occuper les députés sans portefeuille d'un gouvernement à forte majorité. En fin de compte, leur succès dépend ''surtout de la qualité des membres du comité''.

D'après le professeur **Paul Thomas** de l'Université du Manitoba, l'article de Reid a jeté un souffle d'optimisme trompeur, sans répondre ''à d'autres témoignages sur l'existence du simple député qui dénotent un fort sentiment de frustration, presque d'impuissance totale . . . ''. Il déplore le fait que M. Reid ''ne parle pas des obstacles qui empêchent le simple député de jouer véritablement un rôle législatif creatif''. Par contre, il reconnaît que l'article de John Reid ''attire notre attention sur certaines dimensions internes et négligées du processus législatif'' ainsi que sur ''l'importance du fait que le processus représentatif passe par l'intermédiaire des membres du Parlement''.

M. Thomas présente ensuite quelques idées très judicieuses relativement à un renforcement de la Chambre des communes, qui lui permettrait de surveiller l'administration. Ce point de vue rappelle les commentaires préalables de M. Patterson sur les pouvoirs de surveillance du Congrès. Thomas fait valoir avec conviction l'argument que la Chambre devrait reconnaître

> les limites de ses capacités lorsqu'il s'agit de façonner le contenu des lois et se concentrer davantage sur l'examen minutieux du fonctionnement législatif et sur la transmission des revendications populaires au Cabinet et à la bureaucratie . . .

Diverses réformes devraient à l'avenir consolider la fonction de surveillance des membres; et

> grâce à l'amplification de ses activités de supervision, la Chambre pourrait également participer plus souvent à l'élaboration des lois, étant mieux informée sur la nature des opérations gouvernementales.

M. Thomas ajoute quelques commentaires détaillés sur certaines questions spécifiques soulevées par M. Reid et conclut que les simples députés ''se sentent frustrés à cause de leur impuissance, à influencer la politique''. Nombre de suggestions de réformes se présentent. Cet ensemble de suggestions constitue une liste de changements importants de la procédure parlementaire, dont un grand nombre consolideraient le pouvoir et l'influence du législateur individuel. Cependant, l'enthousiasme de M. Thomas pour les changements suggérés est modéré parce qu'il prévoit que la réforme

> continuera de s'amplifier graduellement, aussi bien parce que les gouvernements ne souhaitent pas imposer de changements qui déséquilibreraient la stabilité politique à leur détriment que parce qu'il est difficile de prévoir toutes les conséquences d'un changement quelconque.

La majorité des articles présentés à la conférence analysaient divers aspects internes du processus législatif — élaboration des lois, relations fédérales-provinciales, procédure parlementaire, objectifs et fonctionnement du Parlement et avenir de la démocratie parlementaire. Toutefois, deux des articles traitaient plus précisément de l'influence des institutions et des activités externes sur le cours général du processus législatif et constituaient une tentative d'évaluation des responsabilités de ces institutions lorsqu'elles ont à faire face à des personnes impliquées dans le processus législatif.

Le principal article du **Chapitre 6**, écrit par le professeur **William Stanbury** et intitulé ''Lobbying and Interest Group Representation'',* constitue un sérieux effort en vue d'offrir un cadre analytique global pour l'étude de la représentation des divers groupes de pression au Canada. Les négociations de couloirs étant très répandues au Canada, cette étude présente un grand intérêt.

Les deux principales questions sur lesquelles se penche M. Stanbury dans son article sont la description de l'étendue de la pratique du *lobbying* aujourd'hui au Canada et la dissipation de certains mythes traditionnels relatifs à ces activités et à ceux qui y participent. Bien que le terme *lobbying* provienne probablement de Grande-Bretagne, où des particuliers s'entretenaient avec leurs élus au Parlement dans les couloirs de la Chambre des communes, le stéréotype canadien de l'agent de couloir repose probablement sur sa conception du *lobbyist* américain — ventru, gros cigare à la bouche, voiture tape-à-l'oeil et compte en banque rondelet. M. Stanbury souligne à juste titre qu'il n'y a pas de modèle unique d'agent de couloir ou de ses activités. Il en existe de toutes sortes — associations qui veillent en permanence sur les intérêts de leurs clients, particuliers employés pour certaines tâches spécifiques ainsi que groupes *ad hoc* qui élaborent des campagnes en vue de certaines luttes législatives — et qui mènent leurs affaires de bien des façons différentes.

M. Stanbury choisit comme point de départ le principe selon lequel les négociations de couloirs sont une réalité et font légitimement partie du processus démocratique. Elles sont étroitement liées à l'idéal pluraliste de la théorie démocratique, puisqu'elles offrent un véhicule à l'articulation des intérêts des citoyens ainsi qu'à l'évaluation du poids relatif de ces intérêts. En outre, la croissance ainsi que la complexité des gouvernements modernes exigent qu'il y ait une circulation d'information efficace entre ceux qui gouvernent et ceux qui sont gouvernés. Les négociations de couloirs peuvent concourir à structurer ce réseau.

A la suite de cette valorisation du rôle théorique joué par le *lobbying* au sein d'une société démocratique, M. Stanbury en étudie trois aspects par le menu: ses objectifs, ses véhicules, ainsi que l'opportunité de cette pratique. Il conclut que les agents parlementaires canadiens efficaces (a) traitent principalement avec les ministres du Cabinet et les hauts fonctionnaires, (b) emploient des moyens

---

* Le *lobbying* et la représentation des groupes de pression.

subtils, officieux, non protocolaires pour les approcher (Stanbury parle ''de l'opacité des communications entre les *lobbyists* et les ministres ou fonctionnaires qu'ils veulent atteindre'') et (c) commencent leurs activités dès que possible (l'agent idéal est celui qui fait germer ses propres intérêts législatifs dans l'esprit d'un politicien chevronné, et non pas celui qui se contente de réagir, même efficacement, à ce que d'autres on semé). Tout en esquissant le portrait de l'agent parlementaire canadien efficace, M. Stanbury fait un certain nombre de comparaisons intéressantes entre les agents et les négociations mêmes au Canada et aux Etats-Unis. Le *lobbying* américain semble notamment beaucoup plus ouvert et plus dynamique et les cibles du *lobbyist* américain, soit les législateurs, sont tout à fait différentes de celles de l'agent parlementaire canadien, qui cherche à atteindre les ministres et les fonctionnaires.

M. Stanbury ne s'est pas tiré indemne de la conférence. A partir de son expérience de négociateur pour la défense des intérêts des travailleurs et des femmes, **Johanna den Hertog** conteste l'évaluation que fait M. Stanbury des conséquences bénéfiques qu'ont les négociations de couloirs sur la société canadienne. Elle soutient que ces activités au Canada n'arrivent pas, pour l'heure, à éliminer les différences entre les classes, car elles ne permettent pas à tous les citoyens d'exprimer leurs intérêts, ni aux législateurs d'évaluer l'importance relative d'intérêts rivaux. Au contraire, déclare-t-elle, de nombreux groupes n'ont pas accès au *lobbying* et d'autres ne sont pas qualifiés pour s'en servir. Ceux qui ont facilement accès à la procédure et qui savent l'utiliser, c'est-à-dire les hommes d'affaires, peuvent en profiter; ainsi la différence entre les classes se perpétue-t-elle au Canada. C'est un mythe de croire que le *lobbying* est utile à l'idéal pluraliste — en fait, vue la façon dont le *lobbying* se pratique actuellement au Canada, c'est plutôt une négation de cet idéal.

Andrew Roman, Directeur exécutif et Conseiller général du Centre de défense de l'intérêt public à Ottawa, conteste également certaines conclusions de M. Stanbury. Il pense, par exemple, que bien que de nombreux auteurs théoriques affirment que les agents parlementaires les plus efficaces tentent surtout de négocier avec les politiciens chevronnés, ministres et hauts fonctionnaires, ce sont en fait ceux qui prennent le processus d'élaboration des politiques à la base qui ont le plus de succès à Ottawa. A son avis, les agents les plus efficaces sont ''si discrets et si réservés que l'on ne parle jamais d'eux'', ou alors qu'ils ne sont pas perçus comme tels (cabinets d'avocats et avocats) et qu'ils exercent leurs fonctions sous d'autres ''robes''. Le négociateur astucieux, affirme Roman, sait où et quand percer la ''trame sans couture'' du gouvernement fédéral, qui ''n'est pas une machine que l'on fait fonctionner, mais une série d'événements discontinus et aléatoires: des imprévus que personne ne peut véritablement contrôler à quelque moment que ce soit''. Monsieur Roman conclut en passant en revue les problèmes auxquels font face les associations de défense d'intérêts publics qui organisent des activités de *lobbying,* et il termine en citant le cas de la loi sur la concurrence, dont M. Stanbury a longuement parlé auparavant.

Le troisième commentateur, **Alasdair McKichan**, est Président du Conseil canadien de la vente au détail et, du fait qu'il se trouve au plus haut rang du Conseil, joue le rôle de porte-parole de nombreuses entreprises de vente au détail lors de négociations avec les gouvernements et les législateurs dans tout le pays. Monsieur McKichan passe systématiquement en revue les caractéristiques qu'ont en commun les groupes de pression les plus efficaces (auxquels il intègre les associations de travailleurs, à l'opposé de Mme den Hertog); il rejette l'idée selon laquelle taille, richesse et puissance constituent les garanties du succès de la négociation. Il est convaincu de la véracité du principe pluraliste exposé par M. Stanbury, non seulement en théorie, mais également en pratique. Loin d'admettre que les exemples cités par le conférencier principal (concurrence, révision de la loi sur les brevets et réforme du crédit au consommateur) illustrent bien la puissance du lobby des affaires, McKichan affirme que chaque mesure ''aurait pu tout aussi bien être choisie à titre d'exemple de l'inefficacité du lobby des affaires''. Ses commentaires portent ensuite sur deux thèmes très constructifs — les stratégies adoptées par les *lobbyists* efficaces et quelques recommandations à l'endroit du gouvernement, destinées à faciliter la participation publique au processus législatif. La corrélation qui existe entre un grand nombre de ses recommandations et certaines des réformes préconisées au Chapitre 5 (The Backbencher)* et au Chapitre 8 (Procedural Reform)** mérite d'être soulignée.

Le deuxième article, traitant d'une institution et d'une activité qui s'éloignent quelque peu du courant principal du processus législatif, a été présenté par **Geoffrey Stevens**, commentateur politique d'Ottawa au journal *Globe & Mail*. Malgré la propension journalistique traditionnelle ''à éviter toute introspection'', Stevens présente au **Chapitre 7** un article réfléchi intitulé ''The Influence and Responsibilities of the Media''.* Stevens déclare que ''les media ont tant d'influence et sont tellement en vue en cette époque de journalisme post-Watergate, qu'ils doivent plus que jamais se livrer à l'introspection et à l'autocritique''. Dans un article exhaustif et réaliste, Stevens analyse et critique sa profession. Il n'hésite pas à tirer les conclusions négatives qui s'imposent: ''Le fait est, dit-il, que les organes d'information sont accusés de superficialité, de se concentrer sur des banalités et de négliger les problèmes de fond, de s'attacher au sensationnel et de perdre de vue l'importance tant du fonctionnement que des défectuosités du système.''

Stevens souligne que les organes d'information n'ont que peu d'influence à partir du moment où la législation est présentée au Parlement. C'est plutôt avant qu'ils exercent une influence sur la politique gouvernementale, d'une part à travers les points de vue exprimés dans les éditoriaux et les colonnes politiques et d'autre part, grâce au choix des questions à traiter et à l'orientation imprimée aux informations.

---

* Le député sans portefeuille.
** La réforme des procédures.
* L'influence et les responsabilités des organes d'information.

Stevens estime que ces deux derniers points — sélection des nouvelles et méthode de reportage — constituent les principaux problèmes en ce qui concerne la responsabilité des organes d'information. Il s'attaque aux problèmes de définition et de théorie posés par les termes ''responsabilité des organes d'information''. Responsabilité vis-à-vis de quoi? de l'équité? de l'honnêteté? de la sincérité? de la compréhension? Et responsabilité envers qui? envers soi? envers les éditeurs? les rédacteurs? les lecteurs? Stevens conclut que le journaliste a deux responsabilités principales: il a le devoir de connaître aussi bien que possible les questions sur lesquelles il écrit et d'être ''aussi objectif qu'il est humainement possible'' dans le choix des questions à cerner et dans la manière même de les traiter.

Dans son premier commentaire, M. **Walter Young** critique plusieurs des explications offertes par Stevens relativement à l'incompétence de la presse. Il émet alors l'opinion, peut-être discutable, selon laquelle les propriétaires qui monopolisent plusieurs journaux n'ont rien de croque-mitaines, contrairement au portrait qu'on fait souvent d'eux. A une époque où le ''péché mignon du journalisme'' réside dans son ''faible pour la banalité et sa conviction profonde que le local prime sur le provincial et le national'', Young déclare que les avantages théoriques découlant de la concentration de plusieurs organes d'information entre les mains d'un même propriétaire — reportages plus vastes et plus approfondis — ne sont pas assez mis en valeur. Il affirme que la médiocrité du journalisme est accentuée par sa capitulation devant ''l'emploi judicieux que fait l'exécutif politique des communiqués de presse et des divulgations''. Prisonnière des manipulations politiques, ''la presse a renoncé à une grande partie de sa liberté et c'est pour cette raison qu'elle ne joue plus le rôle qui faisait d'elle un ''quart-état''. Etant donnée la situation du tiers-état, on ne peut que déplorer ce fait.''

Dans le commentaire qui suit, M. **Bruce Hutchison**, auteur et commenta-teur politique chevronné, nous rappelle, ainsi qu'à ses collègues, que les media doivent porter leur regard au-delà de la cohue des questions passagères quotidiennes et le fixer de temps en temps sur les questions plus importantes auxquelles le genre humain fera face dans l'avenir. Il conclut: ''La première responsabilité des organes d'information est donc de préparer le public à un avenir très différent du présent et, du moins je le crains, beaucoup moins confortable.''

La définition de la responsabilité des media, au plan de l'objectivité, donnée par M. Stevens est un thème qui revient souvent dans les commentaires des autres journalistes présents à la table ronde qui suit son allocution lors de la conférence. Les commentateurs ont également soulevé un certain nombre de questions importantes. **Catherine Bergman** évoque les difficultés qu'éprouve la presse francophone au sein de media à forte prédominance anglophone. A l'instar de Stevens, elle estime que le pouvoir réel de la presse est un pouvoir de sélection, mais elle ajoute que ''la presse francophone, quant à elle, n'a pas ce pouvoir. La première page du *Globe & Mail*, par exemple, détermine non seulement l'ordre des informations présentées par la C.B.C. et les premières pages d'un grand nombre de journaux de langue anglaise au Canada; mais également l'ordre des informations de langue française.'' Pareille situation amène Catherine Bergman à penser qu''''il n'y a actuellement aucun organe d'information qui reflète exclusivement le point de vue du Québec, et encore moins le point de vue du Québec en ce qui concerne les affaires canadiennes''.

Pierre O'Neil s'inquiète du fossé qui sépare les journalistes — et les politiciens — d'une part, et les intérêts de l'homme de la rue, d'autre part. Selon lui, cette distance indique peut-être que la presse n'a que peu d'influence, que ce soit sur les politiciens ou sur leur auditoire.

Frances Russell du *Winnipeg Tribune,* qui a fait ses armes à Ottawa et dans plusieurs capitales provinciales, insiste sur l'impact qu'a la politique polarisée sur le souci d'objectivité. Le journaliste politique, souligne-t-elle, doit acquérir et protéger la ''capacité de se tenir en retrait, de jauger les deux côtés d'un oeil toujours critique exempt de tout parti pris''. En pratique, cet idéal professionel a un effet mesurable et bénéfique sur les politiciens, sur le processus législatif et sur le public. Mais au sein d'un climat politique polarisé comme celui de la Colombie-Britannique et du Manitoba, soutient Frances Russell, le commentateur politique sérieux s'expose à ''une expérience désastreuse'' car ''tout comme la nature déteste le vide, la polarité a horreur de l'objectivité. Et bon gré mal gré, on se retrouve avec une étiquette.'' Elle exhorte les organes d'information à résister à ces pressions et à faire entendre ''la voix de la modération et du bon sens contre . . . les 'les partisans sectaires'''. Si l'on considère le ton qui prédomine dans les commentaires précédents, la requête de Frances Russell semble vouée à un sort décevant, ce dont tous les Canadiens devraient se préoccuper sérieusement.

Le **Chapitre 8** nous présente les opérations quotidiennes de notre système parlementaire et son impuissance à gérer les affaires publiques. Dans un article détaillé et sérieux, le professeur **C.E.S. Franks**, de l'université Queen's, analyse les raisons théoriques et les résultats réels des réformes de procédures qui ont été effectuées dans le cadre du système législatif fédéral, particulièrement au cours de la dernière décennie.

Bien que la réforme parlementaire ne soit pas une question à laquelle s'intéresse généralement le public ou même qui fasse l'objet d'analyses théoriques sérieuses — M. Franks déclare modestement que ''sans aucun doute pour bien des gens, s'inquiéter de procédure parlementaire équivaut à discuter vins sur le Titanic'' — ce serait sans doute une erreur que de voir un manque d'importance dans ce qui est en fait un manque de lucidité et d'intérêt. La Chambre des communes est quand même l'organisme le plus en vue et le plus important en ce qui concerne l'élaboration des lois dans ce pays et elle mérite, par conséquent, que les spécialistes et les citoyens prennent le temps d'évaluer sérieusement ce qui s'y passe.

Deux faits frappants relatifs à la Chambre des communes émergent au cours de la deuxième moitié de cette décennie — tous deux dignes d'étude. Il s'agit d'abord du fait que le rendement effectif de la Chambre des communes a diminué ces dernières années. L'un des faits saillants des années Trudeau est le grand nombre de législations importantes qui ont poussé leur dernier soupir au Feuilleton de la Chambre à la fin de la session législative. Toutefois, dans quelques provinces, y compris la Colombie-Britannique, le rendement des assemblées provinciales a remarquablement augmenté. Dans le but d'arriver à ce résultat, un grand nombre de provinces ont rationalisé et considérablement simplifié leur système législatif plutôt rudimentaire. La Colombie-Britannique, notamment, a établi un système de Cabinet fonctionnant par comités (relative-ment efficace) et un système législatif par comités (beaucoup moins efficace). Ces innovations méritent notre attention car elles reposent surtout sur les systèmes des comités législatifs et du Cabinet fédéral, si soigneusement élaborés par le Premier ministre Trudeau. Cependant, en dépit du parallélisme de ces structures, les résultats produits par les deux systèmes sont totalement différents. La création, à l'échelle fédérale, d'une structure de comités simplifiée n'a pas abouti à une augmentation du nombre de lois adoptées par le Parlement; par contre, l'adaptation provinciale de cette structure a produit précisément cette augmentation. Bien que certains facteurs extrinsèques puissent sans aucun doute contribuer à expliquer cette anomalie (par exemple, une grande partie des lois adoptées par la législature de la Colombie-Britannique au cours de la session 1977 — session très productive — étaient de caractère secondaire ou d'intérêt "domestique"), on peut apprendre beaucoup en comparant la marche des processus législatifs aux niveaux fédéral et provincial cette dernière décennie.

Autre fait à noter: le peu d'intérêt que suscite la réforme des Communes au cours des présents débats sur l'unité nationale. Nous savons tous aujourd'hui que le centre des débats sur notre crise nationale ne se situe pas à la Chambre des communes, mais réside plutôt dans la combinaison de la conférence fédéra-le-provinciale et des organes d'information, particulièrement la télévision. Non seulement les Communes ne constituent pas un *forum* pour le débat sur l'unité nationale, mais elles ne sont même pas *objet* du débat. Il y a, à cet égard, un contraste frappant entre la Chambre des communes et le Sénat. Presque tous les personnages politiques importants au plan national — le Premier ministre, Joe Clark, Flora MacDonald, le Premier ministre Bennett, le Premier ministre Davis, par l'intermédiaire de son Comité consultatif — ont souligné l'importance d'une réforme en profondeur du Sénat dans le cadre de la réforme constitutionnelle nécessaire. En fait, certains hommes politiques semblent estimer que la réforme sénatoriale devrait passer avant toute autre réforme constitutionnelle. En un sens, cette passion nationale collective (Henri Bourassa a dit un jour que la réforme du Sénat "frappe de temps en temps, tout comme d'autres épidémies et d'autres fièvres") pour la réforme du Sénat est incongrue. Nous consacrons une énergie intellectuelle intense à la division de l'administration nationale qui élabore les lois, division qui n'a joué qu'un rôle très mince au cours de l'histoire, et, en même temps, nous négligeons presque totalement l'organisme qui est et doit être en réalité le centre vital de notre processus démocratique.

L'article de M. Franks constitue un antidote utile à la préoccupation nationale actuelle à l'égard de la réforme du Sénat. Il reconnaît que la Chambre des communes constitue l'axe du processus d'élaboration des lois du Canada et que la quantité aussi bien que la qualité de nos lois nationales dépendent surtout de l'efficacité de son fonctionnement. M. Franks aborde ce thème et offre plusieurs explications utiles, à deux niveaux. En premier lieu, il fait une étude détaillée et révélatrice du fonctionnement actuel des Communes et, en particulier, du nouveau système législatif par comités. Deuxièmement, à partir de cette étude, Franks arrive à faire un certain nombre de commentaires très pertinents sur la direction que prendra éventuellement la Chambre des communes (il conclut par exemple: "L'un des pires dangers pour le Parlement au cours des prochaines années sera, je le crains, d'être rejeté dans l'ombre tandis que les relations fédérales-provinciales et, éventuellement, l'élaboration d'une nouvelle Constitiution prendront la place d'honneur."). Finalement, M. Franks fait quelques recommandations spécifiques destinées à améliorer le processus parlementaire. Il s'agit de propositions innovatrices et parfois discutables (il suggère, par exemple, que le Comité permanent des comptes publics se réunisse à huis clos) qui constituent une excellente conclusion à l'une des études les plus minutieuses et les plus utiles réalisées sur la Chambre des communes ces dernières années.

John Holtby puise les commentaires qui suivent dans son expérience à titre de Premier greffier adjoint à l'Assemblée législative de l'Ontario pour présenter une perspective provinciale. Il offre une étude subtile et féconde des derniers changements de procedure en Ontario, destinés à mettre en valeur le rôle du simple député, et il passe ensuite en revue les réformes qu'il estime nécessaires pour que le Parlement puisse exercer un contrôle sur les dépenses publiques. Ses recommandations sont empreintes de sens pratique, particulièrement en ce qui concerne les personnes désireuses d'adhérer aux comités, les ressources en personnel ainsi que le volume initial de travail. Par ailleurs, il appuierait toute disposition destinée à augmenter le nombre de débats parlementaires consacrés à l'étude de la politique ministérielle et visant à imposer aux parlementaires l'obligation de se rendre régulièrement dans les territoires relevant de leur compétence.

Monsieur Holtby se rallie à certaines des opinions avancées par M. Franks, celles dont il estime qu'elles visent en somme à simplifier "le travail du gouvernement en limitant le droit de regard des parlementaires sur la gestion gouvernementale". Une lecture attentive de ses commentaires révèle à quel moment il lui paraît important d'avoir un système parlementaire bien adapté aux besoins de la société moderne. "Serait-il bon, demande-t-il, d'envisager la séparation de l'exécutif et du législatif tout en maintenant la période de questions?"

Le **Chapitre 9** présente une allocution prononcée par le professeur **W.H. Charles**, de l'université Dalhousie, qui étudie de longue date le processus législatif et est l'un des premiers à avoir donné un cours de législation dans les facultés de droit du Canada. Dans cet article, intitulé ''Public Policy and Legislative Drafting'',* M. Charles tente de répondre à la question suivante: le rédacteur de lois joue-t-il un rôle créateur lorsqu'il formule des lois ou est-il un simple technicien qui n'exprime que les politiques établies par les législateurs et les fonctionnaires?

L'article de M. Charles a le grand mérite, entre autres, d'être le résultat de sérieuses recherches empiriques qu'il a entreprises pour pouvoir répondre à la question précédemment posée. Il a fait parvenir un long questionnaire à vingt conseillers législatifs canadiens importants, dont la plupart lui on fourni des réponses détaillées. En conséquence, l'article de M. Charles nous donne peut-être la première image nette du rôle et de l'influence des rédacteurs de lois au Canada.

Cet article suggère un grand nombre d'explications utiles et parfois surprenantes. Il semble, par exemple, que l'importance du rôle de concepteur de politiques que joue le conseiller législatif est inversement proportionnelle à celle de la Division de la rédaction du gouvernement. Les rédacteurs qui manifestent des talents créateurs, dans la formulation de politiques, semblent provenir des provinces plus petites, où la bureaucratie gouvernementale est réduite.

Une deuxième partie de l'article de M. Charles présente un grand intérêt: elle traite du rôle des rédacteurs lorsqu'ils préparent des lois secondaires. Deux points à noter: en premier lieu, les règlements sont généralement rédigés par des fonctionnaires du service responsable d'administrer la loi d'autorisation. Deuxièmement, il semble que le rôle du rédacteur, en tant que concepteur de politiques, soit considérable. M. Charles déclare:

> On s'attend de toute évidence à ce que le rédacteur joue un rôle important dans l'élaboration du contenu fondamental des règlements, plus que lorsqu'il s'agit de la rédaction de statuts . . . Compte tenu du volume des lois secondaires adoptées tous les ans, la contribution des rédacteurs à l'élaboration de politiques pourrait être considérable.

Si l'on suppose, à juste titre, que les fonctionnaires ministériels qui rédigent les règlements ne sont pas aussi compétents que les rédacteurs professionnels employés par les conseillers législatifs, une image intéressante se fait jour: le rôle des rédacteurs politiques professionnels dans l'élaboration des politiques est peut-être moins important que le rôle des rédacteurs non spécialisés.

Malgré cette source d'inquiétude potentielle, M. Charles conclut que le conseiller législatif canadien joue un rôle essentiel en tant qu'architecte des programmes statutaires, en tant que rédacteur ou concepteur d'une terminologie qui doit refléter avec précision la politique choisie et, enfin, en tant que

---

* Politiques et rédaction des lois.

"sentinelle et protecteur officieux des droits de l'individu". Quelle que soit leur influence individuelle sur des questions politiques de portée plus vaste, les rédacteurs de lois ont résisté, selon lui, à toute tendance à l'abus de pouvoir grâce à leur "remarquable intégrité personnelle et professionnelle".

Dans un premier commentaire, **J. Douglas Lambert** déclare sans ambages que "la consultation en matière législative ne constitue qu'une partie des fonctions du conseiller législatif". Il soutient que son rôle de concepteur de politiques (de conseiller) peut légitimement être élargi. Il établit une comparaison tout à fait pertinente entre le juriste privé (qui doit conseiller et, en même temps, exécuter maintes fonctions juridiques et techniques) et le rédacteur de lois (à qui bien des gens contesteraient le droit d'exercer les fonctions de consultant), et il conclut que la formation et la compétence de nombreux rédacteurs de lois leur permettent de mener à bien la double tâche de leurs homologues de l'exercice privé. Cependant, tout comme l'avocat privé, l'avocat-conseil ne doit pas s'égarer dans le domaine de la politique auquel il n'est pas rompu. Ainsi, les rédacteurs/conseillers législatifs doivent maintenir et protéger leur indépendance vis-à-vis de leur client (le procureur général ou l'assemblée législative). En d'autres mots, ils lui donnent des conseils sans s'identifier aux promoteurs. En fin de compte, leurs conseils doivent reposer sur "l'objectivité et le jugement qui ne peuvent provenir que du détachement vis-à-vis des conséquences découlant des diverses solutions au problème".

Le professeur **Richard Dole, Jr.**, de l'Université de Houston, présente une perspective américaine. De nombreux rédacteurs de lois aux Etats-Unis ne sont pas juristes et, en conséquence, il faut décider si leur oeuvre est un projet de loi ou de règlement. Leur participation au début de l'élaboration de propositions législatives est très limitée, en partie à cause de la dispersion du pouvoir d'initiation qui existe dans le cadre du système congressionnel et également à cause de la grande complaisance à confier aux tribunaux la question de la constitutionnalité des statuts. Bien que les rédacteurs de lois professionnels américains participent moins à l'élaboration de politiques qu'un grand nombre de rédacteurs professionnels canadiens, M. Dole est convaincu que l'exercice de cette profession va de pair avec un pouvoir et des responsabilités considérables. Il demande que l'on établisse des directives précises permettant que l'on se serve de "l'histoire législative objective comme d'un auxiliaire extrinsèque à la structure statutaire, sans égard à l'ambiguïté apparente des textes statutaires". Il estime que cette façon de procéder est indispensable car les "services législatifs du gouvernement sont trop importants pour que la mise en application de ses politiques [passées en revue par les tribunaux] dépende des termes choisis par un rédacteur professionnel de projets de lois".

A la fin du Chapitre 9 figurent les réponses à plusieurs questions importantes soulevées par les membres de l'auditoire. Cette session a été présidée en totalité par G. Alan Higenbottam, Conseiller législatif de la Colombie-Britannique, dont les rédacteurs de lois ainsi que de nombreux amis au Canada déplorent le décès, survenu l'été dernier.

Au **Chapitre 10**, on trouve quelques opinions très personnelles de feu **John Mackintosh**, alors Membre du Parlement (Berwick & East Lothian) et Chef du Département de Sciences politiques à l'Université d'Edimbourg. C'est avec l'éloquence et l'esprit qu'on lui connaît qu'il aborde le sujet "The Future of Representative Parliamentary Democracy".* Député sans portefeuille influent et indépendant, savant de renommée internationale, M. Mackintosh fait une synthèse adroite des observations des autres collaborateurs et présente quelques remarques d'une vaste portée et incitant à la réflexion sur les mesures de base nécessaires à l'amélioration du système parlementaire. La nouvelle de son décès, survenu le 30 juillet 1978, a attristé ses innombrables admirateurs et amis et déclenché un torrent d'éloges des deux côtés de l'Atlantique. Ceux qui ont eu le privilège de s'entretenir avec lui et de l'écouter à la conférence ont été personnellement sincèrement affectés par sa mort, car c'était un conférencier "combatif et spirituel", "dynamique et stimulant, qui avait le don d'établir des contacts humains simples et naturels" (*The Times,* 31 juillet 1978); ses pairs le décrivaient "comme étant l'un des cinq ou six grands orateurs de sa génération" (*The Scotsman,* 31 juillet 1978). Son comportement, lors de la soirée de clôture d'une conférence très animée et dont chacune des sessions avait attiré toute son attention, confirme et donne encore plus de poids à la sincérité des hommages rendus à un personnage aussi exceptionnel. Sa mort porte un dur coup aux efforts faits tant au Royaume-Uni qu'au Canada pour faire échec à la tendance vers un gouvernement exécutif.

Dans ses remarques, M. Mackintosh exprime quelques doutes pratiques à l'égard de la théorie de surcharge présentée par M. Stanfield, tout en convenant que "nous devons simplement produire un système d'économie mixte qui, tout en ne limitant pas sans raison l'activité gouvernementale, établisse nettement la limite des droits privés et de l'activité économique que le gouvernement ne peut pas contrôler efficacement". Sans charte "des activités gouvernementales légitimes", nous réagirons toujours "aux réclamations incessantes d'actions qui, à leur tour, se transforment en promesses politiques dont les objectifs sont hors de portée et dont l'accumulation jette le discrédit sur le système dans son ensemble".

Dans le cadre du domaine "des politiques réalisables", déclare M. Mackintosh, les Communes et les assemblées législatives doivent regagner leur place de tribunes où sont débattues et prises les principales décisions concernant les affaires publiques. Il fait allusion aux possibilités d'introduire des réformes électorales permettant de mieux représenter "les blocs de pouvoir", les questions régionales et ainsi de suite, dans le cadre du droit, en citant particulièrement le cas de la deuxième Chambre. Il est nettement en faveur d'une plus grande liberté (et responsabilité politique) pour le simple député, faisant remarquer à juste titre que les moyens disponibles sont bien plus évidents que la

---

* L'avenir de la démocratie parlementaire représentative.

"volonté politique du gouvernement et des personnes en questions". Il est convaincu que la réponse repose sur un système efficace de comités dans le cadre duquel les membres deviendraient des investigateurs devant lesquels les organismes publics et les fontionnaires seraient comptables de leurs politiques et de leurs dépenses. Selon lui, cette procédure serait une "activité légitime pour les législateurs au sein d'un système parlementaire et pourrait passer avant l'éthique qui veut que l'on appuie systématiquement son parti"; elle dénoterait un sens des responsabilités plus grand envers les électeurs du fait que "dans le cadre des tâches de militant d'un parti, il existe une tâche secondaire . . . de critique et de contrôle".

L'absence de volonté politique notée plus haut s'aggrave à cause de la confusion croissante qui existe entre les institutions directes et les institutions démocratiques de représentation. Après avoir exclu les référendums s'appliquant au retranchement de certaines clauses spécifiques dans les constitutions écrites, M. Mackintosh exprime son opposition à toute autre tentative destinée à faire fonctionner le pays à coups de questionnaires. Il emploie ici quelques-uns de ses propres exemples "maison" pour donner plus de poids à ses arguments. Ses remarques sont livrées alors que Messieurs Lang et Trudeau expriment leur attachement renouvelé à l'appareil de la "démocratie directe". M. Mackintosh craint visiblement que l'enracinement du système de scrutin "oui-non" entraîne un nouvel affaiblissement d'un système de représentation déjà extrêmement fragile. Des décisions complexes, impliquant l'allocation de ressources rares, ne peuvent être ramenées au "choix entre boutons rouges et boutons bleus".

Ce qu'il faut, plutôt, c'est une démocratie parlementaire réellement représentative, où les législateurs sont comptables de leurs actions, où le soutien du parti ne constitue pas une camisole de force éthique et où les partis tiennent ou tombent selon leurs réalisations, mesurées en regard des programmes électoraux qu'ils ont soigneusement élaborés. Le gouvernement par représentation, ajoute M. Mackintosh, "n'est *pas* un choix médiocre pour diriger la démocratie, mais la façon *adéquate* de diriger une démocratie au sein de toute société moderne".

A l'appui de la nécessité d'établir une législature activiste, M. Mackintosh déclare que le gouvernement (exécutif ou Cabinet) devient en réalité un gouvernement anonyme dominé par des fonctionnaires non élus. Cette tendance a encore élargi le fossé entre le gouvernement et le public et menace d'affaiblir la base d'unanimité tellement essentielle au fonctionnement de la démocratie.

De toute évidence, les remarques de M. Mackintosh ont fait vibrer de nombreuses cordes sensibles, ce qui a donné lieu à une période de questions-réponses très animée.

Chapter Two

The Present State of the Legislative Process in Canada: Myths and Realities

by
*Robert L. Stanfield**

My subject is the governmental process at our federal level. I do not claim my paper to be a learned dissertation, with footnotes and scholarly allusions. I will give you rather the illusions and disillusions of a practising politician; of a practitioner who has tried to observe and understand how we are being governed but has not cluttered his mind with facts exposed or opinions expressed in learned journals, as will probably be all too apparent. I will be stating some propositions rather starkly, without scholarly qualifications. That may have the advantage of provoking discussion even if I am uttering something less than eternal truth. I might also add that I will not be discussing the role of the Senate of Canada.

Changing Role of Governments

When one discusses how well our governmental institutions are performing, it is necessary to recognize the change which has occurred in the conditions or context in which these institutions are performing. It is hardly appropriate to compare the performance of legislatures and governments in the last century with the performance of legislatures and governments today. Changes in society and values have obviously increased enormously the difficulties of legislatures and governments. Fifty years ago citizens in Canada expected little of their governments outside limited areas of responsibility. Governments in Canada were assumed to be inefficient and touched by corruption or tarnished by patronage, but this mattered little to the citizen because he did not ordinarily expect much from government, unless he was looking for patronage. Patronage was a fact of life and was taken for granted. There was plenty of time to argue or exploit the great questions, like provincial rights in 1896 and reciprocity with the United States in 1911. I do not wish or need to push the argument too far in order to remind you that the role of government in our society has changed enormously in the past half century. Fifty years ago the citizen had no more respect for the

---

* The Honourable Robert L. Stanfield, P.C., Q.C., M.P. (Halifax)

politician then he has today, but then it did not matter much because few expected or demanded much from politicians. The role of government was so much more limited than today.

It is not merely that the role of government has expanded enormously, however. Because of changes in our society it is much more difficult than formerly to find a consensus upon which the country can be governed. The effect of the breakdown of tradition has been vast in itself. Party loyalty, for example, is a very thin reed for a government to rely on today. When tradition breaks down and voters get their impressions from the radio or television, governments acquire powerful tools to manipulate public opinion, but a public opinion which can be manipulated is volatile and shifting and consequently a consensus becomes more difficult to maintain. Achieving a consensus becomes particularly difficult as more voters do their own thinking. More than one hundred years ago Walter Bagehot suggested that the British had stable and the French unstable government, because the French were more intelligent and insisted on thinking for themselves. De Tocqueville had a different explanation when he compared France and the United States, but Bagehot had a point. I have long speculated whether democracy would work if a certain percentage of a country obtained a university education *and* insisted on thinking for themselves. Fortunately for government in Canada, in this respect, university education has not yet caused too many Canadians to think for themselves.

Nevertheless, consensus is more difficult to achieve than it used to be when most voters inherited their views. When voters do not follow tradition they must be persuaded; and even with television that is not easy when society consists of highly organized and well financed interest groups, each pushing its own interests and each reluctant to compromise, unless it is made very well worth while to do so. The volatility I mentioned does not apply to the particular interests of special interest groups.

I have had something to say elsewhere about the problems of achieving and maintaining a consensus upon which the country can be governed, and this is not my theme nor my subject today. I mention it simply to remind you that the context in which our legislatures and governments are operating has changed greatly. In assessing how well they are doing one must, therefore, ask how well any other democratic system would work; but one must also ask whether a democratic system that worked well for a simpler and more traditional society is the most appropriate for our society of competing interest groups which gets most of its impressions, if not its opinions, from television. I only raise the question at this stage today to make the point that we are asking parliamentary responsible government to operate in conditions and to perform roles that were not anticipated as parliamentary responsible government evolved. Little wonder it is creaking. The trouble is it is not working well at Ottawa.

Anything I have to say today will relate to the Parliament and government of Canada because I am not familiar enough with the current performance of provincial legislatures and governments to discuss them. While I was a member of the House of Assembly in Nova Scotia from 1949 to 1967, and of the government of that province from 1956 to 1967, I am out of touch with those institutions even in that province. My guess is that many of our provinces are beginning to suffer from the stresses and strains that seem to me to make our federal Parliament and government ineffective. Nova Scotia is a relatively small province where government has its own peculiar difficulties but where the scope of government is much less complex than in Quebec or Ontario. One gets some idea of what has happened to provincial governments, however, when one remembers that at the turn of the century being the premier of Nova Scotia was hardly a full time job; that by 1930 the annual expenditures of the Government of Nova Scotia were of the order of $7 millions (say $40 millions in current dollars); and that the expenditures of the Government of Nova Scotia are now some $1.3 billions. Until fifty years ago provincial governments were, with few exceptions, dealing with matters that members of the legislature understood as part of their daily lives. Now members of the legislature of Nova Scotia have to decide to spray or not to spray — for the spruce budworm — a decision which involves not only emotions but scientific knowledge and expert judgment which are far from the daily lives of most members of the legislature. But when I say that parliamentary responsible government is not fitted for what we are asking it to do I have in mind our federal institutions. A year ago I argued — in giving the George Nowlan lectures at Acadia University in Nova Scotia — that we must make a choice between all-pervasive government and parliamentary responsible government, that we cannot have both. Then last November we had *The Economist's*[1] lament for British parliamentary responsible government based on reasons somewhat different from mine.

Diagnosis of the Problem

However, everyone does not share this gloom. In discussing the failure of the Canadian House of Commons to control government expenditures, *The Globe & Mail,* in a February 4, 1978 editorial was inclined to blame not the institution but the personnel, "those sleek, well salaried, well-pensioned gentlemen don't give a damn how much of our money is wasted." Professor John Meisel[2] of Queen's University has recently expressed the view in a Walter Gordon lecture that "we are eminently governable and not really overloaded but that we do have some problems."

The contrast between the shrill lament of *The Economist* and the gentle accolade of Professor Meisel is striking. For *The Economist,* parliamentary responsible government for all practical purposes no longer exists in Britain. There is instead a dictatorship of the party leadership enforced by party whips. *The Economist's* critique is concerned "less with the jaded cries for electoral

---

[1] *The Economist,* "Blowing up a Tyranny," Nov. 5, 1977.
[2] John Meisel, "The Federal Government: Can It Cope?" Walter Gordon lecture delivered at the University of Saskatchewan, November 18, 1976.

reform as such than with the undignified, inefficient, undemocratic and, above all, unparliamentary government that is Britain's lot today." Professor Meisel, in his paper, reaches the relatively optimistic conclusion that in Ottawa "the legislature, the cabinet and the bureaucracy have shown reassuring capacity to undergo reform and adjust to new conditions."

The Economist in effect says parliamentary responsible government is a sham and a delusion in Britain. Professor Meisel believes that while we have some problems in Canada our institutions have proved adaptable. The only really serious worry Professor Meisel seems to have is whether we can adapt to the strains on our federal system, which is a different question than the performance of our federal parliamentary and governmental institutions.

I must say immediately that the savage attack of *The Economist* on the Mother of Parliaments would seem far from inappropriate if made, with some changes of emphasis and some modifications, on the Parliament and government of Canada. I have great respect for Professor Meisel, but I find it hard to believe he is writing about the Parliament I have been working in for the last ten years and the governments I have been watching for many more years. In my opinion we no longer have parliamentary responsible government in Ottawa.

I assert that parliamentary responsible government is not fitted for what it is being asked to do: that both the government and the Parliament are overloaded to the point that we have poor government; and Parliament cannot cope with government. Professor Meisel does not believe the system is overloaded. *The Economist* does not seem to believe that overloading is the problem either. It seems to believe that the basic problem is the tyranny of the executive and the vested interests of the dominant parties in the present system. "Being a British Member of Parliament is a whipped, degrading and self perpetuating profession, not because it should or need be, but because it is," says *The Economist*. That is a little strongly put, but I know what the editors of *The Economist* mean when they so describe the condition of Members of Parliament. I agree that we must be concerned about the domination of Parliament by the executive. "A great test of the freedom and power of any legislature," says *The Economist*, "is whether it can control its own timetable and whether it can extract information from the executive." Personally I do not believe it would be realistic to expect our House of Commons to control its own timetable much more than it does. I expect the government of Canada would be somewhat surprised to be told that it is in control of the timetable of the House, although it certainly has a high degree of control over the business the House may consider. The government does, moreover, have a high degree of control over information it gives out. The House of Commons could theoretically force the government to give information, but normally the House is controlled by the government. Unnecessary secrecy is a cause for concern which can be corrected.

But I believe that above all we must be concerned about the overloading of both the government and Parliament. There are many reforms required that are important, possible and very worthwhile, but there may well be no way in which we can expect government to do what it is trying to do today and yet give us dignified, efficient, democratic and, above all, parliamentary government, if I may transform the lament of *The Economist* into a description of the goal it would consider desirable.

It is certainly something to read an eminent British journal of opinion predicting for the Britain of the future that "the central Parliament . . . would distance itself from the executive either by a total separation of power and of voting slips, as in America, or some more carefully drafted version of the half-way house attempted by de Gaulle and Debré." That is certainly something, coming from the editorial heirs of Walter Bagehot; but I am not yet persuaded that the United States or French constitutions are any better suited to provide dignified, efficient, democratic and above all, parliamentary government than is our existing constitution. Leaving aside the question of dignity, it remains to be seen how parliamentary the French system is, and we certainly have good reason to doubt the efficiency of the United States system.

Overloaded Ministers

Let me describe, however, the way things seem to me to work or not to work in Ottawa. Consider for a moment what we are asking ministers to do. They represent a constituency, they must seek re-election of themselves and their government, and must therefore devote time and energy to being politicians; they ought to see that their vast sprawling departments operate effectively and report to the House of Commons on their activities; and they must make policy decisions covering an enormous range of subjects. There is no need for me to describe to you the range of decisions government, that is, ministers, must make at Ottawa these days; but think about it. Of course, they get expert advice, but under our system they ought to make their own decisions on matters which are frequently of enormous complexity. Ministers can and do organize themselves into committees and thus divide or share their work to some extent, but they are collectively responsible, and even if they are prepared to delegate a good deal of decision-making responsibility to Cabinet committees, they just do not have the time to be constituency representatives, active politicians, overseers of their departments and intelligent policy makers on the scale being undertaken. For me it is a case of *res ipsa loquitur*. I do not believe the present deplorable condition of our country can be explained simply in terms of the capacity or lack of capacity of members of our federal governments.

Despite the use of flow charts, computers, consultants and memoranda, the government in Ottawa is trying to do far more than it can do intelligently and effectively. It is bound to make many ill-considered policy decisions and it cannot effectively control its own administration. Improvements can be made; important improvements. The Auditor General has recommended more effective financial controls. This is valuable advice. It will not, however, solve the problem of ministers responsible to the House of Commons trying to make and implement policy in the myriad areas into which government has entered or is entering.

It is not simply the scope and complexity of contemporary government that strains the capacity of government. The principle of responsibility or answerability means that so much more comes to the top for decision than would be the case in administering a business corporation where responsibility can be delegated and results measured in terms of profit and loss.

Overloaded M.P.'s

If the ministers have put themselves in an impossible position, consider the poor Members of Parliament. Parliament is not fitted for controlling the kind of all-pervasive government we have today. It cannot cope with it effectively. This would be so even if the House of Commons had not lost financial control of government back in 1965 when it accepted a time limitation on the consideration of Estimates. When I entered the House in the fall of 1967, the consideration of Estimates seemed to me a farce, because ministers were answering only questions they chose to answer, knowing that because of the time limitation they no longer had to give satisfactory explanations in order to get their Estimates passed. I found an emasculated House of Commons which was still capable of greatness on occasion, but which was no longer in effective control of the public purse.

There have been suggestions as to how the consideration of estimates could be improved. Some of these have merit, but they would not restore financial control to the House of Commons. They might well improve surveillance. Frankly, I do not know how the House of Commons can be restored to effective supervision of the government, how we can restore government really responsible to Parliament, except by cutting back on the role of the government and thereby making it possible for Parliament to cope. I am not one of those who glorifies the Parliament of past generations. Except on great occasions, I suspect the House of Commons was usually a pedestrian place, but it did not much matter, because government was not so involved in the lives of Canadians; and the House of Commons could bring government into line when it wished to do so because it could delay the passage of Estimates as long as it liked.

Under current conditions, there is no way of getting back that unlimited power to delay Estimates. No government would agree to that. The government does not have enough parliamentary time now to get its legislation passed. But even if — and this is a basic point — Parliament somehow regained its old power to control the purse, it could not effectively control the manifold operations of the contemporary government in Ottawa. The Cabinet cannot exercise such control. How could the members of the House of Commons?

The frustrations of Members of Parliament are increased by federal-provincial deals, agreements and resulting legislation which confront Parliament as *faits accomplis*. There may be no way to avoid this in contemporary Canada, but federal-provincial arrangements have significantly reduced the role of Parliament.

There can be improvements, important improvements in Parliament and government. My colleague, Gerald Baldwin, M.P. for Peace River, has been fighting for the adoption of freedom of information legislation. This would produce more open government and give Parliament and the public access to much information which the government now keeps secret under claim of confidentiality. Doubtless, too, the House can be better organized. More staff could help committees probing into governmental operations.

But the fundamental lack of effective control would remain. Bear in mind that subject to the rules of the House, the government controls the House and the business before it. We do not have a separation of powers, as in the United States. The House of Commons and the government are not normally adversaries. Only the government and opposition parties are normally adversaries. The majority of the House support the government or the government resigns and calls an election. Whether the United States' presidential system with its separation of powers is more fit for the current scope of government is another question.

We frequently hear minority governments praised. Minority governments are really responsible to Parliament, it is said. I believe genuine minority governments are disastrous. I say "genuine" because we have had minority governments like the Pearson administration which could for all practical purposes act like a majority government because fear of an election among a group of members outside the government party meant they were unlikely to bring the government down intentionally. It seems to me that the Davis government in Ontario can act substantially like a majority government for some time because neither opposition party wants to be blamed for bringing on an election. But where you have a minority government which is struggling and wheeling and dealing to keep afloat, as was the case between the federal elections of 1972 and 1974, you have a mess. One of the great problems in a democracy is to get the hard decision taken. They will certainly not be taken by a minority government.

It is a wonder that the House of Commons does not destroy the minds and souls of its members. I have great respect for the members, by and large, and the effort they make. Many save themselves by spending little time in the House except for Question Period and by devoting themselves to serving their constituencies or pursuing subjects of particular interest, in House committees or elsewhere. The hard and excellent work done by many Members of Parliament is a tribute to them. There are few, however, who are not seriously troubled by the frustrations of Parliament. Opposition members know that their ability to control the government is limited to the sort of digging done by Elmer MacKay, which calls for special talents; to putting the heat on the government on issues of current public interest and concern; and to delaying the passage of legislation or forcing changes through delaying tactics, which is an important but not an inspiring role.

Canadians are electing a House of Commons on the assumption it can control the government, but they are in fact electing a House of Commons which cannot control the government, and this subjects the members to criticism they do not deserve.

I am not suggesting that Parliament is useless or that the members are wasting their time. The role of Parliament is still important, and also the work of its members. My point is that parliamentary control of government is not effective and it is difficult to see how it can be made effective because of the vast scope of government activities.

On the other hand, Parliament has become unsatisfactory to a government trying to do everything under the sun, begrudging time its ministers must spend in the House to the neglect of their other work, and being constantly frustrated by the difficulty in getting its legislative programme adopted. It is perhaps not surprising that Mr. Trudeau and other ministers seem to believe that when an electorate gives a government a mandate, it is the duty of Parliament to respect that mandate and pass the government's legislation and adopt its spending programmes with reasonable dispatch.

Under this view, the House of Commons would become a place where ministers answer questions they choose to answer and where legislation sought by the government and subjects raised by the Opposition could be discussed for limited periods of time. Parliament would become a combination of a bear-pit session and a discussion group. That has not happened yet, because opposition parties have fought against it, but that is the direction in which Parliament is sliding.

I do not agree that the basic parliamentary problem could be resolved by the House of Commons regaining control of the purse, which through the centuries was the basis of parliamentary control of the executive. Such control is still essential to parliamentary responsible government, but such control, even if it could be regained, would not enable the House of Commons to control effectively the activities of all-pervasive government. If the Cabinet has lost effective control, how could the House of Commons hope to establish it?

More and more matters, for all practical purposes, are being decided by and implemented by the bureaucracy. This is inevitable in view of the broadening scope of federal government activities. This represents a change in opinion on my part, because formerly I believed, based on my experience in Nova Scotia, that control of the bureaucracy was not a serious problem. I no longer believe this. We are losing control by democratically elected people both at the parliamentary and the ministerial level. In Sweden, resentment against the power of the bureaucracy has been said to have been a major factor in the recent changes of government.

Alternatives and Choices

There is, I believe, only one choice. We can accept the loss of parliamentary responsible government or we must accept a more limited role for our federal government. If we want the federal government to run just about everything, we will end up with a bureaucracy running just about everything, with ministers floundering more and more, losing more and more public respect and becoming steadily less in charge. If we want to retain — or, more accurately, regain — parliamentary responsible government at Ottawa, we have to accept a more limited role for government at Ottawa. What is involved is recognition that democratic responsible government and all-pervasive government in Ottawa are not compatible. They cannot exist together. We cannot have both. If we want all pervasive government we must accept more and more government by improvisation or by bureaucrats who will become increasingly inaccessible to scrutiny. If we want democratic government with decisions being made by ministers responsible to Parliament, then we must accept a more limited view of the role and activities of our national government and accept an arrangement in which decision making is decentralized.

I am not speaking here simply to provincial governments and municipal governments being given more authority, although there is doubtless room for some desirable readjustment of authority between the different levels of government. The solution must be more drastic, because provincial and municipal government would soon run into the difficulties now encountered by Ottawa, if they have not already done so. We would have to be content to let people run their own affairs to a greater extent than we are today.

I am not arguing for a return to laissez-faire and the abandonment of all government regulation of the economy. I am arguing that the government of Canada cannot do well all it is trying to do and that we would be wise to get the federal government out of areas of responsibility which are reasonably self-regulating or can be made so. That is the point, of course, about the so-called free market. It is frequently not really free, it is certainly imperfect, but it does permit firms and people to make decisions. It is a form of decentralized decision making. The question to be asked whenever we are considering governmental intervention is not whether what we are seeking to improve is working perfectly but whether something else could work better, enable people to have more control over their own affairs, make our society more democratic, bearing in mind the load our government and Parliament are already carrying.

As I emphasized, I am not suggesting that government should turn the country over to economic barons to divide it among themselves. I do not believe a society with great inequalities of wealth is a healthy society. Nor do I admire a society whose principal goal is making money.

Those are different questions than the one I am discussing. We should be concerned about the goals and the values of our society, but I believe we must pursue our goals without overloading our democracy. We ought not to overload our politicians with responsibilities they cannot satisfactorily discharge. Federal politicians are overloaded today and this should concern all of us. We are asking more of government than parliamentary responsible government can perform.

Some believe the need of all-pervasive government activity is essential — so that government can control the giant organizations that exist today, and provide the myriad services they believe government must provide. If so, they must choose: they must abandon parliamentary responsible government. To me that would be the wrong choice, but those who argue for a larger and larger role for government at Ottawa must recognize parliamentary responsible government is not fitted for the job. To me, it is urgent that Canadians recognize this simple truth.

I do not pretend it is easy to cut back on the scope of government in Ottawa when many are demanding more government activity. You may say to me: why talk about this at all in view of these difficulties? The beginning of wisdom is understanding. It is important we understand what is happening to us. We should understand that we do not have dignified, efficient, democratic and, above all, parliamentary government. While we can improve what we have we cannot create effective democratic government simply by changing the system. We have run up against the limits of human capacity to be both efficient and parliamentary. We ought to be concerned.

I do not wish to suggest that everything is wrong at the federal level of politics. I have already paid tribute to the fine work done by some Members of Parliament in pushing good causes. I repeat my statement that being a Member of Parliament is far from being a waste of time, even if a member cannot perform the traditional role of controlling the government or change very much what the government puts through Parliament. Parliament has roles other than controlling the government.

An important role for opposition Members of Parliament is to offer the public an alternative government. Until recently the House of Commons was becoming less and less appropriate as a forum for that role, because more and more voters were forming their impressions from events and discussions covered by television outside the House. Question Period in the House might be good theatre for those present (it was of little use in getting information), but what counted was generally not what had taken place in the House as much as the performance of the actors before the cameras outside the House. I was always sceptical as to how much television in the House of Commons would change this, but experience to date suggests that, however unpleasant televising the proceedings in the House may make working conditions there for members, it may make the House once again a good forum in which parties can discharge some of their political functions, one of which is to provide the public with an alternative to the government. If Parliament cannot control government it may help voters decide whether they should change the government.

Political parties are an important aspect of Parliament and consequently their state of health is important to Parliament and to government. Admittedly they are far from perfect, but I believe they have become somewhat more open and democratic than formerly. Improvements in election financing and the control of election expenses have been important reforms. So also has been provision for leadership review and the increasing attention parties are giving to the democratic choice of delegates to party conventions. We can all think of areas for further reform — such as the procedure for nominating candidates — but parties are aware of the importance of being perceived to be open and democratic and this will continue the momentum of party reform.

Some are concerned that our political parties do not offer voters a clearer ideological choice or offer more ideological leadership. This is not the lament of *The Economist* in its article. "Little did Bagehot realize," says *The Economist,* "that a system designed for Whig and Tory gentle folk would fall into the hands of competing 20th century ideologues, condemning Britain to permanently inefficient sectarianism." A country as diverse as Canada would be an *a fortiori* case for the importance of political parties not emphasizing ideological difference for the sake of ideological differences. A major role of national political parties in Canada is to promote consensus and reconcile differences. This role was probably never more important than today. How well our national parties are performing this role may be debatable, but they are trying. They have the motivation because they must succeed in this if they are to succeed at the polls. Parties are criticized because, it is said, they do not persuade the best people to run. Those who make that criticism should try to persuade those supposedly best people to run — especially if they fear they may have to sit in the opposition. In any event, it is one thing to nominate bright people. It is another thing to elect them. Many bright people could not be elected dogcatcher.

How well does the House of Commons represent the country and reflect the various opinions and interests in the country? Very imperfectly, but this does not bother me as much as it would some others. I should make my bias clear here. It is better to have a government following a coherent programme and providing efficient government based on the views of even a substantial minority than it is to have a government floundering around ineffectively, trying to hold together an uneasy and shifting coalition of groups of differing views and ideology, really pleasing no one and taking the country nowhere. We have so many tensions and reasons for instability in our country that we have to accept, in my view, the simplifying role of our constituency system — simplifying in the sense that it exaggerates for the time being the importance of certain views as the basis of government. I believe this simplification process is made somewhat more acceptable by the federal nature of the country which permits governments representing somewhat different views to co-exist. There can be no such thing as Parliament perfectly reflecting the diversity of opinion in the country, and I am prepared to accept less representativeness than we could theoretically achieve in order to get a tolerable degree of coherence and stability in government. I am prejudiced by the amount of incoherent and poor government we have received at the federal level, despite the presence of some able people, and I do not wish to see a bad situation made worse.

Summary

In summary, I believe that some aspects of our federal parliamentary governmental operations have been improved, that others can be readily improved, that some federal institutions such as political parties are more open and democratic than they used to be, but that the basic institution, parliamentary responsible government, is not working in a dignified, efficient, democratic and, above all, parliamentary way because it is seriously overloaded. We are asking too much of the parliamentary process and the people we elect to operate it.

COMMENTS

GORDON F. GIBSON*

In commenting on the subject, and particularly on the exposition given by Mr. Stanfield, it will be my thesis that our legislative process in Canada has failed us in at least two ways. First of all, there has been the failure of the parliamentary system *per se* relative to other systems, in terms of the democratic process. I will argue that our system does not presently provide for either the sensitive representation of or the proper implementation of the public will. Nor does it provide for adequate democratic control of the executive.

Federal-Provincial Issues

Moreover, our legislative process has failed in terms of its functioning in a federal state. This is very clear. The Lower House is not representative of sentiment in the various regions of Canada, and the Upper House does not perform the regional brokerage task for which it was established. My conclusion is that we can probably continue to bumble on, perhaps with the loss of Quebec and some partition of the rest of the country, but that if we really wish to provide better government for our citizens, truly *radical* modification of our political institutions is necessary.

Mr. Stanfield's overview of the legislative process takes place in the context of a constitutional constraint which he does not mention, probably because it has been an automatic part of the life of every Canadian politician since Confederation. I am referring to the provision that our federal and provincial governments should be similar in nature to the British parliamentary system.

With that simple requirement comes some good things, but some very questionable attributes have been imported into Canada. The British parliamentary system was devised many hundreds of years ago, and has evolved since, as an instrument of governance for a geographically small, unitary kingdom, with a particular kind of social structure. There is no reason to suppose that this particular political framework should be the suitable model for the Canadian legislative process, and I think that if we are really to make progress, we will have to abandon this constitutional limitation. Indeed, the conclusions and analysis of Mr. Stanfield's paper itself give reason only for gloom, if some such escape route is not provided.

Mr. Stanfield's major assertion is that "both the government and the Parliament are overloaded to the point that we have poor government; and Parliament cannot cope with government." In this conclusion I concur with him, and in particular I endorse it in respect of even the government and legislature of

---

* Member of the Legislative Assembly of British Columbia (North Vancouver-Capilano) and Leader of the Liberal Party.

British Columbia, with our far smaller budget and public service. I also agree that the legislature's control of government would only be improved marginally by freedom of information laws and better staffed parliamentary committees.

Mr. Stanfield notes the increased frustration that applies both to the Parliament of Canada and the provincial legislatures of the growing practice of making federal-provincial deals which confront all legislatures with *faits accomplis.* Of course, under the dictatorship of the executive, legislatures are always faced with *faits accomplis,* but under federal-provincial agreements it is far worse. They are so cast in stone from the time of the agreement that even if the opposition were able to convince the government that amendments should be made it would be too late to change things in any significant respect.

It should be noted that while this frustration is understandable, one of the problems of our system is that our national Parliament never has had an effective federal-provincial function. The Senate was, in part, designed for that purpose, but does not in fact accomplish it. The House of Commons is completely hopeless in representing regional interests. Members of Parliament vote for their party. They do not vote for *bona fide* regional considerations, even when a serious issue exists. The exceptions are so rare in the Canadian context as to be near curiosities. Even the minority protection afforded Quebec Francophones arises out of an accommodation with one political party and this does not afford long-term security.

Scrutiny of Expenditures

Mr. Stanfield does not mention a very serious failing of the parliamentary system in several Canadian legislatures, particularly in British Columbia, though less so in Ottawa. I am referring to the refusal of the executive branch, through its control over the legislature, to allow in-depth scrutiny of legislation or expenditures before committees provided with adequate staff and time to satisfy even the minimal duties of surveillance expected by the electorate. In British Columbia we never send estimates to committees (other than to Committee of the Whole), and almost never send legislation. The result is that the often uninformed and hastily prepared comments of political non-experts in any given field have to be substituted in debate for the testimony that could come through the committee system, either of experts or simply members of the public with strong views. The British Columbia example is an extreme case, but it is a clear example of the tyranny that our four-year elected dictatorship can exercise over their legislatures and the democratic process. The net result is that the body elected to represent the people — the legislature — in fact represents them only in terms of talk. In terms of actual power and action, government is not only conducted but also controlled by a small group chosen from the majority party, called the Cabinet.

Importance of Backbenchers

Here we have another clear myth versus reality. Most people think that their M.P.'s and M.L.A.'s are important people. With rare exceptions, they are not, unless they are Cabinet ministers. Government backbenchers are jacks-in-the-box, with a duty of standing up at the proper time, and opposition members are mere mouths, hoping some day to get enough publicity to destroy the current regime.

While the House of Commons (and some of the provincial legislatures) have far better developed committee systems than British Columbia, the underlying fact of the complete control of the legislature by the executive branch is the same in every area. Thus the instrument that is supposed to provide public control over the government does not do so and cannot do so. The only real control is exercised at election time, and that is obviously a very unsatisfactory kind of control. At election time, the public cannot have any real input on individual issues; they simply must accept this group or that group. They may not even have much of a choice in that regard, unless the alternative is credible, as all too often it is not. Many of our provinces are virtually one-party provinces, as far as government is concerned, and there is a similar tendency at the federal level. The absence of real choice means that functional democracy is terribly hampered, and the absence of a free legislature means that issue-oriented democracy is rendered virtually impossible — choices are made in terms of leadership and parties.

After his catalogue of parliamentary difficulties to which I have added, Mr. Stanfield comes to some conclusions. He notes first of all that while the system can be improved with changes in the rules the fundamental difficulties will remain. I concur. Mr. Stanfield comes to the conclusion that if we want to regain parliamentary responsible government, ''we have to accept a more limited role for government.''

Cutting Back

I am extremely concerned about this conclusion. I do not question its truth, as long as we retain our straightjacket of the British parliamentary system. What concerns me is that, in my view, the alternative, which for Mr. Stanfield is the shedding of governmental responsibilities to reduce government to the point where Parliament can control it, is one that is simply not going to happen. It has not happened anywhere else, in a democratic system, in modern times, and we have no reason to believe that it is likely to happen in Canada. In fact, we have much reason to believe exactly the contrary.

Consider the most recent examples in British Columbia and Manitoba where strong majority governments have been elected not just with a mandate but with an almost religious zeal to cut back the scope of government and the public service. What has happened? Almost nothing. In some cases, elements of the private sector that happened to be owned by the government, but were operating with a great deal of autonomy, have been spun off or reprivatized. That has made little difference. In some cases, a few public servants have been fired, a fairly large number transferred to Crown corporations, and a brake put on hiring. That is not major surgery of the kind that Mr. Stanfield must have in mind.

It is probably possible to go through one government after another, and one set of regulations after another, and find 10 percent, 20 percent, perhaps in some cases, even 30 percent of regulations, reporting requirements, orders-in-council, employees, programmes, or even dollars, that one might get some consensus on cutting back, but it is an enormously difficult process as anyone who has even been involved in that kind of exercise will know. And — here is the problem — even if it works, it will not really make that much difference with respect to the workload of M.P.'s or to the overall scope of government activity. This is the problem in a nutshell.

To get around this, we either have to go to a different kind of society, which is really the business of the people, and not the politicians, or go to a different kind of political system. It is my own contention that while the British parliamentary system cannot cope, there are others that can and this suggests to me the clear necessity of radical reform.

Radical Reform

I think that the main elements of this reform are easy enough to spell out, and probably even to obtain some agreement on, but we must recognize at the outset that that does mean that they will be accepted. One of the facts of political life in Canada is that the gatekeepers to reform, the federal and provincial governments in power, are themselves the prime beneficiaries of the existing system. The political system of the day may have many miseries and inadequacies, particularly for the public, but for the political establishment of the day it is the system that placed them in a position of power. Interestingly enough, the main opposition party will generally go along with the government establishment in this regard, as we see Mrs. Thatcher demonstrating in Britain today with her opposition to proportional representation. The official Opposition may deplore the government of the day, but they admire the system that will give them the same untrammelled power on the inevitable day when that happens.

So in ordinary times, radical political reform has virtually zero chance of success. But these are not ordinary times. Canada is in a tremendous turmoil, particularly caused by the current government of Quebec, but by other factors as well, which demonstrate quite conclusively that the current political system is not working very well. *Some change* is going to have to be made in our political process to accommodate this fact. That occasion of change, which will be made concrete by the re-writing of our constitution, should be seized upon as an opportunity to secure the maximum possible reform of our legislative system.

I think that these reforms should follow certain principles. They should, for example, be conservative in the sense of changing as little as necessary for the achievement of the reform we need. There is no need for example, to go all the way to the American, Swiss, or German systems or any other, and indeed, none of these would fit in Canada. The necessary reforms must be cognizant of our existing constitution and our existing social, cultural and economic circumstances. Secondly, the reforms should be such as to reduce confrontation and enhance harmony in our political process. The British parliamentary system is almost unique and counter-productive in the sense that its basic ground rule first requires the demolition of one political group before the other political group can advance. We know very well in British Columbia the impact of this kind of attitude on our labour relations to choose one example. We need a system that does not give all the power to one group, and zero power to another group, but a system that distributes powers and responsibilities in a judicious way, so as to encourage co-operation among the various representatives of society. A party that has something to lose will be responsible; an opposition that has nothing to lose will concentrate single-mindedly on the achievement of power. It is that simple. Honourable men and women may fight this tendency, but the tendency and the ground rule are there, and must never be forgotten, on pain of complete lack of success in the political game. Next, as a general principle, reform should strive for an improvement of the democratic process by which the government is more truly representative of the electorate with a more stable tenure and an effective policy implementation capability.

Based on these principles, it is possible to become a bit more specific as to desirable directions for the structure of governments in Canada.

Canada is in dire need of some machinery for direct democracy. The experience of the United States of America and Switzerland has been very successful — while direct democracy is often inconvenient to politicians, in the sense of providing a device to go around them when they refuse to do something or override their decisions when they wish to do something that the public disapproves of, it is a marvellous safety valve and route of last resort when other more conventional means fail.

To give two examples drawn from British Columbia: governments in this province, until 1972, successfully stonewalled demands for a full Hansard, and a Question Period in the Legislative Assembly. In the end it was only granted through the enlightenment of the newly elected NDP government (and perhaps they came to regret their enlightenment in due course!). It is inconceivable that we would have been denied a Question Period throughout the twentieth century, had there been provision for an Initiative in our constitution. Equally, there is a wide-spread sentiment in British Columbia for electoral reform. It might not, at the moment, have majority support but certainly that sentiment would have been tested from time to time had the Initiative process been available.

At the federal level, the abolition of capital punishment was a massively unpopular move in the country at large. With the right of referendum, given a certain number of signatures, that popular sentiment could have made itself felt. As one who personally believes that in Canada in the 1970s, capital punishment is not appropriate, I would regret the decision, but I would gladly accept it for the sake of the democratic principle.

There are many well-known dangers of direct democracy, having particularly to do with the potential tyranny of the majority, which can and must be guarded against and I certainly do not advocate a full Swiss-style result, but a slight provision for this safety valve would be a great advance in Canada. It is of some encouragement that the Parti Québécois at least considered the general instrumentalities of direct democracy when bringing forward its referendum law, and it is to be hoped that the federal government in considering its referendum law may do the same thing — though again, the gatekeepers to reform do not like to tie their hands.

Whatever one may think of direct democracy, the great bulk of public business will always be done by indirect democracy — through our representatives — and it is here that the most consequential changes need to be made.

The first step to achieve effective control over the government by the representatives of the people must be the restoration of legislative supremacy — which once existed in the British parliamentary system until roughly the twentieth century, at which time party discipline became the instrument for the Cabinet's assertion of control.

Why Are Things as They Are?

One should not speak of reform without asking why things are as they are now. The answer is very simple. Under British parliamentary theory, the executive serves at the pleasure and the control of the legislature, and should they be rejected on any item of consequence, it is their duty to leave office. No one wants to leave office, and continuity in office has become more coveted as government itself has become more important. The Cabinet therefore made the logical move — it arranged to take control over the institution which, in theory, controlled it since under our system, the government has no security without complete control of Parliament.

Any change in this situation must provide for continued executive tenure and only then will the Cabinet release its iron grip on Parliament. That involves a semi-separation of the executive branch, placing their continuity, as between general elections, either completely beyond the reach of the legislative branch, or else affected only in very restricted circumstances. The former is the case in Switzerland and the United States; the latter in Germany. Both in the German and Swiss cases, "semi-separation" is the proper phrase, as there remains a strong connection between the executive and legislative branches for policy integration, which is much more appropriate to our history than the United States example.

In turn, there must be security for the legislative branch by providing it with a fixed term of office removed from the whim of government. That removes the greatest club of government over our elected representatives. Beyond that, the legislative branch must have reasonable control over the management of its own time (though I agree with Mr. Stanfield that the government must have a strong guiding hand) and complete control over its own budget, access to tools such as continuing and wide terms of reference for committees, staff for committees, and a freedom of information law.

The current government of British Columbia, to its great credit, has provided a model for the rest of the country in at least one area of governmental activity, namely control over Crown corporations. A continuing committee of the legislature has been established, with its own budget, and continuing terms of reference to audit the activities of five of British Columbia's most important Crown corporations. The committee does not *control* their day-to-day activities, but it does have the opportunity to become quite expert in the corporations' activities, to exercise the most detailed oversight, and to bring strong moral suasion to bear where appropriate.

Without going into details, control over the government budget is the most complex question for resolution. A legislature with any real power has to have some control over the budget, and a government with any real policy implementation power and policy continuity has to have a considerable control over the budget. We need to give intensive study to this question.

Electoral Reform

Still on the topic of indirect democracy, important improvements in our electoral system would be very desirable. Currently, 20 percent of Quebecers may vote Tory and elect almost no one, and 25 percent of Albertans may vote Liberal and elect no one. This is not a good situation, particularly for a highly regionalized country like Canada where every area should be well-represented in both major parties. The answer is simple: namely, some kind of electoral reform. The German system which provides a half-and-half mixture of constituency representation and proportional representation might be a good model for Canada. The result, I say at once, will very often be coalition governments, in the legislative branch and even in the executive branch. That, in my view, is not a problem. It works perfectly well in other parts of the world, and indeed makes certain that the major interest groups in the country work together — because they must.

On this point I must express a clear disagreement with Mr. Stanfield's paper. He says,

> It is better to have a government following a coherent programme and providing efficient government based on the views of even a substantial minority than it is to have a government floundering around ineffectively, trying to hold together an uneasy and shifting coalition of groups of differing views and ideology, really pleasing no one and taking the country nowhere.

While I will not concede that the alternative is a government "floundering around ineffectively" (for that is certainly not what happens in many other countries) I would like to discuss the first part of the statement — the desirability of "following a coherent program and providing efficient government based on the views of even a substantial minority." I will give two case examples of recent history in Canada where this has happened, and neither supports the case made against coalition government.

The first example of a government elected on the basis of a "substantial minority" was the Barrett government in British Columbia, elected in 1972. With just under 40 percent of the vote, it acquired a strong legislative majority. They proceeded to introduce into British Columbia a philosophical orientation which the majority of voters had never mandated. Only our electoral system made it possible. Had the Barrett government been required to achieve coalition support under a system of proportional representation, their excessive mistakes (and they made some good moves, too) would have never happened. Exactly the same argument applies to Mr. Lévesque's government, elected in 1976. On the basis of proportional representation, Mr. Lévesque would have had to form some kind of coalition to govern his province, and I think we would be more confident about the future of Canada.

Another objection raised by Mr. Stanfield, having to do with the determination of government, must be assessed. He says that, "one of the great problems in a democracy is to get the hard decision taken. They will certainly not be taken by a minority government." In that, he is correct insofar as he refers to the British parliamentary system. That, however, is not the experience of other countries. The continuing coalition governments of France, Germany and Switzerland have proven as apt as the British parliamentary governments of the United Kingdom and Canada at making difficult decisions.

Really, this is not surprising. In countries where politicians are elected under a proportional representation system (or in France, the run-off system), individual politicians know that they have a long-time political future, particularly when they achieve a senior stature. They know that they will have to live with the future that they are creating today, because they can be reasonably certain that they will still be elected ten years hence and probably will be part of a government. Canadian politicians often cannot afford to take such a long-term view. So, there are arguments on both sides.

Mr. Stanfield explicitly excluded the question of the Senate from his remarks, and I will deal with it only very briefly. It is clear that reform of the legislative process in this country must see an Upper House that represents regions, and which votes on regional lines, rather than party lines, to balance the representation by population, party-dominated Lower Chamber, and to protect regional, cultural and linguistic minorities. If one accepts this premise, it is clear that the Upper Chamber, however constituted, cannot possibly be controlled by the executive branch. Thus, in one giant step, we move at least half way to the semi-separation of powers, which is the key to the better functioning of indirect democracy. That done, we might as well make the House of Commons work better too.

Conclusion

My conclusion is that Mr. Stanfield's analysis of responsible parliamentary government as it functions in Canada is essentially correct, and that the current unhappy situation will not be corrected without breaking out of the British parliamentary moldm It will be for others to detail more precisely the ways in which this might be done, but to me Mr. Stanfield's comments make it clear that it *must* be done, because of his demonstration that the present situation is intolerable and because of the impossibility, in my view, of obtaining a solution through the massive withdrawal of government from current areas of activity.

RICHARD GUAY*

In his statement, Mr. Stanfield stressed a certain number of points. I wish to comment on two of them in particular.

The first is the domination of the legislative branch by the executive branch in the British parliamentary system. This is indeed a serious problem because any government expects the full approval of the members of its party in deciding in the last resort which measures are to be enacted. The legislative debates merely fill in time prior to the adoption of a predictable result. Such debates serve but two purposes: to give the illusion of a parliamentary system and to allow the Opposition to make a certain number of adversarial points.

Strengthening Committees

I therefore share Mr. Stanfield's feeling that parliamentary control of government is not effective. However, there are some possible answers to the problem. We are hoping to come up with these proposals for a better legislative system in a special committee of the caucus of the members of the Parti Québécois in the National Assembly. I recently had occasion to intervene publicly on this question in responding to an opinion put forward by a political science professor at Laval University who felt that it was ''useless to think of a change in the role of the member, at least in the legislative area'' because the legislative branch had been shunted aside by the Cabinet and that select group of the civil servants typed by Galbraith as members of ''the technostructure.''

In my response, I suggested that there is a possibility of a larger role for a member and thus a larger control by the legislative branch over the executive branch and, more particularly over the public service. But it is not within the confines of the National Assembly itself, or for that matter the House of Commons, that this control can be exercised, but rather in parliamentary committees. And, in order to do this, I feel that we must look towards the American presidential system.

————f

* Member of the National Assembly of Quebec (Taschereau) and Parliamentary Assistant to the Minister of Communications.

The Quebec National Assembly has already taken a certain number of preliminary measures to enhance the role of its members by the strengthening of parliamentary committees. Thus the rules of procedure in the National Assembly have been completely revamped so that they now add up to less than two hundred articles, a reform that has helped to simplify the legislative process. During the present session, the Minister of State for Parliamentary and Electoral Reform has proposed and the Assembly has accepted the idea that from now on there will be as many parliamentary committees as there are departments within the government and the quorum for each committee has been considerably reduced, allowing members to specialize in a certain number of very specific fields.

Committees Role

The next step, the most important as far as I am concerned, would be that parliamentary committees would no longer be the ultimate captive of a minister; they would become something akin to American Senate or House of Representatives committees. This implies that these committees would no longer be presided over by a neutral person, perceived to be something of an extension of the President in the National Assembly, whose sole responsibility is to see to it that the rules are applied, but rather by a member of the majority who would effectively run the committee, while seeing to it that the rules are followed. Each committee could have a vice-chairman who could be a member of the Opposition. These committees would study the estimates of each department in the presence of the minister who would come before the committee and also the bills relating to the field of their respective competence, which the minister would justify article by article before the committee. These committees could also, without the presence of the minister, exercise a closer control over the way that the public service executes governmental decisions, by having the power to call civil servants before it to study in depth a given problem and to ask specific questions. In the same manner, these committees could hear presentations by groups or individuals within the population, whether in the Assembly itself or elsewhere in Quebec or even outside of Quebec. This would have the added advantage of saving ministerial time from such duties.

In short, what I am proposing is to free ministers and allow them to have more time in order to run their departments while allowing the legislative branch to exercise a closer control over the activities and responsibilities of government.

It follows that these committees would have to be given the necessary personnel in order to allow them to discharge their duties in an efficient manner and to make sure that they are fully conversant with the issues before them. Such a situation already exists in part in the House of Commons in Ottawa but their committees do not have the research staff necessary to function efficiently and their conduct is constrained by an outdated notion of party discipline within the membership.

Some may argue that such a reform puts ministerial responsibility in question. I believe that this is not the case; the members of the majority must, in the last resort, go along with the government, for it implies the political survival of the government and indeed their own political survival. But this necessary discipline does not exclude the debates and the discussions that should be taking place within the framework of the parliamentary system, for if they are not held there, they may be held outside, perhaps in the streets, to the prejudice of social peace. In short, such a reform would allow members to contribute far more to the legislative process and to play their true role. If governments may be tempted to take a closer look at such reform, I suggest that it will be in their interest even if it implies that they may be more accountable to the legislative branch.

Need for Change

Change is necessary for without it we will continue to have the disparities in responsible government so evident when one contrasts the congressional handling of the Watergate scandal and the federal spectacle associated with the Royal Canadian Mounted Police Inquiry.

Because of the separation of powers in the United States, Congress was able to bring an unrelenting exposure on the Watergate matter and, in the end, the American people learned enough on the subject to provoke the resignation of the President of the United States who, had he not done so, would have been impeached by Congress.

In Canada, the Royal Canadian Mounted Police has committed illegal acts. Whether it be the burning of barns, the opening of mail, the stealing of the membership lists of the Parti Québécois, illegal wiretapping, or other acts, we now know that the federal police put themselves above the law, whatever the immediate reasons may have been for this conduct.

But the Parliament of Canada is powerless before such a situation. Was there or was there not prior ministerial approval to the illegal acts of the RCMP and if so, who were the persons responsible? These fundamental questions remain for the moment answerless. It is extremely important that these questions be answered in public for if politicians have also placed themselves above laws voted by Parliament, they are certainly not worthy of the confidence that Canadians have placed in them and should consequently not only resign but also possibly be prosecuted in the courts.

In order to find out some of the illegal acts of the RCMP, it took the initiative of an inquiry commissioned by a provincial government, something that the federal government feared to such a degree that it went before the courts to stop it on constitutional grounds.

If the decision of the Quebec Court of Appeals should be confirmed by the Supreme Court of Canada,[1] there would be two categories of citizens in Canada: those like you and myself who have to obey the laws, and the federal government of Canada and its agencies such as the RCMP, who can place themselves above the laws without provincial governments, who are constitutionally responsible for the administration of justice, being able to do anything about it.

Of course the federal government has set up its own inquiry into the activities of the RCMP, a commission that is remarkable by the fact that it is made up of people who do not offer all the necessary guarantees of objectivity and who, when things get hot, meet behind closed doors so that the people are not able to know what goes on. It is not surprising that the federal inquiry has been embroiled from the beginning in a crisis of confidence and credibility. But during all this time and this is what is more dramatic, the Canadian Parliament, aside from the daily question period, has been powerless because of the domination of the legislative branch by the executive branch.

The second major element of Mr. Stanfield's statement deals with the nature of the Canadian federal system. I fully share Mr. Stanfield's comments when he says that "the government at Ottawa is trying to do far more that it can do intelligently and effectively." The Parti Québécois has, by the way, a solution that would ease the burdens on the federal government, insofar as it deals with Quebec. But whatever the future of Quebec and Canada, it is clear that the present situation is absurd. Canadians and, as far as we are concerned, Quebecers, are overgoverned.

Duplication of Government

It is absurd for the people of Quebec with its population of six million people to be governed by thirty departments whose sole purpose is to look after the welfare of Quebecers, while thirty-four departments within the federal government also deal with the fate of Quebecers in a proportion that one can arbitrarily but realistically set at the same percentage as that of the population of Quebec within the Canadian total, that is to say somewhat over 25 percent.

As a result of this situation, we have two ministers of Agriculture, two ministers of Communications, two ministers of Consumer and Corporate Affairs, two ministers of Natural Resources, two ministers of the Environment, two ministers of Finance, two ministers of Social Affairs, two ministers of Industry and Commerce, two ministers of Justice, two ministers of Labour, two ministers of Immigration, two ministers of Revenue, two ministers of Public Works, two ministers of Intergovernmental Affairs, two ministers responsible for Youth, Leisure and Sports, two ministers responsible for Municipal or Urban Affairs, two ministers of Transport, two presidents of Treasury Board, two ministers

---

[1] *Editorial note: The Keable Inquiry appeal was argued before the Supreme Court of Canada on May 29-30, 1978 and the decision is now awaited.*

responsible for Cultural Affairs and two Executives or Privy Councils dealing wholly or partly with the fate of the population of Quebec in their respective fields.

It is obvious that the citizen, in the last resort, is the loser in this inefficient and overbureaucratized system complicated by the grey areas of the *British North America Act,* the federal government's spending power, and the constant demands of Quebec to administer its own business. The situation continues to worsen as the federal government tries to demonstrate to Quebecers that it is just as much present in their everyday life as the government of Quebec. It is easy to identify the squandering of public funds that follows.

But already, with the jurisdiction that the government of Quebec possesses at the moment, we are witnessing a growth of the influence of the technocracy at the expense of the political power, a situation somewhat similar to that which Mr. Stanfield has described in Ottawa. Therefore, whatever the present or additonal powers the government of Quebec is called upon to assume, it is quite evident that we cannot let the technocrats hold more power over the functioning of the State. Indeed one can conceive, somewhat like Mr. Stanfield has done, that one of the solutions consists in diminishing governmental interventions in the daily lives of our citizens. However, I believe that the role of the State is here to last; indeed it may grow and in the end it is not necessarily such a bad thing for Quebecers because the State of Quebec is really the only collective instrument worth mentioning that we possess by and for ourselves.

Beyond the new powers that the government of Quebec may take over from the government of Canada, the ultimate solution resides in the decentralization of these same powers throughout the territory of Quebec in favour of local and regional institutions. These groups are more able to discharge the tasks that the citizens are asking from their government, rather than have a situation in which we would merely substitute one overly centralized state for another in which everybody waits for decisions from Quebec before doing anything.

These are the thoughts that are at the centre of the debate going on within the government of Quebec. The thrust is to decentralize considerably the activities of the State and to give to local administrations such as schoolboards, municipalities and regional administrations the power to act and the financial means to do so. It goes without saying that these local or regional administrations must be responsible to the people; I hope that this will be the occasion to strengthen democracy at the local and regional level and to get the average citizen to become more interested in public affairs, whether it be in the ward of a city, in the city itself, or in local educational or regional institutions.

Conclusion

In short, instead of administering the State on a basis which in many cases is one of distrust and which implies detailed control by civil servants seeking to justify their own existence, I believe that we must turn to a society of confidence.

This must involve a new confidence by the State in the intelligence and goodwill of citizens to assume their responsibilities at the local and regional level rather than depending constantly on the national government. By taking these steps, we will contribute towards a more genuine system of responsible and accountable government at every level of public activity. This would truly constitute legislative reform.

RONALD I. CHEFFINS*

Mr. Stanfield has very competently outlined many of the concerns that most intelligent observers have with respect to the functioning of our parliamentary institutions. We have all watched the overloading of our governmental institutions with so many responsibilities and demands that the possibility of a coherent and rational allocation of priorities has become increasingly difficult and, at times, seemingly impossible. In fact, the whole process has become so irrational that the federal Parliament, already beset with a plethora of problems, is embarking on programmes in areas of provincial jurisdiction. For example, it has created virtually duplicatory mechanisms in the field of consumer legislation, human rights, and has probably invaded provincial jurisdiction with its proposed legislation in the fields of banking and anti-trust legislation. The foregoing are only a few of the areas in which the federal government has encroached upon provincial legislative fields, at a time when sensitivities about federal and provincial jurisdictions are more common than ever before in Canada's history. It seems increasingly that ministers are being influenced by the push of the bureaucracy, rather than indicating the goals which Canadian society should attempt to achieve.

Growth of Government

Mr. Stanfield is undoubtedly also correct when he indicates that the citizens' expectations from government are growing with increasing rapidity. More and more people expect their pet panaceas to be embodied in legislative schemes of one kind or another, ranging all the way from legislation on obscenity, to permitting or prohibiting abortion, right through to the minutest regulation of the economic market-place. Governments satisfy a few people when they respond to these demands, but at the same time every governmental initiative produces an almost opposite and equal reaction. Governments are expected to balance the budget, and yet stimulate the economy through a variety of potentially inflationary measures. They are expected to support economic initiative, while at the same time guaranteeing a high standard of economic and social security. Within the framework of a single government we see illustrations of strong opposing demands. For example, here in British Columbia we find one

---

* Professor of Law, University of Victoria

minister defending the total integrity of provincial parks, thus responding to the urgings of environmental groups. Another minister presses for some of the parkland to be used for the cutting of lumber, the latter minister, of course, responding to the ever-increasing clamour for jobs for the thousands of Canadians who are unemployed. The role of the Opposition has become one of sniping at this vast bureaucratic policy-making apparatus known as the Cabinet and the public service. The question is whether there is any suitable or preferable option to the existing system.

The instinctive approach of Canadians at this time in our history seems to be to emulate the United States. In fact, in many areas, such as education, we tend to buy ideas that the United States has attempted, and dropped as failures. These rejected concepts then form the basis of the new educational panacea for Canada. Are we going to follow a similar path in Canada? Does the United States in fact have an alternate system from which we can derive ideas to modify and alter our own structure?

American Model — Advantages and Disadvantages

One of the features of the American congressional system that appeal to legislators is that they enjoy a very definite role in the formulation of legislation. They are not, as in Canada, simply responding to the initiatives of the Cabinet, but have in their own right the authority to initiate legislation, including Acts which involve expenditure of public funds. The negative side of this, however, is the tremendous lobbying pressure put on individual members of the United States Congress by very efficiently organized pressure groups. In fact, fourteen members of Congress in recent years are being investigated or indicted for various illegal or unethical activities. This is not because of the greater morality of our legislators, but rather lessened opportunity. The American congressman's vote is definitely up for grabs, and thus he is subject to a whole series of pressures and temptations which do not apply to legislators in Canada. The essence of influencing public policy in this country is persuasion of the Cabinet, be it federal or provincial, but there is some refuge from pressure by virtue of the tradition in Canada of Cabinet solidarity. This means that it affords some protection to a member of the Cabinet from lobbying pressure, which is, of course, not enjoyed by the United States legislator. Similarly, another disadvantage of the American system is the tight control of the legislative process by committees. Chairmen of committees enjoy an authority almost equal to that possessed by Cabinet ministers in our system.

The American legislative system is in many respects slower moving and much more ponderous than our own. In fact, the whole American system of government is designed to ensure that excessive authority is not placed in any particular set of hands, whereas our system places probably an inordinate amount of power in the hands of the executive. It is, as the economists say, a cost-benefit analysis, namely, that one has the often stalemated but probably more participatory mechanism of the United States, as against the more autocratic but probably more efficient system in Canada. There seems little doubt in my mind that, if we had the American system, we would not have the kind of health care system which we presently enjoy.There is no perfect method. There is a cost for whatever legislative mechanism or constitutional structure is adopted.

It is appropriate to ask the question of the extent to which the constitution is a factor in the kind of legislative process which we enjoy. As in so many other matters, the constitution is, to a very considerable extent, silent on the question of how the federal Parliament and provincial legislatures should function. There is in the preamble to the constitution the statement that we should have, ''a Constitution similar in Principle to that of the United Kingdom,'' however there is no further expansion on this theme. A number of constitutional decisions have discussed this statement, but all the judgments have focused on the supposition that this phrase was designed to ensure the continuance of certain basic and traditional civil liberties. There are no judicial decisions that this phrase necessarily implies any particular form of functional arrangement involving the legislatures.

BNA Act — Federal Provisions

There are a number of provisions in the *British North America Act* dealing with federal and provincial legislatures, though they are basically concerned with establishing legislative institutions rather than defining how they function. The key provision is, of course, Section 17, which provides that, ''There shall be One Parliament for Canada, consisting of the Queen, an Upper House styled the Senate, and the House of Commons.'' Section 18 of the Act goes on to define the privileges and immunities and powers to be exercised by the Senate and House of Commons, and relates these to similar privileges enjoyed in Great Britain.

The next key section on the subject of the functioning of Parliament is Section 20, which provides that there will be a session of the Parliament of Canada once at least in every year, though one session of our Parliament only lasted a very few hours. The Act then goes on at considerable length to provide for the composition of the Senate and how it is appointed. There is no evidence from these sections as to how the Senate should function, or the extent to which in reality it should exercise the legal power given to it by the *British North America Act*. One section in connection with the Senate of considerable interest is Section 34, which provides that the Speaker of the Senate is to be appointed by the Governor General. This is an interesting departure from the practice of the House of Commons, which is to elect the Speaker, though, of course, he is selected by the Prime Minister.

The British North America Act then goes on to a number of provisions with respect to the House of Commons, but here again the basic concern is with the structure of the House, that is to say, the number of members, the election of the Speaker, the number of members necessary to constitute a quorum, and that kind of detail. One provision, however, of particular importance is Section 60, which provides that the House of Commons shall not continue more than five years, subject, of course, to being sooner dissolved by the Governor General. Section 91(1), however, does provide that the House of Commons may be continued beyond the five-year limit, if its continuation is not opposed by more than one-third of the members of the House.

Sections 53 and 54 of the *British North America Act* are exceptionally important legislative provisions, in that they contribute substantially to giving the Cabinet a strangle-hold on the legislative process. Section 53 provides that Bills involving the expenditure and raising of public funds must originate in the House of Commons. Section 54 is of particular significance, because it provides that the House of Commons cannot adopt or pass any provision with respect to the expenditure or raising of public funds, unless the appropriate measure has been recommended to the House by a message of the Governor General. The constitutional tradition in this regard is that the Governor General does not provide a message to accompany legislation, unless he is so advised by a member of the Cabinet. This means that the Cabinet has total control over all measures involving the raising or expenditure of public funds. This provision was a carry-over of a similar provision in the *Act of Union* of 1840, designed to curb the practice which had grown in Lower and Upper Canada of members' log-rolling in favour of roads and bridges in their own constituency. It should be noted that the provisions of Sections 53 and 54 are made applicable to the provincial legislatures by virtue of Section 90 of the *British North America Act*. The importance of these provisions cannot be under-estimated, because of the extent to which they reduce the leverage of the private member in introducing legislation.

BNA Act — Provincial Constitutions

In the provincial sphere the most important section of the *British North America Act* is Section 92(1), which essentially provides that, except as regards the Office of Lieutenant-Governor, the provincial legislature has the authority to provide for the constitution of the province. There are, of course, other provisions in the *British North America Act* dealing with provincial constitutions, and particularly provincial legislatures, but once again these essentially involve the establishment of legislatures rather than defining their functioning. Because Ontario and Quebec had to be created by the *British North America Act* of 1867, this Act provides for the creation of legislatures in Ontario and Quebec. With respect to Nova Scotia and New Brunswick, Section 88 merely provides for the continuation of the legislatures in existence in those provinces prior to the passage of the *British North American Act* of 1867. It is interesting to note that both the legislatures of Nova Scotia and New Brunswick were created by the Crown, acting under the authority of the royal prerogative. It might also be observed that a number of the provincial legislatures had as part of their constituent elements Upper Houses, but in every province these have now been eliminated. From a constitutional perspective the two most controversial of these measures were in Manitoba and Quebec, which by ordinary Act of the legislature abolished their respective legislative councils. In neither case was the constitutionality of these measures challenged, though particularly in the case of Manitoba, it seems as if there could have been a strong case made out against the constitutionality of this action.

Experimentation Possible

Just as in the case of the federal Parliament, so with respect to the provincial legislatures, there was and remains considerable room for legislative experimentation at the provincial level. Despite these opportunities the legislatures have all basically stayed with the model of responsible government which had been developed prior to Confederation in both Britain and in the British North American colonies. It should be noted, however, that responsible government had not taken hold in British Columbia, though in the schedule to the Order-in-Council admitting British Columbia to union, it provided for responsible government being a feature of the political functioning of the new province. The only evidence of any significant departure from the existing legislative process was in Manitoba towards the end of the first World War. The legislature of the province passed an Act providing for a method of initiative and referendum for the passage of legislation. This simply meant that a certain percentage of the electorate could make it mandatory for a piece of legislation to be considered by the legislature and, in appropriate circumstances, it could be turned into law by the approval of the electorate in a referendum. The constitutionality of this legislation was questioned, and in a very famous decision it was held by the Judicial Committee of the Privy Council to be unconstitutional, because the Office of Lieutenant-Governor was entirely bypassed, contrary to the provisions of Section 92(1) of the *British North America Act*. This legislation, however, was obviously only to be used in exceptional circumstances, and was not in itself an attempt to change the structure of the legislature or alter its basic functioning.

It is surprising that, with the wide variety of different parties which have held power at the provincial legislative level, there has not been more experimentation in legislative functioning. As indicated earlier, the only restraints really are Section 92, sub-section 1, which protects the Office of Lieutenant-Governor, and Section 54 with respect to money Bills. My own explanation for this lack of experimentation is that under our system governments are usually so satisfied with the degree of power accorded to them by office, that there is no incentive to change. It is not surprising that, finding themselves in this happy position, Cabinets are loath to involve themselves in experimentations which would lead to greater sharing of their authority with the legislature generally. Thus, there is no inducement for a Premier to change a system which gives him a virtual strangle-hold over his own political executive, the institutions of public administration, the appointment of a number of judicial officers, as well as control of the legislature.

Summary

In summary, my point is essentially this, that once again the constitution is not a stumbling block to experimentation in the field of legislative functioning. The constitution remains incredibly flexible in this area as in so many others. The problem once again is a question of political motivation and political will. It seems as though there is considerable dissatisfaction with the existing situation, but considerable uncertainty as to the appropriate remedies. It seems as if most of the attention is now being riveted at the federal level on the reform of the Senate. There does not seem to be much of a consensus evolving as to what should happen with respect to the House of Commons. There does not seem to be emerging any widespread view that the present Cabinet model should be replaced by a congressional system similar to that of the United States. Certainly in British Columbia there appears to be growing fascination with the German model of federalism, but whether this carries through to the functioning of the national German legislature is a matter for conjecture. There are certainly other legislative models, particularly that of France, which hang somewhere between the structure of the United States and that of Canada. But an exploration of its possibilities is beyond the limited scope of this comment. It is sufficient to say, however, that the limitations imposed on experimentation by the constitution are few, and correspondingly the opportunity for change, if we can agree on the kind of change, lies within our grasp.

DISCUSSION

Rapporteur: J. Terence Morley*

In the time available for questions from the floor two fundamental issues were discussed. The first questioner suggested that Parliament had never controlled the policy process even though as a legislature it must formally put a seal of approval on those policies enshrined in legislation. Given this historical generalization, he continued by stating that the role of Parliament is to respond and criticize — to respond to the legislative and policy initiatives of the Cabinet, and to criticize the Cabinet's conduct of government.

Mr. Gibson responded that, while Parliament must inevitably respond to executive initiatives and certainly ought to provide a forum for informed criticism of the government, these were not the only appropriate roles for Parliament to play. Most important was the need for Parliament to respond to public opinion and public sentiment and that this requirement meant that Parliament itself must undertake certain initiatives.

Richard Guay pointed out that in the United States 20 percent of legislation passed by the United States Congress is initiated by Congressmen themselves and not by the President or other members of the executive branch of government. In addition, the Congress has made fundamental and dramatic changes to legislation proposed by the President and other executive branch officers. Canadian parliaments, according to *Mr. Guay,* could profit from this American example and parliamentarians ought to take legislative initiatives.

Robert Stanfield suggested that parliaments have played a significant role in policy making and cited the nineteenth century British example of William Wilberforce and his allies — both in and out of Parliament — persuading the majority in Parliament to abolish the institution of slavery in the British Empire. Mr. Stanfield stated in addition that Parliament does not even respond well to executive initiative and therefore that this narrow view of the appropriate role of Parliament cannot serve as an excuse to forego fundamental parliamentary reform.

The second question concerned what has often been viewed as a fundamental difference between Canadian and American conceptions of democracy. It was suggested that the Executive Council or Cabinet, at least where one party has a majority in Parliament or a provincial legislature, has been elected to conduct the business of the people as it sees fit until a new election. If it loses that support as a result of its policies and conduct of government then it will lose the next election and a new executive, supported by the people, will have a mandate to govern until a subsequent election is held. It was suggested that this system allows the citizen to fix blame (or to award praise and support)

* Department of Political Science, University of Victoria.

on an identifiable group with an identifiable set of policies. He asked who would be seen as responsible for the conduct of public affairs if private members of the legislature and the legislature itself — divided between warring parties — were to assume additional responsibilities for public policies. *Mr. Stanfield*'s central theme that a more limited government was the *sine qua non* of parliamentary reform was also questionable. Would not sunrise and sunset laws modelled on those of several U.S. states and which provide a set statutory life for various boards and commissions established by government be necessary if a more limited government were to become reality? He also suggested that certain public enterprises such as Air Canada should be returned to the private sector as an additional means of limiting governmental activity. He asked *Mr. Stanfield* whether he agreed with these specific proposals.

Mr. Stanfield replied that he did not believe that limited government could simply be achieved by sunset laws. Mr. Stanfield did not comment on the question of the reprivatization of public enterprise. He did, however, speak at some length about the utility of having a dominant executive which can be blamed or praised by the electorate. He stated that the British tradition makes the Cabinet or Executive Council responsible to Parliament, not to the people. The Cabinet does not have a blank cheque between elections to do what it wills and it must maintain the confidence of the House of Commons in order to survive. This, according to *Mr. Stanfield,* gives parliamentarians of all parties a responsibility for ensuring a reasonable government that continues to be reasonable.

Professor Cheffins welcomed the question and agreed that indeed one of the advantages of the parliamentary system was that people know whom to criticize. He pointed out that this is not the case in the United States where Americans all see the President as a kind of elected George III — a chief with considerable prestige and significant power who nevertheless cannot be blamed because he cannot control his legislature. With this system, no one is responsible and it is difficult to achieve change because it is impossible to locate the nexus of political power. *Professor Cheffins* argued that those who wished parliamentary reform of the sort which would make the Canadian system resemble more closely the American should be aware that the disabilities of the American system would also be visited upon Canada; in particular, the inability to take swift decisive action on important public questions.

Richard Guay suggested that the governmental system in the Fifth Republic of France is a model which might possibly provide, in practice, the best of both the British and American systems.

Gordon Gibson responded with Sam Rayburn's aphorism ''where you stand depends on where you sit.'' Sitting as the leader and only member of an opposition party in the British Columbia Legislature, *Mr. Gibson* asserted that in his view *Professor Cheffins'* comments were unsupportable. He said that it was all very well to be able to pin responsibility on the government of the day but without a strong legislature very little, if anything, could be done about their successes and failures. Instead, Mr. Gibson argued for a free legislature which would be sensitive to issues and would be able to deal with public policy in political terms larger than the issue of a government's survival.

Professor Cheffins demanded more details about this alternative and asked whether Mr. Gibson, in fact, had an alternative. *Mr. Gibson* replied that he believed in a semi-separation of powers in which the government was responsible to the legislature only in an informational sense. He suggested that governments should only be removable by a legislature with great difficulty as, for example, in the German system, and that the legislature should be able to turn down executive proposals without fear of causing a general election. *Professor Cheffins* replied that this really meant the elimination of the strong party system as it has developed in Britain, Canada and the Canadian provinces.

Time, the inveterate enemy of all parliamentary debate, forced the discussion period to end at this juncture.

Chapter Three

Federalism and the Legislative Process in Canada

by
*Donald V. Smiley**

My colleague John Gellner tells a story about a young American legal officer who was sent to a Third World country to instruct its army on court-martial procedures. The day he arrived a soldier was brought before a military tribunal and within the space of a few minutes summarily convicted and executed. The American was of course properly shocked and set out to instruct his hosts so that in the future they might do better. When the next court-martial was held it seemed that the lessons had been well learned. In fact, the process dragged on for several weeks with the most fastidious concern by all with the intricacies of procedure. However, there seemed to be no progress in reaching a verdict and the American officer finally suggested to the chairman of the tribunal that this lack of progress was in danger of becoming "cruel and unusual punishment" of the accused. The reply was less than reassuring, "Oh, you don't need to worry about *him* — we shot him the first day."

It would belabour the obvious to connect Gellner's anecdote with the subject of this paper. Like the second court-martial board, the characteristic role of the Parliament of Canada and of the provincial legislatures in federal-provincial relations is to discuss actions which have already been taken. I have little hope that this situation can be changed in any significant way without a radical restructuring of our political institution.

LEGISLATURES AND EXECUTIVE FEDERALISM

To get some concrete idea of the place of legislatures in the ongoing processes of federal-provincial relations it might be helpful to examine briefly how the House of Commons dealt with Bill C-37, enacted in March 1977 as the *Federal-Provincial Fiscal Arrangements and Established Programs Financing Act, 1977*. It is plausible to argue that this is the most important piece of financial legislation ever enacted by a Canadian Parliament. Very large sums of money

---

* Professor of Political Science, York University.

were involved — about one-sixth of total federal expenditures for all purposes and roughly four-fifths of the financial transfers from Ottawa to the provinces. The intergovernmental relations leading up to this legislation engaged both the financial and philosophical underpinnings of Canadian federalism in their most fundamental aspects. Yet despite the importance of this matter, here is what Thomas Courchene, perhaps the most informed academic analyst of Canadian public finance, had to say about Parliament's role:

> The entire negotiation process with respect to the new fiscal arrangements essentially bypassed the Parliament of Canada. It is true that the Fiscal Arrangements Act is an act of Parliament. But our federal representatives were effectively presented with a *fait accompli,* hammered out between representatives of Ottawa and the ten provincial governments. The bulk of the Commons debate on the bill was directed toward sorting out the precise details of its various provisions. There was no debate in the traditional sense of the term. . . . Public opinion was not brought to bear on the new arrangements. This is in marked contrast to the information that has been available in the print and electronic media relating to the upcoming revision of the new Bank Act, for example. Yet the Bank Act revision pales in consequence with renegotiating the financial basis of the federation in terms of the impact on the Canada of tomorrow.[1]

The lack of parliamentary involvement in federal-provincial relations is demonstrated not only in situations where it is restricted to the *post hoc* ratification of actions already agreed upon by the two levels of government, but also by governments bypassing their respective legislatures in announcing future policies. To give a recent example, at the opening of the meeting of the eleven finance ministers on January 25, 1978, the Honourable Jean Chrétien announced ambitious targets for the Canadian economy and a suggested strategy about how such goals might be pursued. These projected federal policies had not been subjected to prior parliamentary debate even in general terms, and if some kind of federal-provincial economic strategy emerges from the series of meetings among ministers which is now (early February) in progress, this will have been developed with almost no involvement of the legislatures to which these governments are at least nominally responsable.

In general then, the actual locus of public decision has increasingly shifted from single governments to a complex network of intergovernmental relations, to what I have elsewhere called "executive federalism." It is misleading to consider our present circumstances in light of an idealized view of the past in which the textbook relations between government and legislature are assumed to have prevailed. There was never such a past in this country, and in his recent book *Government in Canada,* Thomas Hockin speaks of the "tradition of a collective central energizing executive as the key engine of the [Canadian] state."[2] Yet to the extent that there has been and can be effective involvement of

---

[1] Thomas Courchene, "The New Fiscal Arrangement and the Economics of Federalism," Paper delivered to the Conference of the Future of the Canadian Federation, University of Toronto, October 15, 1977, p. 34.
[2] Thomas Hockin, *Government in Canada* (Toronto: McGraw-Hill Ryerson, 1976) p. 7. Hockin is referring to executive dominance in both federal and provincial governments.

the legislature in the policy process, a necessary but not sufficient precondition is that the locus of actual power resides in single collective executives rather than being diffused in a complex of interactions among several governments.

Several characteristics of executive federalism as these bear on the legislative process may be noted.

First, the processes of intergovernmental interaction have come to involve an increasing number of matters. During the quarter-century after the Second World War, Ottawa came to exercise influence in a very large number of fields within the legislative jurisdiction of the provinces through the use of conditional grants and shared-cost arrangements. More recently, the federal authorities have become somewhat less urgent than before in pressing their own judgments on the provinces by these devices. However, this new emphasis on unconditional as against conditional fiscal transfers means that Parliament is called upon to appropriate large sums of money without any assurances about how the provinces will expend such largesse. On the other side, several matters which a generation ago were regarded as being almost exclusively or exclusively federal now involve both orders of government — immigration, broadcasting, control over lending institutions, international, cultural and economic relations, the support of scientific research, stabilization policies, and so on. There is thus hardly any area of public policy which does not in one way or another engage the activities of both the federal and provincial governments.

Second, the responsibilities for federal-provincial relations are diffused within the cabinets and bureaucracies. Fifteen years ago I visited Ottawa and most of the provincial capitals in a study of the administration of conditional grant programs. By present standards, the machinery of federal-provincial interactions was very undeveloped. At the federal level a significant number of middle-rank civil servants were involved with their provincial counterparts in specific activities — the building of the Trans-Canada Highway, hospital construction and other relatively narrowly defined programs in the field of health services, vocational training, the administration of categorical programs of public assistance and so on. At the more senior levels of decision there was what appeared to be somewhat intermittent activity by Treasury and Finance Departments in negotiating the five-year tax arrangements. In this context first ministers were involved only sporadically in federal-provincial relations. How different it is today! At the federal level there is a standing committee of Cabinet on federal-provincial relations chaired by the Prime Minister, a Secretary of State for Federal-Provincial Relations, an adviser to Cabinet on federal-provincial relations of senior deputy minister rank and a burgeoning Federal-Provincial Relations Office in the Privy Council Office, a Federal-Provincial Liaison Division in the Department of External Affairs, and a division of the Department of Finance under an assistant deputy minister with major responsibility for relations with the provinces. Beyond this machinery where concerns are jurisdiction-wide, there are a very large number of federal agencies whose interactions with the provinces are more specific — the Ministry of State for Urban Affairs, important elements of National Health and Welfare, of the Departments of the Environment and of the Secretary of State. So far as I am aware, no one has delineated even in a broad way the contours of influence and power within this complex executive-bureaucratic network — for example, what *is* the role of the Honourable Marc Lalonde as Secretary of State for Federal-Provincial Relations? And until the lines of authority are known it is almost trite to say that Parliament will continue to be frustrated in any efforts to find out what is going on and to exercise a modicum of surveillance or control over these activites.

Third, federal-provincial relations — or at least some of the most crucial aspects of these relations — are carried on in relative secrecy. It must be said on the other hand that the governments involved have not developed any firm conventions about confidentiality, and it is not impossible for assiduous journalists or even professors to penetrate these processes. I have not examined with any care the impact of the recent moves towards freedom of information on federal-provincial relations. However, one of the plausible dodges that those who wish not to divulge information may assert is that such information came by way of relations with other governments.

Fourth, and this is almost trite, the processes of executive federalism are being carried on within the context of a struggle for the survival of the federation itself. There is an atmosphere of unreality about these relations. The governments involved, at least those other than Quebec, must work these complex processes as if the system were a stable and ongoing one. And yet each participant is immediately aware that what he or she does may have some direct or indirect effect on the very survival of Confederation. Thus federal-provincial relations, even those involving very specific and/or highly technical matters, are inevitably highly politicized. I may add almost parenthetically that one of my worries about the existing situation is that almost all of the federal ministers most directly concerned with federal-provincial relations are Francophones from Quebec — of course the Prime Minister himself, the Secretary of State for Federal-Provincial Relations, the ministers of Finance, Communications, Regional Economic Expansion, and National Health and Welfare. I wish not to be misunderstood here, but it seems inevitable to me that these ministers will inevitably and understandably be preoccupied with what might be called "crisis federalism" to the relative neglect of the ongoing processes of federal-provincial relations, and may well be somewhat insensitive to the elements of those relations other than those occasioned by the challenges of Quebec nationalism.

In general terms, I do not see any very promising prospects for the House of Commons — and this applies in almost the same way to the provincial legislatures — to involve itself more effectively in the ongoing processes of executive federalism. It would indeed be difficult to develop a standing committee on federal-provincial relations precisely because the scope of such relations is so broad as to include in one way or another virtually every important activity of the two orders of government. However, a suggestion made by Flora MacDonald some months ago might bring about some modest improvement. At the beginning of each first ministers' conference the governments in turn would state their general positions on the matters under review. According to Ms. MacDonald's proposal, the federal position paper would first be introduced not into the conference but in the House of Commons, with provision for parliamentary debate on the directions the government proposed to take. Such a reform would in some significant way enhance the effective involvement of Parliament in federal-provincial matters.

THE LEGISLATIVE PROCESS AND CONSTITUTIONAL REFORM

In order to make any analysis of the actual or potential role of legislatures in the process of consistutional reform it is useful to review the law and conventions of the constitution as these relate to amendment.[3] There are two major categories of amendment. The first is made up mainly of provisions related to the structures and processes of the central government and in such cases can be effected by the action of Parliament alone. The second category includes provisions relating to entrenched rights and to the legislative powers of Parliament and the provinces. Amendments here are enacted by the Parliament of the United Kingdom acting in response to a Joint Address of the Senate and House of Commons of Canada. By convention, but by convention only, such action is taken by the Parliament of Canada only after the consent of all the provinces is secured.

As is the case with other aspects of federal-provincial relations, the processes by which the most crucial kinds of constitutional amendments are made are dominated by the executive. The provision for a Joint Address ensures that there will be some opportunity for parliamentary debate on a proposed amendment. Yet because such amendments will normally be introduced only after the consent of the provinces has been secured, debate in the Senate and House of Commons will perforce lead to only *post hoc* ratification of an agreement between the federal and provincial governments. It may be noted also that the prevailing conventions of the constitution dictate only that the consent of provincial governments is required rather than that of provincial legislatures. While any provincial cabinet is of course free to submit such a matter to its legislature, of the four amendments effected by the procedure — those of 1940, 1951, 1960 and 1964 — the first was enacted without being referred to any provincial legislature, the second involved the legislative assemblies of Quebec, Saskatchewan and Manitoba, and the latter two only the legislature of Quebec.[4]

---

[3] The Honourable Guy Favreau, *The Amendment of the Constitution of Canada* (Ottawa: Queen's Printer, 1965).
[4] *Ibid.*, pp. 13-15.

In the process of constitutional review which began with the Confederation for Tomorrow Conference in November 1967 and ended with the Victoria Conference of June 1971, the major participants were the federal and provincial governments alone and neither Parliament nor the provincial legislatures played a crucial role. As will be remembered, the Victoria Charter was agreed upon by the federal government and the governments of all the provinces except Quebec at the latter conference. Premier Bourassa offended one of the operating rules of executive federalism and incurred, it is said, the annoyance of his fellow first ministers by not being willing to commit Quebec on the spot and requested an eleven-day period in which to give his government's decision on the Charter. If Quebec's approval had been secured it seems likely that Canadians would have arrived at a very new constitutional settlement after only a perfunctory debate in Parliament and perhaps almost none at all in the provincial legislatures.

There *was*, however, parliamentary involvement in the process of constitutional review through the work of the Special Joint Committee of the Senate and of the House of Commons of Canada on the Constitution of Canada. The government was never enthusiastic about the establishment of such a committee and it was appointed only in response to persistent pressures from the Leader of the Opposition and his party in the House of Commons. During the two-year period of its existence the Committee held one hundred and forty-five public meetings in forty-seven cities and towns. Fourteen hundred and eighty-six persons appeared as witnesses and these hearings provided almost the only opportunity for persons with specialized constitutional knowledge and other citizens not on the payroll of one government or another to have their views about constitutional matters heard. The Committee itself included several persons with established reputations as constitutionalists — Andrew Brewin, Gordon Fairweather, Eugene Forsey, Maurice Lamontagne and Mark Mac-Guigan.

The *Report* of the Joint Committee[5] published in early 1972 was in my view a sensible and constructive program for constitutional reform. However, constitutional discussions among governments for the time being had then been ended by the failure to secure agreement on the Victoria Charter. Further, there are uncertainties about how much consensus there was on the *Report* within the Committee itself. Parliamentary rules preclude minority reports or minority statements being published under the auspices of a legislative committee and within a short time after the *Report* was made public several of the Committee's members voiced their dissents. Apparently the most contentious issue discussed by the group related to Quebec's right to self-determination, and two Quebec M.P.'s asserted that the *Report* was unsatisfactorily equivocal in this regard. Two M.P.'s from the New Democratic Party issued a statement faulting the document for not including recommendations that federal legislative powers

---

[5] The Special Joint Committee of the Senate and of the House of Commons on the Constitution of Canada, *Final Report* (Ottawa: Queen's Printer, 1972).

could be extended to deal with an economic emergency. In several subsequent speeches in the Senate and elsewhere Eugene Forsey made a defence of the existing constitutional system in explicit criticism of the spirit and substance of the *Report*. Despite the quality of the Committee, some of the evidence it compiled and its *Report*, it seems unlikely that its labours will have any profound influence on constitutional developments in the future.

The making and unmaking of constitutions for Canada is thus as much dominated by governments in the 1970s as it was in the 1860s. The Quebec Resolutions, it is true, gave rise to a debate which took up most of six weeks of the time of the Legislative Council and the Legislative Assembly of the United Province of Canada in early 1865. Yet, as today, legislators were frustrated because the constitutional proposals before them were the resultant of a complex bargain among governments and the legislature could only ratify or turn down such a package as a whole but could not modify its contents.

The processes of constitutional reform in Canada are thus dominated by the executive with relatively little involvement by Parliament and the provincial legislatures. And this situation is unlikely to change without a radical restructuring of our political institutions. But I think the existing procedures contain much more promise for piecing Canada together through a new constitutional settlement than do the proposals for taking these matters out of the hands of elected politicians altogether as suggested by the Committee for a New Constitution (CNC).[6] The Committee proposes a ''Constitutional Commission'' of whose members half would be chosen by the government of Quebec and half by the government of Canada, the latter ''on nomination'' of the other provinces. The work of the Commission would be fed in, so to speak, to a popularly elected constituent assembly charged with drafting a new Canadian constitution which would come into effect only after being ratified by a national referendum or plebiscite.

The CNC proposal is based on the assumption that it is possible and desirable to arrive at a new constitutional settlement through a constituent assembly composed of presumably representative and disinterested citizens. I think this is naive in the extreme. If we are to get such a settlement it will come only through a political bargain determining the basic circumstances under which Canadians will continue to be governed under a common political system. The subsequent drafting of a constitution is no more than a technical task for skilled lawyers. It may prove to be true that differences among Canadians are so profound as to make such a settlement impossible. Or if we fail, historians may in the future judge that our elected politicians were insufficiently adept at their calling to evolve a new bargain from the elements amenable to agreement that existed. But what is clearly required are political skills of the highest order, and it

---

[6] For a more detailed account of my criticism of the manifesto of the Committee for a New Constitution, see my ''Distressing Confusion,'' *Canadian Forum*, November 1977, pp. 24-26.

is exceedingly unlikely that these skills exist in abundance outside the circle of those whose claims to power are based on success in the unedifying trial-by-combat of popular elections.

FEDERALISM AND THE REFORM OF PARLIAMENTARY INSTITUTIONS IN CANADA

We are on the verge of a new round of constitutional review in Canada. And of course the stakes are higher than ever before. In the past few years I have become increasingly convinced that if we are to arrive at a relatively stable constitutional settlement, this will include not only a redelineation of the respective powers and responsibilities of the federal and provincial authorities, but also significant reforms in the structures and processes of the central government.[7] Later in this section I shall have something to say about specific changes in the Parliament of Canada. But first I should like to embark on a rather more general analysis of our political institutions.

Canada is a federal country in a very elemental way in the sense that the most politically salient of its interests and attitudes are territorially bounded. There are several provincial/regional economies at very different levels of prosperity and development; French-speaking Canadians are overwhelmingly concentrated in Quebec and in areas contiguous to Quebec in Ontario and New Brunswick; there are significantly different patterns of social and institutional life and of popular attitudes as one travels from one coast to the other. And it is convincingly argued that our political institutions themselves contribute to the territorialization of political issues and frustrate the mobilization of Canadians on other axes.[8] Thus we unite and conflict as westerners, Québécois and Newfoundlanders rather than as poor against rich, the upwardly mobile against those of stable or declining status, or libertarians as against authoritarians.

Now if we take those territorially bounded cleavages of Canada as "givens," there are two polar way in which we can deal with them. The first is to design our political institutions so that these territorial particularisms find an effective and continuing outlet through the institutions of the central government. Karl Lowenstein has designated this as "intrastate federalism."[9] The other alternative is to confer the responsibility for matters about which territorial differences are most profound on the states or provinces according to Lowenstein's "interstate federalism." Most federal systems involve a mix of these two devices, but my general argument is that we have in Canada shifted the balance too far toward the interstate alternative and that we should thus take steps

---

[7] For a more elaborate discussion of the arguments in this section, see my "The Structural Problem of Canadian Federalism," *Canadian Public Administration* 14 (1971): 326-43.

[8] Richard Simeon, "Regionalism and Canadian Political Institutions," in J. Peter Meekison, ed., *Canadian Federalism: Myth or Reality*, 3d ed. (Toronto: Methuen 1977), pp.292-304.

[9] Karl Lowenstein, *Political Power and the Governmental Process* (Chicago: University of Chicago Press, 1965), pp. 405-7.

to ensure the more effective representation of territorial particularisms within the central government. Otherwise it seems likely to me that the provincial governments will assume the almost exclusive franchise to represent attitudes and interests that are territorially bounded. There are many reasons I wish this not to occur, the major one being that in this process the federal authorities will lose their capacity to undertake effective measures of interpersonal or interprovincial equalization.

In order to make this analysis somewhat more concrete, let us see what has happened to Alberta in the eleven federal general elections from 1945 to 1974 inclusive. From several perspectives Alberta is a province "pas comme les autres" — it was the last part of Canada to come under agricultural settlement; the discovery of petroleum at Leduc in 1947 led to its economy being altered more radically than has occurred in any other province and the Alberta economy more than that of any other province depends on the exploitation of non-renewable resources; it has been governed by "minor" parties for fifty of its seventy-three years in Confederation and not since 1911 has it had a provincial government of the same partisan complexion as that in power in Ottawa; and its prevailing public attitudes are alleged to be to the "right" of those dominant elsewhere in Canada. Here then is what has happened to the aberrant province (see Table 1).

- of the 193 Alberta seats in the eleven elections, 51 (26.4 percent) went to the party returned to power in Ottawa and 142 (73.6 percent) to the opposition parties. If we exempt the elections of 1957, 1958 and 1962 in which Conservative governments were returned, only 17 Alberta seats (12.0 percent) were won by Liberals while 125 (88.0 percent) were won by opposition groups. Yet in none of these latter eight elections did the Liberals fail to get at least 20 percent of the Alberta popular vote and in the last two elections gained the support of one of four Alberta voters without winning any of the 38 seats at stake.

- in the period under review Albertans have been sparsely and ineffectually represented in federal Liberal cabinets. Although Jack Horner's reputation in this new role is yet to be established, his predecessors are eminently forgettable — Mackinnon, Prudham, Hays, Olson, Mahoney. Even if we include the Diefenbaker government, Edmonton as Canada's fastest growing metropolitan area has not had a representative in the Cabinet since 1957 apart from Marcel Lambert's two months' incumbency as Minister of Veterans' Affairs in 1963.

Table 1
Alberta in Federal Elections 1945-1974

	% of popular vote				*Seats*		
	C	L	S.C.	NDP/CCF	C	L	S.C.
1945	18.7	21.8	36.6	18.4	2	2	13
1949	16.8	34.5	37.4	9.3	2	5	10
1953	14.5	35.0	40.8	6.9	2	4	11
1957	27.6	27.9	27.8	6.3	3	1	13
1958	59.9	13.7	21.6	4.4	17		
1962	42.8	19.4	29.2	8.4	15		2
1963	45.3	22.1	25.8	6.5	14	1	2
1965	46.6	22.4	22.5	8.3	15		2
1968	50.4	35.7	1.9	9.3	15	4	
1972	57.6	25.0	4.5	12.6	19		
1974	61.2	24.8	3.4	9.3	19		

The result of Alberta's relative lack of strength on the government side of the House of Commons has meant that interests specific to the province are chanelled almost exclusively through the provincial government. And Alberta's unique position among the provinces occasioned by its dependence on fossil-fuel resources has resulted in a situation in which these interests are very specific indeed.

In terms of my general prescription, I shall consider at the end of this paper three possible avenues of reform in the institutions of the Parliament of Canada — reforms in the relations between the political executive and the legislature, in the Senate and in the federal electoral system.

RELATIONS BETWEEN THE POLITICAL EXECUTIVE AND PARLIAMENT.

I have argued that neither the Parliament of Canada nor the provincial legislatures can come to play any effective role in federal-provincial relations unless the workings of our parliamentary institutions are radically changed. We have here the executive dominance of the legislature to a fairly full degree along with, at the federal level at least, the dominance of the Prime Minister and the staff agencies which serve him over the Cabinet and the bureaucracy. It can plausibly be argued also that this prime ministerial apparatus is as yet less fully representative of the territorially based particularisms of Canada than was the Cabinet in the earlier days where at least some of the ministers had regional bases of power giving them a degree of influence independent of the prime minister.

Despite everything my teachers of political science — some of them American professors — taught me a quarter of a century ago, I am now convinced that in the present Canadian circumstances we should move in the direction of the American congressional model. I confess not to have thought out the implications of this position in detail, and in particular whether or not we could move significantly in this direction by gradual steps rather than by an explicit constitutional change providing for the separation of legislative and executive powers. Perhaps we might establish a new convention by which a House of Commons vote of no-confidence would have to be explicitly so framed. Perhaps we might somehow limit the power of a prime minister to recommend dissolution, and with it his power both over his own party and the House of Commons. Certainly any move in this general direction should strengthen the position of the standing committees of the House as against the political executive and bring about a situation where cross-party coalitions in these committees would develop.

THE REFORM OF THE SENATE

There has been sporadic discussion recently of restructuring the Senate so it could more effectively reflect regional and cultural differences. Two distinguished political scientists, Ronald Watts and R.M. Burns, have made careful and detailed analyses of the matter[10] and Flora MacDonald has suggested that the Senate be reconstituted as a "House of the Provinces." Here are my own preliminary conclusions.

First, not a great deal would be gained by reforms which went no further than to change the methods by which Senators are appointed or their terms of office. If the provincial governments were given some influence over appointments this would have no other result than to give provincial Cabinets a further source of patronage. Perhaps something can be said for five or ten-year terms for Senators. My own preferred reform would be a constitutional amendment prohibiting an appointment to the Senate of any person under sixty years of age — appointments at, say, forty are outrageously generous prizes at the disposal of the government of the day.

Second, genuine bicameralism is incompatible with British parliamentary institutions. Comparative experience would suggest that a second chamber, whatever its composition and powers, can play a genuinely equal and co-ordinate role with the other House only in those systems like those of the United States where the political executive is not responsible to the lower chamber. Otherwise, the chamber to which the executive is accountable is where the action takes place, and in Australia even the popularly elected Senate is much less influential than the other house.

Third, there may be more positive possibilities for reform in creating some kind of body in Ottawa which would further institutionalize the processes of federal-provincial relations. Such a reform is compatible with leaving the Senate as it now is. The new "House of the Provinces" might be given the responsibility for approving federal-provincial agreements or appointments to the

---

[10] R.L. Watts, "Second Chambers in Federal Systems," *The Confederation Challenge,* Vol. 2, Ontario Advisory Committee on Confederation, Toronto, 1970, pp. 315-55 and R.M. Burns, "Second Chambers: German Experience and Canadian Needs," in Meekison, *op. cit.*, pp. 188-215.

Supreme Court and some of the major federal regulatory agencies. Here and there it has been suggested that there be a body something like that of the German Bundesrat which consists of delegates of the lander (state) governments. There are several differences between the German and Canadian political regimes which make their experience not immediately applicable to our circumstances. The major difference is that in Germany much of the activity of the lander is in the administration of laws enacted by the national legislature. This is not our way, and is probably incompatible with a regime of parliamentary responsibility. But the major difficulty in such a further institutionalization of federal-provincial relations is that the new body would have to be fitted in with the existing processes of executive federalism. I have limited expectations here. As early as 1945 Premier Drew of Ontario suggested that it was his intention " . . . to designate a minister who is responsible for Dominion-Provincial relations and who will spend much of his time in Ottawa in connection with this work.[11] This intention was never carried out, but with the circumstances of modern air travel and telecommunications it would be quite feasible for Ottawa and the provinces to form a joint council in Ottawa of such ministers as Mr. Drew suggested without radical changes in the existing system of federal-provincial relations. Experience suggests, however, that governments will be very reluctant to give up any significant amount of their independent discretion to any joint authority.

THE ELECTORAL SYSTEM

In a classic article of a decade ago Alan Cairns demonstrated the pervasive impact of the federal electoral system on Canadian politics.[12] Walter Stewart in his *Divide and Con*[13] published in 1973 elaborated some of Cairn's analysis in a journalistic and polemical form. Yet despite the strictures laid on the electoral system by academics and journalists, Flora MacDonald in her recent suggestion that we adopt proportional representation is, I believe, the first contemporary federal politician to recommend changes in this crucial aspect of our political institutions. The essential defect of our electoral system is that it distorts regional and provincial balances in the House of Commons. I need not go into details. Liberal representation is overwhelmingly from Ontario and Quebec and Conservative representation from what Peter Newman has called "outer Canada," and these imbalances are more profound than the relative proportions of popular votes the two parties received from these provinces/regions. At the extreme degree, the shift of a handful of votes in the 1972 general election might well have resulted in a situation where Canada was governed by a minority Progressive Conservative administration with only two seats from Quebec supported by the New Democratic Party with no seats from that province.

---

[11] *Report of the Dominion Provincial Conference* (Ottawa: King's Printer, 1945), p. 16.

[12] Alan Cairns, "The Electoral System and the Party System in Canada 1921-1965," *Canadian Journal of Political Science* 1 (March 1968): 55-80.

[13] Walter Stewart, *Divide and Con: Canadian Politics at Work* (Don Mills, Ont.: New Press, 1973).

Those few people who think of reforming the federal electoral system have generally thought in terms of some form or other of proportional representation (PR). I would oppose PR on two grounds.

First, proportional representation involves multi-member constituencies and this would almost inevitably weaken the role of M.P.'s in serving their constituents in individual and community matters. The major justification for PR is that it works towards the congruence of a party's proportion of the popular vote and the proportion of seats it has in the legislature. Obviously this congruence is closer when there are few electoral districts rather than many, and in most such systems constituencies elect at least five members. This regime would obviously result in very populous constituencies in Canada and thus complicate the constituency role of M.P.'s, even if they were applied only to the larger metropolitan centres with other areas being organized on the single-member basis. Just as crucially, the diffusion of responsibility for constituency service among several M.P.'s from an area would probably result in such services being performed ineffectually.

Second, PR would probably result in the establishment of splinter parties whose appeal was limited to particular areas and thus contribute to the fragmentation of the party system. There are devices by which this fragmentation might in part be arrested, as by the rule governing the election of the West German Bundestag according to which only those parties which win 5 percent or more of the national popular vote are eligible to share in the distribution of the half of the members of that chamber who are elected by PR. But even with such a provision, I would expect proportional representation in Canada to contribute to the strength of minor parties less disposed than are the major political groupings toward accommodation on a nation-wide basis.

My own proposal for electoral reform would proceed along these lines. Voters would cast their ballots as they now do and the same number of M.P.'s would be elected from single-member districts. But the House of Commons would be enlarged to include one hundred "provincial" M.P.'s, with Prince Edward Island having one of these and the rest distributed among the other provinces in proportion to their respective populations. The "provincial" members would have the same standing in the House as their other colleagues and be given services in their respective provincial capitals and travel privileges to and from those capitals. The provincial M.P.'s would be chosen by ranking in each province those candidates who had received the highest proportion of popular votes to the winning candidates. Thus in Newfoundland, which according to the 1971 census would gain two seats under my proposal, the provincial members would be those two who had come nearest to capturing the seven seats in the province.

I have had some calculations made of the impact of this proposal if it had been in effect from 1957 onward. Table 2 presents the results from the two most recent federal elections on the assumption — not unreasonable — that this reform would not have affected the way in which people did in fact vote.

Table 2
Seat Distribution in the House of Commons

		1972 Actual		Smiley Reform		1974 Actual		Smiley Reform
Newfoundland	L	3	L	4	L	4	L	4
	PC	4	PC	5	PC	3	PC	5
PEI	L	1	L	1	L	1	L	2
	PC	3	PC	4	PC	3	PC	3
NS	L	1	L	3	L	2	L	5
	PC	10	PC	11	PC	8	PC	9
					NDP	1	NDP	1
NB	L	5	L	7	L	6	L	8
	PC	5	PC	6	PC	3	PC	4
					Ind	1	Ind	1
Quebec	L	56	L	72	L	60	L	71
	PC	2	PC	5	PC	3	PC	14
	SC	15	SC	23	SC	11	SC	17
	Ind	1	Ind	2				
Ontario	L	36	L	52	L	55	L	74
	PC	40	PC	56	PC	25	PC	39
	NDP	11	NDP	15	NDP	8	NDP	11
Manitoba	L	2	L	4	L	2	L	2
	PC	8	PC	10	PC	9	PC	12
	NDP	3	NPD	4	NDP	2	NPD	4
Sask.	L	1	L	1	L	3	L	3
	PC	7	PC	8	PC	8	PC	10
	NDP	5	NDP	8	NDP	2	NDP	4
Alberta	L	0	L	7	L	0	L	7
	PC	19	PC	19	PC	19	PC	19
BC	L	4	L	10	L	8	L	9
	PC	8	PC	10	PC	13	PC	19
	NDP	11	NDP	13	NDP	2	NDP	5

These reforms would contribute to a more appropriate regional balance among the parties in the House of Commons. In terms of the 1974 elections:

- 81.2 percent of the Liberal seats came from Ontario and Quebec. Under the new proposal this would be reduced to 78.4 percent. But more crucially, the Liberals would have won seven seats in Alberta.
- 67.3 percent of the PC seats came from "Outer Canada," outside Ontario and Quebec. Under the new proposal this would be reduced to 60.7 percent. The PC's would have won eleven more seats in Quebec.

This reform would also have the same effect as PR in making more nearly congruent their proportions of the popular vote and the proportion of seats gained by parties in the House of Commons as shown in Table 3.

Table 3
Number of Votes Per Seat

| | 1972 | | 1974 | |
	Actual	*Smiley Reform*	*Actual*	*Smiley Reform*
L	34,112	23,195	29,098	22,177
PC	31,622	25,063	35,467	24,958
NDP	55,275	40,798	91,734	56,452
SC	49,198	32,086	43,748	28,308

This reform would not only do something to redress the regional/party balance in the House of Commons and make the government party more fully representative of regional interests, but would also increase competition among the major parties throughout Canada. When one of the parties is denied parliamentary representation from a particular area, the results are almost always unfortunate. In some cases the party organization comes to be controlled by those who are more interested in patronage for themselves than in electoral competition. Sometimes the national party fails to expend resources in grass-roots organization and seeks to build its strength by recruiting local or provincial notables. In the House of Commons and in the higher echelons of the national party, the demands of a province or region disaffected from that party are often articulated by outsiders with few direct claims to an understanding of that province or region. Such results could in part be mitigated by the reform I have proposed.

CONCLUSION

I see relatively few possibilities under our existing parliamentary regime for the Parliament of Canada or the provincial legislatures to be effectively involved in federal-provincial relations, including not only the ongoing interactions between the two orders of government but also the processes of constitutional reform. But the more crucial defect of our regime in terms of the challenge to national unity is that the institutions of the central government do not adequately represent our regional and provincial particularisms. Remedying these defects would require us to proceed in the direction of a congressional system: the strength of the national government of the United States vis-à-vis the states can be explained in large part by the circumstance that local and regional interests find an effective outlet through the Congress and a fragmented executive branch. In general terms, the current disposition to deal with our discontents by enhancing the power of the provinces without reforms in the institutions of the central government can lead only to unfortunate results.

COMMENTS

LOU HYNDMAN*

Professor Smiley's paper is to be welcomed as a contribution to reasoned debate concerning the role of the Parliament of Canada and of the provincial legislatures in federal-provincial relations. To a great extent Canadian politics is the politics of federalism. Few, if any, issues which are discussed in Canada today do not in some fashion impinge on federal-provincial relations.

While I agree with Professor Smiley's perception that changes are required in our federal system if it is to cope with the challenge to national unity, I disagree with his emphasis on institutional and electoral reforms. If Canada is to survive as a nation, changes to central institutions and to the electoral system will not suffice by themselves. What is also required is a fundamental change in attitude on the part of governments, and especially the bureaucracy of the central government in Ottawa. A further point of departure I have with Professor Smiley's paper relates to his basic premise that a stronger central government is required to resolve Canada's problems. On the contrary, I see Canada as a nation where the federal government and each provincial government are balanced and complementary in their roles and responsibilites, not where the provinces are subordinate to the federal government. Given the geographic, economic, cultural and linguistic diversities in the regions of Canada — a factor recognized by Professor Smiley in his paper — there is a need for strong provincial governments which can reflect the needs and aspirations of their constituents. The federal system must be made more responsive to the particular needs and preferences of the provinces and regions if the quality of federalism in Canada is to improve and become relevant to the 1970s and 1980s.

Executive Federalism

Given my responsibilities as Minister of Federal and Intergovernmental Affairs for Alberta, I feel it is important that I comment on the processes of what Professor Smiley has called "executive federalism." It is a reality that interaction amongst the governments in Canada is extensive, encompasses virtually all areas of public policy, and if activity related to the most recent First Ministers' Conference is an indication, is on the increase. The standard criticism of this process is that it downgrades the activities and the position of the legislative bodies. As Government House Leader in Alberta, I disagree.

In my view the processes of "executive federalism" come under minute scrutiny in the Assembly. In Alberta these processes are discussed during question period, in debate, and during estimates. There are opportunities galore

---

* The Honourable Lou Hyndman, Minister of Federal and Intergovernmental Affairs, Government of Alberta and Government House Leader, Alberta Legislative Assembly.

for government or opposition M.L.A.'s to take part. Hardly a sitting day goes by when a member of the House does not pose a question to a minister which involves some aspect of federal-provincial relations. For example, recently I was asked in the legislature whether we were negotiating an agreement with the federal government on the Alcan Pipeline. The member wanted to know the terms and conditions of a possible agreement. The week before that, I was asked what involvement we have had with the federal government on the multilateral trade negotiations. Correspondence between Premier Lougheed and Prime Minister Trudeau is, in most cases, tabled in the House. The above illustrates the fact that the opportunity is there for legislative participation and input into these important questions, not only before discussions, but also during negotiations and after agreements are signed.

A particular reference in Professor Smiley's paper is to the recently concluded *Fiscal Arrangements and Established Programs Financing Act*. I think it fair that I describe the process of the negotiations from a different perspective. Provincial governments were aware that for the First Ministers' Conference in June 1976, a new proposal respecting certain shared-cost programs would be forthcoming (indeed in the 1975 June budget the Minister of Finance had already indicated that the federal government would terminate the *Hospital Insurance and Diagnostic Services Act* — without advising the provinces!). Approximately one week before the First Ministers' Conference, provincial officials, after exerting some pressure on the federal government, had an opportunity to see the federal working document. The purpose of this advance consultation was to give the provinces an opportunity to prepare their responses for the First Ministers' Conference. The federal paper was presented simultaneously to the First Ministers and to Parliament. The paper contained principles which were debated at the federal-provincial meeting and which could also be debated in Parliament.

The June 1976 First Ministers' Conference was followed by a Finance Ministers' Meeting in July 1976, a Finance Ministers' Meeting in December 1976, a First Ministers' Conference in December 1976, and a Finance Ministers' Conference in January 1977. I should add that the premiers discussed this matter at the Premiers' Conference in August 1976, as did the provincial Ministers of Finance and Treasurers prior to the December 1976 meetings. While it is true that these meetings were not open to the press, the fact that they were being held was known and there were questions and speeches in Parliament and in the legislatures. Throughout this time, as events unfolded, there was full opportunity for the important questions of principle outlined in the federal paper to be discussed throughout Canada: in Parliament, in provincial legislatures, in academic circles, and in the media.

Certainly in June 1976 no firm positions had been taken by the provinces. The negotiations took place over a seven-month period which gave an opportunity for those interested to raise questions. I should add that the federal government's policies with respect to cost limitations on Medicare contained in

Bill C-68 were matters that could be debated in Parliament. Bill C-68 placed a ceiling on cost-sharing for 1976-1977 and subsequent fiscal years. An earlier federal policy (1972) which established a ceiling on federal contributions towards post-secondary education costs of 15 percent per annum could have been debated in Parliament. My point is that too frequently critics point to the end result, and overlook the long and arduous process which has led to that result. Even before the Established Programs Financing Proposal was unveiled, major changes in those programs were subject to public debate and scrutiny.

Let us look at the problem from a slightly different perspective by studying a second example. Alberta entered the federal Anti-Inflation Program only after an enabling Act had been approved by the provincial legislature. That Act and Alberta's position with respect to our participation was fully debated in the Assembly. Only after the Act was given Royal Assent did detailed negotiations on the agreement take place. The life of our Act was approximately eighteen months. To extend our agreement with the federal government beyond March 31, 1977 required further legislative action. The government decided to continue in the program for an additional nine months. The matter was again fully debated in the provincial legislature, as an amendment was necessary. Debate took place at second reading and during committee study.

A further example of legislative input involved Alberta's position on the amending formula during the interprovincial discussions on the constitution in the fall of 1976. Alberta's position was set out through a resolution of the legislature but it was the government itself which instituted the debate in the Legislative Assembly. The matter was fully discussed and the resolution secured support from both sides of the House. Indeed an amendment to the resolution introduced by the official Opposition formed part of the final resolution.

Constitutional Reform

On the question of constitutional reform, I share Professor Smiley's concerns regarding a constituent assembly. This type of body would seriously reduce the accountability of elected officials to electors. Government leaders are the ones working within the confines of the constitution. As such, they must be directly involved in the process of developing a workable constitution. Having said that, however, it should also be stated that government leaders are very much aware of a continuous basis of proposals and ideas that come forth from a variety of sources.

Some mention has been made of the package of constitutional proposals that the federal government will be putting forth later this spring. My understanding is that this package will be introduced in Parliament first. There has been no attempt to secure prior agreement from the provinces, nor have we been privy to federal thinking on the matter.

Parliamentary Reform

In examining proposals pertaining to parliamentary reform I have some concerns. I have already discussed executive federalism and believe that it is very much a part of the operation of our constitution and should be institutionalized. I have to ask the question, however — are reforms which are presented under the guise of reforming the federal system, reforms which are designed to improve the parliamentary system? One frequently hears criticism of the role of legislatures today. I think we should be very clear about our objectives before we start to reform Parliament. Thus, while Senate reform may be one solution to the problems of federalism, it may completely distort the workings of the parliamentary system based on the Westminster model. For example, some proponents of Senate reform have not addressed themselves to the question of how such a body will deal with the federal budget. That document certainly has a direct impact on the provincial governments. Nor have they really addressed the effect such a major change would have on the functioning of the party system in Canada and the operation of caucuses. Nor have they really considered the long-term effect such an institution will have on Cabinet government at either the federal or the provincial levels. Which government will be accountable for decisions?

While the American congressional model has many important federal features, the altering of legislative-executive relationships in Parliament is an area that requires very careful assessment. The congressional model is not without its critics or problems. The basic question is, do we want a parliamentary form of government? We should answer this fundamental question before embarking on a new course.

As far as electoral reform is concerned, my only comment is that Professor Smiley's proposal is thought-provoking. The difficulty with such a proposal is that once set in place, we do not know what its consequences will be. Will the provincial M.P.'s be thought of as second class M.P.'s because they came second in the general elections? I would also imagine that their term of office would be relatively short, given the uncertain nature of politics. Moreover, as Table I indicates, third parties also benefit considerably from this proposal. As such, the proposal could lead to the fragmentation of the national party system by encouraging the formation of splinter parties.

Conclusion

To me, Canada has developed its own unique system of giving expression to what Professor Smiley calls "regional and provincial particularisms." That system is the federal-provincial process of bargaining. Executive federalism, while perhaps not perfect, provides an opportunity for a full discussion between governments in Canada. Before we embrace the German model or the American model or indeed, any other, we must study the defects of these systems and gauge the full consequences of their adoption in Canada. In grafting parts of other political systems onto the Canadian system, we must ensure that we are not creating worse problems than the ones we are attempting to solve.

To sum up, I believe that the intergovernmental trends in federal-provincial relations are entirely compatible with the parliamentary system, although it may well be necessarv to develop different links between this relatively new mechanism and Canadian legislatures. It is an important and valuable new dimension in Canadian federalism and holds real promise as an adaptable, constructive mechanism for future intergovernmental relationships.

NORMAN J. RUFF*

Events over the past few months have provided further confirmation of Professor Smiley's description of the contemporary nature of the federal-provincial policy process as "executive federalism." The February 1978 meeting of the First Ministers on the economy and the preceding series of sectoral meetings provide not only a further illustration of the ever increasing scope of intergovernmental negotiations, but also the extent to which this body has become a forum of policy formation to the exclusion of parliamentary institutions. In addition to comprehensive briefs emanating from Ontario ("An Economic Development Policy *for Canada*"), and from British Columbia ("Toward a *National* Economic Policy"), the conference also was the occasion for the suggestion by two federal Cabinet ministers, Mr. Horner and Mr. Lalonde, that private sector groups and "regional or local decision makers or interest groups" be directly involved in consultation between the federal and provincial governments. If the latter were to become part of the regular conduct of federal-provincial relations then this would be a very fine tuning of executive federalism.

In addition, the proposal by Premiers Bennett and Lougheed for provincial participation in the nomination of members of federal regulatory bodies has much to commend it, but it too further enhances the ties of executive federalism in an increasingly significant area of public policy removed from close parliamentary scrutiny.

Role of Parliament in Constitutional Debate

The virtually undetectable participation of the House of Commons in the post-1976 discussions of our constitutional future and the search for "renewed" federalism further illustrate the limited participation of Parliament in federal-provincial matters. The earlier role played by Parliament in the abortive 1968-1971 review through the Special Joint Committee on the Constitution was

* Assistant Professor, Department of Political Science, University of Victoria.

not an entirely wasted exercise. Despite the fate of its report, the Committee's hearings conducted throughout the country did provide a valuable opportunity for the mobilization of regional views, and were an excellent example of the institution acting in its primary role as an instrument of political communication.

In our new concern for national unity, this role has been given to the Pepin-Robarts Task Force, and the House has thus far been confined to a three day debate in mid-1977 on the motion that the members "dedicate themselves anew to the continuing unity of Canada." If nothing else, a parliamentary committee would have saved us from the embarrassment of the search for Quebec representation on the Task Force, and the newly found electoral aspirations of some of its members and senior staff.

I agree with Professor Smiley that the role of Parliament in the formal process of constitutional amendment is ordinarily a limited one but disagree that it is necessarily confined to merely *post hoc* ratification. Two exceptions immediately spring to mind. In 1936, a joint address proposing restrictions on provincial brrowing and an extension of provincial tax powers was turned back and effectively killed by the Senate. And, in 1960, once again the Senate acted independently and revised the proposed constitutional amendment concerning the retirement age of judges, so as to exclude references to district and county courts.

These two examples may lend some credence to the possible utility of a reformed Senate as a vehicle for regional representation at the federal level and a parliamentary presence in federal-provincial relations — or perhaps one should say in the light of the interest in a German style House of the Provinces, composed of provincial Cabinet representatives, as a provincial presence in the federal legislative process. Without dwelling on the dangers inherent in the import of political institutions — we are already struggling with the question of British parliamentary institutions and complicating the situation still more by contemplating the grafting on of an addition with roots in the pre-1918 German Empire — we should be especially cautious of adopting the highly bureaucratic and secretive elements of the work of the Bundesrat which relies heavily for its success on deliberations held in camera by committees of state officials. The existing network of federal-provincial conferences already embodies such features and there can be little advantage to a further institutionalization of them within our parliamentary framework.

Proportional Representation

I am uneasy about the prospect raised by Professor Smiley of adding a further one hundred seats to a House whose membership is destined to reach an estimated three hundred and ten seats by 1981 under the existing representation formula. However, I find Professor Smiley's proposal for "provincial M.P.'s" a far more imaginative one than Senate reform, and an idea which more effectively addresses the problem of adequate regional representation in Parliament. In following the details of his scheme, however, I sense that those awarded "provincial seats" as runners up, if not entirely to be regarded as second class M.P.'s, could hardly be considered as potential Cabinet material to boost weak regional representation. In some respects the proposal is a step along the way toward a combination of the existing simple plurality system and proportional representation.

Such a scheme has already been aired in the Province of Quebec. One third of the seats in the National Assembly would be allocated in proportion to the total vote with a ten percent cut-off to qualify for such representation. This is itself a variation of the West German electoral system and represents a combination which avoids the loss of constituency contact which is feared under simple proportional representation, and the difficulty of status that I see in Professor Smiley's "runner-up" concept of "provincial" M.P.'s.

My personal preference would be for an extra allocation of "provincial" seats in the House of Commons but with their occupants chosen on the basis of the proportion of votes cast for provincial lists of party candidates. The voter would cast one vote for the local constituency M.P. and a second for a "provincial" list drawn up by the party. All existing seats per province would be allocated according to the proportions of the second vote with the lists being drawn upon to make up the difference between the number of M.P.'s elected on the constituency votes and the total for which the party would now be eligible. Where a party's seats exceed its due proportion these would be retained and the total number of seats from a province enlarged accordingly. I should add that at heart I am skeptical as to the receptiveness of the public and our politicians to electoral reform at the federal level — even in the face of such sensible proposals. It should also be noted that lack of adequate parliamentary representation, which Professor Smiley has so well documented in the case of Alberta, does not confine regional interests to provincial government channels or act as a total hindrance to the exertion of influence on the federal government. As our experience of the success of western mining interests in regard to the Carter Commission's proposals for tax reform demonstrates, other productive means of access in the form of organized group activity are also available.

Conclusion

The underlying question of the relevancy of Parliament to the processes of executive federalism and Parliament's ability to perform effectively a surveillance function in this area is, of course, but one aspect of the total pattern of its relationships with the Cabinet and the offices of the Prime Minister and the Privy Council. The position of the House in the field of external affairs raises still more serious doubts as to the efficacy of Parliament. While some of the solution to Parliament's general difficulties may lie in such institutional questions as allocations of time and the role of committees, attention must also be given to the capability of the individual M.P., both opposition and government backbencher, to effectively confront the centres of power in the PMO and PCO as well as the federal-provincial conference. Though now subject to an *ad hoc* partisan formula, the funding of research assistance begun in 1968 and the televising of the House go some way to redress the balance, and enable the House to begin the function as the major institution for political communication it was designed to be. More freedom of action for the M.P. and wider access to background and preparatory papers which precede Cabinet policy initiatives would further enhance the work of Parliament.

Finally, we should also be reminded that the weaknesses of Parliament are in large part human weaknesses, and more particularly those of the parliamentary parties. In the face of our current financial, economic and constitutional difficulties I find it startling to see reported in a recent poll that, when asked which federal party was best able to handle such problems, 45 percent of the respondents could not name such a party. If our parliamentary system is in difficulty, it lies primarily in its failure to adequately frame responses to our economic, social and constitutional problems. Their solution lies not in Senate, electoral or procedural reform, but rather in the talents and policy alternatives produced by our parliamentary parties. In this sense the critical failings of Parliament are not those of the institution but rather of the parties that form it.

R.M. BURNS*

It is pretty generally accepted that the comparative study of institutions in different governmental systems is less productive than we might wish it to be. Nevertheless, there is much that can be learned from the experience of others and from their mistakes and we would not be well advised to pass by too quickly. In his paper in Chapter 4, Professor Patterson has given us some interesting insights into the operation of the United States Congress and while I feel no strong attachments to congressionalism there may be some lessons, particularly in its committees, that could be valuable to us.

Like most of you, I suspect, I have had my reservations about the workability of our parlimentary system. Having spent too many hours in the galleries of both Ottawa and some provinces, I have often come away convinced that were I there a better job would be done. It has only been since I have taken the time to examine objectively what members were up against that a more realistic appreciation of the situation has taken over.

I am by no means sure that the reform of our institutions or their processes in itself is likely to provide a cure for our national malaise. The fault may be much closer to our own perceptions of our just claims on the community. But as it is the institutions and processes with which we are concerned here, I will

---

* Director, Executive Development Training Programme, School of Public Administration, University of Victoria; Chairman, Advisory Committee to the B.C. Cabinet Committee on Confederation.

regretfully refrain from expounding on the moral shortcomings of present day society which may be more at the root of the matter.

There are two main legislative institutions with which we must concern ourselves, the House of Commons (or in the provinces, the legislatures) and the second chamber, the Senate. My main concern is with the latter as a possible instrument of federalism. But despite Mr. Stanfield's apparent, if reluctant, conviction as to the critical state of the Commons, I cannot refrain from a few gratuitous and I hope constructive suggestions.

Commons Reform

The melding of legislative and executive responsibilities in the parliamentary system has much to commend it. But we must acknowledge that in a federal system some related problems follow. One of the more obvious of these is the inevitable tendency for the most routine processes to become politicized with the involvement of the executives in almost every aspect of government at both national and regional levels.

In the process the role of the legislator has become sadly eclipsed. I am not at all sure what we can do about it. It may be that it is a necessary price of having any effective government at all. The legislative branch is certainly not an effective administrative instrument nor should it be. Parliament, being what it is, is going to be preoccupied a good deal of the time with politics, which in itself is hardly to be criticized. But while much of what it does is pertinent to government overall, some even vital, a good deal of often meaningless rhetoric about peripheral matters follows, designed more to attract the attention of the media (and presumably the voter) than to contribute to better government.

While it is, I believe, an almost inevitable part of any modern governmental system that the executive be dominant, there are a couple of things that might be done to redress the balance. There could be considerable merit in limiting somewhat the extensive power that the Prime Minister has over the life of the Commons and the political concerns of its members through his power over dissolution. This might be controlled in a reasonable way if the government could only be defeated after a vote following a specific resolution of want of confidence, probably not too different to the situation as it has been developing since February 1968. Failing such a vote, dissolution should only come at the end of a fixed period of four or five years. This is by no means an original idea. The West German parliament has such a fixed life. No doubt there would be difficulties but it is worth some serious consideration.

The second possible change is one that has already been seriously approached in the last few years and involves a greater reliance on the committee system. John Stewart in his excellent study of the Canadian House of Commons goes into this in some depth. The objectives have obviously been desirable but the performance considerably less than ideal. What appears to be missing is a committee status more independent of the strict party discipline which characterizes the Commons. If the committees are to have real influence, their performances must be based on the merits of the case rather than on the convenience of the government. I do not suggest that the elimination of party discipline is in itself a desirable end but it should have a sufficient place in the House to satisfy us. I have been tempted to suggest that the power of these committees be further extended, perhaps even to the point where they might actually cut estimates or recommend that a bill be turned back. Probably in theory those powers already exist but under present discipline they are not often exercised.

There are obvious objections to such changes and I would need to know a great deal more than I do to actively embrace them. I suspect that only someone who has actually served in the Commons would be in a position to make any judgments of value on such matters.

There is one further problem which directly involves our electoral system. Due to the prevailing nature of our political regionalism, we have no truly national party insofar as seating in the House of Commons is concerned, although all of the major parties make respectable showings on a national basis in terms of popular vote.

Dr. Smiley has looked at this and made certain proposals. The need for a cure is obvious but I am less than enamoured of the idea of adding a hundred additional seats to an already large house. With Dr. Ruff, I lean rather toward some adaptation of the West German system of two electoral slates, equally divided, one made up of individual single-member constituencies, the other of a party slate. With the minimum safeguards the Germans have provided, I believe this could remedy in some part at least the regional representational defects that currently distort our federal system. I have not done the arithmetic but at least the regional balance would be improved.

But the House of Commons is only part of the story. Parliament consists of two Houses and it is the role and functions of the second chamber, the Canadian Senate, to which I think prior attention should be given, if only for reasons of some greater practical possibilities of accomplishment.

Senate Reform

Second chambers in a federal system have two distinct, if related, responsibilities. First, they have the basic function of review of the legislative actions of the lower house, in effect a curb on the powers of the executive. This function is common to second chambers whether in a federal or a unitary state. The second basic function is limited to federal systems and it is in the representation of regional interests and viewpoints in national decision making. If there was a clear, independent and co-ordinate division of authority between the two levels of government and if all units were of more or less equal power, there would be no need of such a representative authority. But with the wide discrepancy of representation that results regionally under a system that is basically one of "rep by pop," it is generally accepted that some compensating regional influence should be provided.

It is a common complaint of Canadian provincial governments that they are heavily influenced in their independent policy making by the powers of the national government. No doubt this has been true. But it is by no means a one-way street and we have now in this country a situation where political actions of provincial governments can have important effects on national policies without any direct political responsibility being attached. Thus we have power without responsibility and it is in the interests of correcting this deficiency that I think changes should be considered. I believe that the country can only survive if there is a national identity supported by a strong central authority cognizant of regional as well as national interests. National policies belong properly to the government and Parliament of Canada.

If the Senate of Canada fulfilled the role which the Fathers of Confederation originally intended for it, regional representation in the Parliament of Canada would have been a fact, although one must agree that the primary power would still have been the responsible elected government. But it never has and certainly does not now, even allowing for some of the very useful tasks it does perform from time to time. It is for this reason that increasing attention is being paid to Senate reform. Two important factors have to be considered — the form of appointment and the powers.

It has been suggested that a second chamber would be more suitable to provincial interests if it were elected or if it were to be appointed in whole or in part by provincial governments. No doubt the changes would have some effect but there is little experience in other parliamentary federations to indicate that an elected Senate would better represent regional interests or that a Senate appointed by the provincial governments would be of higher calibre than the one we have.

West German Model

It is perhaps a recognition of the importance of political responsibility that there is an increasing interest in the system which has been developed in the Basic Law of the Federal Republic of Germany since World War II. Essentially what the West German system does is recognize that the best way to make the regional governments responsible in matters of national concern is to have them directly represented in the national parliament. Thus in the Federal Republic, the second chamber or Bundesrat is made up of the executive governments of each state or land (or their appointed delegates) voting en bloc in each case with a scaled representation of five to three votes depending on the size.

A very careful attempt has been made to combine the two functions of the second chamber in a practical way. Federal powers have been divided into two parts, "Simple Laws" passed by the Bundestag (the elected house) and those of primarily national concern, and over these the Bundesrat has only the power of suspensive veto which may be overridden by the Bundestag. "Laws of Consent" are those which are of direct concern to the States. In these the Bundesrat has an absolute veto.

The system has provided a reasonably effective process by which the actions of the popularly elected Bundestag can be reviewed by the second chamber without interfering too radically with its powers. At the same time the system appears to provide very well for the protection of vital state interests. Admittedly it is a system that leans heavily on the bureaucracy both in the development of policies and in the settling of differences. But it is a bureaucracy under some control, and in any event I suspect this reliance is a price we have to pay for government in the complex world of today. It will be noted that we do have some related experience in this through our operational structure in federal-provincial relations. But the solution is not easily transferred for it is not as straightforward as it looks on the surface and its effectiveness rests on three facts in particular: the division of federal powers into those of primarily national and those of state concern, the influence of strongly integrated party interests at the national and state levels, and the fact that administrative responsibility for many federal laws is vested in the states. One might also suggest that the historical German preference for strong central authority has been an important influence in making the system work. This has inhibited the Bundesrat in any tendency toward an over-emphasis on state-rights.

While the system has obviously worked well in West Germany, we should not automatically assume that it will be easily adapted to a long-established intergovernmental relationship in different circumstances. We must remember that the Basic Law of Germany was developed in the aftermath of chaos and not superimposed on the vested interests of one hundred and eleven years.

I am not at all confident that we have the will or the ability to agree on the division of national powers as has been done in West Germany. Nor do I see any obvious willingness to agree to extensive administrative devolution. And as Dr. Corry has said, all significant problems of federalism being political in the deepest sense, I am less than optimistic that our fragmented party system will respond in the same way that has contributed to the success of the German system.

But acknowledging all the difficulties and the dangers of the present tendency to oversell the solution, there is much to be learned from the West German approach. Certainly the idea of introducing political responsibility into provincial demands for a voice in national policy making has much appeal. It should not be beyond our capacities to find some workable system given the will to do so.

ARTHUR TREMBLAY*

Professor Smiley points out in his paper that "there is an atmosphere of unreality" about the conduct of federal-provincial relations at the present time. It will come as no surprise to learn that this observation is strongly felt in Quebec, maybe more strongly than anywhere else in Canada. It will be no surprise for you either if I confess that such a feeling is even stronger for me as a member of this panel where I am expected, I presume, to approach issues in all serenity and detachment.

Be that as it may, feelings of this kind being part of the complexities of the situation, let us take them as a sort of background without questioning them and let us try to act as if things could follow their normal course.

In that perspective I have a few comments to make on Professor Smiley's paper. In the first place, there are several points raised by Professor Smiley which call for clarification. For example, he argues that there are

> relatively few possibilities under our existing parliamentary regime for the Parliament of Canada or the provincial legislatures to be effectively involved in federal-provincial relations, including not only the ongoing interactions between the two orders of government, but also the processes of constitutional reform.

And then he observes:

> In general terms, the current disposition to deal with our discontents by enhancing the power of the provinces without reforms in the institutions of the central government can lead only to unfortunate results.

Am I correct in assuming that his approach to constitutional reform consists of a two stage approach, namely: first, the reform of the institutions of the central government, possibly "in the direction of a congressional system" according to the United States model; and, second, the constitutional reform itself, that is the modifications to the BNA Act relating to the distribution of legislative powers and so forth? Am I correct in understanding that in his view the first stage is a sort of prerequisite or precondition before we could embark on the second?

If this is the case, I must express my concern that many matters of crucial importance might happen in Quebec even before we would have entered the first stage.

My second comment relates to Professor Smiley's diagnosis that:

> the processes of constitutional reform in Canada are dominated by the executive with relatively little involvement by Parliament and the provincial legislatures. And this situation is unlikely to change without a radical restructuring of our political institutions.

* Professeur, École nationale d'administration publique à l'Université du Québec; Sous-ministre des Affaires intergouvernementales, Québec, 1971-77.

Quebec National Assembly and Executive Federalism

I will assume that this diagnosis is correct for the Parliament of Canada and the legislatures of other provinces as well. However, it is quite incorrect in the case of the National Assembly of Quebec. For many years the National Assembly has been involved in and has been debating a wide range of federal-provincial issues.

How is it then that there is presumably such a difference between Quebec and the rest of Canada in that respect? The answer is possibly explained by institutional factors. The establishment in 1963 of the Department of Inter-governmental Affairs and the appointment of a Minister of the Crown to be responsible for those affairs before the National Assembly have provided the Quebec M.N.A.'s with the proper channel to challenge and debate the policies and actions of the government in its dealings with the rest of Canada.

I know from my own experience that the debate on the estimates of the Department of Intergovernmental Affairs, not to mention other instances, has always been the occasion when the minister had to defend the general policies of the government as well as its specific actions in the field of federal-provincial relations. In that sense the existence of a minister and department in charge of those relations has definitely been a factor in the relatively more intensive involvement of the Quebec National Assembly in federal-provincial issues. I do not think though that it has been the most significant one.

The basic factor, it seems to me, has to be found in the attitudes and concerns of the Quebec people themselves. For decades the Quebec community has felt deeply involved in matters of federal-provincial relations and for a very simple reason: the people of Quebec have always felt that their own destiny as a community was at stake in those relations, namely in what I might describe as the balance of power between the more remote federal government and the provincial government in which they could perceive a better image of themselves. Democracy means just that after all. Involvement of the parliaments or legislatures starts in community involvement and in turn communities involve themselves when they feel that some important aspects of their own destiny are in question.

Constitutional Reform Time Constraint

It may well be that for many years, at the federal level at least, we have been living under a regime of what Professor Smiley calls ''executive federalism.'' I am far from certain that this will continue to be the case in the future even if the radical type of changes proposed by Professor Smiley and others are not adopted. We are running out of time for the changes necessary to bring together the creative energies of this country, and if there is hope for responsive restructuring it must involve the initiative and zeal of the general population, the average citizenry.

Outside Quebec, in all Canada, it seems to me that some genuine involvement is now taking place. I do not care if this new concern for the future of Canada as a nation has been provoked by the shock following the election of the PQ in Quebec. I do not care either if there is some confusion and much trial and error in the process.

The fact seems to be there that more and more people in all parts of Canada want to be involved and are involving themselves in the future of this country and in the reconsideration of its intergovernmental institutions. I sensed this momentum quite clearly last June in Toronto at the Destiny Canada seminar. I also sensed it recently in Banff at the regional conference sponsored by the Canada West Foundation. It remains to be seen how much the participants in such gatherings represent the attitudes and concerns of the average citizen. I hope they do.

Otherwise, if the average people of Canada are not yet ready to go in the direction of significant changes in the *status quo*, I am afraid that politicians will not be inclined to go very far in that direction. I guess I should not expect too much from the platforms of the national parties in the next federal election, for instance.

I do not want to appear too pessimistic, but I must say, should matters remain unchanged, that it will be very agonizing for me as a Quebec citizen in search of a real and significant "third option" between the *status quo* and "souveraineté-association" to exercise an intelligent choice at the referendum in twelve, maybe eighteen months from now.

I know of course that as a Quebec citizen I have to define for myself my own "third option" and I do not want others to do my homework in my place. But surely I should know clearly what my fellow Canadians have in mind for the Canadian federation of tomorrow when I vote in the referendum. They have to tell me. They have to tell me within a year or so. Otherwise, when the time comes to take my stand at the referendum, I will be left to my solitude in a decision of crucial consequences for them as well as for myself.

Je suis bien conscient, que ces commentaires n'ont peut-être pas toute la sérénité et le détachement qui caractérisent habituellement les conférences d'un institut de recherche. Je suis bien conscient qu'ils ont peut-être été abusivement influencés par la conjoncture dans laquelle je me trouve placé comme citoyen du Québec qui se perçoit lui-même comme authentiquement québécois dans l'ensemble canadien.

J'espère néanmoins qu'ils auront contribué de quelque manière à notre réflexion commune, à notre recherche commune des renouvellements nécessaires à la survivance canadienne.

FLORA MACDONALD*

In a recent paper on the constitution, Professor J.A. Corry, a past principal of Queen's University, offered the view that "[b]ecause of Quebec and the great regional diversities from sea to sea, Canada is an *incorrigibly* federal country." That is an intriguing phrase, "an incorrigibly federal country," and it states a truth about Canada that many people particularly, if I may say so, in Central Canada have refused to acknowledge for many years.

Need for Regional Representation at the Federal Level

This nation is, by its very nature, and right down to its roots, an incredibly diverse one. That fact is not going to change and it must be accommodated in any feasible proposals for constitutional change.

Professor Corry also makes another important point. So far as formal constitutional doctrine and powers are concerned, "Canada is properly described as having one of the most decentralized federal constitutions in the modern world." This reality has profound implications for our freedom to manoeuvre effectively in our present circumstances. It means that although decentralization has become very much of a catchword in some circles, it is not a certain road to national salvation. We certainly need some decentralization. But, most of all, we need a decentralization of attitudes in Ottawa. We need to root out of the structures of power in Ottawa the idea that the centralized way of doing things is the only way.

It is my contention that the balance between strong regions and a strong nation can only be maintained by more effective *regional* representation at the *federal* level. The answer to some of our present problems is not to parcel out to the regions the powers required by the central government to fulfill its national mandate. It is rather to put the regions back into the federal government. It is to change Ottawa from being a *central* government to being a truly *federal* government.

Need for Balance

The major question for Canada is simply this: how can we restore the crucial balance essential to any federal system, a balance which recognizes the need both for strong regions and for a strong national community?

That balance, that delicate equilibrium between our regional and national interests, is one that has had a special fascination for me over the years. As a Canadian born and brought up in the Maritimes, who has spent parts of my

* Member of Parliament (Kingston & The Islands). Subject to minor changes, the Comment follows Miss MacDonald's remarks to the Alternatives Canada Conference sponsored by the Canada West Foundation in Banff, Alberta, March 28-29, 1978. Permission to reprint is gratefully acknowledged.

working life in both Western Canada and Quebec, and who now represents an Ontario constituency, I have long been keenly aware of the distinctiveness of the social and political cultures of each part of the country.

This distinctiveness is as much attributable to historical influence as it is to geographical factors. But because it exists, the needs and aspirations of the various regions differ. And because they differ, they must be met with sensitivity and fairness when formulating national policies. All too infrequently has that been the case in recent years.

The kind of country we now have is one that bears the stamp of domination by central Canadian interests. More and more we are being made to realize that these interests are not shared by the other parts of Canada. What is good for Toronto is not necessarily good for Antigonish in far-off Nova Scotia. And as we have seen many times, an idea drafted in Ottawa, while it might possibly work in Montreal or Toronto, may not work in Red Deer. We have already learned — perhaps too late — that what is good in Ontario may not wash in Quebec. Our anglophone theories do not automatically fit francophone practice and wishes. Now the voice of protest is being heard in Newfoundland and in the West. Atlantic Canada is increasingly skeptical of Upper Canadians and Westerners are cool, very cool, toward business priorities "down East."

Many of our present troubles arise from the failure of our system to reconcile national and regional interests effectively. Canada is simultaneously one country, a partnership between two language groups, five regions, and ten provinces and vast northern territories. Somehow our governmental structures must be rebuilt to reflect these realities and to make creative dialogue possible.

There are many reasons for the present strains in Canada but I shall focus for the moment on just two of them: one is the lack of adequate regional input into national decision making and its consequences for the country; the other is the changing and expanding roles of government at both levels.

In recent years, there has been a growth of government at both levels. Make no mistake. People want governments to do things for them. And governments have responded. The problem, of course, is that we seem to have gone too far, too fast. (And some of us were using that line long before the Prime Minister discovered it.)

Growth of Federal-Provincial Formal Interactions

The provincial governments had the legal power and Ottawa had the money. So Ottawa jumped in — with lots of programs — and the result is the present tangled mess. Federal programs were dreamed up in Ottawa and applied uniformly across the country. Often those programs reflected neither the priorities of the provinces nor the needs of the people. To sort out some of the many problems that resulted, there has occurred a build-up of consultations between Ottawa and the various provinces in an attempt, after the fact, to recut the cloth to fit the different provincial figures.

The result of these developments has been an increasingly counter-productive tension between federal and provincial interests. The tension was, of course, brought into the open and intensified by the situation in Quebec — especially following the 1976 election victory of the Parti Québécois. But even before that, it was becoming more and more apparent that not only Quebec had complaints against Ottawa — nearly all the provinces did. There has been a rising chorus of discontent in all parts of the country, and even mutterings of separation in the West.

These developments say something about the inability of our political institutions to cope adequately with the explosive growth in the role and functions of government. What are we to do about that inability? One of the mechanisms that has emerged is in effect a new kind of political institution — the federal-provincial conference. Its emergence has been properly observed by Professor Smiley as one of rapid growth carrying very crucial implications for Canadian federalism.

The whole intergovernmental structure has become a massive one in the last decade. Aside from the well-publicized First Ministers' conferences, there are conferences at all levels of government and there are literally hundreds of committees. Look at Alberta as an example. In 1975, this province took part in four federal-provincial conferences at the First Ministers' level; 76 at the ministerial level; 73 at the deputy-ministerial level; 40 at the level of assistant deputy minister and in 144 meetings of officials — for a total of 337 formal intergovernmental meetings which is more than the total daily sittings of the House of Commons and the Alberta legislature combined.

In an earlier work discussing the development of the federal-provincial conference, Professor Smiley analysed the establishment in 1955 of the Continuing Committee on Fiscal and Economic Matters and described it as a "breakthrough in the institutionalization of federal-provincial fiscal relations." But he points out that the committee was authorized only to share information and discuss technical matters and that it had no responsibility for either recommendation or action. A conference communique stated: "The committee will not take collective action but each of its members will report to his own government on the subjects discussed."

Now, let us compare the limited mandate of that 1955 conference with that of the recent conference of First Ministers. In his invitation to the Premiers, the Prime Minister stated that the upcoming conference would be "a concerted attempt to restructure the Canadian economy in order to make it more effective and efficient over the medium term."

Without discussion whether that would be a good or a bad idea, I want to impress on you the implications of the Prime Minister's objective for that conference. In just over twenty years the federal-provincial conference has apparently been changed from a forum for sharing information — to which nobody could object — to a wholly new instrument of executive power and decision making and all without a single mention of formal constitutional change.

What Is Parliament's Role?

I do not want to suggest that change in federal-provincial conferences is a bad idea. I do not want to suggest that we should do away with federal-provincial conferences. What I do want to suggest, however, is that it is time to ask some pertinent questions. How can we ensure that we make the most of this new mechanism for federal-provincial consultation on a continuing basis? How can the legislatures and Parliament share the vast burden of work this powerful new mechanism has imposed on and apparently restricted to the executive level of government? How do we ensure that the fundamental principle of public accountability in our parliamentary system, at both the federal and provincial levels, is not only maintained but enhanced in the process?

We have in place a costly and growing network of federal-provincial negotiations for the sorting out of problems. The challenge now is to build this still evolving network from a curative into a positive system of regional input to national policy making and to do so without creating a new tier of government. There is no easy or simplistic solution. But we can at least make a start by facing up to the choices that are open to us. I shall mention three; there may be others.

First, we can maintain the *status quo*. We could allow the accommodation of regional needs to take place — or fail to take place — through the present (more or less) random system of federal-provincial conferences. This option, however, raises all the serious questions of accountability. Do we want more and more "government by conference"? Or, do we want to bring about more effective and sensitive government by our legislatures and our Parliament? As more and more decisions are made at the conference table, and fewer and fewer in Parliament, I have my own private fantasy that we might soon have to donate the Speaker to the federal-provincial conference and turn the House of Commons into a museum.

Second, we could try to solve the problem of regional diversity by extreme decentralization. That means handing over most of Ottawa's important powers to the provinces and leaving it up to them to keep out of each other's jurisdiction. There are two things wrong with this option. Whatever might be the distribution of powers, it is very difficult to disentangle governments in a federation. As Professor Corry said earlier this year:

> The draftsman who could frame a sharp-edged distribution of powers over the environment which would keep federal and provincial governments out of one another's hair hasn't been born yet.

So serious entanglement is probably not on. The second thing wrong with this option is that if we go overboard in handing powers to the provinces, we will end up with a country that is no longer a country. It will be no more than a weak association of ten mini-countries. That is no way to save Confederation. Carried too far, it ensures the demise of confederation.

Proposed Changes

I want to concentrate on the third suggested choice. Let us not weaken the central government to the point where we give up the dream of a Canada of shared interests and mutual responsibilities. Instead, we ought to build on those values. We need an option that does not deny the value and importance of regionalism. Our alternative must reconcile the dual impulses of a strong, united Canada and strong, diverse regions within the institutions and processes of the central government. This approach means remaking the central institutions to give them a new measure of legitimacy as genuine expressions of both regional and Canada-wide interests.

Senate Reform

Part of the answer may rest in changing the Canadian Senate. The Senate could be changed to become a more vital force in knitting the country together by providing an ongoing forum for federal-provincial dialogue. I have spoken before of the possibility of turning the Senate into a House of the Provinces. If any such reform of our Parliament were considered, my personal preference would be to have a majority of the new chamber's members delegated by the provincial governments, with a minority appointed by the federal government.

This would not remove the need for continued consultation at the federal-provincial executive level. But it would provide for incorporating the results of these consultations more directly into the deliberations of Parliament. It would not change the need, for example, that was recognized at the Kingston meeting last September between the Leader of the Opposition and the four Conservative premiers, for annual consultation among First Ministers on economic and fiscal policies and goals.

We could have a chamber with some of the present capabilities of the Senate to assist in the legislative process. It could examine in depth some of the major social and economic issues of the country. It could, for example, examine the impact of tariff, transportation and taxation policies upon regional growth with a view to maximizing the national industrial potential of each region. But, most of all, it could guarantee that there is a direct voice in Parliament of the interests of the various regions as they are understood and represented by the elected governments of the provinces.

Such a House of the Provinces could be the vehicle through which we would ensure that no federal policy was implemented without its being given prior scrutiny for its implications for the various regions of the country. Naturally, this would not guanantee that such policies would be appropriately modified. But it would make certain that the government and the people would appreciate more precisely the probable consequences of important proposals.

Approached with imagination and a sense of Canada's contemporary needs, a reformed Upper House could contribute significantly to the achievement of the balance essential to our federal system. It would give the provinces a direct input into federal decisions which affect them. On the one hand, this responds directly to the lack of full regional representation in Ottawa and enhances the provincial role. It would also ensure that the provinces will be more aware of the national dimensions of their actions. On the other hand, it would ensure greater federal sensitivity to regional interests and would avoid the dangers of generalized decentralization. While not replacing the myriad of federal-provincial negotiations, it would substantially integrate this process into Parliament itself. In doing so it could make this process permanent, institutionalized, more open and accountable, and hence more legitimate.

Increased Provincial Input

There are various other less substantive reforms at the national level that would also assist the process of federalizing (if I may use the term) the central government.

Several federal agencies, among them the Bank of Canada, the Canadian Wheat Board, the Canadian Radio-television and Telecommunications Commission, the National Energy Board and the Canadian Transport Commission, now exercise extensive powers which have important implications for the regions, and in areas in which the provinces are active. The legitimacy and effectiveness of these agencies require that the provinces have some voice in appointments to their governing boards.

Finally, in every federal system, the Supreme Court plays a crucial role as the final arbiter in matters of the interpretation of the constitution. It is therefore vital that its judgments and membership are seen as legitimate by all who are subject to its authority. The unilateral appointment of Justices of the Supreme Court of Canada by the federal government erodes this basic legitimacy, however even-handed the members of the Court are in practice. A provincial role in appointments is therefore essential.

''Federalization'' pursued in this manner would do much to reconcile the twin drives of country-wide development and regionalism which so characterize our national crisis.

There are many other aspects of our parliamentary process that cry out for reform if we are not to go on forever searching for alternatives. They include:

- the principle of accountability, so badly eroded in recent years, must be re-established by the development of a renewed respect on the part of government towards Parliament;
- accessibility to information through the enactment of a *Freedom of Information Act* that would reduce government secrecy to a minimum. In this day of big government, such a move towards greater openness would strengthen the democratic process;

- examination of the electoral system to determine whether party representation in the House of Commons could be made more representative of the votes cast;
- strengthening the role and powers of committees could further enhance our parliamentary system.

Conclusion

There is so much that we need to tackle. We would be kidding ourselves to talk of any one alternative as the grand resolution to all our discontents. A country as diverse as Canada does not work that way. Rather, the goal should be to improve the framework and rules within which the continuing debate and dialogue between regional and national interests are presently taking place.

It is dangerous to put too much stock in search of a grand once-and-for-all solution. Constitutional remedies such as those we have been discussing will not themselves alter deeply ingrained attitudes. But by having our constitution and institutions more accurately reflect our regional diversities, we will have set the stage for a better understanding of the aspirations of all Canadians, and have begun the task of breaking down the barriers that for too long have divided us.

DISCUSSION

Rapporteur: R.M.A. Lyons*

In response to the commentators, *Professor Smiley* reaffirmed his belief in a federal system for Canada, including a strong central government. He argued that our federalist state is a necessary vehicle for achieving broader regional representation on problems which are cross-regional in character and where majority reconciliation by provincial governments alone might unduly prejudice some regions. He stated, " . . . the real legitimation of federalism is to achieve the ability to make the *hard* decisions, for example in our present framework, those involving energy and unemployment." He also commented that some provinces assume the role of "paper tigers" on many issues, as we saw when some provinces, in the midst of the energy crisis, decided we needed a national energy policy.

On the matter of adding "provincial" M.P.'s to the Commons, *Professor Smiley* observed that the idea was hardly radical; Cabinet traditionally has had a regional dimension to its composition and the Leader of the Opposition, Mr. Clark, has indicated his willingness to draw Cabinet ministers from the Senate if necessary to achieve regional balance.

Several people disagreed with *Mr. Hyndman's* suggestion that the legislatures in the provinces have the ability to "minutely scrutinize" executive decisions. One characterized executive federalism as a "four-year dictatorship" in which the federal government ruled by negotiated agreement with provincial Cabinets. *Mr. Hyndman* disagreed. He felt the criticisms of executive federalism were largely misinformed and he indicated a greater inclination to accept the existing status of federal-provincial relations than other speakers. *Mr. Hyndman* supported the concept of federal-provincial agreements — "They will be the form of Canadian federalism in the next two decades."

Pursuing this point, a question was raised on whether Canada could afford the costs of intergovernmental relations — the staff required at the federal and provincial levels, the time required to achieve results, the frustration of negotiations. Panelists seemed to agree with *Mr. Hyndman's* reply that the linear geography and heterogenity of this nation imply some cumbersome arrangements, some additional costs, and a unique form of federalism.

The next question directed the focus of discussion away from the institutional framework implied in Professor Smiley's paper toward the "people problem." It was pointed out that established institutions are the result of past behaviour, and that they are run by people. When there are political problems in the United States, it was suggested, it is accepted that the people are wrong and the institution is right; in Canada we find the fault in the institution. Where do the

* Department of Agricultural Economics, University of Manitoba.

political parties with their lawyers and technicians, their brokerage systems, and political bureaucrats fit into an identification (and solution) of our federalist problems?

Miss MacDonald pointed out that *Mr. Stanfield* had referred to the role of political parties in his opening remarks. He had referred to making parties more open, to achieving more grass roots support, and to reform of the *Election Expenses Act. Miss MacDonald* indicated that her own hope had been that overhaul of the parties would have resulted in more people becoming involved and seeking election. She concluded, however, that this has not happened, and that she has been disappointed by the response to a real effort to involve more grass roots activity with the parties. "We must," she said, "determine why parties are not considered more legitimate."

A BASIC BIBLIOGRAPHY

FEDERALISM AND THE LEGISLATIVE PROCESS IN CANADA

Burns, R.M. *Political and Administrative Federalism.* Canberra: Australian National University, 1976.

Black, E.R. *Divided Loyalties: Canadian Concepts of Federalism.* Montreal: McGill-Queen's University Press, 1975.

Cairns, A.C. "Governments and Societies of Canadian Federalism." *Canadian Journal of Political Science* 10 (December 1977): 695-725.

Canada. Parliament. Special Joint Committee of the Senate and of the House of Commons on the Constitution of Canada. *Report.* Ottawa: Information Canada, 1972.

Cheffins, R.I. and Tucker, R.N. *The Constitutional Process in Canada,* 2d ed. Toronto: McGraw-Hill Ryerson, 1976.

Corry, J.A. and Hodgetts, J.E. *Democratic Government and Politics,* 3d. ed. rev. Toronto: University of Toronto Press, 1960.

Crepeau, P.A. and Macpherson, C.B., eds. *The Future of Canadian Federalism.* Toronto: University of Toronto Press, 1965.

Dawson, R. MacGregor. *The Government of Canada,* 5th ed. Toronto: University of Toronto Press, 1970.

Hodgetts J.E. "Regional Interests and Policy in a Federal Structure." *Canadian Journal of Economics and Political Science* 32 (February 1966): 3-14.

Hopkins, E.R. *Confederation at the Crossroads: The Canadian Constitution.* Toronto: McClelland and Stewart, 1963.

Kwavnick, D., ed. *Royal Commission of Inquiry on Constitutional Problems.* Toronto: McClelland and Stewart, 1973.

Laskin, Bora. *Canadian Constitutional Law,* 4th ed. rev. Toronto: Carswell, 1975.

Lederman, W.R. *The Courts and the Canadian Constitution.* Toronto: McClelland and Stewart, 1964.

Lederman, W.R. "Unity and Diversity in Canadian Federalism: Ideals and Methods of Moderation." *Canadian Bar Review* 53 (September 1975): 597-620.

Lesson, Howard A. *External Affairs and Canadian Federalism.* Toronto: Holt, Rinehart and Winston, 1973.

Lyon, N.J. and Atkey, R.G., eds. *Canadian Constitutional Law in a Modern Perspective.* Toronto: University of Toronto Press, 1970.

Mallory, J.R. "Canadian Federalism in Transition." *Political Quarterly* 48 (April-June 1977): 149-63.

Mallory, J.R. "Confederation: The Ambiguous Bargain." *Journal of Canadian Studies* 12 (July 1977): 18-23.

Mallory, J.R. *The Structure of Canadian Government.* Toronto: Macmillan, 1971.

Meekison, J.P., ed. *Canadian Federalism: Myth or Reality,* 3d. ed. Toronto: Methuen, 1977.

Meisel, John. (1976) "Citizen Demands and Government Response." *Canadian Public Policy* 2 (Autumn 1976): 564-72.

Mundell, D.W. "Legal Nature of Federal and Provincial Executive Governments." *Osgoode Hall Law School Journal* 2 (1960): 56-75.

Rogers, N.M. "The Genesis of Provincial Rights." *Canadian Historical Review* 14 (March 1933): 9-23.

Rogers, N.M. "The Political Principles of Federalism." *Canadian Journal of Economics and Political Science* 1 (August 1935): 337-47.

Royal Commission on Dominion-Provincial Relations. *Report* (Rowell-Sirois Report). Ottawa: King's Printer, 1940.

Simeon, R. *Federal-Provincial Diplomacy: The Making of Recent Policy in Canada.* Toronto: University of Toronto Press, 1972.

Simeon, R. *The 'Overload Thesis' and Canadian Government."* Canadian *Public Policy* 2 (Autumn 1976): 541-52.

Simeon, R. ed. *Must Canada Fail?* Montreal: McGill-Queen's University Press, 1977.

Smiley, D.V. *Canada in Question: Federalism in the Seventies.* Toronto: McGraw-Hill Ryerson, 1976.

Smiley, D.V. *Conditional Grants and Canadian Federalism: A Study in Constitutional Adaptation.* Toronto: Canadian Tax Foundation, 1963.

Smiley, D.V. *Constitutional Adaptation and Canadian Federalism Since 1945.* Ottawa: Queen's Printer, 1971.

Smiley, D.V. ed. *Royal Commission on Dominion Provincial Relations* (Rowell-Sirois Report). Toronto: McClelland and Stewart, 1963.

Smiley, D.V. "The Structural Problem of Canadian Federalism." *Canadian Public Administration* 14 (Fall 1971): 326-43.

Smiley, D.V. "Two Themes of Canadian Federalism." *Canadian Journal of Economics and Political Science* 31 (February 1965): 80-97.

Stanley, George. *A Short History of the Canadian Constitution.* Toronto: Ryerson Press, 1969.

Strayer, B.L. *Judicial Review of Legislation in Canada.* Toronto: University of Toronto Press, 1968.

Trudeau, P.E. *Federalism and the French Canadians.* Toronto: Macmillan, 1968.

Van Loon, R.J. and Whittington, M.S. *The Canadian Political System.* Toronto: McGraw-Hill, 1971.

Western Premiers' Task Force on Constitutional Trends. *Reports.* Victoria: Queen's Printer, 1977, 1978.

Whyte, J.D. and Lederman, W.R. *Canadian Constitutional Law.* Toronto: Butterworths, 1975.

Chapter Four

Congressional Government — Continuity and Change in the U.S. Legislative Process

by
*Samuel C. Patterson**

Both the Canadian Parliament and the United States Congress have roots which extend back to British parliamentary experience and practices of the eighteenth and nineteenth centuries. They have much in common, sharing a similar heritage. The national legislatures of both North American countries were adapted to federal constitutional structures, and to patterns of representation suitable to the governance of societies spanning a large continent. Of course, the Canadian Parliament is much more faithful than its congressional neighbour to the British form of parliamentary government. The United States Congress developed in a constitutional system in which the independence of the legislature from the executive could flourish. Members of Congress, elected quite separately from the President, soon acquired and have largely sustained a basis of electoral support independent from that of the chief executive. By the same token, in a system of constitutional separation of powers, the President is not dependent upon a congressional majority for his continuation in office. Moreover, Congress evolved in a society which, from the turn of the nineteenth century, became increasingly populist, insistent upon highly public government. Although by fits and starts, and sometimes by steps backward, Congress has in a remarkably persistent fashion developed as an ''open'' legislative assembly, conducting its business with an unusually high degree of publicity and a minimum of secrecy. As a legislative institution, Congress has proved to be highly autonomous, adaptive to changes in its political environment, very open to public scrutiny, and highly permeable to the representation of a wide variety of interests and constituencies.

* Professor of Political Science, University of Iowa; an extended version of this paper, under the chapter heading of ''The Semi-Sovereign Congress,'' will appear in the *The New American Political System* (1978) edited by Anthony King (Washington, D.C.: American Enterprise Institute for Public Policy Research). The Institute's consent to reproduce substantial portions of the original chapter in a form intended for a mainly Canadian audience is gratefully noted.

Congress is not unique. It belongs to a class of political institutions which, generically, are called representative assemblies.[1] There are more than a hundred major institutions of this sort in the world today. They exhibit many structural differences and variously perform their representative functions. The comparative study of these representative institutions is one of the important challenges of modern political inquiry.[2] At the same time, Congress is probably the most impressive specimen of its genre. Among other things, it is a very powerful *legislative* body. In an era in which lawmaking has in most countries fallen heavily into the hands of executives, the American Congress continues to be a significant, independent lawmaking institution, capable of legislative innovation and able to undertake the creative act of lawmaking without executive leadership if necessary.[3]

In this appraisal of continuities and changes in Congress, especially in the 1970s, the focus is upon three central questions: (1) what changes have been taking place in the relationship between Congress and its constituency? (2) how has Congress changed as a legislative organization? and (3) what changes have occurred in congressional decision making? These are questions for which very extensive answers are possible. In contrast to most national representative assemblies, the American Congress has been singularly observed, investigated, and analysed. The study of Congress has propagated since the mid-1960s, so that today there is quite a rich literature dealing with the institution.[4] This chapter can only provide selective attention to a highly complex, intricate, and hoary national legislature.

Many changes, large and small, have taken place in the organization and procedure of the Congress of the 1970s. Of the previous decade and before, Ralph Huitt said, "Congress changes, as all living things must change; it

---

[1] One compendium which provides information about 56 national representative assemblies is Valentine Herman and Françoise Mendel, eds., *Parliaments of the World* (London: Macmillan, 1976).

[2] See Gerhard Loewenberg and Samuel C. Patterson, *Comparing Legislatures* (Boston: Little, Brown, 1978).

[3] See Gary Orfield, *Congressional Power: Congress and Social Change* (New York: Harcort Brace Jovanovich, 1975); Ronald C. Moe and Steven C. Teel, "Congress as Policy-maker: A Necessary Reappraisal," *Political Science Quarterly* 85 (September 1970): 443-70; John R. Johannes, "Congress and the Initiation of Legislation," *Public Policy* 20 (Spring 1972): 281-309.

[4] Little, Brown and Company of Boston has published an excellent group of books about Congress in The Study of Congress Series; see Lewis A. Froman, Jr., *The Congressional Process: Strategies, Rules, and Procedures* (1967); Randall B. Ripley, *Majority Party Leadership in Congress* (1969); John S. Saloma III, *Congress and the New Politics* (1969); Charles O. Jones, *The Minority Party* (1970); John F. Manley, *The Politics of Finance* (1970); Richard F. Fenno, Jr., *Congressmen in Committees* (1973); and Robert L. Peabody, *Leadership in Congress* (1976). Important additional studies include Randall B. Ripley, *Congress: Process and Policy* (New York: Norton, 1975); Norman J. Ornstein, ed., *Congress in Change* (New York: Praeger, 1975); David R. Mayhew, *Congress: the Electoral Connection* (New Haven: Yale University Press, 1974); Harvey C. Mansfield, Sr., ed., *Congress Against the President* (New York: Praeger, 1975); Lawrence C. Dodd and Bruce I. Oppenheimer, eds., *Congress Reconsidered* (New York: Praeger, 1977); Roger H. Davidson and Walter J. Oleszek, *Congress Against Itself* (Bloomington: Indiana University Press, 1977); Morris P. Fiorina, *Congress: Keystone of the Washington Establishment* (New Haven: Yale University Press, 1977); and Susan Welch and John G. Peters, eds., *Legislative Reform and Public Policy* (New York: Praeger, 1977).

changes slowly, adaptively, as institutions change.''[5] The pace of congressional change has quickened. There are, accordingly, more changes for the observer of Congress to study than in most of the years before the 1970s. But, perhaps paradoxically, the meaning of congressional change is in many respects, still difficult to weigh. We cannot promise to unravel the profound effects of recent changes in the institution, but we can bring some order to the complexity of these changes and thereby take a step in the direction of understanding what congressional changes mean.

CONSTITUENT CHANGES IN CONGRESS

The bicameral Congress is composed of a Senate in which each state is represented by two senators, and a House of Representatives apportioned among the states on the basis of their populations. Because the Constitution gives each state two senators regardless of population, the one hundred senators represent widely disparate numbers of people. The senators from the largest state, California, represent more than twenty-one million people, while the senators from small states like Alaska and Wyoming represent fewer than four hundred thousand people. In contrast, the House of Representatives has always been representative on the basis of the states' populations. Furthermore, since the landmark reapportionment decisions of the U.S. Supreme Court in the 1960s, the four hundred and thirty-five House members have been elected in single-member districts which are more-or-less equal in population. It has been a significant feature of the concept of representation in the United States that legislative districts should, above all, be made up of an equal number of citizens, in accord with the prevailing doctrine of ''one person, one vote.''

Two facets in the relationship between Congress and its constituency have been especially notable: the operation of the congressional election system, with its growing propensity to the re-election of incumbents; and the increasing activities of congressmen in servicing their constituents. In the post-World War II era, the Democratic party has been dominant in the congressional houses, and the character of the electoral system helps to maintain this dominance. The growing rate of the return of incumbent House and Senate members is the result of various features of the election system and the politics of the 1970s, but the expansive activities of members of Congress in their states and districts have made an important contribution to the enhanced incumbent return rate.

The Congressional Electoral System

The Republicans have only succeeded in winning a majority of seats in the Congress twice since World War II (in 1946 and in 1952). In the 95th Congress, Democrats occupied 67 percent of the House seats and 62 percent of the Senate

---

[5] Ralph K. Huitt and Robert L. Peabody, *Congress: Two Decades of Analysis* (New York: Harper & Row, 1969), p. 229.

seats. As figure 1 shows, the party margins in the House of Representatives have fluctuated since the 1940s, although Democratic hegemony has generally increased. Figure 1 also shows the Democratic and Republican votes in House elections, indicating since the mid-1950s a greater yield in seats for Democratic votes, and a smaller proportion of seats in relation to Republican votes.

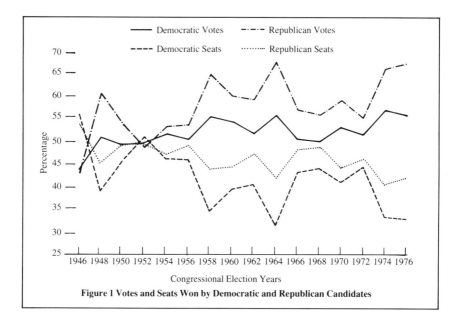

Figure 1 Votes and Seats Won by Democratic and Republican Candidates

Figure 2 displays the general relationship between votes and seats for the House of Representatives. In the post-World War II years, neither party's candidates have garnered fewer than 40 percent of the total vote, or more than 60 percent. As figure 2 shows, the Matthew Effect[6] is quite pronounced, and generally advantageous to the Democrats inasmuch as they have been in the dominant party (a 1 percent increase in their general election vote yields approximately 2 percent of the seats in the House). The Democrats have always dominated southern congressional elections. Until the mid-1960s, the electoral system systematically advantaged the Republicans in the northern states, but since then the system has favoured the Democrats in both North and South. These changes in the payoff of the electoral system stem from changes in the distribution of Democratic and Republican voters. Today there are more Democratic safe seats than there were in the 1960s and before, there are fewer

---

[6] This electoral system bias is called the Matthew Effect after the proverb in Matthew 13:12: "For whosoever hath, to him shall be given, and he shall have more abundance; but whosoever hath not, from him shall be taken away even that he hath."

marginal Republican seats, and Democratic voters are somewhat "over-represented" because their low rate of election turnout means that the number of voters is lower in Democratic districts than in Republican districts.[7]

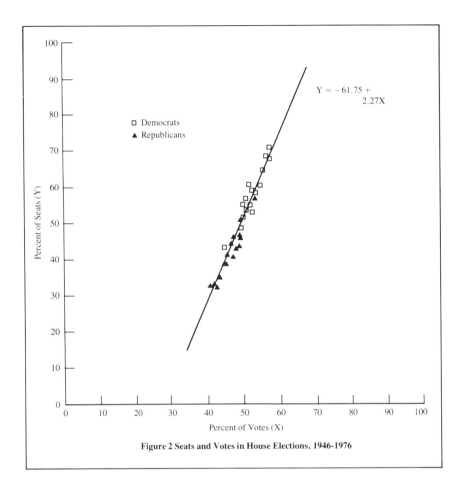

Figure 2 Seats and Votes in House Elections, 1946-1976

The performance of the American electoral system is highly characteristic of single-member district, plurality vote systems. It confers a large congressional majority on the party which captures a majority (or a very large plurality) of the popular votes. The system is about equally responsive to Democratic and Republican votes, but because of its post-World War II dominance at the polls in congressional elections, the bias of the system favors the Democratic party. On

---

[7] See Edward R. Tufte, "The Relationship Between Seats and Votes in Two-Party Systems," *American Political Science Review* 67 (June 1973): 540-54; and Robert S. Erikson, "Malapportionment, Gerrymandering, and Party Fortunes in Congressional Elections," *American Political Science Review* 66 (December 1972): 1234-45.

average, about 48 percent of the popular vote could yield a majority of House seats to the Democrats, while the Republicans require slightly over half of the popular vote to win a majority of House seats. In actuality, of course, Democratic candidates have won considerably more than a majority of popular votes in most post-war elections.

Within this electoral framework, incumbent candidates for House and Senate seats have a marked tendency to be re-elected. While a very large proportion of seats are contested in every election, incumbents have always been advantaged in the outcome. The ''incumbency effect'' in congressional elections has, moreover, become more striking, especially in House elections since the mid-1960s. The magnitude of this effect is portrayed in tables 1 and 2. Of the incumbent House members running for re-election in 1976, three were defeated in primary elections and thirteen lost the general election, producing an incumbent return of nearly 96 percent. The 1974 election had been a Democratic landslide — more than a fifth of the Republican incumbents seeking re-election were defeated by Democrats.[8] Of the seventy-nine new Democrats elected to the House in 1974 or afterward, seventy-eight sought re-election in 1976 and seventy-five were successful.

Table 1
The Re-election of Incumbents to the U.S. House of
Representatives

Year	Incumbents Seeking Re-election	Those Losing in the Primary	Those Losing in the General	Those Returned	As a % of Those Seeking Re-election	As a % of the Total House
1956	411	6	16	389	95	89
1958	394	3	37	354	90	81
1960	403	5	26	372	92	86
1962	393	11	14	368	94	85
1964	397	8	44	345	87	79
1966	407	5	40	362	89	83
1968	404	3	5	396	98	91
1970	398	8	12	378	95	87
1972	381	7	13	361	95	83
1974	391	8	40	343	88	79
1976	384	3	13	368	96	85

Source: Charles O. Jones, ''Will Reform Change Congress,'' in Lawrence C. Dodd and Bruce I. Oppenheimer, eds., *Congress Reconsidered* (New York: Praeger, 1977), p. 254; *Congressional Quarterly* Weekly Report, 34 (November 6, 1976): 3121-22.

---

[8] For a thorough analysis of the 1974 Congressional election, see Walter Dean Burnham, ''Insulation and Responsiveness in Congressional Elections,'' *Political Science Quarterly* 90 (Fall 1975): 411-35.

Table 2
The Re-election of Incumbents to the U.S. Senate

Year	Incumbents Seeking Re-election	Those Losing in the Primary	Those Losing in the General	Those Returned	As a % of Those Seeking Re-election
1956	28	—	3	25	89
1958	31	—	11	20	65
1960	29	—	1	28	97
1962	35	1	5	29	83
1964	36	4	4	28	78
1966	32	3	1	28	88
1968	28	4	4	20	71
1970	30	1	6	23	77
1972	27	2	5	20	71
1974	27	2	2	23	85
1976	25	—	9	16	64

Source: Congressional Quarterly Weekly Report, various issues.

On the whole, the rate at which Senate incumbents have been returned in elections is considerably lower than for House incumbents. Only 64 percent of Senate incumbents seeking re-election in 1976 were returned, the lowest post-war return rate. Nine incumbents were defeated in the general election, eight incumbents did not seek to be re-elected, and Governor Wendell Anderson of Minnesota was appointed to replace Senator Walter Mondale, who became Vice-President.

There is no reason to believe that the high rate of return of incumbents to Congress sharply distinguishes it from parliaments in most other countries where there are no constitutional or other restrictions on the number of terms which a representative may serve. The presence of a substantial proportion of incumbents in the legislature provides it with an important measure of continuity, and allows for the development of expertise on the part of members. A legislative body like the House of Representatives, all of whose seats are up for election every two years, could not function effectively if a large number of its members could not be re-elected over a number of elections, thus acquiring experience both in representing their constituents and performing as legislators.

Congress is increasingly criticized because of the high rate of return of incumbents on the ground that this indicates rigidification, locking the institution into a changeless and stultifying pattern of complacency and lack of responsiveness. This criticism would carry greater weight if there were some evidence to support the claim made that undemocratic and otherwise undesirable consequences flow from the present congressional incumbency rate. No one knows what an optimal incumbency rate would be for Congress; admittedly, it probably would not be desirable for a representative institution to experience no change in its membership over extended periods of time. But this is far from the case. Both House and Senate receive what seem to be quite ample injections of "new blood" because of turnover of membership at a rate greatly under-exposed by focusing merely upon the high rate of incumbency return in a period as short as two years. Moreover, what evidence there is about the responsiveness of winners of congressional elections (mostly incumbents) to the views of their constituents strongly suggests that they are more likely to be in harness with the constituency than their challengers, and that policy agreement between congressmen and constitutents is more robust for members elected in safe districts than for those representing competitive districts.[9]

In House races, the advantages of incumbency have increased. Systematic estimates of the incumbency advantage vary in magnitude. One set of estimates suggests that "the gain to a candidate from running as a incumbent for the first time and the loss to a party when its incumbent retires increased from roughly two percent to about five percent of the vote" between the 1950s and the 1960s.[10] Other estimates corroborate the increased advantage of incumbency since the mid-1960s, and indicate an average incumbency advantage in elections between 1966 and 1974 of around 6-7 percent of the vote.[11] There is evidence that the importance of incumbency increased in Senate elections between 1946 and 1970.[12] But the Senate incumbency advantage has not increased as much as for House incumbents, and Senate incumbency is not as great an advantage as House incumbency. States are more socially and eocnomically diverse than congressional districts, and thus are less politically homogeneous and more competitive. The relatively poor showing of Senate incumbents in 1976, plus a more normal responsiveness of the 1972-1976 House elections to shifts in voter preferences, suggests the possibility that the incumbency effect has "bottomed out."[13] Or perhaps more precisely, it may be that the electoral process has begun to stabilize around a generally lower level of intra-district competitiveness than characterized it before the mid-1960s.

---

[9] For suggestive studies, see: Warren E. Miller, "Majority Rule and the Representative System of Government," in *Mass Politics: Studies in Political Sociology*, ed. by Erik Allardt and Stein Rokkan (New York: Free Press, 1970), pp. 284-311; John L. Sullivan and Robert E. O'Connor, "Electoral Choice and Popular Control of Public Policy: The Case of the 1966 House Elections," *American Political Science Review* 66 (December 1972): 1256-68; and, Charles H. Backstrom, "Congress and the Public: How Representative Is the One of the Other?" *American Politics Quarterly* 5 (October 1977): 411-35.

[10] Erikson, "Malapportionment, Gerrymandering and Party Fortunes in Congressional Elections," p. 1240; and Robert S. Erikson, "The Advantage of Incumbency in Congressional Elections," *Polity* 3 (Spring 1971): 395-405.

[11] Albert D. Cover and David R. Mayhew, "Congressional Dynamics and the Decline of Competitive Congressional Elections," in *Congress Reconsidered*, ed. by Dodd and Oppenheimer, p. 60.

[12] Warren L. Kostroski, "Party and Incumbency in Postwar Senate Elections: Trends, Patterns, and Models," *American Political Science Review* 67 (December 1973): 1213-34.

[13] The 1972-1976 "swing ratio" increased to 2.3 afrer a marked decline in the 1960s (1960-64 = 1.7; 1966-70 = .7). The swing ratio, which is the estimated slope of the regression of votes and seats, indicates the responsiveness of the partisan division of legislative seats to changes in the partisan division of the general election vote. Of course, calculating the swing ratio from election triplets implies confidence in statistical comparisons based upon very small frequencies. As the graphic presentation in figure 3 shows, the votes-seats relationship in the United States has produced a very tight linear fit over all postwar congressional elections. See Tufte, "The Relationship Between Seats and Votes in Two-Party Systems," p. 550.

The increase in the incumbency effect in congressional elections — the propensity of voters to re-elect incumbents — and the concomitant decline in the competition of congressional contests appear to stem largely from changes in patterns of voting behaviour. There is evidence that political party identification accounts for a declining proportion of the congressional election vote.[14] There has been since the mid-1960s some increase in the proportion of independents in the electorate. But more importantly, partisan cues for voting behaviour appear to have become less important for those who have a political party attachment of some kind. Defections from party in congressional voting have increased in the electorate, even among "strong" party identifiers. Defections among voters from their party identification have significantly advantaged incumbents since the mid-1960s, and there has been an especially sharp increase in partisan defections among those identified with the party of the congressional challenger. The spurt in defections to the congressional incumbent among voters identified with the challenger's party in 1972-1974 may have occurred as many dismayed Republicans voted for Democratic incumbents in reaction against the Nixon presidency and the Watergate affair. But the evidence indicates a more profound weakening of partisan cues in congressional election voting, and a tendency for congressional elections to be increasingly responsive to national forces (such as the state of the economy and the perceived performance of the President), although local forces continue to have a sizeable impact on constituents' voting.[15] When partisan cues for voting are weakened, and when incumbent congressmen can effectively appeal to voters in terms of highly salient national political concerns which they can capitalize on without being expected to resolve, the electoral advantage of incumbency can be enhanced.

Weakened partisanship in the electorate presumably increases the difficulty of mounting an effective challenge to incumbents in their districts. Congressmen can "run for Congress by running against Congress," or against the President, or in the name of solutions to the host of national problems the solutions of which he or she cannot be held accountable for as merely one member of a collective body. Incumbents have acquired very handsome resources for use in their districts to present a posture of helping the district, to claim credit for the distributive largesse of the national welfare state, and to appear to be struggling faithfully, if helplessly, against great national crises, evils, and policy problems.

---

[14] See Robert B. Arsensau and Raymond E. Wolfinger, "Voting Behavior in Congressional Elections," paper presented at the 1973 Annual Meeting of the American Political Science Association, New Orleans.

[15] Edward R. Tufte, "Determinants of the Outcomes of Midterm Congressional Elections," *American Political Science Review* 69 (September 1975): 812-26; Francisco Arcelus and Allan H. Meltzer, "The Effect of Aggregate Economic Variables on Congressional Elections," *American Political Science Review* 69 (December 1975): 1232-39; Howard S. Bloom and H. Douglas Price, "Voter Response to Short-Run Economic Conditions: The Asymmetric Effect of Prosperity and Recession," *American Political Science Review* 69 (December 1975): 1240-54; Samuel Kernell, "Presidential Popularity and Negative Voting; An Alternative Explanation of the Midterm Congressional Decline of the President's Party," *American Political Science Review* 71 (March 1977): 44-66.

Accordingly, incumbency cues for voting may have become more important in voters' choices.

Servicing the District

There is no doubt that congressmen are in a far better position today to nurse their constituencies than was true twenty years ago. First, members are authorized a far larger number of trips to their districts or states, and they spend more time at home. In the early 1960s, House and Senate members were authorized to take three government-paid trips home. That number was doubled in 1966, and doubled again in 1968; in 1973, eighteen round trips were authorized; in 1976, House members were given twenty-six trips home, and senators more than forty; in 1977, the House authorization was increased to thirty-two round trips a year. Interviews with two hundred and nineteen House members indicated that in 1973 members went home an average of thirty-five times and, altogether, spent 38 percent of their time in their districts (nearly a third went home every weekend).[16]

Second, the traffic in mail between congressmen and their constituents has markedly increased. The House Commission on Administrative Review reported in 1977 that incoming mail to the House had grown threefold between 1971 and 1977, and that members were getting an average of 31,600 letters annually. The outgoing mail has increased dramatically, as well. About 40 million pieces of franked mail were sent out by House and Senate members in 1954; by 1970 the amount had grown to about 200 million.[17] This change far exceeds the rate of population growth; in 1954 about one in every four Americans could have received a letter from a member of Congress; 1970, the mail averaged one letter for every American. The amount of franked congressional mail has climbed in the 1970s, stimulated by a new "constituent communication allowance" in the House permitting members to send two newsletters to constituents a year at congressional expense. The volume of franked mail is notably larger in election years than in non-election years.

Third, members' staffs have increased substantially. In the early 1960s, House Members could have a staff of nine persons; now a staff of eighteen is authorized, with a total "clerk hire" allowance of $225,114. Senators' staffs have doubled since 1960; depending upon the populations of the states, Senators are now authorized staff allowances ranging from $413,082 to $844,608. But probably more important than the growth in the sizes of congressional staffs is the burgeoning of district and state offices. Constituent service activities have increasingly been moved out of members' Washington offices and to the offices

---

[16] Richard F. Feno, Jr., "U.S. House Members in Their Constituencies: An Exploration," *American Political Science Review* 71 (September 1977), p. 890.
[17] David R. Mayhew, "Congressional Elections: The Case of the Vanishing Marginals," *Polity* 6 (Fall 1974): 295-317, reprinted in *New Perspectives on the House of Representatives* 3rd. ed., ed. by Robert L. Peabody and Nelson W. Polsby (Chicago: Rand McNally, 1977), p. 38.

in their districts. In 1960, 14 percent of House members' staffs were assigned to their district offices; this had grown to 26 percent in 1967, 34 percent in 1974, and 36 percent in 1977.[18] For the 95th Congress, House members averaged nearly two district offices each, and Senators more than two state offices. In 1977, 16 percent of House members had assigned half or more of their staff to their district offices. Senators have established more than three hundred branch offices in the states, staffed by more than four hundred aides who dispense constituent services.[19]

Fourth, the volume of "casework" for constituents and constituency projects has expanded a great deal in the 1970s as the coverage of welfare laws and veterans' benefits has been enlarged and as federally funded projects in states and communities have proliferated. Although there is no systematic monitoring of this growth, the Senators from the largest states, New York and California, now have casework loads ranging between 30,000 and 50,000 cases a year, and for about two-thirds of Senate offices this work has been transferred to the state offices. A study of Senate staff activity conducted in 1972 showed that two-thirds of the staff dealt with constituency projects once a day or more, and more than 40 percent of the Senate aides estimated that they handled casework more than once a day.[20]

Finally, candidates for Congress are spending more money in their election efforts. In 1976, average spending by Democratic House candidates was $80,965, for Republican candidates $77,400. Senate Democratic candidates averaged $569,902 in campaign spending, Republicans $616,501. Although these are large average amounts, the average cost per vote for House candidacies was only $1.22; for Senate candidacies the cost per vote was $1.52. Moreover, campaign expenditures vary sizeably from place to place. Senator William Proxmire (D., Wisc.) got 72 percent of the vote with a total expenditure of only $697. In contrast, Senator H. John Heinz III (R., Pa.) spent $3 million. In the House races, half of all of the campaign money spent was expended by 10 percent of the candidates, and 43 percent of the candidates spent less than $15,000 each. At the other extreme, in California's 27th congressional district the Republican victor spent $403,675 and the Democratic opponent spent $637,080.[21]

In 1974 and 1976 Congress enacted new legislation regulating campaign spending. The main provisions of the new law limited spending in primary and general elections, limited contributions which could be made to campaigns, and required detailed reporting and disclosure of campaign financing. A Federal

[18] Percentages for 1960, 1967 and 1974 are from Fiorina, *Congress: Keystone of the Washington Establishment*, p. 58. Figures for 1977 were calculated from the 1977 *Congressional Staff Directory*.
[19] U.S. Congress, Senate, Commission on the Operation of the Senate, "Constituent Service," by Janet Breslin in *Senators: Offices, Ethics, and Pressures*, Committee Print (Washington, D.C.: Government Printing Office, 1977), p. 19.
[20] Harrison W. Fox, Jr. and Susan Webb Hammond, *Congressional Staffs* (New York: Free Press, 1977), p. 186.
[21] *Congressional Quarterly Weekly Report* 35 (June 25, 1977): 1291-94, and (October 29, 1977): 2299-2311.

Election Commission was created to implement the new campaign regulations. There has been persistent controversy over the limitations and reporting requirements of the campaign law, and concern expressed about the presumed advantages conferred on incumbents by the law. In 1976, although House incumbents spent more and were overwhelmingly re-elected, money and incumbency provided little help to the third of the Senate incumbents who were defeated. On the whole, campaign spending appears to add little to the already very substantial advantages of incumbency.[22]

The impact of the growth in constituency service activities is not easy to assess precisely. It has been demonstrated that the frequency with which House members travel to their districts and their allocation of staff resources to their districts are not correlated with the members' election margins — safe seat congressmen do not differ significantly in these matters from those elected in marginal districts.[23] Increased constituency nursing has not brought about a change in the proportion of Americans who can recall the name of their congressman, and so incumbents have no greater advantage in name visibility over challengers than was the case twenty years ago.[24] Nevertheless, it is possible that an increased proportion of constituents are responding to incumbent congressmen *qua* incumbents, based more on voters' evaluation of members' constituency service performance than on their party or their policy-making activities in Washington.[25]

A Harris Survey conducted for the House Commission on Administrative Review in January 1977 provides some shreds of evidence about the impact of congressmen's contacts with constituents and their constituency service activities. Some of the results of this survey are given in Table 3. Half of the respondents could recall the name of their House member; 54 percent made favourable and only 13 percent made negative comments when they were asked to mention things their congressman "has done in office or what he (she) stands for." Although only 15 percent reported that they or a member of their family had directly requested help from their congressmen, nearly 70 percent of those who had asked for help said they were satisfied with the help they received. Sixty-six percent reported having received mail from their congressman, and 68 percent said they had read about their congressman's activities in the press or heard about the member on television.

---

[22] On the effects of campaign spending and regulation, see Lawrence Shepard, "Does Campaign Spending Really Matter?" *Public Opinion Quarterly* 41 (Summer 1977): 196-205; Gary W. Copeland and Samuel C. Patterson, "Reform of Congressional Campaign Spending," *Policy Studies Journal* 5 (Summer 1977): 424-31; Gary C. Jacobson, "The Electoral Consequences of Public Subsidies for Congressional Campaigns," paper presented at the 1977 Annual Meeting of the American Political Science Association, Washington, D.C., and Timothy A. Hodson and Roland D. McDevitt, "Congressional Campaign Finance: The Impact of Recent Federal Reforms," paper presented at the 1977 Annual Meeting of the American Political Science Association, Washington, D.C.

[23] Fenno, "U.S. House Members in Their Constituencies," pp. 890-97.

[24] John A. Ferejohn, "On the Decline of Competition in Congressional Elections," *American Political Science Review* 71 (March 1977), p. 170; Cover and Mayhew, "Congressional Dynamics and the Decline of Competitive Congressional Elections," p. 67.

[25] This is Fiorina's argument in *Congress: Keystone of the Washington Establishment.*

Table 3
Americans' Attitudes Toward Congressmen, 1977

Survey Item	Percentage
"Very" or "fairly" interested in the activities of Congress	58
Can recall congressman's name	50
Comments positively about congressman's activities or stands	54
Read newspaper story or heard television story about congressman	68
Received mail from congressman	66
Sent letter or telegram, or signed petition, to congressman	29
Met congressman or heard congressman speak at a public meeting	26
Respondent or family members requested assistance from member of Congress or staff	15
Contributed financially to candidate	11
Personally visited congressman	8
Campaigned for congressional candidate	7
Own congressman "excellent" or "pretty good"	40
Same as or better than other congressmen	63
Congress "excellent" or "pretty good"	22

Source: Based upon interviews in January 1977 with 1,510 respondents conducted by the Harris Survey for the U.S. House of Representatives' Commission on Administrative Review.

In addition, the survey showed that constituents evaluate their congressman quite positively, more so than Congress as a whole. Forty percent rated their own congressman as "Excellent" or "Pretty Good" (38 percent said they were not sure about their members' performance), but only 22 percent rated Congress equally highly (and only 14 percent were not sure). There are no survey data which conclusively establish that increased constituency nursing has brought about wider salience for incumbents among their constituents, but some of the evidence is consistent with the claim that this has been the case.

CHANGES IN THE CONGRESSIONAL ORGANIZATION

The most acclaimed changes in Congress in recent years have been in the congressional organization itself. The organization's membership has changed, and its workload greatly altered. These changes have not necessarily been inexorable, but they have not been very susceptible to deliberate manipulation by Congress itself. Changes in the organizational mechanics of Congress — in the committee structure, the party leadership, and the staff — have aroused spirited congressional debate, and precipitated deliberate legislative reorganization. Moreover, Congress has made new attempts to cope with the burgeoning information technology of the 1970s. Congress had attempted to cope with massive increases in the workload by reshaping the committee systems of the two houses, and drawing upon the expertise of the growing numbers of congressional staff.

The Pressures of Work

The workload of Congress has steadily increased, particularly since the 1960s. As figure 3 shows, the extent of floor sessions and committee or subcommittee meetings has escalated. This growth is particularly telling in the House, where the number of committee and subcommittee meetings doubled between the 84th and 94th Congresses. Since Congress has not grown in

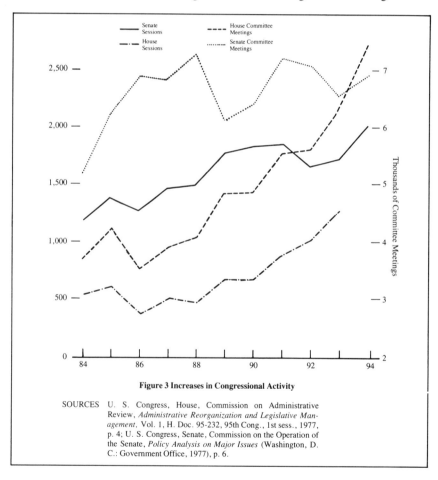

Figure 3 Increases in Congressional Activity

SOURCES U. S. Congress, House, Commission on Administrative Review, *Administrative Reorganization and Legislative Management*, Vol. 1, H. Doc. 95-232, 95th Cong., 1st sess., 1977, p. 4; U. S. Congress, Senate, Commission on the Operation of the Senate, *Policy Analysis on Major Issues* (Washington, D. C.: Government Office, 1977), p. 6.

membership, this means that members are much more heavily burdened in their performance of legislative work. In addition, members serve on more committees and subcommittees. In the 95th Congress, three hundred and forty-seven House members had two or more committee assignments, and two hundred and fifty-seven members had four or more subcommittee assignments. In the 94th Congress, the average senator served on four committees and fourteen subcommittees. Consequently, overburdened work schedules and a morass of conflicting meeting times have been a mounting congressional problem.

Both houses have attempted to alleviate the work pressures on members by establishing special commissions to recommend improvements in work scheduling. The House Commission on Administrative Review (the so-called Obey Commission, after its chairman, David R. Obey, D., Wisc.) established during the 94th Congress, and the Commission on the Operation of the Senate created in 1975, conducted thorough studies of House and Senate operations. Both commissions found that members worked an eleven-hour day on the average, that they were required to engage in too many legislative activities because of their multiple committee assignments, and that work schedules had become overly demanding and filled with conflicting obligations. Both Commissions agreed that members' days had become "long, fragmented, and unpredictable." Both made recommendations for changes in scheduling of legislative work and administrative practices, and quite a few of these recommendations were adopted. But the fundamental problem of congressional coping with accelerating demands for policies and services lay in the committees and the congressional staffs.

Congressional Committees

The most striking feature of congressional organization is its decentralization, and congressional government by subcommittee has grown in the 1970s. Table 4 shows the growth in the number of subcommittees in selected years since 1945.

In the 95th Congress, the House had twenty-nine committees (twenty-two standing and seven select) with one hundred and forty-nine subcommittees. Persistent efforts have been made to streamline the House committee structure since the passage of the *Legislative Reorganization Act* of 1946. A Select Committee on Committees (called the Bolling Committee after its Chairman, Richard B. Bolling, D., Mo.) was created in 1973, and it proposed a thorough modernization of House committees. However, its proposals did not get supported in the Democratic party caucus when they were considered in 1974.[26]

---

[26] For a very perceptive, insiders' analysis of the Bolling Committee's work and its fate, see Davidson and Oleszek, *Congress Against Itself.*

Table 4
Congressional Subcommittees, 1945-1977

Year	Number of Subcommittees of			
	House Committees	Senate Committees	Joint Committees	Total
1945	106	68	6	180
1959	121	100	8	229
1961	131	109	13	253
1968	139	104	15	258
1970	138	104	15	257
1975	146	139	14	299
1977	149	113	5	267

Source: Malcolm E. Jewell and Samuel C. Patterson, *The Legislative Process in the United States,* 3rd ed. (New York: Random House, 1977), p. 39; *Congressional Staff Directory,* 1977.

Instead, the Democratic House majority adopted committee proposals formulated by its own caucus Committee on Organization, Study, and Review, chaired by Julia Butler Hansen (D., Washington). The result was the Committee Reform Amendments of 1974, which further dispersed committee power to the House subcommittees.[27]

The Senate of the 94th Congress had twenty-four committees with one hundred and thirty-nine subcommittees. Former Senate Majority Leader Mike Mansfield (D., Mont.) once observed that he thought "this body is getting subcommittee-happy." In 1976, the Senate established a temporary Select Committee to Study the Senate Committee System, chaired by Adlai E. Stevenson III (D., Ill.). Late in that year, the reform committee issued recommendations for a sweeping overhaul of the Senate committee system. These proposals were greatly modified by the Senate Committee on Rules and Administration and on the Senate floor, but in February 1977 the Senate adopted a resolution providing for extensive committee changes. The major changes involved reducing the number of committees, and revising committee jurisdictions so that work on major new legislative responsiblities could be more effectively concentrated. Most committees were left intact, and some were renamed, but major jurisdictional changes were made in order to recreate the old Interior and Insular Affairs Committee as the new Committee on Energy and Natural Resources with control over most energy matters. The reform resolution also prohibited full committees from creating subcommittees without the approval of the full Senate.

---

[27] An analysis of the work of the Hansen Committee from 1970 to 1973 is in Norman J. Ornstein, "Causes and Consequences of Congressional Change: Subcommittee Reforms in the House of Representatives, 1970-1973," in *Congress in Change,* ed. by Ornstein, pp. 88-114.

The new Senate committee arrangements have served to reduce policy fragmentation in that body but the problem remains in the House. In the first five months of the 95th Congress, 1,956 measures had been referred to more than one committee. The policy fragmentation of the House committee system is poignantly illustrated in the cases of energy and health in table 5. Energy bills are especially widely dispersed across the committee structure. Nineteen committees handled energy bills, and although a plurality were referred to the Committee on Interstate and Foreign Commerce, five other committees considered 8-10 percent of the energy bills. Health legislation was more concentrated, with Interstate and Foreign Commerce and the Committee on Ways and Means dealing with most of them, but fourteen other committees handled some health legislation.

Table 5
Energy and Health Bills Referred to House
Committees in the First Five
Months of the 95th Congress
(in percentages)

Committee Referred to	Energy	Health
Agriculture	4	2
Appropriations	1	1
Armed Services	1	1
Banking, Finance, and Urban Affairs	9	1
Education and Labor	3	-
Government Operations	3	10
House Administration	1	1
Interior and Insular Affairs	10	1
International Relations	8	1
Interstate and Foreign Commerce	27	45
Judiciary	4	3
Merchant Marine and Fisheries	5	1
Post Office and Civil Service	1	2
Public Works and Transportation	9	1
Rules	1	1
Science and Technology	9	-
Small Business	3	-
Veterans' Affairs	-	2
Ways and Means	2	28
Total	100	100

Source: U.S. Congress, House, Commission on Administrative Review, *Administrative Reorganization and Legislative Management,* Vol. 2, H. Doc. 95-232, 95th Congress, 1st sess., 1977, p. 33.

When the House got President Carter's energy legislation in early 1977 something had to be done to co-ordinate the handling of this complex package. Speaker O'Neill got House approval to establish an *ad hoc* subcommittee on energy which could provide comprehensive consideration of this major policy area in addition to its separate consideration by the standing committees. More recently, consideration was begun in November 1977 of the President's omnibus welfare reform bill by a twenty-nine-member *ad hoc* subcommittee drawn from the memberships of the committees on Agriculture, Education and Labor, and Ways and Means. These temporary arrangements are symptomatic of House committee fragmentation, and indicate the difficulties which the House has in attempting to come to grips with major policy questions which cut across the dispersive power structure of subcommittee governments.

Committee work has not only proliferated, but also it has become more public. In 1973, the House adopted a resolution requiring most committee meetings to be open to the public and the press. Two years later the Senate adopted a similar rule, and both houses approved open meetings of joint House-Senate conference committees. As figure 4 shows, the proportion of closed meetings had declined before these "sunshine" resolutions were adopted, particularly after House Appropriations subcommittee sessions were opened to the public in 1971.

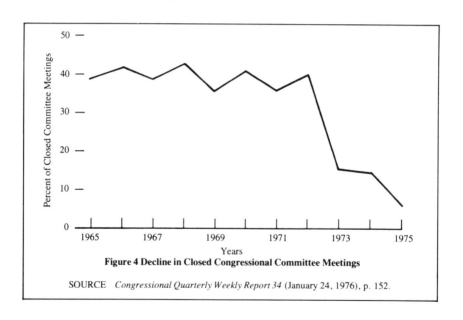

Figure 4 Decline in Closed Congressional Committee Meetings

SOURCE *Congressional Quarterly Weekly Report 34* (January 24, 1976), p. 152.

Congressional Staffs

Twenty years ago, only a few hundred staff people worked on the Hill. Today, their numbers are counted in the thousands. The Capitol and the House and Senate office buildings are literally bursting with staff offices. So abundant have staff resources become that a study for the House Commission on Administrative Review reported in 1977 that "approximately three more office buildings similar to the existing buildings would be required before the facilities of the House would approach those of the executive branch.''[28]

The growth of congressional staffing for the last thirty years is depicted in figure 5. The rate of growth of House members' personal staffs has been particularly sharp. As was noted earlier, a considerable proportion of these staff people are in members' districts, mainly performing constituent service tasks. The most important single realm of growth for the personal office staffs of senators has been in the addition of legislative assistants. Major increases have occurred in both professional and specifically investigative staffs of committees. The relatively large influx of new staff people since the mid-1960s has brought a substantial number of young people to work on the Hill, many serving in very influential policy positions.[29] Members' staffs are especially denoted by their loyalty to the congressman or senator; committee staffs operate in a more closeted environment, constrained by norms of specialization, anonymity, and limited partisanship.[30]

Increased congressional staffing has had at least three important consequences: (1) it has heightened the need for managerial skills on the part of Representatives and Senators, a growing proportion of whom are now required to manage in a bureaucratic sense; (2) it has greatly enlarged the presence of members in their districts or states; and (3) it has contributed to the fragmentation of the congressional policy process by strengthening committees, and especially subcommittees. Twenty years ago there was a crying need for increases in staff assistance to congressmen. Today, concern about the consequences of burgeoning staffs is more often expressed. The House Commission on Administrative Review concluded that

> Committee staffs have grown and tended to become entrenched. As a consequence, committee staffs often appear, at least to some Members, to be more concerned about the power interests of their committees than about what is good for the House.

Moreover, the Obey Commission concluded that

> there has been increasing concern that Members are becoming too dependent on a permanent bureaucracy of staff aides, particularly committee staff aides, who by virtue of their tenure and expertise 'control' policy decisions.[31]

---

[28] U.S. Congress, House, Commission on Administrative Review, *Administrative Reorganization and Legislative Management,* Vol. 2, H. Doc. 95-232, 95th Congress, 1st sess., 1977, p. 127.

[29] For a good recent analysis, see Harrison W. Fox, Jr. and Susan Webb Hammond, *Congressional Staffs* (New York: Free Press, 1977).

[30] See Samuel C. Patterson, ''The Professional Staffs of Congressional Committees,'' *Administrative Science Quarterly* 15 (March 1970): 22-37.

[31] U.S. Congress, House Commission on Administrative Review, *Administrative Reorganization and Legislative Management,* Vol. 2, H. Doc. 95-232, 95th Congress, 1st sess., 1977, p. 59. Also, see Michael J. Malbin, ''Congressional Committee Staffs: Who's in Charge Here?'' *Public Interest* 47 (Spring 1977): 16-40.

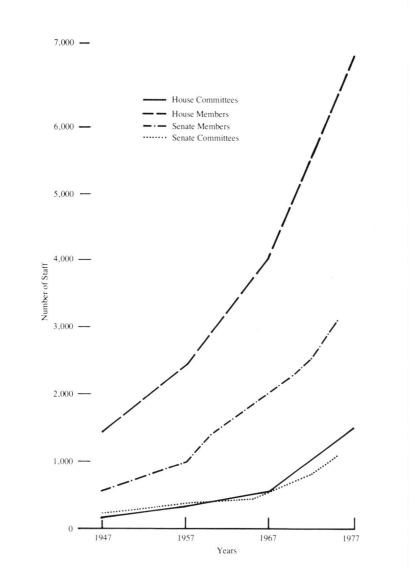

Figure 5 Growth of Congressional Staffing

SOURCE: U. S. Congress, House, Commission on Administrative Review, *Administrative Reorganization and Legislative Management,* Vol. 2, H. Doc. 92-232, 95th Cong., 1st sess., 1977, p. 3; U. S. Congress, Senate, Commission on the Operation of the Senate, *Senators: Offices, Ethics, and Pressures* (Washington, D.C.: Government Printing Office, 1977), p. 6; Harrison W. Fox, Jr. and Susan W. Hammond, "The Growth of Congressional Staffs," in *Congress Against the President,* ed. by Harvey C. Mansfield, Sr. (New York: Praeger, 1975), p. 115.

In addition to the staffs of members and committees, four support agencies assist in the work of the Congress. The Congressional Research Service, an arm of the Library of Congress, provides wide-ranging research services for congressmen and committees. In 1977, it had more than eight hundred employees. The General Accounting Office, in addition to performing a range of auditing assignments, supplies reviews of the economy, efficiency and effectiveness of government programs to Congress; more than a third of the work of the GAO staff now responds to direct requests from congressmen and committees. Its 1977 staff exceeded five thousand people. The Office of Technology Assessment provides policy analysis for Congress on subjects having to do with science and technology; OTA is authorized to have one hundred and thirty employees in 1978. Finally, the Congressional Budget Office, with a staff of about two hundred, furnishes fiscal and economic research for Congress, and is intended to work in tandem with the new House and Senate Budget Committees. Since 1970, the CRS and GAO have been given a larger role in providing research and policy analysis for Congress. The OTA opened for business in 1973, and the CBO was created by the *Congressional Budget and Impoundment Control Act* of 1974.[32] These support agencies provide a very impressive "policy analysis" capability for the Congress; whether congressional leaders and committees can use policy analysis effectively is an issue subject to reservations and debate.[33]

Allied to the growth of congressional staffing has been the development of computerized information systems for Congress. In the "technetronic era" Congress has, however reluctantly, coped with the massive inflation of information by establishing computer facilities for the use of members and committees.[34] For instance, the House Information System created by the House Committee on Administration has a staff of more than two hundred members.[35] In 1977, about two hundred and fifty House offices were equipped with remote computer terminals through HIS, and ninety-seven of the one hundred Senate offices had terminals linking them either to the Library of Congress computer or to various private data banks.[36]

---

[32] A thorough evaluation of these support agencies was prepared for the Commission on the Operation of the Senate. See U.S. Congress, Senate, Commission on the Operation of the Senate, *Congressional Support Agencies,* Committee Print, 94th Cong., 2nd sess., 1976.

[33] See Allen Schick, "The Supply and Demand for Analysis on Capitol Hill," *Policy Analysis* 2 (Spring 1976): pp. 215-34, and Roger H. Davidson, "Congressional Committees: The Toughest Customers," *Policy Analysis* 2 (Spring 1976): 299-323.

[34] The term "technetronic era" refers to the age of technology and electronics. See Zbigniew Brzezinski, *Between Two Ages: America's Role in the Technetronic Era* (New York: Viking Press, 1970).

[35] U.S. Congress, House, Committee on House Administration, *Computer-Based Information Resources for the United States House of Representatives,* Committee Print, 94th Congress, 1st sess., 1975.

[36] *Congressional Quarterly Weekly Report* 35 (May 28, 1977). 1045-51.

DECISION-MAKING CHANGES

Decision-making changes have manifested themselves in Congress in changes in voting patterns, and in modifications of processes related to the decisional autonomy of the congressional houses. Structurally, the proliferation of subcommittees has meant an enlargement in the number of decisional units in the House and Senate, and this structural fragmentation probably is, in general terms, the most important change in congressional decision making. As it has been said, "it is not easy for a feudal system to make national policy."[37] At the same time, the strengthening of subcommittee government, and particularly the enhancement of committee staffing, has contributed to the independence and autonomy of Congress, especially in its relations with the executive branch.

Since the mid-1960s, Congress has strengthened its autonomy as a legislative institution in a variety of ways. The pace of congressional oversight of executive agencies has quickened markedly, especially in the House. House committees have increased the time which they spend in oversight activities from 39 percent in the 91st Congress (1969-1970) to 54 percent in the 94th Congress (1975-1976).[38] The growth in the number of oversight subcommittees and investigative staffs, partly stimulated by mounting congressional hostility to the Nixon Administration, accounts for this expanding oversight activity.

Congress sought a larger degree of control over the federal budget when it enacted the *Congressional Budget and Impoundment Control Act* of 1974. The Act placed limitations on the ability of the President to interdict the expenditure of appropriated funds, and expanded the scope of participation in the congressional budget process. New Budget Committees were established in the House and Senate, and the Congressional Budget Office was created to provide Congress with budget information and analysis. The new congressional budget process permits greater control over appropriations, budgetary priorities, and fiscal policy.[39]

Finally, Congress has become much more active in the realm of foreign policy. The *War Powers Act* of 1973, enacted despite the President's veto, established congressional review powers regarding the commitment by the President of the United States armed forces abroad. The *Executive Agreements Act* of 1972 requires the President to transmit international agreements other than

---

[37] Ralph K. Huitt, "Congress, the Durable Partner," in *Congress: Two Decades of Analysis,* by Ralph K. Huitt and Robert L. Peabody (New York: Harper & Row, 1969), p. 229.

[38] Joel D. Aberbach, "The Development of Oversight in the United States Congress: Concepts and Analysis," paper presented at the 1977 Annual Meeting of the American Political Science Association, Washington, D.C., p. 26. For the development of oversight activities prior to the 91st Congress, see Lawrence C. Dodd and George C. Shipley, "Patterns of Committee Surveillance in the House of Representatives, 1947-70," paper presented at the 1975 Annual Meeting of the American Political Science Association, San Francisco.

[39] For details, see Allen Shick, "The Battle of the Budget," in *Congress Against the President,* ed. by Mansfield, pp. 51-70; and John W. Ellwood and James A. Thurber, "The New Congressional Budget Process: The Hows and Whys of House-Senate Differences," in *Congress Reconsidered,* ed. by Dodd and Oppenheimer, pp. 163-92.

treaties to Congress so that it is informed about such commitments. Congressional oversight of intelligence activities, once sacred cows, has expanded, and congressional activism in foreign policy has generally accelerated. The executive-legislative consensus on foreign policy which was exemplified in such post-World War II policies as the Truman Doctrine, American participation in the United Nations, the Marshall Plan, or the more recent Gulf of Tonkin Resolution has largely evaporated, and Congress has become much more an adversary of the President in the fields of national security and foreign affairs. The device of the "legislative veto" — which permits Congress to override actions of the President — has been included in foreign policy legislation in the 1970s much more frequently than before as a way to assure congressional involvement in foreign policy implementation.[40]

CONCLUSION

Thirty years ago, the architect of the *Legislative Reorganization Act* of 1947 wrote:

> . . . Congress lacks adequate information and inspection facilities. Its internal structure is dispersive and duplicating. It is a body without a head. Leadership is scattered among the chairmen of 81 little. legislatures who compete with each other for jurisdiction and power. Its supervision of executive performance is superficial. Much of its time is consumed by petty local and private matters which divert its attention from national policy-making. Elected by the people to protect the public interest, it yields too often to the importunities of lobbyists for special-interest groups. It lacks machinery for developing coherent legislative programs and for promoting party responsibility and accountability. Its posts of power are held on the basis of political age, regardless of ability or agreement with party policies. And its members are overworked and underpaid — the forgotten men of social security.[41]

Congress has acquired impressive staffs and information processing facilities; improvements have been made in its system of committees; oversight of the executive has expanded measureably; far less of its time is spent on merely parochial issues; it is substantially more impervious to special-interest pressure; seniority is no longer an automatic guarantee of committee power; and certainly its members are not underpaid (a 1977 increase raised members' pay to $57,500 a year).

Congress has great political power, and an enormous capacity to frustrate the legislative ambitions of the President, as President Jimmy Carter has discovered in the course of his first year in the White House. It tasted sovereignty during the exhilarating days of 1973 when it nearly removed a President, Richard

---

[40] See U.S. Congress, House, Committee on International Relations, *Congress and Foreign Policy-1976*, Committee Print (Washington, D.C.: Government Printing Office, 1977). Also see Fred Kaiser, "Oversight of Foreign Policy: The U.S. House Committee on International Relations," *Legislative Studies Quarterly* 2 (August 1977): 255-79.
[41] George B. Galloway, *Congress at the Crossroads* (New York: Thomas Y. Crowell, 1946), p. 334.

Nixon, from office, and surely would have had he not resigned. We do not have congressional government in the United States in the sense that an omnipotent Congress makes all the laws, which the President and the executive branch merely dutifully enforce. Such a simplistic system never existed. But Congress is far more formidible as a political body today than it was in the more quiescent days of the 1950s and early 1960s. Congress is semi-sovereign.

It remains, nevertheless, a peculiar institution. The electoral connections of its members are highly individual and localized. Although its membership has become more ideologically homogeneous, and accordingly somewhat more partisan, its party leadership remains relatively weak. Its internal power structure continues to be highly dispersed, with legislative influence over policy decisions scattered over a large number of members manning its many subcommittees and conducting business in a remarkably open and public manner. It jealously guards its independence, enlarges the scope of its legislative activities, strengthens its capacity to scrutinize the executive, and demands a greater role in realms of policy previously left largely to the President. Its aggregate decision making is "individualistic" in the sense that party or committee influence on members' voting is not compelling. In short, Congress is an unusually democratic legislative institution. This makes it a very frustrating policy-making body for those politicians and intellectuals who have the "received truth." And, its democratic character makes it often seem painfully slow and incompetent to its attentive constituents. Its own internal dynamic, along with these external frustrations and annoyances, brings about cyclical pressures for reform. So, it surely will be true that the Congress of the 1980s will not be much different from the Congress of the 1970s — but it will not be the same.

Congress is a more formidible parliamentary institution than its North American cousin, the Canadian Parliament, especially in its independence from the executive branch. It is also a more public body, operating with very little secrecy about its processes, policies, and political machinations. Although this semi-sovereign Congress may be well-suited to the peculiar politics of the United States, it probably is not very exportable. Moreover, obviously the parliamentary system of government does not lend itself especially well to an autonomous legislative body. Nevertheless, Canadians may find Congress a useful study, both for what to do and what not to do to improve the effectiveness of their own parliamentary institutions.

Chapter Five

The Backbencher and the Discharge of Legislative Responsibilities

by
*John M. Reid**

The concept of "legislative responsibilities" is a very considerable one, and much more than is generally recognized, it penetrates the day to day existence of the backbencher. While some members come with causes or interests to advance, it is by no means clear that they will be able to participate most effectively in the legislative process. That requires the development of special skills, seldom found outside the political process. That educative experience, however, is the subject of another paper.

We usually use the term "legislative process" when we consider new legislation or the amendment of existing legislation, this latter category being by far the area most dealt with by Parliament. It also includes legislation by regulation, an increasing practice. Such a concept has a certain solidity about it but I would go farther and argue that it also includes administrative actions as well. The concept of legislative responsibilities goes beyond that to where a member becomes an advocate of a particular set of measures or ideas. He then becomes an educator in attempting to win the broad general support which is required to develop a legislative solution to the problem at hand.

Members can become advocates for legislation as a result of the work they do in their ridings which provides them with an excellent window on how well a particular programme may or may not be working. This information, I might add, is not generally available to either ministers or senior civil servants; it is really available only to someone placed like an M.P. who can understand the problem which brought forth the original legislation and can follow the working out of the legislative solution.

THE HOUSE COMMITTEE SYSTEM

Another important source of ideas and involvement for members is the committee system. If one wants to understand what the government is doing, and

---

* Member of Parliament (Kenora-Rainy River); appointed Minister of State for Federal-Provincial Relations November 24, 1978.

how well it is discharging its function, the committee system is one of the best facilities available for members. It allows members to learn in depth about those things which interest them, and it opens the door to important contacts both within and outside government. For the backbencher, the committee system is both his best opportunity and his greatest frustration. Additionally, it is within the committee system where the member has his greatest opportunity to influence the actual words of the law.

I would point out that the committee system is a substantial one. At present, nineteen individual committees are listed in the Standing Orders. I estimate that about sixty-five members carry the workload of the committees. The membership of the committees ranges from twelve to thirty members. Although committees have the power to establish their own quorum for the purpose of hearing witnesses, they usually accept the quorum necessary for decisions which is 50 percent plus one. Of course, this practice impedes the orderly operation of committees, but members are not inclined to relax this practice. It wastes a great deal of the time of the conscientious member who must wait for a quorum to appear.

From time to time Special Committees are established by the House. For example, we have a Special Committee on Rights and Immunities of Members, one on the Implementation of Television in the House and in its committees and a Joint Committee with the Senate on the National Capital Region.

In addition to the sixty-five members who really maintain the committee system, there are another twenty to twenty-five "floaters." There are the people who seldom show up for the hard, difficult work of committees but who are very much in presence during the final days of the discussion of a bill, or especially when there is the hope of a scandal. These people, from all parties, are well-known to the long suffering committee members.

PRIVATE MEMBERS' BILLS

What are the outlets for the legislative urge of members? There are several, and I would like to deal with them in turn. But I should add that there are not many members who are really interested in the various aspects of the legislative process as it operates. Most are interested only as it happens to apply to their interests of the moment. Often, because these members have not acquired the necessary skills, they find it difficult to perform their legislative function. I estimate that perhaps twenty to twenty-five members really know their way through the legislative process.

In first place by tradition is the private members' time. It is divided into three sections, one allowing a member to present a proposal for a change or an addition to the public law in the form of an actual bill to the House. The second is the right of a member to present a proposal in the form of a resolution. This form has fewer restrictions than the previous option. The third is the time allotted for members to present private bills dealing with private matters. These are limited at the present to the establishment of banks and the incorporation of certain other companies whose federal charter demands a decision by Parliament — for example, a private member's bill currently before the House to amend Bell Canada's Charter. To indicate how this practice is dying out as a result of changes to the law, this is the only bill of its nature presented in this session; in the previous one, there were only two.

By and large, the function of private members' hour is to allow members to present ideas for debate. Since a good many of them do come up for debate, the government must make some response. Whether the government likes it or not, it must take the proposals seriously and present its arguments to the House, since it knows that most members (from whatever side of the House) regard the passage of private members' bills as a significant achievement for the backbench. Consequently, government must take note of these bills, and determine how to respond to the ideas contained in them.

Over the past six years, a surprising number of these bills have been considered. For example, the House recently approved my motion, seconded by Jim McGrath, a Conservative M.P., to send six bills dealing with the obscenity section of the Criminal Code to the Justice Committee, which is holding hearings on them as this paper is being written. That took some negotiations with all parties in the House. Backbenchers are not without the power to negotiate.

On some occasions, a member may utilize the private member's time for purposes other than the debate of a pet bill. This strategy nonetheless may produce legislative action by the government and also by provincial administrations. For the member most interested in legislation, the private members' hour is an important opportunity, not only for what response the government must make, but also because it allows the member to carry on his work of educating the public, the press, and the government. In my own career, I have found the private members' hour to be invaluable.

Allow me to give a somewhat lengthy personal example of the impact of a private member's bill which was not debated.

Two or three years ago I was approached by an individual who was receiving an indexed Canada Pension Plan disability pension. As a result of union-management decisions, he was also covered by a private plan, which guaranteed him a monthly sum of money. As his CPP was indexed, it went up with the cost of living, but the insurance company's obligation went down, since its contract called for it to maintain his gross income at a particular level.

I entered into lengthy correspondence with the Minister of National Health and Welfare. I spend considerable time with the officials of the Department. They told me they could do nothing since the insurance company was only doing what its contract called for, and the solution was outside federal jurisdiction. I tried to deal with the Ontario lawmakers, but was not able to accomplish much.

At this point, I decided to draft a private member's public bill to deal with the problem and discussed the matter with the Department of Justice. Then I set to work, with the help of the Parliamentary Law Clerk to construct a private members' bill to deal with this situation. Because of the constitutional situation, the bill was less than satisfactory since I was trying to achieve a desirable result by indirect means.

Within a few days of the bill's introduction in the House of Commons, I received a number of phone calls from NHW officials and others. One of the most interesting was from the trade association representing the insurance industry. Their spokesman told me they recognized the problem, wanted to help solve it, indicated they disagreed with my bill, but felt it had pointed the way to a possible solution.

This turn of events prompted contact with the Ontario Pension Commission which regulates the operations of pension funds in that province. After some months of discussion and deliberations, in which I did not take part, the Ontario Pension Commission changed its regulations. The result was to eliminate the abuse by which private plans had secured an unwanted advantage from the advent of indexed public plans to the considerable detriment of retired employees.

I was not the first person to have picked up this problem but I was the first to propose a concrete solution however unsatisfactory it may have been. The solution came from an agency of a provincial government, with the full co-operation of the affected private sector. It gives an indication of the complexity of our governmental system and the need for those who would legislate to seek out allies.

And the bill, incidentally, was never called for debate in the House of Commons. Yet it served its purpose even better than most of those which are debated. Without the use of the private member's bill, this story might have had quite a different ending.

DEBATES AND COMMITTEES REVISITED

The House, when dealing with legislation, really is a forum for the parties. The House is a party battleground and if one wishes to go charging out into someone else's war, one must be prepared to take the consequences.

That statement should be qualified, however, because in reality the debate between the parties is concluded within two or three days. At that point, since the House has yet to discipline itself to the use of its time, the debate is likely to drag on, unnoticed by the press and public alike. Creative members then have an opportunity to develop ideas in the general area covered by the legislation. Out of relief, everyone will listen to something new! But the House generally is not an accommodating arena to the backbencher interested in legislation unless, of course, he is a part of a party's team on that subject.

At the committee stage, however, the circumstances change somewhat for the better. While opportunities to change a particular bill significantly are rare and few, there are possibilities for action by individual members when a bill encounters significant opposition from the public or strong interest groups.

Competition policy is an excellent example. The Commons Finance Committee, at the end of last session, released a report on competition policy which is likely to be influential in determining how the government will deal with this problem. Those members who participated in that work will have made, in all likelihood, a significant contribution to that particular legislative idea. Comparable opportunities for input by backbenchers have accompanied the growing use of government background papers (formerly called white and green papers) and their reference to committees for study and report. In the hearings devoted to members, through this study and hearing representations on these proposals, the committee members have required a greater opportunity to participate directly in the legislative process. Additionally, there is the use of references to committees, the most interesting recent example being the report of the Justice Committee on the Penitentiary System, and the Committee's subsequent demand to be kept informed as to the government's implementation of the series of changes recommended by the Committee.

A further example of the ability of the backbencher on the government side to react to legislative proposals is contained in the sage of gun control legislation. The first proposal put forward by the government was treated harshly at the committee stage and when it reached the House at report stage it became clear that there was not sufficient government backbencher support to ensure its passage. The internal opposition to the bill came from government supporters who represented rural areas.

In the next session, a much modified bill was introduced and after some considerable difficulties, it eventually passed. The final version was significantly different from its predecessor. Those changes would not have taken place if a number of government backbenchers had not had the support of opposition backbenchers — or, depending on your point of view, vice versa.

There is a further aspect to committee work in the legislative sense, and that is in the area of debating Supply or Estimates. According to the Standing Orders, the government must bring down its spending estimates for the forthcoming fiscal year and have them referred to the various Standing Committees by March 1st. The committees then have to May 31st to deal with them. At the conclusion of the process, an appropriation bill based on these Estimates is presented to Parliament in late June. In conjunction with the Supply process, the opposition parties have twenty-five days in the House of Commons, spread throughout the parliamentary year, but concentrated in May and June. During those days, they choose the topic for consideration. In addition to attacking the government, they can and do advance ideas requiring a legislative solution.

The most significant factor for the private member at the committee stage of considering Estimates is that the committees are unfettered by terms of reference set by the House. Anything coming under the responsibilities of a department whose estimates have been referred to a committee is grist for that committee's mill. The committee can investigate any aspect of that department's activities in the broadest possible sense.

In terms of the educative process, participation in the work of committees is probably the most effective forum for members, although much of the work is arduous and detailed, and worse from a pragmatic point of view, it generates little or no publicity unless one can discover a scandal of appropriate dimensions. Since committees have come on the scene, the opportunities for learning what government does and does not do have greatly expanded, and the ability to pose questions directly to ministers and senior civil servants, in my opinion, has had a beneficial impact on all. Members can confront the people running programmes directly with their concerns; and then can deal with the policy aspects either with the minister in committee or take them to the House. The Opposition member has an advantage at this stage as he and his party have access to the twenty-five supply days, an opportunity denied to government backbenchers.

A particular opportunity for backbenchers arises with the establishment of Joint Committees with the Senate, such as the Joint Committee on the Constitution or the Committee on the National Capital Commission. These Joint Committees tend to have greater clout than Special Committees established by either chamber.

Finally, I must underline the significance for backbenchers of committees set up to deal with particular issues or those special priorities.

Public Accounts is a committee which works closely with the Auditor General. It has had opportunities to influence legislation as a result of investigations carried out following suggestions in the Auditor General's annual report. For example, the recent background paper on Crown Corporations resulted as a direct consequence of the Public Accounts Committee's investigation into Atomic Energy Canada.

The Regulations and Statutory Instruments Committee has one of the more interesting and important jobs to do. Its task is to check up on all of those orders issued by the federal government coming under its title. Since there has been a tendency for Parliament to entrust more regulatory power to the government, this role is most important. This function, at times, resembles that of a quasi-court. It provides an important check on the use of delegated legislative powers. Additionally, this committee is currently studying the government's background paper on "Freedom of Information."

The most important constraint on the role of the private member is his party affiliation. With the advent of television in the House of Commons, great attention is being paid by political parties to the articulation and perception of party policy. This operates to constrain members for now the party feels it must present as uniform a position as possible on a wide variety of issues. The emphasis on the uniformity of policy statements thus affects every member in a much more pervasive manner than previously experienced.

I cannot emphasize this point too much. Members are conscious that they entered the House as party members. This fact is part of the environment of politics. It limits what role a backbencher can envisage for himself. It is necessary, as well, for the functioning of the House. The effort needed to develop the necessary discipline in the House with its two hundred and sixty-four members (after the next election this will be two hundred and eighty-two), all with a sizable ego, would be virtually impossible without the use of team discipline. Another consideration is that there are no rigid rules as to how or what a member can do when he is elected. There is no one role. Often members are overwhelmed by their choices in the relatively unstructured atmosphere of the House and of politics in general. Some thrive in this arena, and others find it impossible.

CONCLUSION

For members, the changes in developing the committee system, begun in 1965 and brought to the present status in 1967, have opened the system to permit more direct personal involvement in the legislative process. This system has provided him with a great deal of relevant information, broken down barriers between the civil service, ministers and M.P.'s and developed I believe, a much better feedback mechanism for all participants in the legislative process.

Although I did not mention it before, the committee system has also opened the legislative system to ''outsiders'' by allowing them to come and make direct presentations to committees. This ventilation has been helpful to all, even though it has not been without its pains.

The traditional means of participating in the legislative process are still of considerable importance. The time devoted to private members' business is vital to members with a legislative bent. It is still used extensively and there have been a number of reforms to ensure that the opportunity to use this time is spread around more equitably than before. In addition, there appears to be a willingness by the government to co-operate more fully to ensure that private members' bills get more decent treatment than the hasty burial experienced in the past.

One of the more important areas where a backbencher is able to exercise a legislative function arises in his participation in the development of party policy. In some ways, this can be the most important part of a backbencher's legislative outlook. I have not dealt with that aspect of his activities. I have not dealt with the impediments to reforming the legislative function which is implicit not so much in the nature of the system itself, but rather from the fact that the floor of the House of Commons, and to a lesser extent in all of its emanations, is a battleground between parties and, occasionally, ideas.

For those members with a legislative bent (we do not all share that impulse), the opportunities are more readily available now than they have been in the past. As one associated closely with the parliamentary process for some fourteen years, I believe that members will continue to persevere for more opportunities to participate more directly in the legislative process by making it more accessible to individual initiatives and less susceptible to the constraints imposed by party.

COMMENTS

JOHN A. FRASER*

The title of John Reid's paper, *The Backbencher and the Discharge of Legislative Responsibilities,* raises several issues.

The first is the role of an individual backbencher in promoting and achieving a particular legislative measure. After referring to the general process of government sponsored legislation, Mr. Reid observes that

> [t]he concept of legislative responsibility goes beyond that (the legislative process) to where a member becomes an advocate of a particular set of measures or ideas.

Private Members' Bills

Mr. Reid cites the private members' time, including private members' bills, private members' motions and private bills dealing with private matters such as banks and federally chartered corporations. It is true that the private member does have an opportunity to present "a particular set of measures or ideas" to use Mr. Reid's words. Sometimes these proposals are eventually incorporated into law. But the chance of this happening is very limited.

I do not have available any statistics on the number of private members' bills or motions that have actually become law over the years. However, if one refers to the Order Paper and Notices of Monday, March 20, 1978 it will show that two hundred and thirty private bills have been introduced for hearing since the start of this Session in October 1977. Of these, one bill concerns Bell Canada and another two are Senate bills dealing with exemptions to marriage law and specific proposed marriages but which require the sponsorship of a member of the House of Commons. The two Senate bills were passed. The Bell Canada bill was referred to the Standing Committee on Transport and Communications.

Of the remaining two hundred and twenty-seven bills which are what could be termed true private members' bills, only nineteen bills have been debated. Of the nineteen, eight are name changes of electoral ridings resulting out of redistribution and were all passed, almost as matter of course. Thus it can be seen that only eleven bills really come within the kind of legislative initiative contemplated by Mr. Reid. Ten of these dealt with pornography and were referred to the Standing Committee on Justice and Legal Affairs. The one remaining bill, entitled the *Parliament Hill Curator Act* is aimed at preserving all aspects of the appearance and setting of Parliament Hill. It was referred to the Standing Committee on Justice and Legal Affairs. It should be noted that of the eleven private members' bills that ought to be considered for the purposes of this discussion, none was passed, although all were referred and may, in some form or another, contribute to eventual legislation. Also, it is important to remember

---

* Member of Parliament (Vancouver South)

that of the two hundred and twenty-seven, many of these bills have been introduced session after session and no doubt many will be re-introduced at a future date.

Mr. Reid mentioned resolutions introduced by private members under notices of motion. Again, citing the Order Paper and Notices for March 20, 1978, twenty-six notices of motion were introduced since the start of this Session. A number were debated but were talked out without a vote and have reverted to the bottom of the list where they slowly work their way back up the list again unless withdrawn. Only one, proposing the establishment of a National Administration School for Public Servants, was referred to the Standing Committee on Miscellaneous Estimates. None was passed.

As a point of interest, of the forty-one notices of motion in the last Session, from October 1976 to October 1977, only one was passed and only one was referred to a standing committee.

Private members' bills cannot propose the expenditure of money, except in a minor incidental way. Therefore, this procedure is limited in terms of subject matter. However, resolutions or notices of motion can call on the House to adopt measures involving public expenditure. A member can introduce as many bills as desired, but no member can introduce more than one notice of motion during a Session.

It can be seen from the foregoing that while there are opportunities for a backbencher to propose legislation, it is a very limited opportunity. The fundamental rule still prevails, and that is that the government of the day initiates legislation. The backbencher — or as I prefer to say, the individual member — considers it, amends it sometimes, and either votes for it or against it.

Dealing with Government Legislation

This leads me to some comments on the legislative responsibility of the individual member in dealing with government legislation. John Reid argues that

[w]hile opportunities to change a particular bill significantly are rare and few, there are possibilities for action by individual members when a bill encounters significant opposition from the public or strong interest groups.

I agree with Mr. Reid's statement in general, especially when a majority government tightly controls its own members who, in turn, control the committees. Under majority conditions, it takes considerable persuasion to obtain changes, and as Mr. Reid says, the chance will only arise if the public is aroused. However, there are times when even government members will concede a bill is badly drafted or, sometimes, faulty in concept and detail. An example of this was the first Gun Control bill which ran into heavy weather in committee and which was never passed in its original form. I believe that at one point, when the first version was before committee, at the urging of members from both sides of the House, the government came in with over fifty amendments to its own bill.

It is a very different situation when there is a minority government because the opposition outnumbers the government both in committee and in the House. Under such circumstances individual members have some real leverage. If the opposition can agree, the argument ends there. But rather than lose the bill in its entirety, the government members needing the support of some of the opposition develop an amazing propensity to make a deal. In my opinion the committee system worked much better during the minority regime from 1972 to 1974 than it has under the present majority Parliament.

Mr. Reid's paper is weighted toward the member's "opportunity" to propose legislative measures. I believe this is a legitimate and useful subject for inquiry. But the words used in the topic heading concern "the discharge of legislative responsibilities." While the proposing of legislation is a part of a member's responsibility — and I suppose that can apply to both the government and opposition members — the question of what is the responsibility of an individual member varies depending whether they are in opposition or government.

Role of Opposition M.P.'s

However one might wish it otherwise, Parliament is an adversary system and the government has a political stake in its own legislation. As a consequence, governments expect their members to get the legislation through with as little fuss as possible. The opposition, however, sometimes really disagrees with the principle of the legislation. When this happens, the responsibilities of the government members are different from those of the opposition members. If the opposition is totally opposed to a bill they have a responsibility to do two things: within the rules to try to stop it; failing that, to try to repair it or delete parts of it that are most offensive. But, as Mr. Reid has admitted, to do this sometimes requires mobilizing public opinion. To get public opinion mobilized may require delay, protracted debate, and endless amendments in order to hold the bill in committee, and then further amendments at report stage and further debate at third reading.

This sort of situation raises some interesting questions. If, in the case of a minority government, the combined opposition dug in their heels, the government would probably withdraw the bill rather than see it defeated. But in a majority situation it would eventually pass, unless the government really had second thoughts. This can happen — it did with Bill C-16, the *Borrowers and Depositors Protection Act*.

The responsibility of the opposition member, if really opposed to the bill, is to try to stop it. But what about the government backbencher who may believe the bill is a mistake? As I said, the first pressure on a government member is to help get the bill passed. Is there any way around this dilemma? I think there is, and it lies in re-examining the present committee system and removing the party lines to a considerable degree in committee. Once the party lines are lifted, a competent government committee member, no longer compelled automatically to support the legislation, or every part of it, could view the bill in a much more objective manner. If, in addition, committees were properly staffed in terms of independent resources, the result might be a more productive use of members' time, and, I believe, would result in individual members taking greater interest in the area of concern of the committee.

Just as government members are not always entirely in support of a government bill, likewise, opposition members are not always in favour of their party's stand on a bill. A little bit more independence might not do any harm. I have often wondered what would happen in the House if the secret ballot were introduced. There might be some stunned party leaders — and, afterwards, out in the corridor, individual backbenchers from both sides heading off for a joint celebration. I am not advocating secret votes — members must stand and be counted. I am just observing that party discipline often goes beyond necessity, and by its very nature forces members to forfeit at least one of their primary responsibilities and that is to think for themselves. Gilbert and Sullivan's famous song is still applicable: "I always voted at my party's call, And never thought of thinking for myself at all!"

Parliamentary Committees

I want to mention a problem that does affect the individual member's duty to be responsible and it concerns committees. Often, members who attend committee meetings just do not know what the real effect of the bill before them will be. For instance, the Labour Committee has just ended its consideration of Bill C-8 which makes significant changes in the *Canada Labour Code*. I doubt if most members had read the bill, and I am certain that few of them knew enough about the code to understand what some of the proposed amendments were all about. It was impossible to exercise judgment on most of the amendments unless the member had some understanding of the following:

(1)   the present law and how it worked;
(2)   why the change was being proposed;
(3)   the effect of the change; and
(4)   how these changes would relate to the ten provincial labour codes.

All of this should have been presented, at the commencement of consideration of the bill, in the form of a properly researched paper which would be something more than a propaganda sheet. The responsibility for bringing this information before the Committee fell almost entirely on the opposition, although I am quick to point out that, before the hearings ended, as the opposition labour critic, I did receive considerable co-operation from the deputy minister and his officials. I am not telling tales out of school, however, when I relate that one public servant remarked that maybe the Department should have prepared the necessary background information, but then added: "but is that really our responsibility?" My answer is that it is someone's responsibility, and not that of the individual backbenchers because they just do not have the resources, or the time, in most cases to do the job properly.

Mr. Reid referred to committee work on Supply (Estimates) and I think he is saying that here the backbencher has an opportunity to investigate a department's activities. The implication in Mr. Reid's comments is that a member has the chance to raise matters and at least has a forum for ideas and proposals. To a degree this is true. But the real task of a committee studying estimates is to exercise that control of the public purse that the public expects from Parliament. In this I am not convinced the system is working. Mr. Peter Dobell, the Director of the Parliamentary Centre, stated in a recent article in the *Globe and Mail:*

> Between 1969 and 1977, Parliament approved about 235 billion dollars of public expenditure. During those years Parliament made only two cuts: $19,000 in supplementary funds for Information Canada in 1973 and $1,000 dollars from moneys being voted for the Canadian Broadcasting Corporation in June, 1973 . . . In sum, in nine years Parliament has pared the grand total of $20,000 from government spending proposals of 235 billion dollars.

Surely the control of expenditure is a responsibility of every members. And yet, usually more time is taken up in committee on Estimates by members pursuing some aspect of a government policy relating to the department than giving any real examination to the figures. There are a number of reasons for this state of affairs, but in fact, whatever the reasons, very little responsibility is being exercised.

Conclusion

Mr. Reid speaks from a position of far more experience than I do. Maybe the backbencher today has more opportunity to have, in Mr. Reid's words, "direct personal involvement in the legislative process," than some years ago. However, there is much room for improvement, and, in my view, the system as it now functions is not conducive to allowing the individual member much initiative, and indeed, at times works against the members' fulfilling their most basic responsibilities. The Cabinet and the bureaucracy really run the show and all too often the backbencher ends up as an onlooker, just waiting for the division bells to ring.

DONALD C. MACDONALD*

The backbencher's capacity to participate effectively in the legislative process depends on two conditions: first, his/her own abilities and desire to participate; and second, reform of the machinery of Parliament so as to provide a greater opportunity for participation.

---

* Member of Provincial Parliament of Ontario (York South), Leader of the Ontario New Democratic Party, 1961-70.

Ability and Desire to Participate

With regard to the first condition, there are many examples of elected representatives who have had neither the ability nor the desire, and yet have survived for an unconscionable length of time — if they look after the folks back home. Their participation in the legislative process can be, at best, nominal, sporadic and routine; but if they are good constituency members, all will be forgiven by the voters at the next election.

But another critically important factor has emerged in recent years: even if members do have the ability and desire to participate effectively in the legislative process, they are seriously inhibited from doing so because they are swamped by the routine and time-consuming details of servicing their constituents. They are, in the words of the recent Ontario Commission on the Legislature, victims of the "case work syndrome." They have become little more than "social workers," helping their constituents to cope with the bureaucracy which can, and often does, affect every conceivable phase of an individual's life. To survive, let along operate effectively, there is need for adequate office space and equipment; adequate legislative and constituency staff; adequate opportunity for communication, both to travel and by telephone. With these facilities and staff, which have been provided in greater measure in recent years, there is at least an opportunity for the member to service his constituency and have enough time and energy to be a legislator.

More Opportunity to Participate

All of which brings me to the second condition, with which John Reid has dealt in some detail: reform of the machinery of parliament to permit the member to participate more meaningfully in the legislative process. My observations will be an elaboration of the points which he has raised, with greater emphasis on the provincial scene, notably in Ontario, with which I am most familiar.

The initiation of new legislation, or the amending of existing statutes, is an open field through private members' bills. Imagination and energy are all that are needed both at the legislative level, and in developing a public crusade, when needed, to win broad enough support for ultimate enactment. The current efforts of Ged Baldwin, M.P. for Peace River, in relation to freedom of information legislation provide a classic example. The member here becomes both a legislator and an educator.

As Mr. Reid points out, this process sometimes results in the government's accepting the proposed legislation. But even if the government does not respond, the member is left to pursue his interests through a private member's bill, it is to be hoped that reforms in that connection will soon permit enactment with greater frequency. Usually legislation has been regarded as the exclusive prerogative of government, with the private member reduced to little more than an objector or a rubber-stamp supporter.

If the proposed legislation involves the expenditure of public money, which is rightfully the prerogative of government, then approval of it in principle can be sought by way of a resolution which, it is hoped, the government will heed once the House has given its approval.

Experience with private members' bills has been extremely varied. In some provinces (Nova Scotia, for example), considerable time has been allotted to them. The whips are off; often Cabinet ministers will be on opposite sides of an issue brought forward by an opposition member; and a vote is permitted at the conclusion of the debate.

Ontario's experience is in striking contrast. For years, the handling of private members' bills was a mere ritual — left to the concluding days of the session, and often called after midnight in sessions extended throughout the night to achieve adjournment of the House by Easter. There was even one case when the Premier called such an opposition bill when the sponsor was away briefly for a dental appointment, and thereby disposed of it without debate!

Current experiments with the rules in a minority government situation open up the possibility of some improvement. Private members' bills are debated at greater length; and can be voted upon. However, if twenty members of the legislature wish to block a vote, they can do so; and twenty government members, on strictly party lines, usually do rise to forestall any vote on an opposition member's bill. The spirit of the experiment is being breached; and the prospect of even this small measure of progress surviving is unlikely, should the government regain a majority.

Committee Work

A second outlet for the legislative urge is to be found in committee work. In standing committees, where there is the opportunity for extra-parliamentary input, or where party lines are often less stringently maintained, the backbencher can often have a significant impact on details, and sometimes even on more fundamental changes. However, the organization and operation of committees have been the bane of parliamentary life. They have ranged from committees related directly to a ministry, or group of ministries, to a smaller number of omnibus committees. In the Ontario experience, experiments in this process have gone on endlessly for the past twenty years without having achieved a satisfactory result. Usually, there are too many committees to be fitted into the limited time available; or too many of them are operating at the same time, so that the legislative operation becomes a two or three-ring circus into which the individual member has difficulty fitting. As John Reid comments, "for the backbencher the committee system is both his best opportunity and his greatest frustration."

Select committees, which meet only when the House is not in session, as opposed to standing committees which meet to deal with matters referred to them by the legislature, offer another fruitful area for backbench participation. They provide the opportunity to enquire in depth into some matter of growing public concern, and thereby permit the member to become something of an expert in the subject under enquiry. In Ontario, select committees have often been used as the vehicle for involving, and thereby maintaining the interest of, the backbenchers of a big majority government. In my experience, their achievements depend very much on the quality of the staff of the committee. Without staff to do the basic research work, the member with his many other responsibilities simply does not have the time to do an in-depth study. But with adequate staff, they can become an effective body to assess the details of a complicated subject, and make policy recommendations that can have a direct and beneficial effect on future legislation.

Committees can also provide a useful forum for backbenchers to work through the details of new and controversial legislation. The Ontario experience recently with legislation on industrial health and safety and with family law provides good examples. Extended hearings, with a great deal of public input, have not only provided the backbencher with a realization of the impact of such legislation but with an opportunity to share in the development of a consensus which will command public support.

Consideration of Estimates for the coming year's expenditures is another area of committee work in which the backbencher can plan an important role, whether it be done in Committee of the Whole House or in a standing committee of the legislature. Not only is there an opportunity for the backbencher to become familiar with the details of a ministry's operation, and thereby glean information of great value for future changes in policy, but he or she is involved in the critical scrutiny of public monies. That has rightfully been considered as one of the main responsibilities of the private member, particularly on the opposition side of the House, and nowhere can that role be played more effectively than in committee work on Estimates.

Here, as Mr. Reid points out, committee work is an educative process, with a direct relationship not only with ministers and their deputies, but also with senior civil servants heading various branches of the ministry. Unfortunately, this highly important work requires a greater measure of dedication, for it usually generates little or no publicity unless related to a scandal which captures the attention of the media. It is to be hoped that current experiments with television coverage to provide electronic Hansard coverage may open up possibilities for communicating more of this important work of legislative bodies to the people whose business has too often been conducted in virtual secrecy.

Summary

To sum up, the task of making the role of a backbencher more meaningful in all phases of the legislative process is a growing preoccupation of both the political scientist and the serious elected member. The common characteristic of modern legislative bodies is the growing dominance of the executive branch to a point where the private member has been reduced to little more than a rubber stamp for decisions that have been made in the bureaucracy of government, and have come from the Cabinet to the House in a form and manner that permit of very little revision.

Private members' bills and committee work are the major areas for improvements, but there are many other aspects of the legislative process, smaller in themselves, but accumulative in their impact, where the role of the backbencher can be meaningfully developed. But that requires detailed study and a great deal of persistent hard work. Legislative processes are notoriously tradition-bound so that often the most progressive members instinctively resist change. However, changes must be made if legislative bodies are going to be able to cope effectively with the massive flow of public business, and if the backbencher is to feel that his role in the process is really of some influence.

PAUL G. THOMAS*

My remarks will be divided into two parts, First, I would like to present some brief comments on John Reid's paper. Secondly, I would like to explore, in terms of some practical reforms to Commons procedures, how we might provide those greater opportunities for backbenchers to participate more directly in the legislative process which John Reid mentions in the final sentence of his paper.

Increasing the Opportunities for Participation

In choosing to pick up on the final point in the paper, I reveal some of my disappointment with the paper. Here we have a paper by an intelligent, articulate and experienced backbencher with fourteen years of service in the House, yet there is little hint in the paper that the system poses serious or insurmountable obstacles to backbench involvement in the legislative process, provided that M.P.'s are crafty and diligent. I find the general tone of satisfaction with the system surprising for several reasons. Surprising first, because John Reid has campaigned for several years, particularly through his work on the Standing Committee on Procedure and Organization, for reforms that would strengthen the role of the ordinary M.P. and has probably earned for his efforts the reputation among some Cabinet ministers of being a nuisance.

It is surprising also because the other available accounts of a backbencher's existence reveal a strong sense of frustration, bordering on futility, that characterizes M.P.'s outlooks towards their parliamentary careers. Two books that have captured better than any dry, political science study could, the frustrations, boredom, pressures, strains and the occasional moments of excitement and genuine accomplishment in an M.P.'s everyday life are by Mr.

* Assistant Professor and Head of the Department of Political Studies, University of Manitoba.

Gordon Aiken, *The Backbencher* and by Mr. Douglas Roche, M.P., *The Human Side of Politics*.

My own interviews with seventy-five M.P.'s in 1972 revealed a vague, generalized sense of discontent about the role of the ordinary M.P. within the legislative process. Among younger, better educated, abler M.P.'s, the malaise seemed to be even more pronounced. The fact is that the system under-utilizes (the more cynical observer would say wastes) the talents and efforts of intelligent and conscientious members. This fact accounts in part for the phenomenon of the ''parliamentary drop-out,'' those apparently foolhardy members who voluntarily surrender all those ''perks'' which indignant editorialists regularly attack: the $26,000 salary; $10,600 for expenses; free air travel; generous pensions; secretarial assistance; constituency offices; junkets abroad; and even invitations to the annual press gallery dinner!

As a class of citizens, M.P.'s regularly receive more abuse than they deserve. Part of that abuse is due to ignorance on the part of some commentators. John Reid is correct in his attempt to counter the popular image, often conveyed by journalists and some academics, of M.P.'s as a tribe whose emblem is servitude; who regularly and passively accept the will of their ministers irrespective of their own opinions and/or the wishes of their constituents. However, in setting out to provide a more accurate, balanced portrait of the work of the M.P., he chose not to discuss the impediments to a creative legislative role by backbenchers. In its tone and in some specific statements that I will discuss shortly, the paper tends to minimize the constraints on the private member.

Let me say first, that many critics of Parliament, and some scholars who adopt a ''scoreboard'' approach towards parliamentary effectiveness, tend to mistake debates, amendments and votes on the floor of the House and in the standing committees for all of the legislative process. In fact, such activity is the proverbial tip of the iceberg. Most of the important activity of M.P.'s occurs in the form of private discussions with ministers, participation in the caucus, informal contacts with the bureaucracy, participation in closed meetings of Commons' committees when reports are being drafted, and contributions in public sessions of the committees in ways that cannot be easily quantified and measured by empirical social scientists.

John Reid's paper draws our attention to these neglected, private dimensions of the legislative process. The invisible nature of such activity, however, poses a problem for M.P.'s in convincing the public that they earn their keep and deserve to be re-elected.[1] For this reason, many M.P.'s have sought in recent years to supplement their private role with a more visible public role in the

---

[1] See John Meisel, *Working Papers on Canadian Politics* (Montreal: McGill-Queen's University Press, 1972) p. 31. According to Meisel's data on the factors influencing voters' decisions in the 1968 election, the work of the elected M.P. ranked as a distant fourth factor (8 percent of the sample) far behind the party leader and the general image of the party.

legislative process and in attempting to do so they have run up against some difficult obstacles.

Problems of Reform

While I wish to deal mainly with the M.P.'s role in the handling of bills and estimates, what follows is not an argument against the role of the M.P. as "liaison agent" to government on behalf of his constituents. M.P.'s are not sent to Ottawa only to serve as "philosopher kings" debating the great issues of the day. Dealing with constituents' problems should not be beneath their dignity and cannot be if they hope to be re-elected. "Putting a human face" on the operations of modern government is a vital function of the M.P. and should not be belittled on the ground that it detracts from their role as national legislators or inclines them to be narrow and parochial in their approach to legislation and spending. Therefore, I agree with John Reid's emphasis on the importance of the representation process working through M.P.'s. The M.P.'s awareness of governmental programmes from the side of the public is valuable as a source of feedback on the effects of programmes and as a means of ensuring bureaucratic responsiveness and accountability. Indeed, I would argue that, given the complexity of modern public policy, the need for coherence in policy making, the constitutional autonomy of the Cabinet, and the fact of disciplined political parties, it is impossible to return to a situation, if such ever existed, where the legislature is able to generate a significant portion of the policies applied in our society.

It is necessary to disclose such a perspective because inevitably our judgments and prescriptions are conditioned by our underlying assumptions about what roles the House of Commons can legitimately and effectively perform within the political system. There is no model of the "ideal" House of Commons which commands unanimous or even overwhelming support. However, in my view, the House of Commons presently remains too mesmerized by its traditional legislative role and has paid far too little attention to its role as a continuous source of interchange between authority and those subject to authority. This is not to say that the policy process cannot be opened up to allow for more involvement of the legislative branch; recent reforms to the committee system were adopted partly with this aim in mind. But the function of the Commons which could most profitably be strengthened is that of overseeing the administration. By recognizing its limited capacity to shape the content of legislation and concentrating more upon the scrutiny of executive performance and the transmission of popular demands to the Cabinet and the bureaucracy, the Commons could establish an important and viable role for itself.

At present the surveillance function seems to be little understood or accepted by the politicians and the public. The facilities for the review of administrative activities are underdeveloped and what opportunities do exist are little used; a point which is illustrated below. By increasing its supervisory activities the Commons could also increase its opportunities for participation in lawmaking since it would be better informed about the nature of government operations. Many of the bills introduced in each session are administrative in nature, such as amendments to existing statutes incorporating the lessons learned by the bureaucracy in attempting to apply the original legislation. Moreover, a significant and growing portion of the activity of government which impinges on our everyday lives occurs in the form of administrative actions and regulations.

Improved standing committees of the Commons should eventually reach a point where they would discover such administrative problems almost as soon as the departments. Therefore, future reforms should involve the following balancing of interests. In return for the assurance that they will normally obtain the passage of their legislation in good order, governments should permit committees far greater insight into the internal workings of departments and programmes. More knowledgeable committees could assist the government in developing public understanding of and support for programmes. Such committees could also help governments to solve the problem of the accountability of the bureaucracy by providing an institutionalized means for reviewing programmes and operations. In the words of Professors Hansen and Wiseman,

> Relieving the frustrations of the backbencher and making officialdom more amenable to democratic — as distinct from merely sectional — pressures are two complementary aspects of the same process.[2]

Private Members' Bills and Resolutions

With my bias thus disclosed, let me offer some more detailed commentary on John Reid's paper. His discussion of the legislative opportunities begins with private members' bills and resolutions. It is suggested that these occasions are valuable to members as an opportunity to publicize their policy ideas and to exert some pressure on the government. It is suggested that "a surprising number of these bills over the last six years have been considered." We must be clear that the latter phase does not mean enacted. According to my calculations the number of private members' bills enacted in the ten parliamentary sessions between 1963 and 1972 totalled thirty-one and many of these dealt with minor matters (twenty-one were simply enacting a readjustment of the electoral boundaries or names of particular constituencies), which is not surprising since technically they cannot involve the expenditure of money. When one considers that seven hundred and eighty private members' public bills were introduced over the four sessions of the 28th Parliament, one gets an idea of the odds against an M.P. seeing his ideas reflected in legislation.

---

[2] A.H. Hanson and H.V. Wiseman, "The Use of Committees by the House of Commons," *Public Law* (Autumn 1959) p. 279.

As the paper points out, the practice has developed of referring related bills to standing committees, which may enable M.P.'s to have their ideas investigated more thoroughly. On occasion this can actually lead to government action such as occured in the case of Mr. Barry Mather, who conducted a persistent and eventually successful one-man campaign for health warnings on cigarette packages. Such successes remain rare, however. Even though more bills are sent to committees, the actual percentage of private members' bills handled by committees has dropped since M.P.'s (in an apparent case of contagious masochism) have introduced an increasing number of bills in each recent session.

Notices of motions are more flexible than bills. Since they simply urge the government to consider a particular course of action, such as the establishment of a parliamentary inquiry, they may involve the expenditure of money. Moreover, they need not be drafted in statutory language. Once again, however, they are seldom productive of government action. Out of the several hundred notices of motion introduced in the first and second sessions of the 28th Parliament, fewer than fifty were debated and only a handful were passed. Despite these frustrations, M.P.'s continue to regard bills and resolutions as a valuable means by which to express opinion.

Committees

The paper moves on to a discussion of participation by members in the standing committees. The new Standing Orders adopted in December 1968 assigned to the committees the three tasks of reviewing legislation, examining Estimates, and conducting general inquiries. The principal motive of the Trudeau government in transferring more work to the committees was to expedite the handling of its increased legislative workload, but the reforms were also heralded as a breakthrough on behalf of the private member. In practice, the committees have become the main working units of the Commons. As John Reid notes, the committees now represent the backbencher's "best opportunity and his greatest frustration."

In my view the procedural changes of 1968 did not expand greatly the scope for backbench and committee involvement in the formulation of legislation.[3] While almost all government bills are now referred to the standing committees after second reading, the government remains protective of major pieces of legislation when substantive amendments are proposed. The traditional notion that a fundamental change to government policy represents a defeat or severe political setback apparently persists in the minds of most ministers and M.P.'s, even though that defeat is likely to occur in the relatively freer atmosphere of the standing committee rooms and normally will go unreported in the press. Most of

---

[3] I have elaborated on this theme in "The Influence of Standing Committees of the Canadian House of Commons on Government Legislation" (A paper presented to the Conference on Legislative Studies, York University, October 13-15, 1977).

the successful amendments originate with the government. Many of the amendments introduced by opposition parties involve substantive policy differences with the government. These are not expected to pass and are presented mainly for their propaganda value. The case for a particular amendment is clearly strengthened, as the paper notes, by the presence of outside pressure from influential groups or the provinces. There are a number of other factors that affect the influence of committees on government bills, including the general political situation, the nature of the legislation involved, the attitudes of the minister and his advisers, and the types of changes being sought. The legislative process is variable and precise generalizations are difficult to formulate.

The Estimates

I am less optimistic than John Reid regarding what M.P.'s can accomplish through the new procedures for dealing with the Estimates. Undoubtedly the new Supply process represents an improvement upon its century-old predecessor, but even it involves problems. No longer is it necessary to waste fifty to seventy-five days of House time with political gamesmanship. In the old Committee of Supply (discarded in 1968), members made political speeches rather than probing for information on departmental affairs. Ministers replied in kind. Now Supply is voted regularly, the Estimates receive at least some real attention, and the right of the opposition to criticize in front of the press gallery has been preserved through the device of "supply" days.

The greatest weakness of current practices is that policies and programmes continue to be looked at piecemeal, usually on a short-term basis, and rarely in conjunction or comparison with each other. Most committees fail to study policy changes implicit in the annual Estimates, to assess the success of departments in attaining policy objectives, or to investigate the administrative efficiency of departments in any thorough or systematic fashion. Members are presently not prepared to do the hard, dull, grinding work of scrutinizing the Estimates. Attendance at committee meetings devoted to the Estimates is usually lower than for bills or general investigations. This lack of enthusiasm for the scrutiny function is partly caused by the handicaps under which the committees work. All the Estimates are tabled at the same time. The rush to study them and report before the deadline dates means that many committees are meeting simultaneously. Members find it impossible to attend all the hearings on the Estimates that interest them or affect their constituency. Ministerial attendance is usually limited to several hours and public servants are prohibited from answering policy questions, so that the time available for policy discussions is limited.

I disagree with the statement that the Estimates provide an opportunity for committees "to investigate any aspect of a department's activities and often areas that are not covered by the department's activities." In theory, the committees are expected to limit their attention to the financial basis of departmental operations and the government has used this doctrine on occasion to restrain the committees. On April 10, 1974, Mr. G.W. Baldwin quoted in the House part of a letter written by the parliamentary secretary to the government House Leader and sent to all committee chairmen. It read in part:

> For your information and guidance please note that reports from standing committees dealing with estimates should consist of approval, reduction or elimination of estimates only. Reports of a substantive nature, including recommendations on items relating to or contained in the estimates, are clearly not allowed. In carrying out your responsibilities vis-à-vis the committees' consideration of estimates, please try to ensure that this principle is at all times maintained.[4]

Another problem is that members do not have the benefit of the departmental studies that support spending decisions. Frequent changes in the format of the Estimates in recent years mean that members have difficulty using the so-called "Blue Book." The presentation of Estimates seems more designed to meet certain accounting principles than to assist the M.P. in understanding government spending. For example, under the PPB format of Estimates' presentation a great amount of detail on spending has been lost. In theory this should raise the sights of the M.P. from the trivial and parochial to the broad issues involved in government spending. In fact, the details were often " the indispensable handles" that M.P.'s used to come to grips with a $40 billion-plus budget. Moreover, specifics and details are what concern constituents on whose behalf members attempt to raise matters on the Estimates.

The pell-mell pace of the committees in March, April and May gives members little time to prepare, digest and reflect upon the information which is available. Reports to the House are prepared in haste. Usually they consist of nothing more than a short statement recommending the approval of the Estimates. Not surprisingly, these reports have seldom occasioned a House debate.

This process may be educational for some members as John Reid suggests. Through it they may be introduced to some of the mysteries of the modern budgetary process, but the House of Commons plays a negligible role in scrutinizing, influencing and restraining government expenditures. The fundamental question we must ask is whether the House of Commons is any longer capable of assessing the "economy" and "efficiency" of governmental operations. My own view is that the notion of an annual pre-audit of *all* government spending is beyond the capacity of the House, no matter how many committees are established or how well staffed such committees are.

General Inquiries

I agree with John Reid that the most promising area for greater backbench influence is through general inquiries focused perhaps on government white

---

[4] *Debates,* April 10, 1974, p. 1319.

papers or green papers. Committees and individual members obviously feel freer to criticize the government when they are considering discussion papers or conducting studies in areas where an official government policy has not been declared. A number of committees have attempted to use their hearings as a means of increasing citizen involvement in the policy process, but their success has been limited.

Consistent with the model of the Commons outlined above, I would like to see more annual reports of departments referred to the committees. Then the committees could select freely which aspect of departmental operations they wished to investigate and they would be freed of the time constraints and the financial focus which characterizes their studies based upon the Estimates. The government would likely object to such a suggestion because it would take time away from the committees' more routine work on bills and estimates. The government believes that already too little time of the committees is devoted to government business. There may be some merit in their complaint when one considers that in the third Session of the 28th Parliament, by my calculations, 29 percent of the committees' time was spent on legislation; 38 percent of their time was spent on financial business (estimates and public accounts), and 33 percent was spent on general inquiries. Since the government receives more political credit for launching new programmes than for successfully administering established ones, there is always a temptation to cram more legislation into a normal session than can possibly be handled. "Politicians are, after all, more interested in takeoffs than in landings."

Suggestions for Reforms

Having suggested that private members — on both sides of the aisle — are frustrated by their incapacity to affect policy, let me turn to some suggestions for reforms that might improve their situation. Obviously it is not possible in the time available today to present a detailed plan for reform of the Commons. Also, I am conscious of the danger of making glib pronouncements about how the operations of the Commons could be improved. The various functions of the institution are interrelated so that changes in the procedure for performing one function can have a detrimental impact on other aspects of the Commons' operations.

Yet there is reason for some optimism about the prospect for institutional reform, once the next federal election is out of the way. In the last decade the House of Commons has witnessed more deliberate change in parliamentary organization and procedure than in any other period. Some of the reforms have served to improve the position of the backbench member. Partly because of the relative improvement in their situation, backbench pressures for further change will continue to exist. Any proposals for reform must be assessed not only in technical terms, but also in political terms, how they will affect the powers of government and opposition, and the frontbenches and the backbenches. To ignore the political context in which procedure is formulated is to ensure that good advice will often be ignored.

On the other hand, we should not worry exclusively about the immediate political acceptability of specific reforms. Many of the past improvements in the Commons' procedure, such as referral of Estimates to the committees, were once seen as heretical and dangerous. Fortunately, notions of what constitutes proper political practice change over time. In the time available, let me present some suggested reforms in "shopping list" fashion:

- the number and size of standing committees should vary according to the function performed by individual committees, but generally the committees should be reduced in size;
- there should be established a large forty-five member committee on public expenditures and economic policy that would serve to bring together in one forum the taxing and spending decisions of government for purposes of analysis and public discussion;
- a system of periodic recesses of the House should be established to enable committees to operate free of conflict with sittings of the House and to enable M.P.'s to keep in closer touch with their constituencies;
- chairmen of committees should be selected from a list of nominations from the whips of all parties in order to promote a more positive, co-operative attitude in the committees;
- committees should be granted the right to initiate studies by means of requests to the House;
- minority reports from committees should be officially allowed within Commons' procedure;
- opposition parties should be prepared to set aside perhaps five of their twenty-five supply days for purposes of debating reports of committees on estimates and general topics;
- committees should be granted a small annual budget to hire staff, up to perhaps five or ten members. In the event that a committee wished to undertake a major study, it could request funds for additional staff through a report to the House;
- in connection with bills, the government should attach an explanatory memorandum to each bill when it is introduced, preferably at the time of the Throne Speech. Such a memorandum would explain the origins (including interest groups that were consulted), purposes, main provisions, the type of regulations that are anticipated and the relationship of the bill to existing and forthcoming legislation;
- the financial basis for the consideration of government operations should be dropped. Reviews of departmental policies and programmes should be carried on by the standing committees through the vehicle of the annual reports of the departments. The task of scrutinizing estimates should be performed by subcommittees of the proposed new public expenditure committee;

- the office of the Auditor General should extend its role beyond that of a narrow accounting operation into the area of evaluation of the effectiveness of programs;
- a *Freedom of Information Act* should be passed and in return for the more expeditious passage of its legislative programme, the government should grant the Commons more insight into the internal workings of departments and programs.

This list of suggestions could be expanded, but I have already exposed myself to enough criticism. My own prognosis would be that future changes in parliamentary procedure will be incremental in character, both because of a desire by governments not to foster changes which would upset the existing political balance to their detriment and because of the difficulty of forecasting all the consequences of any change.

A BASIC BIBLIOGRAPHY

THE BACKBENCHER AND THE DISCHARGE OF LEGISLATIVE RESPONSIBILITIES

Aiken, Gordon. *The Backbencher*. Toronto: McClelland and Stewart Limited, 1974.

Bishop, P.V. "Restoring Parliament to Power." *Queen's Quarterly* 77 (Summer 1970): 149-56.

Blair, Ronald. "What Happens to Parliament." In Trevor Owen Lloyd and Jack McLeod, eds., *Agenda 1970*, pp. 217-40. Toronto: University of Toronto Press, 1968.

Black, E.R. and Cairns, A.C. "A Different Perspective on Canadian Federalism." *Canadian Public Administration* 9 (March 1966): 27-44.

Brownstone, M. "The Canadian System of Government in the Face of Modern Demands." *Canadian Public Administration* 11 (Winter 1968): 428-39.

Byers, R.B. "Perceptions of Parliamentary Surveillance of the Executive: The Case of Canadian Defence Policy." *Canadian Journal of Political Science* 5 (June 1972): 234-50.

Clarke, H.D. and Price, R.G. "A Note on Pre-Nomination Role Socialization of Freshman Members of Parliament." *Canadian Journal of Political Science* 10 (June 1977): 391-406.

Corry, J.A. "Adaptation of Parliamentary Processes to the Modern State." *Canadian Journal of Economics and Political Science* 20 (February 1954): 1-9.

Crossman, R.H.S. "Canadian Issues as Seen from Outside." In Gordon Hawkins, ed., *Order and Good Government*, pp. 139-43. Toronto: University of Toronto Press, 1965.

Fox, Paul, ed. *Politics: Canada*. Toronto: McGraw-Hill Ryerson, 1977.

Franks, C.E.S. "The Legislature and Responsible Government." In Norman Ward and Stafford Duff, eds., *Politics in Saskatchewan*, pp. 20-43. Toronto: Longman Canada, 1968.

Franks, C.E.S. "The Reform of Parliament." *Queen's Quarterly* 76 (Spring 1969): 113-17.

Fulton, D., Jewett, P. *et al.* "Parliament and the Public." In Gordon Hawkins, ed., *Order and Good Government*, pp. 43-90. Toronto: University of Toronto Press, 1965.

Hanson, A.H. and Wiseman, H.V. "The Use of Committees by the House of Commons." *Public Law* (Autumn 1959): 277.

Hockin, T.A. *Government in Canada*. New York: Norton, 1975.

Jackson, R.J. and Atkinson, Michael M. *The Canadian Legislative System*. Toronto: Macmillan, 1974.

Jewett, P. "The Reform of Parliament." *Journal of Canadian Studies* 1 (November 1966): 11-16.

Kornberg, Allan. *Canadian Legislative Behaviour: A Study of the 25th Parliament*. New York: Holt, Rinehart and Winston, 1967.

Kornberg, Allan. "Parliament in Canadian Society." In A. Kornberg, L.A. Musolf, *et al.*, eds., *Legislatures in Developmental Perspective*. Durham, N.C.: Duke University Press, 1970.

Kornberg, Allan. "The Rules of the Game in the Canadian House of Commons." *Journal of Politics* 26 (May 1964): 358-80.

Kornberg, Allan. "The Social Bases of Leadership in a Canadian House of Commons." *Australian Journal of Politics and History* 11 (December 1965): 324-34.

Kornberg, Allan and Thomas, Norman C. "Representative Democracy and Political Elites in Canada and the United States." *Parliamentary Affairs* 19 (1966): 91-102.

Landry, P. "The Future of the Canadian Speakership." *The Parliamentarian* 53 (April 1972): 113-17.

Landry, P. "Procedural Reform in the Canadian House of Commons." *The Parliamentarian* 50 (April 1969): 155-57.

Lloyd, Trevor. "The Reform of Parliamentary Proceedings." In A. Rotstein, ed., *The Prospect of Change: Proposals for Canada's Future*, pp. 23-39. Toronto: McGraw-Hill, 1965.

Lovinck, J.A. "Parliamentary Reform and Governmental Effectiveness in Canada." *Canadian Public Administration*, 16 (Spring 1973): 35-54.

Lovinck, J.A. "Who Wants Parliamentary Reform?" *Queen's Quarterly* 79 (Winter 1972): 502-13.

Mallory, J.R. *Structure of Canadian Government*. Toronto: Macmillan, 1971.

March, Roman R. *The Myth of Parliament*. Scarborough: Prentice-Hall, 1974.

Matheson, W.A. *The Prime Minister and the Cabinet*. Toronto: Methuen, 1976.

Meisel, John. *Working Papers on Canadian Politics*. Montreal: McGill-Queen's University Press, 1972.

Ontario. Select Committee on the Legislature. *Reports, Vols. 1-5*. Toronto: Queen's Printer, 1973-1975.

Power, C.G., Michener, D.R., *et al.* "Focus on Parliament." *Queen's Quarterly* 63 (Winter 1957): 478-573.

Punnett, R.M. *The Prime Minister in Canadian Government and Politics*. Toronto: Macmillan, 1977.

Robertson, R.G. "The Canadian Parliament and Cabinet in the Face of Modern Demands." *Canadian Public Administration* 11 (Fall 1968): 272-79.

Roche, Douglas J. *The Human Side of Politics*. Toronto: Clarke, Irwin, 1976.

Smith, Denis. "President and Parliament: The Transformation of Parliamentary Government in Canada." In Thomas A. Hockin, ed., *Apex of Power*, pp. 224-41. Scarborough: Prentice-Hall, 1971.

Stewart, John B. *The Canadian House of Commons: Procedure and Reform*. Montreal: McGill-Queen's University Press, 1977.

Thorburn, H.G. "Parliament and Policy-Making: The Case of the Trans-Canada Gas Pipeline." *Canadian Journal of Economics and Political Science* 23 (November 1957): 516-31.

Van Loon, R.J. "The Frustrating Role of the Ottawa Backbencher." *Globe & Mail,* April 5, 1971.

Van Loon, R.J. and Whittington, M.S. *The Canadian Political System,* 2nd ed. Toronto: McGraw-Hill, 1976.

Chapter Six

Lobbying and Interest Group Representation in the Legislative Process

by
*W.T. Stanbury**

I. INTRODUCTION

The Ubiquity of Lobbying

In a democratic pluralist society interest group representation or, less euphemistically, lobbying, is a ubiquitous activity. Berry points out that "the act of lobbying is, in very general terms, an act of representation. . . . An interest group is an intermediary between citizens and their government. . . . "[1] The leaders of important interest groups in Canada "assume a critical role in formulating the claims of their various constituencies and hammering out an accommodation among such claims with political elites." Such representatives play "direct, continuous and active roles in the Canadian political apparatus."[2] Van Loon and Whittington emphasize the ubiquitous nature of interest group activity:

> Interest groups are active everywhere in Canadian politics. The industry-financed Canadian Tax Foundation criticizes and examines the whole financial structure of government in Canada. The Canadian Bar Association often works closely with the Federal Department of Justice and various provincial attorneys-general. Nationality associations are vital to the operation of the Department of Manpower and Immigration. The commercial banks work hand in hand with the Bank of Canada. At times, the Canadian Federation of Agriculture appears to be almost an extension of various departments of agriculture. Federal and provincial Departments of Labour work very closely with labour unions. The tie-in between the Canadian Medical Association (and its provincial constituents) and the various departments of health hardly requires highlighting. The list could be multiplied endlessly. Wherever government turns its hand, there it will

---

* Associate Professor and Chairman, Policy Analysis Division, Faculty of Commerce and Business Administration, University of British Columbia and Director, Regulation and Government Intervention Program, Institute for Research on Public Policy. The author wishes to acknowledge the most valuable comments of Dr. Frederick Thompson, Visiting Associate Professor, Faculty of Commerce and Business Administration, University of British Columbia.

[1] Jeffrey M. Berry, *Lobbying for the People* (Princeton, N.J.: Princeton University Press, 1977), p. 5.
[2] Robert Presthus, *Elite Accommodation in Canadian Politics* (Toronto: Macmillan, 1973), pp. 8-9.

find some kind of organized group operating — and wherever groups operate they find that government activities overlap their own.[3]

McKie's study of 176 Ontario-based companies with more than 100 employees conducted in 1971 and 1972 found that 70 percent of the firms used an interest group to approach government and that 61 percent "of the senior executives of the companies hold or have held executive office in an interest group, a position which might be expected to entail a spokesman role."[4] Only 27 percent of the senior executives reported appearing before a legislative committee; 33 percent reported "regular direct contact with government"; and 29 percent were members of a government advisory board or commission. Forty-six such boards were mentioned.[5] In the case of large firms (those with more than 500 employees, n = 97), 38 percent of the executives reported appearances before a legislative committee, 41 percent reported regular direct contact with government and 40 percent of the senior executives were members of a government advisory board or committee.

More recently, a sample of 703 Canadian firms indicated that just over one-half the firms engaged in "communications with political leaders" or "communications with civil servants" at the federal level. Forty-two percent of the firms made individual representations to federal government departments, boards and commissions.[6] The proportion of large firms (over 500 employees) which made individual representations to the federal government was almost twice as large (55.8 percent vs. 28.2 percent) as for small firms.[7]

Although he provides no documentation in support of his estimate, Robert Lewis[8] asserts:

Lobbying in Ottawa is a $100 million-a-year industry that assumes various guises: associations permanently on guard for the special interests of their clients,[9] hired guns on special assignment and *ad hoc* groups who gear up for a specific legislative fight. If Canadians wonder why politicians never seem to listen to them, the reason is that official

[3] R.J. Van Loon and M.S. Whittington, *The Canadian Political System,* 2 ed. (Toronto: McGraw-Hill Ryerson, 1970), p. 286.

[4] Craig McKie, "Some Views on Canadian Corporatism," in C. Beattie and S. Crysdale, eds., *Sociology Canada: Reader,* 2d ed. (Toronto: Butterworth, 1977), p. 231.

[5] *Ibid.,* p. 231.

[6] Institute for Political Involvement, *A Report on the Prospects for Increased Involvement of Business People in the Canadian Political System* (Etobicoke: 1978), p. 5.

[7] *Ibid.,* p. 6.

[8] Robert Lewis, "The Hidden Persuaders: Guns Don't Make Laws, but Gun Lobbies Damn Well Do," *Maclean's,* June 13, 1977, pp. 40b, c, h, i.

[9] Lewis states, "There is even what amounts to a lobby of lobbyists, the Institute of Association Executives . . . [with] 1200 members . . . IAE's membership is one of the few clues to the size of the Ottawa lobby: its 'chapter' in the capital has 304 members" (Lewis, *op.cit.*, p. 40i). Baxter found 135 interest groups listed in the Ottawa telephone directory in 1975 (Clive Baxter, "Lobbying — Ottawa's Fast-Growing Business," in Paul W. Fox, ed., *Politics: Canada,* 4th ed. (Toronto: McGraw-Hill Ryerson, 1977), pp. 206-10). Blunn states, "There are probably 200 associations, firms and individuals who practice the art [of lobbying]" (Ron Blunn, "The Lobbyists: They're Discreet, Don't Twist Arms and Affect Almost All of Ottawa's Rules," *Financial Times of Canada,* January 30, 1978).

Ottawa is too busy heeding special pleaders to hear the unorganized . . . lobbying is the fourth — occasionally the senior — arm of government.

Definitions

It is useful at the outset to define what is meant by an interest or a pressure group and by the term lobbying. Truman defines an interest group in very broad terms. In his view it is "any group that, on the basis of one or more shared attitudes, makes certain claims upon other groups in the society for the establishment, maintenance, or enhancement of forms of behavior that are implied by the shared attitudes."[10] Much of the activity of interest groups is directed toward governments with a view to influencing public policy. This point is emphasized by Pross when he states, "pressure groups are organizations whose members act together to influence public policy to promote their common interest."[11] Lobbying is a general term describing the specific activities associated with influencing the actors in the public policy process.[12] Nadel states, "The term originally referred to those seeking special favors from the government by huddling with legislators in the lobbies of Congress and state legislatures; it was in general use by the 1830s."[13] The term probably originated in Great Britain where it referred to the activities of individuals seeking to influence members of the House of Commons in the lobbies outside the Chamber itself. Milbrath defines lobbying as "the stimulation and transmission of a communication, by someone other than a citizen acting on his own behalf, directed to a governmental decision maker with the hope of influencing his decision."[14] More pungently, Lewis states, "If politics is the art of the possible, lobbying is the art of greasing the skids to make the possible probable."[15]

Stephen Duncan[16] raises the obvious question, "What is a lobbyist?" He then tries to answer it by asking more questions:

Is a Toronto comporate executive who bends the ear of a visiting cabinet minister, or MP, lobbying? . . . Is he a lobbyist if he flies to Ottawa to do the same thing? Is a consultant in Ottawa lobbying if he phones a civil servant, or just seeks information? If the civil servant phones the consultant for reaction to a proposed policy change, is that lobbying? From the

[10] David Truman, *The Governmental Process* (New York: Alfred A. Knopf, 1951), p. 33.
[11] A. Paul Pross, ed., *Pressure Group Behaviour in Canadian Politics* (Toronto: McGraw-Hill Ryerson, 1975), p. 2.
[12] Truman states, "Virtually all groups are pressure groups. The group pursues its interests by organizing its members to exert their concerted power on those who can help them or hurt them. The targets of pressure groups may be individuals, other groups or the state" (Truman, *op.cit.* p. 454).
[13] Mark V. Nadel, *Corporations and Political Accountability* (Lexington, Mass.: D.C. Heath, 1976), p. 43. Nadel quotes a letter from James Buchanan to Franklin Pierce in 1852: "The host of contractors, speculators, stock-jobbers and lobby members which haunt the halls of Congress all desirous . . . on any and every pretext to get their arms into the public treasury are sufficient to alarm every friend of his country. Their progress must be arrested" (p. 43).
[14] Lester Milbrath, *The Washington Lobbyists* (Chicago: Rand McNally, 1963), p. 8.
[15] Lewis, *op. cit.,* p. 40i.
[16] Stephen Duncan, "MP's Bothered — But Stymied — By Lobbyists," *Financial Post,* February 19, 1977, p. 7.

MP's point of view: when does assistance to constituents become activity on behalf of a lobbyist.[17]

As we shall indicate in Part IV of this paper, interest group representation or lobbying can take a wide variety of forms: the presentation of a brief to a minister or parliamentary committee, informal meetings/telephone conversations with civil servants, M.P.'s or members of the Cabinet or a mass media campaign of paid advertisements aimed at showing support for or opposition to a particular policy. The Canadian preference is for the informal, unrecorded meeting with senior civil servants (policy advisers) and/or members of the Cabinet.[18]

Structure of the Paper

Part II of the paper examines some of the explanations why lobbying or interest group representation is an inevitable part of any democratic system. Part III looks at the pluralist ideal and the reasons for its failures in practice. In Part IV, we advance a framework for the analysis of interest group activity in Canada. It focuses our attention on the targets, vehicles and timing of lobbying. Finally, Part V presents a case study of lobbying activity: the attempts to reform Canadian competition policy between 1966 and 1978.

---

[17] Duncan (p. 3) quotes Progressive Conservative House Leader Walter Baker, who has introduced a private member's bill aimed at the disclosure of lobbying activity, as saying the definition of a lobbyist centres on a consultant "whose principal function is to lobby on behalf of others . . . not those whose occupation is administrative or whatever, but who occasionally must defend their interest by contract with politicians or officials." U.S. legislators have been struggling with the same problem recently. Attempts to reform the *Regulation of Lobbying Act* passed in 1946 have been before the Senate Government Operations Committee for over two years. On June 9, 1975 *Business Week* (p. 98) editorialized, "Under their proposal, the regulations would not only apply to anyone whose job involved lobbying as a substantial purpose. They would also extend to anyone who spent more than $250 a quarter or $500 a year 'to influence the policymaking process' and to anyone who talked, on separate occasions, to eight employees of Congress or the executive branch.

This definition could cover half the population of the District of Columbia, not to mention busloads of bird watchers, businessmen looking for government contracts, and schoolboys demanding a pamphlet on how to raise white mice.

Everyone covered would have to file detailed reports each quarter on expenditures, on communications with government agencies, and on the policy decisions he seeks to influence. The resulting deluge of paperwork would be so great that it would frustrate the true purpose of the bill: to make the activities of professional lobbyists an easily accessible part of a public record.

The reformers should narrow their definition of lobbyist to exclude the citizen who simply wants to exercise his constitutional right to tell his government what he thinks."

A year later, a *Business Week* (May 24, 1976, p. 110) stated: "The Senate Government Operations Committee, however, has gone back to the drawing board and produced a more workable law. The bill it is now proposing puts the emphasis on the organization that sponsors a lobbying effort rather than on the individual. Any organization with paid officers, directors, or employees would come under the act if it paid $250 or more per quarter for someone to do its lobbying or if it made 12 or more oral approaches to Congress during the quarter. Moreover, any organization that spent $7,500 or more encouraging others to write or call congressmen would have to register and report its activities. This would throw a healthy light on the carefully contrived letter-writing campaigns that masquerade as 'grass roots' reactions."

[18] See the discussion of "vehicles" in Part IV below.

II. LOBBYING: AN INEVITABLE PART OF A DEMOCRATIC SYSTEM

Why is interest group representation an inherent part of the political system, more narrowly, the legislative process?

First, we live in an interdependent society. Our individual actions and those of our governments make waves which rock (and occasionally swamp) other people's boats. There is a need to actively communicate to other actors (particularly to those with the power to effect decisions) in the political system the actual and potential implications of previous public policy decisions and proposed policy actions. Decision makers *need* to know the potential outcomes of the policy alternatives arrayed before them if they are to choose rationally. No one sitting in Ottawa, Toronto, Victoria or Halifax can predict with much accuracy how a policy action will affect those remote from the centre. Interest group representation can provide accurate and valuable information or expertise not available inside the government. Former federal Minister Donald Macdonald has stated:

> In the process of preparing legislation and also in considering general policy changes, the government requires as much information as possible about the areas to be affected and the possible implications of any proposed changes.[19]

In many cases it *is* necessary (in the jargon of the advertising trade) to "run it up the flagpole and see who salutes" — or howls in disgust.[20] Failure to consult with the relevant interest groups may result in counterproductive outcomes unanticipated by the decision makers. This is not to say policy makers should accept all the claims made by such groups.

Second, a democratic society moves by persuasion, not force. The quality of public decisions depends on two important factors: their technical or analytical sophistication *and* the level of acceptance the decision enjoys among the persons most affected by it. Lobbying is an attempt to influence public policy by persuasion. Blunn[21] quotes Conservative House Leader Walter Baker as saying:

---

[19] As cited in J.E. Anderson, "Pressure Groups and the Canadian Bureaucracy," in Kenneth Kernaghan, ed., *Public Administration in Canada: Selected Readings,* 3d ed. (Toronto: Methuen, 1977), p. 297.

[20] Gordon Sharwood, a prominent Liberal and then president of Acres Limited, has commented on this process in a speech given in 1972: "Trudeau has .. adopted a curious method of introducing new policy. A minister (such as Basford, with his Competition Act, or Benson, with his tax policy, or Herb Gray, with his foreign ownership report, or Kierans, with Communications) is invited to initiate a program, is given no obvious support by Cabinet or Prime Minister and is sent out to "play in the street." If he comes back alive, we have a massive new government initiative; if he does not, Trudeau withdraws the initiative and the minister concerned may not survive.

Even if we disregard the question of fairness to the minister involved, this method of introducing policy warrants criticism for its failure to involve major interest groups in the early stages of policy formation. A small task force is delegated with the responsibility of preparing a report with recommendations for the inception of new policy.

The resulting proposals have often turned out to be impractical, illiberal and immoderate. Regardless of the extent to which concessions are granted before final legislation is passed, the climate of hostility that invariably follows such proposals is not conducive to cooperation. It also has a disturbing impact on the market mechanism" (as cited in W.T. Stanbury, *Business Interests and the Reform of Canadian Competition Policy, 1971-1975* (Toronto: Carswell/Methuen, 1977), pp. 201-2.

[21] Blunn, *op. cit.*

" . . . lobbyists do exert a lot of influence in Ottawa. Their power comes not from force, threat, or even size, but primarily through the art of persuasion."

Blunn also quotes the president of the Automobile Parts Manufacturers' Association of Canada as distinguishing between acceptable and unacceptable forms of lobbying: "About 95% or so of the lobbying done in Ottawa is above board, helpful to the government and brings about better legislation for all Canadians."

True, not all the information supplied by interest groups is correct. Some "facts" are not facts. In other words, one must recognize the propaganda element in the process. But compared to the stronger forms of influence, most lobbying seems to be part of the democratic process. The right to petition one's government for the redress of wrongs is strongly entrenched. Regrettably, the modern manifestation is that of an ombudsman defending the individual *against* the government.

Third, the growth of government has, itself, been a cause of increased lobbying activity. As intervention increases (in the form of taxes, expenditures and regulations) more individuals and groups feel the need to influence the nature and direction of government policy. Blunn argues that the amount of lobbying in Ottawa has increased in recent years. He quotes a lobbyist as follows:

> "A few years ago we spent about 10% to 15% of our time dealing with Ottawa," says Robin Palin, public affairs officer for the Canadian Electrical Association. "I don't know what the figure would be now, but it's a lot higher and it will continue to increase.
>
> Government decisions affect us a lot more than 10 or even five years ago, and so we've got to be able to affect those decisions ourselves as much as possible."[22]

If a person is to be subject to public policy it is not surprising that he or she would want to participate in its formation. The extent and nature of public participation in the political process has changed:

> The emergence of the public participation movement is one of the hallmarks of the past decade. This development represents a sharp departure from traditional patterns of social and political activity in Canada. Since Confederation, public participation has meant a visit to the polling booth at election time. Beyond the ballot box, it was superficially expressed in the political lobbies of vested interest groups and more solidly founded on a tradition of voluntary involvement in community development. But *genuine* public participation, in the sense of individuals and groups sharing in the formative stages of decisions which affect them, was largely absent and unrequested. The ground swell for this new ethic came with the social activism of the sixties. In its early form, public participation was reactive, concerned with battling development schemes which had adverse environmental and social impacts. The role of adversary groups in challenging city hall and other bureaucratic structures continues as a major element of the field, but public participation also appears to be becoming a more integral part of government decision-making. This role is especially evident in the arena of environmental management and is embodied in a considerable amount of policy and legislation. As a result, David Lowenthal claims that no decisions can now safely be made in this field

---

[22] *Ibid.*

without feeling the popular pulse. This assessment underlines the impressive advances which have been made over a very short span of time.[23]

Schultze[24] suggests that as government intervention increases, interest group bargaining over the terms of such direct intervention becomes an alternative to the allocation of goods and services by market forces (accompanied by indirect intervention). Blunn points out the symbiotic nature of the relationship between civil servants and lobbyists:

> The fact is, most senior civil servants welcome lobbyists with open arms.
> As an official in the Department of Transport puts it, "We're often as anxious to meet them as they are us. On any important policy matter it's vital that we get industry's ideas and criticisms. If we don't understand what they say and why, we only open ourselves up to trouble later on."[25]

Governments themselves have been the creators of "enforced consultation." The public policy process now requires formal cooperation or at least consultation with a larger number of actual or potential interest groups both within the government and without. Everybody must be consulted. Proposed policies/decisions must be "cleared" with a wider circle of stakeholders. Kaufman[26] points out that this trend in policy making has contributed to the commonly perceived problem of excessive "red tape."

Fourth, reasonable notions of efficiency in government require the grouping or aggregation of individual interests. A thousand voices, even saying the same thing, are not as intelligible as one person speaking on behalf of the group. Clarity of signals requires fewer speakers making representations in an organized fashion. It is interesting that business interests in Canada currently feel there are too many voices claiming to speak for business. In a recent *Financial Post* story, Worth quotes the head of a Toronto-based multinational as saying, "The fragmentation of business groups across the country has what amounts to a lot of disjointed babbling. We just aren't talking effectively to governments or the people any more."[27] A Halifax executive is quoted as saying,

> The system of business representation through the traditional channel — the Canadian Chamber of Commerce, Canadian Manufacturers' Association and other business groups — has simply broken down.[28] The national organizations can't be all things to all people.

---

[23] John Amatt and Barry Sadler, "Background to the Bibliography," in *Public Participation: A General Bibliography and Annotated Review of the Canadian Experience,* prepared for the Canadian Conference on Public Participation, Banff, Alberta, October 4-7, 1977. (Footnotes have been omitted).

[24] Charles L. Schultze, *The Public Use of Private Interest* (Washington, D.C.: Brookings, 1977).

[25] Blunn, *op. cit.*

[26] Herbert Kaufman, *Red Tape: Its Origins, Uses and Abuses* (Washington, D.C.: Brookings, 1977).

[27] Roger Worth, "Blue Ribbon Group Will Make the Case for Business," *Financial Post,* April 30, 1977, p. 7.

[28] A dissenting view would be registered by Harold Crosby, president of the Canadian Chamber of Commerce. Speaking of his organization, the Canadian Manufacturers' Association, the Business Council on National Issues and the Canadian Federation of Independent Business, Crosby has stated: "All these national organizations have a vital role to play in making government aware of the needs of the business community. Of all these groups, however, I believe the Canadian Chamber of Commerce [which has nearly 3000 corporate members] draws together the widest spectrum of interests, and in that sense, can claim to speak with the broadest mandate on behalf of the private sector overall" *(Financial Post,* Sept. 17, 1977, p. 24).

Its impossible, for example to represent big business and small, the multinationals and the corner-store merchants — to say nothing of fundamental regional differences.[29]

One of the principal forces seeking to reduce the multiplicity of voices in a given interest area has been government. Ministers and senior bureaucrats like to "keep things simple" and avoid cognitive dissonance from what they feel should be a fairly homogeneous entity. Fewer voices and fewer groups simplify the proccess of consultation and the aggregation of interest group preferences.

M.W. Bucovetsky points out that interest groups can perform the function of obtaining goal-consensus — so necessary to a government unit's growth. He states:

> The symbiotic relationship between government agencies and their clientele is a well-known administrative phenomenon. In particular, the effective functioning and growth of a government bureau depends on its having a strong goal-consensus. The more homogeneous a bureau's clientele and the more clearly defined the clientele's interests, the more it will be to the bureau's own advantage to adopt goals that are harmonious.[30]

Government departments have also funded, sponsored and supported the creation of organized interest groups where none existed. As Pross indicates, "it is not unusual for Canadian governments to create pressure groups in order to foster relations with 'special publics' and to promote a demand for policies which particular departments are anxious to adopt".[31]

Fifth, elected representatives seem to be unable to provide adequate representation for the variety of interests (many conflicting) even within their own geographic constituency. They simply cannot inform themselves well

---

[29] Worth, *op. cit.*, p. 7. William D. Archbold, President and Executive Director of the Business Council on National Issues (an organization comprised of 125 chief executive officers of large Canadian corporations), in describing the reasons for forming BCNI in 1976 stated, "It was apparent that effective participation in the policy formation process required the *coordinated* presentation of carefully substantiated positive recommendations in readily understood terms." (William D. Archbold, "Business Council on National Issues: A New Factor in Business Communication," *Canadian Business Review* 4, no. 2, 1977: 13-15). For more detail on BCNI see Patricia Anderson, "CEO's Only, Big Business Lines Up Its Ottawa Lobby," *Financial Times of Canada,* February 21, 1977, pp. 1, 10, 12. Referring to "the diversity of views of which the [Financial] Post and others observe," A.R. McMurrich, president of the Board of Trade of Metropolitan Toronto stated that such perceptions are accurate, "because business in our society is a kaleidoscope, as diverse in its problems and aspirations as the country itself . . . But while business in the generic sense covers a multitude of interests within the private sector, there is a single theology where there is not one collective voice-free enterprise; the carrier of economic advancement for all Canadians in all regions of this diverse country." ("The Voice of Business," *Journal of the Board of Trade of Metropolitan Toronto,* Christmas 1976, p. 9).

[30] M.W. Bucovetsky, "The Mining Industry and the Great Tax Reform Debate," in A. Paul Pross, ed., *Pressure Group Behaviour in Canadian Politics* (Toronto: McGraw-Hill Ryerson, 1975), p. 107.

[31] A. Paul Pross, ed., *Pressure Group Behaviour in Canadian Politics, op. cit.,* p. 19.
Hannam, the first president of the Canadian Federation of Agriculture, indicates how the then Deputy Minister of Finance, Clifford Clark, informally suggested the establishment of a national farm organization and he used Clark's prestige to enlist support for the organization of the Federation (H.H. Hannam, "The Interest Group and Its Activities," Institute of Public Administration of Canada, *Proceedings of the Fifth Annual Conference,* 1953, pp. 172-73). Anderson states, "The Canadian Drug Manufacturers' Association was organized upon the suggestion of a civil servant and acted as a rival to the long established Pharmaceutical Manufacturers Association of Canada." (J.E. Anderson, *op. cit.,* p. 297). See also S.D. Clark, *The Canadian Manufacturers' Association* (Toronto: University of Toronto Press, 1939), pp. 48-49; and R. Manzer, "Selective Inducements and the Development of Pressure Groups: The Case of the Canadian Teachers' Association," *Canadian Journal of Political Science* 2, no. 1(1969): 103-17.

enough of the various interests/concerns and they have insufficient time to articulate those interests. One might also argue that individual backbenchers — particularly those in the opposition — have limited effectiveness in the legislative process. Given that individuals play multiple roles (worker/executive, consumer/producer, etc.), it is not surprising that existence of multiple interests requires multiple representation. Lobbying by organized interest groups, although not provided for in the Constitution, is almost a parallel form of representative government. Writing forty years ago Clark concluded,

> Cutting across the boundaries of constituencies and provinces to give representation to groups organized upon the basis of common interests, the lobbyists express, more completely than Members of Parliament, the diversified needs of the national community.[32]

If interest groups are to constitute an informal ''estates general,'' we might be concerned that they are not subject to the panoply of written and unwritten rules within which traditionally elected representatives operate. Interest group representation is a shadow form of representation.

For these and other reasons it is time we looked more carefully at both the process and outcomes of interest group representation. Canadians are somewhat naive both about how lobbying works and the impact it can have in some cases. Recently, columnist Marjorie Nichols has pointed out,

> Lobbying is (or can be) an honourable profession. It is often useful to the lawmakers to solicit expert information and opinion from [lobbyists].
>
> The difficulty is that there is a reluctance on the part of this government to concede that Ottawa has a lobby industry and that, given the influence over the operations of government by these lobbies, perhaps some effort should be made to identify them.[33]

Our attitude toward lobbying in the Canadian legislative process can be likened to that toward sex. At one and the same time they are perceived as healthy and natural acts, and they are also seen as embarrasing or slightly taboo activities to be removed from polite conversation. Both forms of prudery seem to be on the wane, but our inability to come to terms with lobbying seems greater than it is with respect to sex.

III. THE PLURALIST IDEAL AND INTEREST GROUP REPRESEN-TATION

The Pluralist Ideal

Interest groups and their representational activity are at the heart of the pluralist ideal. The interest group is the means by which individuals are able to achieve their individual objectives and communicate their values to other

---

[32] S.D. Clark, ''The Canadian Manufacturers' Association,'' *Canadian Journal of Economics and Political Science* 4 (1938): 505-23.

[33] Marjorie Nichols, ''Lobbying: Ottawa's Growth Industry,'' Vancouver *Sun*. January 29, 1977, p. 4.

individuals, groups and governments. As a political ideal, pluralism is concerned with the diffusion of power among a wide variety of competing interests, with multiple sources of initiative for both private and public policy and with the recognition that each individual is the locus of a complex set of overlapping and conflicting loyalties and roles. In the pluralist conception of the political process, the State is given the task of assisting in the resolution of conflict through the facilitation of bargaining, negotiation and compromise. Blaisdell points out, ''Theoretically, pressure groups compete with each other on equal terms, have equal bargaining power, with none enjoying an advantage over the other.''[34] Citizens, when aggrieved, make use of the right of petition and mobilize opinion. The state defines the rules of competition, and its executive rewards the rightful winner. Latham indicates that the legislature ''referees the group struggles, ratifies the victories of the successful coalitions and records the terms of the surrenders, compromises and conquests in the form of statutes.''[35] Neil Jacoby urges interest groups to assert their claims. ''In a pluralistic society, every institution has a right — if not a duty — to do what it can to survive. Pressure upon government for this purpose is a legitimate expression of a fundamental drive.''[36]

The Failures of Political Markets

Canadian political scientist D.C. Corbett claims that ''It goes without saying . . . that pressure groups are a natural phenomenon in social life, and that their abundance and vigour is the special glory of democratic life.''[37] Lowi is not so sure. He argues that we have elevated the pressure group ''from power to ideal.''[38] In general we have been more concerned with the imperfections and failures in economic markets than we have in ''political markets.'' If economic markets break down because of the existence of public goods (in the technical sense), externalities, indivisibilities and natural monopoly, why should we be surprised that the markets (forums is a better word) for political activity are immune from similar diseases. In practice, the pluralist ideal is not achieved. In terms of interest group representation, significant market failure is present.

---

[34] Donald J. Blaisdell, assisted by Jane Greverus, *Economic Power and Political Pressure*, Monograph no. 26, TNEC (Washington, D.C.: Government Printing Office, 1941), p. 13.

[35] Earl Latham, *The Group Basis of Politics* (Ithaca, N.Y.: Cornell University Press, 1952), p. 35.

[36] Neil H. Jacoby, *Corporate Power and Social Responsibility* (New York: Macmillan, 1973), p. 150. See also John T. Bart, ''The Duty to Lobby,'' *Financial Times of Canada*, May 16, 1977, p. 11.

[37] D.C. Corbett, ''The Pressure Group and the Public Interest,'' Institute of Public Administration of Canada, *Proceedings of the Fifth Annual Conference, 1953*, reprinted in J.E. Hodgetts and D.C. Corbett, eds., *Canadian Public Administration* (Toronto: Macmillan, 1960), p. 455.

[38] Theodore J. Lowi, *The End of Liberalism* (New York: Norton, 1969), p. 74.

(a) All Interests Not Represented

Not all significant interests manage to get organized and to compete actively for a say in the formation of public policy. While Truman[39] recognized the existence of unorganized interests, he argued that such interests would be protected and advanced by both elected and appointed officials at all levels of government. However, the idea that government will represent the unrepresented is at variance with reality. Professor Milton Rakove has remarked:

> The theory of democratic politics is that people are elected to deal with public interests. But once they get into office, they realize that the only way to stay there is by appealing to private interests at the expense of public interests.[40]

Daniel Bell reminds us that there are two special requirements for equity in ''a representative republic.''[41] First, all interests must be represented, and second, all issues must be viewed as a negotiable. Real world pluralism satisfies neither requirement.

In general, producer interests dominate consumer interests and the intensely felt interests of the few become well articulated relative to the more diffuse interests of the many. Power grows out of the ability to mobilize vocal political support in such a way that the cost to the effective coalition of decision makers of resisting the pressures of the interest group are greater than those of acceding to its demands.

As Dahl reminds us,

> The making of governmental decisions is not a majestic march of great majorities united upon certain matters of basic policy. It is the steady appeasement of relatively small groups. Even when these groups add up to a numerical majority at election time, it is usually not useful to construe that majority as any more than an arithmetic expression.[42]

Even if the interests of a larger number of individuals are threatened by the actions of government in response to the pressures of the organized interest groups, we seldom see a ''countervailing'' force come into existence. Yet the conventional interest group theory of politics holds that ''any interest seriously threatened by a proposed policy could force supporters of the policy to bargain with it and make substantial concessions.''[43] This idea has been properly branded by Schubert as ''a vague but fervent transcendentalism.''[44]

---

[39] Truman, *op. cit.*

[40] As cited in William Grieder, ''A Little Bit of Money Makes the Politics Go Down,'' Vancouver *Sun,* January 4, 1977, p. 5.

[41] Daniel Bell, ''The Revolution of 'Public Entitlements','' *Fortune* (April 1975), p. 185.

[42] Robert Dahl, *A Preface to Democratic Theory* (Chicago: University of Chicago Press, 1956), p. 146.

[43] James Q. Wilson, ''The Politics of Regulation,'' in James W. McKee, ed., *Social Responsibility and the Business Predicament* (Washington, D.C.: Brookings, 1974), p. 165.

[44] Glendon A. Schubert, '''The Public Interest' in Administrative Decision Making: Theorem, Theosophy or Theory?'' *American Political Science Review* 51 (June 1957), p. 359.

Why do important interests not get represented in the public policy process? Mancur Olson[45] offers the explanation that interest group representation for large numbers creates a *public good* for all those people having a similar interest. The essential characteristics of such public goods are: (1) once they are created they are available to all and the consumption by one individual in no way reduces the amount available to others. Because of their "jointness in supply" such goods are not divisible and appropriable by individuals; (2) no one can be excluded from the benefits of such goods (or it is uneconomic or socially unacceptable to do so).[46] Suppose an individual or a small group of individuals is able to persuade the Canadian Transport Commission to reduce airfaires between Toronto and Vancouver. This benefit is available to all who fly this route, whether they participated in the action or not. They have no incentive to participate in financing the representation so long as they can receive the benefits for free. This is known as the "free rider" problem (no pun intended!).

Public goods will only be provided if the benefit to an individual or a small group is greater than the estimated cost of generating the public good. The larger the group, Olson points out,[47] the less likely the benefit to any individual will be sufficiently large to have that person finance the cost of creating the good rather than doing without it.

Large, unorganized groups, even those such as consumers, who do have a real economic interest, will remain as latent groups unless: (1) they are funded by a government or foundation (for example, about 40 percent of the budget of the Consumers' Association of Canada comes from the federal government), (2) members of the group can be *coerced* into paying dues to finance the lobbying or other representational activities, or (3) group membership and financial support are necessary to obtain some other non-collective benefit.[48] This, Olson[49] calls the "by-product" theory of large pressure groups.

While Olson's theory assumes individuals act in a rational self-interested fashion, he also implicitly assumes they do so in purely *economic* terms.[50] How

---

[45] Mancur Olson Jr., *The Logic of Collective Action* (Cambridge, Mass.: Harvard University Press, 1965).

[46] For a brief discussion of the nature of public goods in the technical sense see John F. Due, *Government Finance: Economics of the Public Sector,* 4th ed. (Homewood, Ill.: Irwin, 1978), pp. 8-9. For a more comprehensive discussion see John G. Head, "Public Goods and Public Policy," *Public Finance* 27, no. 3 (1962): 197-219.

[47] Olson, *op. cit.*, pp. 33-36.

[48] The Consumers' Association of Canada, like a number of other broadly based "public interest" groups (see J.M. Berry, *op. cit.*, p. 39) publishes a magazine, *Canadian Consumer*. For the $8 per annum CAC membership, an individual receives six issues per year — each of which has a newsstand price of $1.50. Therefore, the inputed price of belonging to CAC as an organization is *minus* $1 per year. Morningstar states, "Today CAC sees its main functions as representing, educating and protecting consumers and doing independent research on consumer problems and comparative testing of consumer products. Whether by design or in reaction to public expectations, the Association has also become a vast 'sounding board for and interpreter of what the people of Canada are thinking and saying about the goods and services offered to them." (Helen J. Morningstar, "The Consumers' Association of Canada — The History of an Effective Organization," *Canadian Business Review* 4, no. 4(1977), p. 31).

[49] Olson, *op. cit.*, p. 132.

[50] Olson describes non-economic associations as philanthropic organizations (those whose primary concern is not the welfare of their exclusive membership). He views their behaviour as highly irrational and admits it cannot be explained by his theory (Olson, *op. cit.*, p. 159-65).

do we account for the considerable number of "public interest groups"? Berry defines such a group as "one that seeks a collective good, the achievement of which will not selectively and materially benefit the membership or activists of the organization."[51] Berry[52] excluded from consideration any organization that received 20 percent or more of its funds from government.

When one takes into account *solidarity incentives* (rewards obtained from the socializing and friendships involved in group interaction) and *purposive incentives* (benefits one receives from the pursuit of non-divisible goods), the rationale for individuals supporting public interest organizations becomes more apparent.[53] Berry concludes purposive incentives are the most important; "it is the more ideological, policy-oriented motivations of individuals that make it possible for most public interest groups to exist".[54] Two-thirds of the eighty-three groups in Berry's sample "were begun by entrepreneurs working without significant disturbances[55] [serious fluctuations in the economy; passage of laws; authoritative decisions by the President, administrative agencies or the courts; international or domestic conflict; the formation of adversary interest groups; and rapid changes in technology] as additional stimuli."[56]

(b) What is the Pluralist Optimum?

The second major failing of pluralism in practice is that the "socially optimum balance" may not be achieved. This whole concept is based on a particular view of what constitutes "the public interest." Pluralists argue that at any one time, "political reality can be grasped scientifically as a 'parallelogram of forces' among groups, and the public interest is 'determined and established' through the free competition of interest groups: 'The necessary composing and compromising of their differences is the practical test of what constitutes the public interest'."[57] If the public interest "must necessarily represent a working compromise and be subject to continuous definition, as need arises, in the process of achieving an often delicate balance among conflicting interests,"[58] how can one define the social optimum except in terms of the *process* of interest group competition? In other words, pluralism is to be valued not for the outcomes it produces, but more as a political process compatible with the value

---

[51] Berry defines a collective good as "any public policy whose benefits may be shared equally by all people, independent of their membership or support of a given group." (J.M. Berry, *op. cit.*, pp. 7-8.)

[52] *Ibid.*, p. 9.

[53] *Ibid.*, p. 21.

[54] *Ibid.*, p. 43. Thirty percent of Berry's sample of 83 public interest groups did not have individuals or other groups as members (*Ibid.*, p. 27).

[55] An excellent example of such an interest group is the Canadian Federation of Independent Business — see footnote 86.

[56] J.M. Berry, *op. cit.*, p. 24.

[57] As cited in Lowi, *op. cit.*, p. 75.

[58] A.J. Boudreau, "Public Administration and the Public Interest," *Canadian Journal of Economics and Political Science* 16 (August 1950), p. 371.

judgments of the majority (or at least the influential). A cynic might argue that the influence, even control, by the Canadian "Establishment" goes far beyond that usually ascribed to specific interest groups. Real power lies not in determining the outcome of a specific issue or even in defining the agenda.

Real power lies in determining the *process or framework* with which the agenda will be established and the decisions made. Newman[59] argues, "Operating outside the constitutional forms, the Establishment's adherents exercise a self-imposed mandate unburdened by public accountability."[60] The ultimately powerful interest group may not have to co-ordinate their efforts closely to advance their interests. Newman observes:

> The men who belong to the Canadian Establishment ["a surprisingly compact self-perpetuating group of perhaps a thousand men who act as a kind of informal *junta*, linked much more closely to each other than to their country"] have little need to conspire. They think the same way *naturally*. Most of their ideas mesh perfectly. They recognize so few conflicts of interest because their broad interests seldom conflict. That what is good for them, their careers, and their bank accounts might not also be good for some of Canada's less exalted citizens is not a proposition they are prepared to entertain.[61]

In Clement's view (and as amply demonstrated by Newman) "the powerful have direct access to state leaders and do not have to be organized into 'interest groups' which provide a facade of importance but lack the substance of direct access."[62] He argues that such work as Presthus'[63] ignores "direct interaction by corporations and their elite with members of the state elite."[64]

(c) Other Problems with Pluralism in Practice

There are some additional undesirable aspects of pluralism in practice. Lowi points out that "programs following the principles of interest-group liberalism create privilege."[65] What makes this hard to bear is that such privilege is "touched by the symbolism of the state."[66] More than the spectre of the iron law of oligarchy is raised. One of the results of clear and effective representation of an interest by a group in the policy formation process is that membership in the

---

[59] Peter C. Newman, *The Canadian Establishment, Vol. 1* (Toronto: McClelland and Stewart, 1975), pp. 387-88.

[60] Newman *(op. cit.,* p. 388) points out: "There is no single monolithic Establishment in this country, but rings of establishments, and the most important of them all — because it is so concentrated, so powerful and influences so many others — is that formed by the businessmen who control the Canadian economy's private sector."

[61] *Ibid.,* p. 387.

[62] Wallace Clement, *The Canadian Corporate Elite: An Analysis of Economic Power* (Toronto: McClelland and Stewart, 1975), p. 360.

[63] Robert Presthus, "Interest Groups and the Canadian Parliament: Activities, Interaction, Legitimacy and Influence," *Canadian Journal of Political Science* 4 (December 1971):444-60; "Interest Group Lobbying: Canada and the United States," *Annals of the American Academy of Political and Social Science* 413 (1974): 44-57; *Elite Accommodation in Canadian Politics* (Toronto: Macmillan, 1973); *Elites in the Policy Process* (London: Cambridge University Press, 1974).

[64] Clement, op. cit., p. 360.

[65] Lowi, *op. cit.,* p. 87.

[66] *Ibid.,* p. 88.

group becomes implicitly less voluntary.[67] Furthermore, as organized groups become larger and are seen to ''represent'' defined interests, the greater the likelihood that their internal pluralism will be diminished.

One of the basic assumptions of the interest-group liberalism version of the pluralist model is that ''organized interests are homogeneous and easy to define, sometimes monolithic.'' Furthermore, ''any 'duly elected' spokesman for any interest is taken as speaking in close approximation for each and every member.''[68] An example of the conflict between diminished internal pluralism and the appropriateness of this assumption would appear to be the Canadian Chamber of Commerce with its conflict between large firms and small, and the Canadian Labour Congress with the conflict between national and international unions.

Another of what Lowi calls the ''costs of interest-group liberalism'' is that ''government by and through interest groups is in its impact conservative in almost every sense of that term.''[69] In particular, such a government is strongly resistant to change for offically recognized oxen refuse to be gored. Put another way, '' . . . few if any programs organized on the basis of direct interest representation or group self-administration have ever been eliminated.''[70]

IV. A FRAMEWORK FOR THE ANALYSIS OF INTEREST GROUP REPRESENTATION IN CANADA

Theories exist which attempt to explain the origin of interest groups[71] and their failure to exist in certain circumstances.[72] Theories exist which attempt to explain the macro-determinants of interest group success.[73] There exists a large-scale study of the process by which elite groups, including interest groups, interact and accommodate each other in the Canadian political process.[74] And there exists a considerable number of studies of the activities of particular interest groups or the action of a number of groups in regard to a specific policy issue or decision.[75] There remains, however, a need for an *analytical framework* to act as

---

[67] For a discussion of this issue in U.S. trade associations see Desmond D. Martin and William J. Kearney, ''External Policy and Control in Large Scale National Trade Associations,'' *Journal of Business Administration* 1, no. 1(1976): 29-37.

[68] Lowi, *op. cit.*, p. 71.

[69] *Ibid.*, p. 89.

[70] *Ibid.*, p. 84.

[71] J.M. Berry, *op. cit.*

[72] Olson, *op. cit.*

[73] Van Loon and Whittington, *op. cit.*, p. 301-5; Ronald W. Lang, *The Politics of Drugs* (Lexington, Mass.: Saxon House/Lexington Books, 1974).

[74] Presthus, *Elite Accommodation in Canadian Politics, op. cit.; Elites in the Policy Process, op. cit.*

[75] See, for example, G.R. Berry, ''The Oil Lobby and the Energy Crisis,'' *Canadian Public Administration* 17(December 1974): 600-635; P. Brimelow, ''Business: The Shopkeepers' Shopkeeper,'' *Maclean's*, July 11, 1977, pp. 51-52; Bucovetsky, *op. cit.*; Clarke, *op. cit.*; Helen Jones Dawson, ''An Interest Group: The Canadian Federation of Agriculture,'' *Canadian Public Administration* 3(June 1960): 134-49, ''The Consumers' Association

a tool box which may be used to fashion more sophisticated theories to explain the process of interest group representation and to evaluate the existing theories of interest group behaviour in Canada.

The framework outlined below recognizes that interest groups must take certain key kinds of choices. These relate to the *timing, target(s)* and the *vehicle,* or mode of delivery, for their representations. By focusing on the range of alternatives and the criteria for choice relevant to each of these key choices, we hope to explain in part why it is that, where other things are equal, some groups succeed while others fail. Of course we recognize that other things are *not* equal. Interest groups differ in terms of their wealth, size, access to key decision makers, and so forth. Furthermore, insofar as differences in these and other attributes constrain the choices available to a group, they have direct bearing on the use of the framework. The timing, targets, vehicles framework recognizes that interest groups have limited resources, including access to key decision makers, and hence must make critical choices in respect to these three variables. By abstracting from the host of micro and macro characteristics (attributes) of interest groups, we hope to see their essential behavioural elements laid bare. In this way, we may gain useful insights into the common elements of interest group representation in the Canadian political process.

---

[75] *continued*
of Canada,'' *Canadian Public Administration* 6(March 1963): 92-118, "Relations between Farm Organizations and the Civil Service in Canada and Great Britain," *Canadian Public Administration* 10 (December 1967): 450-70; L. Dion, "A la recherche d'une méthode d'analyse des partis et des groupes d'intérêt," *Canadian Journal of Political Science* 2 (March 1969): 45-64, "Politique consultative et système politique," *Canadian Journal of Political Science* 2 (June 1969): 226-44; G. Bruce Doern, "Pressure Groups and the Canadian Bureaucracy: Scientists and Science Policy Machinery," in W.D.K. Kernaghan, ed., *Bureaucracy in Canadian Government: Selected Readings* (Toronto: Methuen, 1969), pp. 112-19; Douglas Fisher, "An Argument for Complete Openness," *Executive,* August 1977, p. 58; G. Granatstein, *Marlborough Marathon: One Street Against a Developer* (Toronto: James, Lewis and Samuel, 1971); Hannam, *op. cit.;* J.W. Kieran, "Lobbying," *Executive,* April 1969, pp. 33-37; David Kwavnick, "Pressure Group Demands and the Struggle for Organizational Status: The Case of Organized Labour," *Canadian Journal of Political Science* 3 (March 1970): 56-72, *Organized Labour and Pressure Politics* (Montreal: McGill-Queen's University Press, 1972), "Pressure Group Demands and Organizational Objectives: The CNTU, the Lapalme Affair and National Bargaining Units," *Canadian Journal of Political Science* 6 (December 1973): 582-602; Lang, *op. cit.;* Lewis, *op. cit.;* Library of Parliament, "Pressure Groups in Canada," *Parliamentarian* 51 (January 1970): 11-20; I.A. Litvak and C.J. Maule, "Interest Group Tactics and the Politics of Foreign Investment: The Time-Reader's Digest Case Study," *Canadian Journal of Political Science* 7 (December 1974): 616-29; Manzer, *op. cit.;* George S. Mooney, "The Canadian Federation of Mayors and Municipalities: Its Role and Function," *Canadian Public Administration* 3 (March 1960): 82-92; Morningstar, *op. cit.;* Robert E. Olley, "The Canadian Consumer Movement: Basis and Objectives," *Canadian Business Review* 4, no. 4 (1977): 26-29; Brian Owen, "Business Managers' Influence [or Lack of Influence] on Government," *Business Quarterly* 41, no. 3 (1976): 58-69; Larry Pratt, *The Tar Sands: Syncrude and the Politics of Oil* (Edmonton: Hurtig, 1976); A. Paul Pross, "Canadian Pressure Groups in the 1970's: Their Role and Their Relations with the Public Service," *Canadian Public Administration* 18 (March 1975): 121-35; Stanbury, *op. cit.;* H.G. Thorburn, "Pressure Groups in Canadian Politics: Recent Revisions to the Anti-Combines Legislation," *Canadian Journal of Economics and Political Science* 30 (June 1974): 157-74; Carolyn J. Tuohy, "Pluralism and Corporatism in Ontario Medical Politics," in Rea and McLeod, eds., *Government and Business in Canada,* 2d. ed. (Toronto: Methuen, 1976), pp. 395-413; Hugh Winsor, "Lobbying: A Comprehensive Report on the Art and Its Practitioners," *The Globe Magazine,* February 27, 1971, pp. 2-7; W. Wronski, "The Public Servant and Protest Groups," *Canadian Public Administration* 14 (Spring 1971): 65-72; M.L. Friedland, "Pressure Groups and the Development of the Criminal Law," in P.R. Glazebrook (ed.) *Reshaping the Criminal Law: Essays in Honour of Glanville Williams* (London, 1978).

TIMING

We begin with the essential question: "When in the policy/legislative process can an interest group make an input?" While it is practically difficult to separate the question of timing from those of targets and vehicles (mode of delivery) we try to do so for analytical purposes. Obviously, the variables are quite interdependent in many circumstances.

The effective interest group must have a good understanding of the various steps in the public policy formation process. In particular, it must recognize that much of the activity in the pre-parliamentary and post-parliamentary stages is invisible to outsiders. Yet, as we shall see, it is vital to begin making inputs as early as possible in the process.

We have divided the process into three stages, each of which has a number of recognizable steps.

(a) The Pre-Parliamentary Phase

The pre-parliamentary stage is primarily concerned with issue identification, the drafting of policy papers for submission to Cabinet (and its committees) and the "testing" of the general thrust of the policy proposals with key interest groups. In general, we can identify the following steps in the pre-parliamentary phase:

- perceiving the need for change (including the opportunity for purely partisan political gains)
- development of policy ideas/concept (maybe external to the government, political or bureaucratic sides)
- writing of a policy paper for internal circulation in PMO, PCO, or one of functional Departments
- "trial balloons" in the media, circulation to outside experts (political and technical), provincial governments
- interdepartmental circulation of policy paper and consultation
- checking with key interest groups
- preparation of a Cabinet document specifying the proposed policy in considerable detail, submitted to Cabinet by a minister.

(b) The Parliamentary Phase[76]

This phase can be divided into the Cabinet process and the legislative process.

(i) The Cabinet Process

- consideration of policy in a subject-matter committee and decision or recommendation (the original proposal may be modified)

---

[76] The outline is adapted from the *Canada Year Book* (Ottawa: Information Canada, 1973), p. 109.

- Cabinet confirmation of committee decision (the committee decision or certain details may be modified)
- the responsible minister issues drafting instructions for legislation to Department of Justice
- a draft bill prepared by Department of Justice and approved by responsible minister
- consideration of draft bill by Cabinet Committee on Legislation and House Planning
- Cabinet confirmation of committee decision and Prime Minister's signature.

(ii) The Legislative Process

- First Reading in either Senate or House of Commons (reading of title and brief explanation of bill; all money bills must be introduced in the House of Commons, most bills begin in the Commons)
- Second Reading in same House of Parliament (debate and vote on principle of bill)
- consideration by appropriate parliamentary committee (clause by clause examination of bill)
- Parliament Report Stage and vote on any amendments prepared by committee
- Parliament Third Reading and vote
- introduction of bill into other House of Parliament and repetition of the process
- the Governor General in presence of Senate and House of Commons assents to bill and signs it into law.

The output of the Cabinet process is a draft bill, the output of the legislative process is a new statute or amendments to an existing statute. From the point of view of the interest group, the legislative process of the parliamentary stage is easier to follow as the official steps are conducted in public and recorded in easily available documents. Also, changes in the policy may be detected, even if the reasons for them are not discernible.

(c) The Post-Parliamentary Phase

- writing of regulations by the department (or agency) charged with the administration of the legislation
- administration and enforcement of the legislation and regulations
- judicial (and quasi-judicial) interpretation of legislation

Criteria for the Timing of Interest-Group Representations

Because it is the most visible phase of the public policy process, it is often assumed that interest group representations will be focused on the parliamentary phase. A wise (and effective) lobbyist knows better. Although much lobbying is *reactive*, the truly compleat lobbyist seeks to plant the seed of his own ideas (beneficial to the interest group he/she represents) very early in the policy process. Baxter quotes "a highly successful lobbyist for some years now" as saying,

> First of all you have to keep a good lookout on what is going on, on how the government is thinking. That means knowing, and keeping in with, cabinet ministers and some senior civil servants. But that is only part of the craft.
>
> Really, most new ideas begin deep in the civil service machine. The man in charge of some special office . . . writes a memo suggesting a new policy on this or that. It works its way slowly up and up. At that stage civil servants are delighted, just delighted, to talk quietly to people like us, people representing this or that corporation or industry directly involved. That is the time to slip in good ideas. Later it oozes up to the politicians and becomes policy. By the time it is a government bill it takes the very devil to change it. Then you have real trouble.[77]

Put very simply, get your oar in early, but do so with a modicum of taste. Blunn quotes an Ottawa lobbyist as saying, "the quickest way to push your way out of influential Ottawa circles is to push your way around."[78] But there is a conundrum here. How do you know that a policy proposal of interest is brewing — before it becomes public knowledge? This is the critical resource of access.

Access is usually thought of as the ability to gain entry to key decision makers to make a representation. "Real access" is knowing *very early* what issues are under review that are potentially important to an interest group.

The second principle of effective lobbying activity is to recognize there are, as indicated above, quite a number of stages at which lobbying can be done. Failure to achieve the desired result early in the process should not be taken as a signal to withdraw from the field. Rule three is persistence; never give up. The passage of a law does not mean it will have the effects its advocates thought it would have. There is "many a slip between cup and lip" in the implementation or post-parliamentary phase.[79] The regulations accompanying new legislation are often very important in determining the actual impact of the words of the statute. Although it is perhaps more difficult to "get at" the drafters of the regulations, lobbyists offering "expertise" and evidencing a desire to be "helpful" can become involved in the process of creating regulations. Even beyond this stage, there is the possibility of pushing for "bureaucratic repeal" of legislation or regulations. Lobbyists can seek to pressure the civil servants responsible for administering and/or enforcing the legislation to fail to do so. At the very least, they can seek to have civil servants restrain their enthusiasm for carrying out their legislative mandate. Such efforts by lobbyists do not often involve corruption. The fact is that much legislation puts a generous amount of discretion in the hands of its civil servant administrators. For example, in the case of

---

[77] Baxter, *op. cit.*, p. 207.

[78] Blunn, *op. cit.*

[79] Jeffery Pressman and Aaron Wildavsky, *Implementation* (Berkeley: University of California Press, 1975); Eugene Bardach, *The Implementation Game: What Happens after a Bill Becomes Law* (Cambridge, Mass.: MIT Press, 1977).

competition policy, few restraints of trade will be taken to court if few investigations are initiated, few convictions will be obtained if few charges are laid, and few real remedies will be obtained if the Crown fails to make strong representations in respect to possible penalties/remedies provided for in the Act.

TARGETS

At whom is lobbying directed? Which individuals or entities constitute the potential targets at which interest group representations are directed? First, one must identify the actors in the policy process. Second, one must determine who are the *important* actors — those that can determine choices or significantly influence them. Third, one must determine if the interest group representatives have access to the important actors. As Jackson and Atkinson point out, *"access* to decision-makers at important stages becomes a necessary condition of success. The existence of an access point is not a guarantee of influence, but without access almost nothing else is possible."[80]

For analytical convenience, we have divided the targets into two groups: those inside the parliamentary/bureaucratic system and those who are usually defined to be outside it. The result is that interest groups are faced with strategic choices involving direct and indirect approaches to their intended targets, that is, persons able to influence policy choices/outcomes.

Targets *inside* the parliamentary/bureaucratic process:

(a) departmental[81] civil servants who initiate, develop and influence policy (includes special advisers retained from outside the government to work on a particular issue)

(b) minister of the department which is or is likely to initiate a policy change (often this is done through his/her Executive Assistant or Parliamentary Secretary)

(c) other Cabinet ministers (potential rivals or allies of (b))

(d) civil servants of other departments, that is, other than those in (a)

(e) government M.P.'s (backbenchers)

(f) opposition M.P.'s

(g) members (Government and Opposition) of the House committee to which the proposed legislation will be referred. The Chairman may be particularly important

(h) staff of the relevant House committee.

(i) members of the Senate committee which will review the proposed legislation. The Chairman may be particularly important

(j) members of departmental advisory committees or councils.

---

[80] Robert J. Jackson and Michael M. Atkinson, *The Canadian Legislative System: Politicians and Policy-Makers* (Toronto: Macmillan, 1974), p. 33.

[81] This refers to the federal department which is or is likely to initiate and sponsor a policy change, e.g., new legislation, new regulations or new spending/taxing plans.

Targets *outside* the parliamentary/bureaucratic process:

    (a)   other interest/pressure groups, that is, to form coalitions, gain allies (or to neutralize them)

    (b)   the media: daily newspapers, trade publications, magazines, T.V., radio

    (c)   the Party of the party in power — in many cases, the most important members of the national party hierarchy are the key fund raisers (''bagmen'')

    (d)   the parties in Opposition

    (e)   administrative/regulatory agencies outside the departmental structure — these are usually charged with implementing policy and/or acting in an adjudicatory fashion, for example, CTC, CRTC, NEB.

In general, the targets defined to be outside the parliamentary/bureaucratic process are *indirect* targets. For example, for many of the years of debate (1971-1978) over competition policy, business interests (individual firms and groups) have made their case to the newspaper and trade press media sufficiently well that they were able to obtain widespread sympathetic coverage for their views, and extensive editorial support for their opposition to the proposed legislation.[82]

Traditionally, one thinks of specific interest groups external to government lobbying M.P.'s, Cabinet ministers and civil servants to support or block a proposed policy action. Probably as much lobbying takes place *within* the parliamentary/legislative process among the formal actors (M.P.'s, civil servants, Cabinet ministers, special advisers, etc.) as is done by the representatives of groups external to the government in respect to the formal actors. In addition to the purely internal lobbying, internal participants lobby potentially influential groups *outside* the government to gain allies and build support for (or to block) the initiatives taken by ''insiders.''[83] Figure 1 illustrates the possible combinations of the directions of lobbying activity.

Criteria for the Choice of Targets

Which targets are the most important? The answer to this question, of course, is not completely independent of the question of the timing of lobbying activity, which we have already discussed. In any event, there appears to be substantial agreement that Cabinet ministers (particularly the minister(s) sponsoring new legislation or regulations) and civil servants who act as policy advisers are the most important targets. Political scientist Hugh Whalen puts the

---

[82] Stanbury, *op. cit.*

[83] John Fisher makes the interesting argument that business interests should support the Consumers' Association of Canada, not as an ally, but as a defence against more extensive government regulation: '' . . . the business community needs a strong, well researched and organized consumer movement — if they don't do the job that's needed, then government certainly will, and there are lots of votes in this motherhood area.'' *(Marketing,* July 4, 1977, p. 17).

Figure 1: The Directions of Lobbying Activity

Location of *initiating* actor(s)

		inside the government	outside
Location of the *target* group	inside the government	e.g., a Cabinet minister lobbies his Cabinet colleagues to gain support for legislation he wishes to pass	e.g., an interest group such as the CMA, submits a brief to a parliamentary committee
	outside	e.g., a federal department seeks support of interest group (e.g., farmers) in advancing a new price support program	e.g., an interest group seeks a coalition with other group(s) to block certain legislation

matter this way: "Notwithstanding our elaborate mythology on such subjects as parliamentary supremacy, ministerial responsibility and the rule of law, it is now clear that officials design and execute policy because of their technical skills, and because of the wider discretion that accompanies the growth of governmental functions."[84]

The Cabinet and the Bureaucracy

A senior civil servant, as quoted in an article in the *Financial Post*, described the locus for influencing government in the following way:

> People who really want to guide and influence government policy are wasting their time dealing with members of Parliament, senators and, usually, even ministers. If you want results — rather than just the satisfaction of talking to the prominent — you deal with us, and at various levels. . . . To produce results you need to see the key planners, who may be way down in the system, and you see them early enough to push for changes in policy before it is politically embarrassing to make them.[85]

Writing about John Bulloch, president of the 43,000-member Canadian Federation of Independent Business,[86] Brimelow observes,

---

[84] Hugh Whalen, "The Peaceful Coexistence of Government and Business," *Canadian Public Administration* 4 (March 1961): 1-15.

[85] Baxter, *op. cit.*, p. 206.

[86] Bulloch formed the CFIB in mid-1971 following his experience with the Canadian Council on Fair Taxation which he formed to lobby against Finance Minister Benson's tax reform proposals in 1969. By June of 1975 the Federation had 27,000 members; by August of 1976 the number had been increased to 36,000. By mid-1977 they numbered 43,000. Total revenues of the Federation in 1977 were $2.5 million. (A. Ross, "How to Join the March to the New Politics," *Quest* 8 (February 1977), pp. 40-42, 44, 46, 48). "It has more than 60 field representatives, paid $7,500 to $30,000 depending on their ability to recruit members and persuade them to vote in the monthly postal referendums [the president of the organization] uses to determine policy. .. Bulloch is confident the new

He has to deal mainly with civil servants, he notes wryly, whereas his U.S. counterparts lobby legislators: 'We're more relevant than the opposition, and I don't like it'.[87]

Presthus provides some more general empirical support for the proposition that Canadian interest group representatives focus their efforts on bureaucracy, while their American counterparts expend their energy on individual legislators. He asked almost one thousand directors of interest groups, "Which three of the following elements in the political system receive the greatest amount of attention from you and your association?" In terms of the proportion of respondents ranking each target first, he obtained the following results:[88]

Target of Interest Group	*U.S.*	*Canada*
Bureaucracy	21%	40%
Legislators	41	20
Legislative committees	19	7
Cabinet	4	19
Executive assistants	3	5
Judiciary	3	3
Other	9	6
	100%	100%
	N = 604	393

These results should not be surprising, given the different political structures of the two countries. The Canadian system of Cabinet government, characterized by the discipline of party-line voting, has resulted in the reduced influence of backbenchers. McGillivray quotes a lobbyist as saying, "power of the individual member of Parliament or senator is just about zero."[89] Presthus states: "backbenchers are largely excluded from policy determination."[90] He quotes a federal M.P., "If they lobby, they lobby the Cabinet and deputy ministers. They know we have no power." A Quebec deputy is quoted as saying, "An ordinary member can't do enough to make it worthwhile for a lobbyist to see him. It occurs at a higher level."[91] Van Loon and Whittington summarize the

---

[86] *continued*

department [Secretary of State for Small Business] can be captured for his members. In the recent Commons debate on small businesses, eight of the twelve speakers dwelt on the CFIB's feat, one of which is to keep MPs informed of their local entrepreneur's opinions . . .)" (Brimelow, *op. cit.,* p. 51.) The CFIB sponsored the publication of a book on small business in Canada (Rein Peterson, *Small Business: Building a Balanced Economy* (Toronto: Press Procépic, 1977), apparently by agreeing to purchase 50,000 copies. A total of 76,000 copies were printed — an enormous volume in the Canadian context.

[87] Brimelow, *op. cit.,* p. 52.

[88] Presthus, *Elites in the Policy Process, op. cit.,* p. 255.

[89] Don McGillivray, "Lobbying at Ottawa," in Paul Fox, ed., *Politics: Canada,* 3d ed. (Toronto: McGraw-Hill, 1970), p. 164.

[90] Presthus, "Interest Group Lobbying: Canada and the United States," *op. cit.,* p. 46.

[91] Presthus, *Elites in the Policy Process, op. cit.,* p. 248.

view that the Cabinet and the civil service are where the real decision-making power resides:

> Modern government in Canada concentrates the bulk of power in the cabinet and the bureaucracy. Parliament, therefore, is not likely to provide interest groups with a successful arena. As one experienced lobbyist said, "When I see members of Parliament being lobbied, it's a sure sign to me that the lobby lost its fight in the civil service and the cabinet". He might have added that while the group lobbying MPs may occasionally win some temporary victory, its chances of success in the longer run are slight unless they can convince some cabinet ministers as well. Most interest groups and their agents in Ottawa acknowledge this fact, yet it is surprising how much effort occasionally goes into a pressure Campaign when legislation is before Parliament.[92]

Backbenchers

Since power tends to seek power, interest groups devote their efforts to the Cabinet and the key figures in the bureaucracy. If this is true, why do legislators in the figures given above slightly outrank the Cabinet as the prime target of the interest groups activities? Presthus attributes it to the growing importance of committees in the Canadian legislative process. Of particular importance are certain members of committees, for example, the chairman.[93] More important, says Presthus, is the apparent division of labour between the Cabinet and backbenchers. The former concentrates on substantive policy issues, while the latter deals with the demands of constituents.[94] Since "a high proportion of Canadians feel considerable diffidence[95] in approaching federal (and, by inference, provincial) officials," they use interest group representatives to intercede on their behalf.[96] Apparently for some groups, or for some issues, backbenchers constitute the preferred point of access. There are some other reasons for talking to backbenchers, despite their alleged lack of importance in the policy process: (i) a significant number of lobbyists may simply not understand the system and not realize that backbenchers have little influence; (ii) lobbying backbenchers may be seen to be an investment in the future. Jackson and Atkinson remark,

> . . . lobbying both the individual legislator and the committee system represent long-term interest group investment. In majority governments and even in minority situations,

---

[92] Van Loon and Whittington, *op. cit.*, p. 293.

[93] Salter A. Hayden, Chairman of the Standing Senate Committee on Banking, Trade and Commerce for over a quarter of a century provides an outstanding example. See Philip Teasdale, "Senators with Clout: Expert Group Hard at It Despite All the Sniping," *Financial Post,* April 2, 1977, p. 7; Stanbury, *op. cit.*, pp. 145-49. On the role of Senators as lobbyists or quasi-lobbyists see John McMenemy, "Influence and Party Activity in the Senate: A Matter of Conflict of Interest?" in Paul W. Fox, ed., *Politics: Canada,* 4th ed., (Toronto: McGraw-Hill Ryerson, 1977), pp. 454-61; and Richard Cleroux, "Competition Act Study Raises Conflict Issue," *Globe and Mail,* February 12, 1975.

[94] Presthus, *Elites in the Policy Process, op. cit.*, p. 248.

[95] Surely this diffidence does not apply to the corporate, legal and media elite, see Clement, *op. cit.*, and Newman, *op. cit.*

[96] Presthus, *Elites in the Policy Process, op. cit.*, p. 248.

individual legislators are unable to alter dramatically the course of public policy. Throughout the legislative system responsibility and control of legislation rests in the hands of the government. The Canadian Parliament, as we have already suggested, does not make laws, it passes them.[97]

Alternatively, one can point out that some backbenchers obviously become Cabinet ministers in time. A little gentle courting in the past is probably remembered when the M.P. is elevated to the Cabinet. In any event, an interest group would be unwise to openly snub backbenchers even if they possess limited influence. Ignoring M.P.'s ignores the potential influence of the party caucus. Jackson and Atkinson state:

> Before a bill is introduced in the House an outline of the new policy direction is given to the government caucus. At the weekly meetings which follow, caucus members are given opportunities to express the sentiments and grievances of interest groups. Even when the bill has been introduced for first reading in the House, caucus continues to debate the bill and sometimes prevents the moving of second reading.[98]

Jackson and Atkinson also point out:

> Members may also become good public relations agents for various interests. Although most members do not acknowledge much interest group influence in their own elections, there are strong possibilities for group activity in those constituencies where group interests are concentrated. But the major reason for constant group pressure on the backbench may be the belief that a changed opinion there may force an alteration in cabinet's position.[99]

Backbenchers themselves provide similar reasons why lobbyists try to influence individual members. Presthus' data "indicate the majority of members (in the sample) believe that lobbyists think, however wrongly, that if they can persuade a sufficient number of backbenchers to support a given policy, they may be able, in caucus, to change the mind of the relevant minister."[100]

The Senate

As we shall describe in Part V of this paper, the attempts to reform Canadian competition policy illustrate the more important role the Senate can play in certain cases — notably those involving specialized financial and/or economic legislation. As McMenemy[101] indicates,

> Some scholarly studies of the Canadian Senate exhibit an unrealistic disregard for the substance of power . . . When senators are discussed, scholars stress their role as superannuated party supporters. Such jejune analyses usually avoid or minimize the intensive and influential activities of nearly a quarter of the senators (Trudeau-nominated

[97] Jackson and Atkinson, *op. cit.*, pp. 37-38.
[98] *Ibid.*, p. 36.
[99] *Ibid.*, p. 37.
[100] Presthus, *Elites in the Policy Process, op. cit.*, pp. 249-50.
[101] McMenemy, *op. cit.*, pp. 454, 461.

senators who continue to be active key Liberal party officials). These activities relate particularly to the scrutiny of proposed legislation affecting (large) corporate organization, practices and activities, and political party organization and fund raising.[102]

The Senate committees often provide a congenial forum for the representation of business and economic interests. By holding hearings on competition policy *prior* to the House committee in respect to Bill C-227 (later numbered C-7 and C-2) in 1974 and 1975, and again in respect to Bill C-13 in early 1978, the effect was to build up a climate of opinion adverse to the proposed legislation. By holding hearings at the same time as the House committee, the Senate committee provided opponents of the legislation with a second forum to put forward their views to the government.

Colin Campbell describes the Senate as "the lobby from within" and emphasizes that "senators' lobbying activities are paid for by the people of Canada and not by the business firms and groups whose interests they advance."[103] Campbell describes Senate lobbying and legislative activity as "business review." It typically operates as follows:

> First senators hear grievances from the business community members who feel that civil servants and Cabinet Ministers have ignored them. Then, senators astutely wield their corporate reputations through the powerful Banking Committee to persuade the department in charge of a bill that certain "technical" changes must be made within it. If the department's Minister finds the case convincing, he will arrange for the government to sponsor amendments which would accommodate the senators' concerns. Cumulatively, "technical" changes often water down such bills, and this result is the aim of lobbying from within. With the help of senators, in other words, business has been able to get its main points across to the government.[104]

The Canadian pattern of elite accommodation can be seen in its extreme form in the Senate "by paying the salaries of business lobbyists, giving them full membership in the community of legislators, and protecting them from public review of their tenure."[105]

Another way in which the Senate or a Senate committee can wield more influence in the policy process is through delay.

> Business efforts aimed at slowing down progress of the legislation through the parliamentary machinery can be reinforced by the dynamics of the legislation process itself. The minister is faced with a fight for House time, with opposition threats to filibuster (often to achieve victories in other areas) and the emotional drain of committee hearings in both the House and Senate. Toward the end of each session the inter-ministerial manoeuvering for time becomes fierce. In almost all these circumstances compromise to get the bill through, particularly in view of the total amount of time taken

---

[102] Despite the recent Green Paper, *Members of Parliament and Conflict of Interest* (1973), "there is no federal law requiring parliamentarians to disclose, let alone restrict, directorates, property and financial holdings, and legal or other activities which might be construed as lobbying." (McMenemy, *op. cit.*, p. 455).

[103] Colin Campbell, *The Canadian Senate: A Lobby from Within* (Toronto: Macmillan, 1978), p. 11.

[104] *Ibid.*, pp. 69-70.

[105] *Ibid.*, p. 11.

by the legislation in its earlier form, becomes increasingly attractive. As the total time in process lengthens, the ability to maintain intellectual and emotional commitment is reduced. After the "pressure cooker" atmosphere and exhaustion have taken their toll, the ardent advocates of reform may not recognize what has been wrought by compromise.[106]

The Media

It should be obvious that interest groups can, in some cases, "leverage" their positions and expand their influence by skillful use of the media. The pressure of daily deadlines (or in the case of radio or television, of hourly deadlines) can often be used to advantage by sophisticated interest groups. Pratt describes the problem well when he says,

> . . . too often reporters and commentators rely heavily on press handouts from the corporations and governments for their information. That it is a difficult, tiresome, expensive nuisance to generate alternative information, particularly on highly technical issues is true; but it is a lame excuse for not trying harder.[107]

One of Canada's most respected journalists, Robert Fulford, has pointed out that the generalist still dominates newspaper reporting. He states:

> Most reporting, on TV or in the papers, is done by men and women who appear innocent of serious knowledge in the fields they describe. You have a sense, as you listen to them or read them, that all they know of the subject is what they heard from the last expert they met. In the Press Gallery in Ottawa there are about 175 reporters, but I don't believe there is one of them who could be called an expert on, say, foreign policy. There isn't a single man or woman who could speak with independent authority on defence, on welfare policy, or on constitutional law. A politician or civil servant speaking to a reporter usually — not always, but usually — expects to encounter profound ignorance of whatever subject is on the agenda. After a while he comes both to fear that ignorance and to depend on it.[108]

He should have also pointed out that such ignorance can be a most useful condition for the "p.r." men of the interest groups who provide the "handouts" which are often repeated verbatim in news stories.

VEHICLES

How do interest groups communicate their messages to the targets of their lobbying efforts? The following constitute the most important modes of communication:

    (a) *informal discussions,* face to face and by telephone (with important targets such as Cabinet ministers, key civil servants or outside advisers)

    (b) *personal letters* (to the same group indicated in (a))

---

[106] Stanbury, *op. cit.,* p. 178.

[107] Pratt, *op. cit.,* p. 18.

[108] Robert Fulford, "Notebook: You See, the Trouble with Journalism is Journalists," *Saturday Night,* October 1977, p. 14.

(c) *formal briefs* (presented to the relevant minister(s) and/or House and/or Senate committee studying the proposed legislation or general area of policy

(d) *mass campaigns,* that is, multiname petitions, parades, rallies, group visits to Parliament Hill — includes the creation of "media events" and general "rent-a-crowd" tactics[109]

(e) *indirect approaches,* that is, gaining and using allies among other interest groups, creating a favourable impression in the media, the use of campaign contributions.

Criteria for the Use of Specific Vehicles

The mode of communication obviously depends upon the target of the lobbyists' efforts and the timing of the input in the policy process. The "media" must be capable of carrying the message. For example, while an informal conversation can effectively convey the lobbyist's tone in respect to certain tax legislation, a formal brief is needed to spell out in detail the objections to the proposed legislation. The method of communication must be consistent with the values and expectations of the message's target. As Jackson and Atkinson state,

> . . . some organizations have employed tactics which violate accepted norms. For example, the government cancelled Local Initiative Projects for groups which publicly demonstrated to have their grants extended. The norms of mutual accommodation exclude the type of ultimatum conveyed by demonstrations. In Canada the standard practice is negotiation of individual group claims, a rule which is violated at a group's peril. Thus, the legislative system demonstrates a certain rigidity in interest group relations.[110]

Causey *et al.* emphasize the nature of the "Canadian style" of government — interest group interaction:

> If the American way of getting things done is one of dramatic overstatement, the ideal Canadian way of making arrangements (between governments and business) has been one of elegant understatement; the politics of keeping things pleasant, dull and controlled. Influence comes from very private meetings with very important people. Public displays of power and verbal abuse are vulgar and should be avoided.[111]

Jerry McAfee, Chairman of Gulf Oil Corporation and former chairman of its Canadian subsidiary, has spoken nostalgically of the style of lobbying and access enjoyed by large firms in Canada:

> "Canada has things in small enough doses that you can get your arms around it. You can deal on a personal basis with some of the prominent government people — both federal and provincial." . . .

---

[109] A detailed account of one such unsuccessful mass campaign is *The Rally Story* (Vancouver: Women Rally for Action, 1976).

[110] Jackson and Atkinson, *op. cit.,* p. 41.

[111] T.F. Causey *et al., Managing the Political/Regulatory Environment* (London, Ont.: University of Western Ontario, School of Business Administration, 1976), p. 89.

In the U.S., "there's a greater antipathy from government toward business", McAfee says. "There's a greater reluctance for government people to have direct contact with decision-makers in industry, particularly in the oil industry.

We are daily directed by all sorts of bureaucrats in Washington . . . but their contact with us is on a very arms-length — and many times hostile — basis. We ought to be on the same side in solving our energy problems. We can't afford the luxury of that type of war."[112]

J.E. Anderson states that "consultation between civil servants and pressure group officials is often informal rather than formal or institutionalized."[113] He points out that even the "rules of the game" are cloaked in secrecy, a state of affairs with advantages to the pressure groups, the civil servants involved and the government.[114] Blunn escribes the informal contacts between lobbyists and civil servants:

> While constantly defending their line of work as honorable, lobbyists do admit that the kind of relationships they have with people in government can make a difference in how their message is received.
>
> And the best way to get to know civil servants is casually, over a drink or a meal at Ottawa's elite Rideau Club, or even better, the fairway of the Royal Ottawa Golf Club.[115]

John Bulloch, president of the Canadian Federation of Independent Business, was also creator of the Canadian Council on Fair Taxation which lobbied for changes in the tax reform legislation of 1969. He describes the vehicles of communication between interest groups and the government:

> I began to see how the system is stacked in favour of those who own all the lawyers. I found out that the big corporations, without being conspiratorial, control the knowledge factory in this country. All the positions that government takes are the results of conversations, the chinwags, that go on between the experts who are owned by the major corporations and the trade unions, and the experts who work for government. It's a mandarin-to-mandarin process[116]

Formal briefs (and letters) to ministers, and to House and Senate committees can constitute an important means of communication. On certain issues, the number of formal briefs can be enormous. With respect to the 1971 *White Paper on Taxation,* the House of Commons Committee on Finance, Trade and Economic Affairs received 520 briefs.[117] The Senate Banking and Commerce Committee received 343 briefs on the same issue. Between 1969, when the Economic Council's *Interim Report on Competition Policy* was published, to mid-1977 when the Stage II amendments were analyzed by the House and Senate Committees, a total of 522 briefs were submitted on the various proposals to

---

[112] *Toronto Star,* "Yes, Ottawa, Jerry Likes You," July 16, 1977, p. A-7.

[113] J.E. Anderson, *op. cit.,* p. 293.

[114] *Ibid.,* p. 302.

[115] Blunn, *op. cit.*

[116] Quoted in Alexander Ross, "How to Join the March to the New Politics," *Quest,* February 1977, p. 47.

[117] Campbell, *op. cit.,* p. 15.

reform Canadian competition policy. Competition policy has no monopoly on the ability of proposed legislation to call forth a blizzard of briefs. Consider the response to the *Working Paper on Patent Law Revision* issued in June of 1976:

> The patent-law revision — technical and complex — has made few headlines. . . . But it has been the source of a spirited response by many companies, large and small. In the six months since the original patent-law working paper was released, they have flooded Ottawa with briefs and letters, almost 100% of them opposed to all or parts of the new proposals.
>
> The response has astounded many officials here. At last count, 236 briefs and letters had been received at Consumer & Corporate Affairs, with copies often sent also to the Finance Department and Industry, Trade and Commerce, to cabinet ministers and MPs.
>
> "I can't recall ever seeing so much paper go over my desk concerning a single issue, not even counting the competition policy review a few years ago," says one senior official.[118]

The proposed *Borrowers & Depositors Protection Act* also sponsored by Consumer and Corporate Affairs, attracted a considerable number of briefs. Again, they were mainly adverse. Given their financial and political weight (they included the chartered banks, sales finance companies, trust companies, the provinces and even the Consumers' Association of Canada), it is not surprising that the bill did *not* get reintroduced in the session of Parliament beginning in the fall of 1977.[119]

---

[118] Stephen Duncan, "Patent furor spurs rights rewrite," *Financial Post,* January 29, 1977, p. 11. Like competition policy, the proposed patent law revisions have had few vocal supporters. Duncan states: "So far, the only support for patent revision has come from the Economic Council of Canada and Consumer & Corporate Affairs," says one senior government official. "Most Canadians — including a lot of companies — don't realize the impact on their everyday cost of living, or on the cost of doing business, of a patent system that confers benefits in excess of those required to stimulate invention and innovation."

There are many specific objections to the proposed law (in fact many of the briefs run to 70-80 pages). But essentially, the debate is over monopoly rights and what the costs and benefits are of extending those rights.

CCA (and the Economic Council's recent report on intellectual property) argue that the existing system is costing the Canadian public (both corporate and private consumers) too much.

But the proposed law's numerous critics argue CCA would swing the pendulum too far, that the new law's provisions would so reduce the value of patents in Canada that the result would be less research and innovation.

Melvin Sher ("Ottawa heeds protests over patent law," *Canadian Business,* July 1977, p. 25) quotes the Assistant Deputy Minister for Intellectual Property as saying of the more than 250 briefs and letters, "There was everything from letters saying we heard there's a new Patent Law and we don't like it, to well thought out, well reasoned briefs expressing legitimate concerns."

[119] The bill, given First reading on October 26, 1976 as C-16, was the subject of extensive hearings before the Commons Health, Welfare and Social Affairs Committee (a rather surprising choice). An Ottawa *Citizen* story (June 27, 1977, p. 25) said, " . . . easy passage might have been expected for the bill. It has not turned out to be so — for a bill with such generally laudable objectives as a uniform and high disclosure in consumer credit transactions and the suppression of loan-sharking. Instead the Standing Committee on Health, Welfare and Social Affairs of the House of Commons has been met with a steady flow of largely critical briefs. Nor have the criticisms been restricted to the credit industry. Several provincial governments have also expressed serious misgivings — on constitutional as well as other grounds — and likewise the Consumer's Association of Canada. As a result the government has found itself on the defensive, forced to prepare numerous amendments to accommodate some of the criticisms."

Although it was mentioned in the fall Speech from the Throne, Conservative M.P. and finance critic Sinclair Stevens is quoted as saying, "I wouldn't give it a snowball's chance in hell of getting through." ("Conservatives to renew fight against federal consumer bill," Montreal *Gazette,* October 13, 1977, p. 5). See also *Winnipeg Free Press,* October 13, 1977, p. 8. For one editorial in support of the anti-loan sharking aspects of *BDPA* see the Toronto *Star,* July 5, 1977, p. B4. Lawyer/academic Jacob S. Ziegel appraised the bill in an article in the *Financial Times of Canada,* June 20, 1977, p. 8. More recently (March 18, 1978, p. 4) in an article entitled "Its pragmatism all the way to the election," Stephen Duncan of the *Financial Post* argues that the new pragmatism in Ottawa "has

In many instances, formal briefs simply reinforce the private conversations between lobbyists and ministers, key civil servants and other influentials. They may simply be a form of "window dressing" which legitimizes outcomes negotiated in private. It is precisely the opaque character of the communications between lobbyists and their ministerial and civil service targets that has prompted Conservative House Leader Walter Baker's bill to regulate lobbying in Canada. Baker "wants as much lobbying as possible to be carried (on) out in the open 'so people can see who is trying to influence what.' "[120] The same point is made in a recent *Business Week* editorial which said, "The problem (in reforming U.S. lobbying legislation) is to distinguish honest lobbying from covert pressure tactics."[121] Jackson and Atkinson point out that:

> Eventually, interest groups employ every tactic and approach, every available target of influence. Among the tactics used are personal representations to members of the legislative system, public relations activities, the enlisting of membership for mail campaigns, and the presentation of briefs containing expert opinions and information.[122]

Occasionally, we find an example of lobbying activity which involved almost all of the vehicles for putting pressures on the government. One such case was that of the *Time* and *Reader's Digest* efforts to retain their special tax status in Canada. Litvak and Maule summarize the vehicles used:

> In defending their corporate interests, Time and Reader's Digest were able to manoeuvre within the two North American political units. The parent companies petitioned for assistance from their home government in Washington; at the same time their Canadian subsidiaries worked at mobilizing support locally. Thus, they enjoyed advantages and were able to muster resources unavailable to competing Canadian publishers. They exploited policy-input channels fully and launched an extensive campaign that employed simultaneously an array of pressuring techniques. At times their methods seemed more appropriate to a congressional form of government than to Canada's parliamentary system. Besides soliciting aid from the U.S. government, Time and Reader's Digest presented oral and written submissions to the Royal Commission on Publications, attempted to influence Canadian public opinion in their favour through their Canadian editions, mobilized the support of employee associations dependent on their operations, mailed written presentations to each member of Parliament and personally contacted a number of

---

[119] *continued*

spelled an end, temporarily, to the proposed Competition Act and the Borrowers and Depositors Protection Act. The tone and objectives of both bills antagonized and worried large parts of the corporate sector; on the other side, there is little apparent support for the bills among consumers."

[120] Duncan, *op. cit.*, p. 3.

[121] *Business Week* (May 26, 1976, p. 110). *Business Week* (May 23, 1977, p. 31) reports: "Business may soon find that it is doing a lot of its Washington lobbying in a fish-bowl. A recent U.S. Court of Appeals decision holds that once a government agency asks for public comment on a rule proposal, its officials should refrain from discussing the proposal privately with interested parties. If such discussions do take place, full memoranda on what was said must be put in the public record."

The magazine quotes the judgment as saying, "The public record must reflect what representations were made to an agency so that relevant information supporting or refuting those representations may be brought to the attention of the reviewing courts by persons participating in agency proceedings."

[122] Jackson and Atkinson, *op. cit.*, p. 34.

members of Parliament and cabinet ministers, and eventually inspired the creation of a trade organization that gave Canada's major publishers an interest in the *status quo*.[123]

V A CASE OF EFFECTIVE LOBBYING: COMPETITION POLICY, 1966-1978

Overview: A Chronology of the Policy Process and the Opportunities for Interest Group Input

The reform of Canadian competition policy serves to illustrate both the length of time the public policy process can consume and the numerous points at which interest group representations can be and were made. The following chronology highlights the major discrete steps in the process and the points at which major documentary inputs were made.

(a) Pre-Parliamentary Stage (Bill C-256).

- July 1966, Reference on competition policy given to the Economic Council by the Prime Minister.
- 1966-1968, briefs sent to the Council, outside experts consulted by the Council.
- July 1969, the Council's Report published — it was a "consensus" report signed by all twenty-five members — including a score of prominent businessmen.
- 1969, 23 briefs on the Report sent to the Minister of Consumer and Corporate Affairs.

(b) Parliamentary Stage (Bill C-256).

- 1970 to early 1971, preparation of Bill C-256 by Department of Consumer and Corporate Affairs and Department of Justice.
- 1970 to early 1971, intra-departmental consultation.
- June 1971, Bill C-256 given First Reading; as planned, the Bill was allowed to die without being given Second Reading and being sent to committee.
- October-November 1971, series of nine seminars across Canada for businessmen, lawyers and academics in Ottawa (the Conference Board in Canada, September 1971) and Kingston (Queen's University, January 1972).
- 197 briefs received in 1971 and 1972 by Department of Consumer and Corporate Affairs on Bill C-256.

In January 1972, Bill C-256 was allowed to die on the Order Paper as planned. However, strong opposition to Bill C-256, as evidenced in the briefs

---

[123] Litvak and Maule, *op. cit.*, pp. 619-20.

and seminars for businessmen and lawyers, resulted in the replacement of Mr. Basford as Minister of Consumer and Corporate Affairs in January 1972 by Mr. Robert Andras. In March, Mr. Andras announced that a revised bill would be prepared and it would incorporate substantial changes over C-256. Thus began the process leading up to the Stage I amendments to the *Combines Investigation Act*.

(c) Pre-Parliamentary Stage (Stage I amendments)

- March-April 1972, series of seminars for businessmen and lawyers to make representations for changes in C-256.
- October 30, 1972, a federal general election is held, the Liberal Party is returned, but as a minority government; Herb Gray is appointed Minister of Consumer and Corporate Affairs in November.
- July 18, 1973, the Minister of Consumer and Corporate Affairs announces the new competition policy will be introduced in stages.

(d) Parliamentary Stage (Stage I amendments)

- late 1972 to fall of 1973, preparation of Stage I amendments to the *Combines Investigation Act* (originally Bill C-227).
- interdepartmental consultation and consultation with the provinces.
- November 1973, Stage I amendments given First Reading as Bill C-227 (later C-7 and C-2).
- May, October-December, 1974; February-April, June 1975, Senate Committee received 41 briefs and held hearings.
- November-December 1974, February-June 1975, House Committee received 82 briefs and held hearings.
- December 1975, a significantly amended version of Bill C-2 was given Royal Assent and became effective January 1, 1976 (with the exception of the application of S.32 to services, July 1, 1976).

(e) Pre-Parliamentary Stage (Stage II amendments)

- Spring 1975, Skeoch-McDonald Committee (containing two well-known businessmen and a lawyer) began report on Stage II. At the same time, the Williams and Whybrow papers on class actions were commissioned along with several other studies which did not have a direct bearing on the Stage II amendments as eventually introduced.
- June 1976, Skeoch-McDonald report *(Dynamic Change and Accountability in a Canadian Market Economy)* and Williams and Whybrow papers *(A Proposal for Class Actions Under Competition Policy Legislation)* published by the Department of Consumer and Corporate Affairs.
- July-September 1976, 24 briefs submitted on Skeoch-McDonald report and Williams and Whybrow papers.

- September 1976, Queen's University Conference on Skeoch-McDonald report attended by businessmen, lawyers, academics and officials of the Bureau of Competition Policy.
- Fall 1976, informal meetings (re Stage II proposals) of representatives of the Canadian Manufacturers' Association, Canadian Labour Congress, and the Consumers' Association of Canada with officials of the Bureau of Competition Policy and the Minister.

(f) Parliamentary Stage (Stage II amendments)

- Fall 1976 to early spring 1977, preparation of the Stage II amendments by Department of Consumer and Corporate Affairs and Department of Justice; extensive interdepartmental consultations, also consultations with the provinces.
- March 16, 1977, Bill C-42 (the Stage II amendments to the *Combines Investigation Act)* given First Reading in the House of Commons.
- March 25, 1977, Bill C-42 referred to the House of Commons Standing Committee on Finance, Trade and Economic Affairs.
- April, May 1977, two major conferences in Toronto on Bill C-42 (over 400 lawyers and businessmen — along with officials of the Bureau of Competition Policy attend).
- June 1977, hearings before the House and Senate Committees; 147 briefs sent to the House Committee.
- July 6, 1977, the Senate Committee on Banking, Trade and Commerce presents its "Interim Report on Bill C-42."
- August 5, 1977, the House Committee presents its report on C-42 entitled *Proposals for Change.* It contained 94 recommendations for changes in the Bill.
- August 1977-November 1977, Bill C-42 is redrafted by Departments of Consumer and Corporate Affairs and Justice.
- November 18, 1977, Bill C-13 (a revised version of C-42) is given First Reading in the House of Commons.
- November 29, 1977, conference on C-13 held in Vancouver for businessmen, academics and government officials.
- February to April 1978, Senate Committee on Banking, Trade and Commerce holds hearings on C-13. Representatives of five business associations, the Canadian Federation of Agriculture, briefs, the author of this paper and Dr. Skeoch and Mr. McDonald are heard.
- June 29, 1978, the Senate Committee issues its Report on Bill C-13.
- Parliament recesses before Bill C-13 is given Second Reading in the House of Commons.

It should be apparent from this record that the policy process in respect to the reform of competition policy has provided for a host of times for "input" from interest group representatives. And this record does *not* include the almost countless informal contacts between interest group representatives and the civil servants directly and indirectly responsible for the policy and their political masters. Nor does it include communications directed at these decision makers through the vehicle of the newspapers, and trade magazines.

Briefs — Formal Representations

Although the preferred mode of communication may be the informal face-to-face meeting between lobbyists and those whom they seek to influence, the other vehicles of communication are not neglected. Competition policy provides an excellent example of the use of formal briefs (and letters) in response to the government's policy initiatives. The flood of briefs began in 1969 following the publication of the Economic Council of Canada's *Interim Report on Competition Policy*. Perhaps because it was a "consensus" report from an independent, advisory body and hence did not represent an expression of government policy, only twenty-three briefs were submitted to the Minister of Consumer and Corporate Affairs. Predictably, sixteen of the submissions came from individual businesses or trade associations. In addition, the *Interim Report* was extensively reviewed by two academics.[124]

Following the introduction of Bill C-256 in June of 1971, a veritable avalanche of briefs (197) descended on the Minister. Few were favourable.[125] Bill C-256 was not introduced as a regular bill. It was described as an "exposure draft" which would be modified in light of the representations received from the affected interest groups. While the minister in speeches in 1971 repeated the theme that he was willing to change the bill, he also indicated that "the government [was] firmly committed to the principles laid down [in Bill C-256] and the objectives it is designed to fulfill. We are satisfied," he said, "that the bill as presently written answers these principles in all important respects."[126] However, most of the briefs[127] attacked the objectives, philosophy *and* the substantive components of the bill. Both the bill and minister (Mr. Basford) were doomed.

The Stage I amendments, first introduced in November 1973, brought forth 82 briefs which were submitted to the House Standing Committee on Finance, Trade and Economic Affairs. Forty-one briefs were submitted to the Senate Committee, which, as we have noted, began hearings on the proposed legislation before the House Committee. Eighteen of the 82 briefs submitted to the House

---

[124] James Gillies, *A Review of the Economic Council's Interim Report on Competition Policy* (Montreal: Private Planning Association, Canadian Economic Policy Committee, 1969); Bruce C. McDonald, "Canadian Competition Policy: Interim Report of the Economic Council of Canada," *Antitrust Bulletin* 15 (Fall 1970): 521-46.

[125] Stanbury, *op. cit.*

[126] As cited in Stanbury, *op. cit.*, p. 202.

[127] The authors of 24 of the 197 briefs refused to have them made public (14 individual firms, 5 lawyers and 1 individual).

Committee were also submitted to the Senate Committee. Four-fifths of the briefs came from individual firms and trade associations.

The two reports,[128] released in mid-1976, by outside experts which served as advisory "input" to the Stage II legislative proposals attracted another two dozen briefs to the Minister. None has been released to the public. In addition to these written submissions, selected interest groups (e.g., the Canadian Manufacturers' Association, the Canadian Labour Congress, and the Consumers' Association of Canada) had one or more confidential meetings with the minister and his senior civil servants. While these groups were not shown copies of the draft bill, the substance of certain key provisions were outlined and their reactions recorded. In addition, extensive discussions were held within the bureaucracy between the Department of Consumer and Corporate Affairs and the Departments of Finance, Industry, Trade and Commerce, Transport and Justice.[129] As a result of these exchanges, the draft bill was modified in a number of ways. Provincial governments were not left out of the consultative process. Department of Consumer and Corporate Affairs officials met with their counterparts of all the provinces to discuss the major elements of policy to be contained in the Stage II proposals.

When Bill C-42 was introduced in March 1977 and quickly referred to the House Committee on Finance, Trade and Economic Affairs, another flood of briefs was directed to the Committee. Some 81 of the 147 briefs came from firms or trade association, while 40 came from agricultural products marketing boards, farm organizations or provincial agriculture departments. The latter collection of briefs was stimulated by sections 4.5 and 4.6 of the Bill.[130] The Canadian Federation of Agriculture, with the informal assistance of the federal Department of Agriculture, did an excellent job of rousing the farm interests and deploying the shock troops in Ottawa. Their lobbying against the bill had the effect of showing, once again, what the Food Prices Review Board in 1976 called "the marked reluctance on the part of politicians of all stripes to speak out against agricultural interests."[131]

The Senate Committee, which, as we have seen, was much less active in reviewing Bill C-42, received a total of twenty-six briefs. Virtually all of these were also sent to the House Committee. The latter Committee held fourteen

---

[128] L.A. Skeoch and Bruce C. McDonald, in consultation with M. Belanger, R.M. Bromstein and W.O. Twaits, *Dynamic Change and Accountability in a Canadian Market Economy* (Ottawa: Supply and Services Canada, 1976); Neil J. Williams, "Damages Class Action Under the Combines Investigation Act," and Jennifer Whybrow, "The Case for Class Actions in Canadian Competition Policy: An Economists Viewpoint," both in *A Proposal for Class Actions Under Competition Policy Legislation* (Ottawa: Information Canada, 1976).

[129] Less extensive consultation occurred with External Affairs, Agriculture (this is surprising in light of certain provisions of Bill C-42 affecting provincial marketing boards), Communications, Labour and National Revenue.

[130] These sections provided that provincial and federal marketing boards would not be exempted from the Act if the board was controlled by representatives of the procedures or if the board did not regulate as it was expressly empowered to do so and in a way that expressly directed its attention to the conduct in question.

[131] Food Prices Review Board, *Final Report: "Telling It Like It Is"* (Ottawa, February, 1976), p. 34. Bill C-13, which replaced Bill C-42, effectively exempted marketing boards from the purview of the *Combines Investigation Act*.

sessions at which thirty-eight groups or individuals testified. The Senate Committee held only three public sessions and heard from only eight groups. By holding hearings on Bill C-13 (which was given First Reading on November 18, 1977) while the bill was bottled up in the Commons, the Senate Committee received yet more briefs on the proposed legislation. No doubt, Canada's paper industry is pleased with this aspect of interest group behaviour.

Intra-Bureaucratic Lobbying

In the case of changes in competition law proposed in the period 1971-1975, some comments on intra-bureaucratic lobbying should be made. First, there is some evidence to suggest that Cabinet support for Bill C-256 (1971) and Bill C-227 (1973) was not strong. It is believed that without the personal intervention of the Prime Minister, the Stage I amendments in the form of Bill C-227 would not have been approved and sent to the Commons. Interest groups recognized the limited support for the legislation in the Cabinet and lobbied weak supporters or non-supporters to oppose or increase their opposition to the proposals. Obviously a legislative proposal which does not make it through Cabinet or Cabinet committee can hardly become law. Second, the competition policy proposals faced very fierce opposition within the federal government. The normal requirements for "clearances" were greatly expanded and transformed into pitched battles between the bureaucracies within the Departments of Finance, Industry, Trade and Commerce, Transport and Consumer and Corporate Affairs. In addition, the Department of Justice which is responsible for actually drafting all federal legislation held strong views as to its content. This may be because: (i) between 1946 and 1966 the office of the Director of Investigation and Research under the *Combines Investigation Act* was housed administratively in the Department of Justice, and (ii) all prosecutions under the Act, following the investigation and preparation of a summary of the evidence by the Director, are the exclusive responsibility of the Department of Justice. Historically, Justice has been quite conservative in its approach to the prosecution of combines cases. Unlike the Antitrust Division of the U.S. Department of Justice, the Canadian Department of Justice has shown only a very modest amount of imagination in the theories it has advanced in respect to the interpretation of the words of the statute.

Backbenchers

An example of an instance where a strong appeal to backbenchers *did* result in a change in legislation occurred in respect to s.31.4(7) of the *Combines Investigation Act* in the Stage I amendments. This section prevents the application of orders made by the Restrictive Trade Practices Commission in regard to market restriction agreements by franchise soft drink bottlers or franchise food outlets. The pressure for the amendment, referred to as "the bottlers amendment," came from the Canadian Soft Drink Bottlers' Association during committee hearings on the Stage I amendments to the *Combines Investigation Act* in the fall of 1975. Unable to persuade the minister or his civil service advisers of the merit of the exemption, the Bottlers' Association, upon the advice of their Ottawa-wise counsel, prepared a special brief which was sent to every M.P. This tactic carried more weight than usual because most bottlers are local businessmen who hold an exclusive territorial franchise for a name brand product. Most constituencies will have one or more franchise holders. The tactic was more successful (i.e., obtained a complete exemption) than had been anticipated by the Association's counsel.[132]

The Senate

How did the Senate handle competition policy in the 1970s? The Senate's activity centred on Senator Salter A. Hayden's Senate Standing Committee on Banking, Trade and Commerce. The process of reform can be traced back to 1966, but it began in earnest in June of 1971 when Bill C-256 was given First Reading. Business opposition to the proposed legislation was both widespread and loudly articulated. In July 1973, after Mr. Basford, the sponsor of Bill C-256, had been removed as Minister of Consumer and Corporate Affairs, the new Minister, Herb Gray, announced the reforms were being split into two stages and would take the form of amendments to the *Combines Investigation Act* rather than an entirely new Act. In November 1973, the Stage I reforms (Bill C-227, later C-7 and C-2) were given First Reading in the Commons. On March 27, 1974 Senator Hayden asked for authorization from his colleagues to have his committee "examine and report on any bill relating to competition . . . in advance of the . . . bill coming before the Senate." A number of senators commented on how well equipped the Committee was to deal with competition policy because of the great experience of its members.[133] Approval of this motion a week later enabled the Senate Committee to hear interest group representations some nineteen months before the draft legislation was sent to it by the House of Commons. On the Committee's first day of work on Bill C-227 (May 1, 1974) a large delegation from the Canadian Manufacturers' Association presented a brief and testified on the details of the bill. The second day of hearings saw the Canadian Chamber of Commerce and the Canadian Real Estate Association present briefs and testify.

What effects did the Senate committee have on the process of trying to reform the nation's competition legislation? Primarily, it was able to provide a "showcase" for the views of business interests — virtually all of whom were

---

[132] This point was made by their counsel to the author. "The effect of the bottlers amendment will be to preserve local or regional monopolies for the brand name soft-drink bottlers, e.g., Coca-Cola, Canada Dry and Pepsi Cola. While competition, primarily of the non-price variety, will continue to exist between the brand name bottlers, the effect of the amendment will be to reduce the total number of direct competitors in any given market. This will make oligopolistic coordination on price and other variables easier. The final result is most unlikely to benefit consumers" (Stanbury, *op. cit.*, p. 183).

[133] *Ibid.*, p. 144.

seeking to amend the draft legislation in their favour. Henry Aubin of the Montreal *Gazette* said that the reason that the Senate was ''taking the unusual step of viewing the legislation in advance of the House was so that the complaints made by the witnesses at its hearings may have more impact on the Department of Consumer and Corporate Affairs . . . when it redrafts the bill.''[134]

The Senate Committee held hearings on the proposed Stage I amendments to the *Combines Investigation Act* in May 1974, and then again in October, November, and December following the general election in July which saw the Liberals move from a minority to a majority government. In 1975 Senator Hayden's Committee held hearings in February, March, April, and June. The Senate Committee received 41 briefs and heard testimony from the representatives of 29 firms, trade or professional associations. Although the House Committee[135] received more briefs (82) than the Senate Committee, it heard testimony from only half as many groups (16) as did the Senate Committee. By starting early, the Senate Committee was able to present its important first ''Interim Report'' on March 18, 1975, over two and one-half months before the House Committee presented its final report (June 5, 1975).[136] In terms of generating media reports adverse to the legislation, the Senate Committee was always one step ahead of the Commons Committee. Seven of the interest groups appearing before the House Committee also appeared before the Senate.[137]

The overwhelming proportion of briefs and appearances before both Committees came from the ''vested interests.''[137a] The effect of the Senate Committee's hearings was to create an environment hostile to the proposed competition legislation. This occurred largely because the statements of the interest group are transmitted by the media unaccompanied by an analysis of the opinions expressed or ''facts'' expostulated. While the activities of the Senate cannot be clearly tied to specific changes in the draft legislation, by providing a congenial environment for the business groups, the effect was to create an enormous headwind which could be translated into changes in the House Committee either through amendments introduced by the minister or recommended by the Committee and accepted by the minister.[138]

The Senate Committee played a similar role in respect to the Stage II legislation introduced as Bill C-42[139] on March 16, 1977, although it may have

---

[134] Montreal *Gazette*, January 9, 1975, p. 8.

[135] Standing Committee on Finance, Trade and Economic Affairs.

[136] It should be remembered that the bill was not *formally* referred to the Senate Committee (following Third Reading in the Commons) until October 1975.

[137] Stanbury, *Business Interests . . . op. cit.*, p. 156.

[137a] See W.T. Stanbury, ''The Background of Bill C-13: The Stage II Amendments in Historical Perspective'' in J.W. Rowley and W.T. Stanbury (eds) *Competition Policy in Canada, Stage II, Bill C-13* (Montreal: Institute for Research on Public Policy, 1978) Table 1, pp. 28-29.

[138] The exact process here is impossible to determine. For example, it is believed that the minister met with Senator Hayden to bargain over changes in the legislation.

[139] Department of Consumer and Corporate Affairs, *Proposals for a New Competition Policy for Canada, Second Stage* (Ottawa: Supply and Services Canada, 1977).

misgauged the tempo of the review of Bill C-42 by the House Committee in June 1977. While that Committee received 147 briefs and heard testimony from the representatives of 38 firms, trade associations or agricultural groups, the Senate held only three days of hearings, heard testimony from only 8 firms or trade associations and received only 26 briefs. However, it did manage to publish its report[140] on Bill C-42 condemning the bill one month before the House Committee published its report[141] containing 94 recommendations.

On November 18, 1977, a modified version of the Stage II proposals, Bill C-13[142] was given First Reading. Because it was not given Second Reading, it could not be referred to the House Standing Committee on Finance, Trade and Economic Affairs. Not to be caught short, the Senate Committee on Banking, Trade and Commerce began hearings on Bill C-13 on February 2, 1978. After two sessions during which no witnesses were present, the Committee received briefs and heard testimony from the Canadian Petroleum Association on February 23. A week later it played host to a six-man delegation from the Canadian Chamber of Commerce. So while Bill C-13 was dormant in the House of Commons in the face of what appeared to be a general election in the fall of 1978, the Senate Committee has been able to provide a forum for the drum beat of business representations urging that major surgery be performed on the Stage II amendments to the *Combines Investigation Act*. The Senate Committee's report on Bill C-13 was issued on June 29, 1978.[143] As expected, it was highly critical of the bill and called for the elimination of several key sections of it.

Summary

It would appear that by offering so many opportunities for input from the business and legal communities (and more recently, agricultural interests), the government has seen its policy successively "watered down" and delayed for an inordinate length of time. Bill C-13 was described in an Ottawa *Citizen* editorial as "a living, dying and resurrected tribute to the failure of the Liberal government in forming economic policy and in coping with the pressure of the business community."[144] At the same time, the *Financial Times of Canada* offered an editorial entitled "Let's end the joke now." It began by saying, "the

---

[140] "Interim Report . . . on Bill C-42," *Proceedings of the Senate Standing Committee on Banking, Trade and Commerce,* Issue No. 48, July 6, 1977.

[141] *Proposals for Change,* Fourteenth Report of the House Standing Committee on Finance, Trade and Economic Affairs Respecting Stage II Competition Policy (Ottawa: Supply and Services Canada, August 5, 1977). For a critique see M.T. MacCrimmon and W.T. Stanbury, "Policy Death by Administrative Restriction: The House Committee's Report on Bill C-42, the Competition Act of 1977," *Osgoode Hall Law Journal* 15, no. 2 (1977): 485-500.

[142] A number of analyses of Bill C-13 can be found in J.W. Rowley and W.T. Stanbury, eds., *Competition Policy in Canada: Stage II, Bill C-13* (Montreal: Institute for Research on Public Policy, 1978).

[143] See *Debates of the Senate,* vol. 125, no. 91, June 29, 1978, Appendix pp. 1004-20.

[144] Ottawa *Citizen,* November 26, 1977, p. 6.

time it has taken to revise Canada's competition law is a national joke,'' and concluded that Bill C-13 was in the public interest and ''the government should get on with its enactment.''[145]

Warren Allmand, the fifth Minister of Consumer and Corporate Affairs in as many years, has commented on the lobbying in respect to competition policy as follows:

> In their lobbying efforts, I think the powerful opponents have taken advantage of the complexity of the economic issues underlying effective competition legislation and, by clouding the real issues, by oversimplifying and sometimes intentionally distorting them, they have managed on occasion to confuse and sidetrack the public understanding of this vital area of economic policy.[146]

This is a fitting summary of the behaviour of business interest groups in this case study.

CONCLUDING NOTE

This paper has been an analysis of interest group representation in the Canadian federal legislative process. In general, it has been critical of the way lobbying works in practice. The narrowly focused, well-organized constituencies tend to influence policy outcomes more in their favour than do the significant (large scale) but diffuse interests. It is naive to be against all lobbying activity because the system works imperfectly. Instead, we should seek to reduce the imperfections in political markets in order to bring reality closer to the democratic pluralist ideal.

---

[145] *Financial Times of Canada,* November 28, 1977, p. 8.
[146] Warren Allmand, speech in Vancouver, November 29, 1977, p. 12.

COMMENTS

ANDREW ROMAN*

I have been asked to comment on Professor Stanbury's paper. My general view is that there is not much to disagree with, as everything Professor Stanbury has said is solid and well documented. Yet the paper does not really communicate the drama and the terror that lobbying can produce. Techniques such as counting the number of briefs received in relation to particular legislation are not terribly helpful because it is obvious that some briefs have much more impact than others.

The Case of Bill C-256

In 1971, I was a special assistant to the Honourable Ron Basford, then Minister of Consumer and Corporate Affairs, when the first version of the *Competition Act,* Bill C-256, was introduced into the House of Commons. Little did I know when I saw Mr. Basford rise in the House and introduce the bill that C-256 and its successors would provide a full-employment programme for the Canadian lobbying industry including a large number of members of the legal profession.

Senator Hayden, a critic of the bill, was at that time the chairman of the committee of the Senate examining C-256. His name is also the first of a long list of names on the letterhead of a large Toronto law firm which made a number of trips to Ottawa on behalf of clients opposed to some or all sections of the bill. We are not used to thinking of lawyers as lobbyists and the law firms themselves may not recognize that this is the nature of their activity, but many of the law firms do a great deal of it and in relation to C-256, several of the largest firms in the country followed a well-worn track to Ottawa with substantially recycled briefs replete with horrifying interpretations of the statutory provisions. Many of these briefs took the position ''what a disaster it would be if a court were to interpret the new law in such and such a way,'' when they should have known full well that such an interpretation — while never impossible — was very highly improbable. I was much disappointed that several of Canada's leading legal lights took public positions on the bill which were, in my opinion, misleading, if not downright hysterical. For example, a number of the briefs said that the effect of the privative clause in Bill C-256 would be an absolute bar to any judicial review. Those of you who are lawyers know that this is not by any means the case. The privative clause in C-256 was by no means unique. Such clauses are found in a large number of federal and provincial statutes, and are frequently, if not always, ignored by the courts if the tribunal has significantly exceeded its jurisdiction.

---

* Executive Director & General Counsel, The Public Interest Advocacy Centre, Ottawa.

Some of the country's most senior lawyers made speeches containing a litany of hypothetical horrors about the bill. This no doubt did little to harm their billings, but I did not notice that any law society went after them for advertising or for soliciting. The lesson seems to be not that you cannot advertise or solicit, but that you must do so in a way that is subtle and preferably directed to established corporate interests.

The Hidden Nature of Lobbying

To come back again to Professor Stanbury's paper, I want to express some sympathy for the difficulty of his task. Writing authoritatively about lobbying is as difficult as writing authoritatively about the practice of espionage. Anyone who has any relevant current information is likely not to be writing about it but practising it, yet will not tell you how, or with what success. The activity of lobbying itself is so difficult to define, and most of its successful practitioners so secretive that they are impossible to identify. In Canada, obvious lobbying loses its value. Hence any attempt to quantify the number of lobbyists, their annual revenues, and other specifics of that sort is likely to be futile and misleading. Thus Stanbury quotes Blunn as stating that "there are probably 200 associations, firms and individuals who practice the art of lobbying." How does Blunn know this? Almost every sizeable law firm does some gentle lobbying, and there are far more than 200 of them. All kinds of people who call themselves consultants — or even some Senators — spend a great deal of their time in activities indistinguishable from lobbying. Are these included within the magic circle of 200?

While Professor Stanbury has done a good job of surveying the literature, I feel that he has taken some of it too literally and has accepted too much at face value. Moreover, care should be exercised to distinguish the use of U.S. and Canadian sources because the lobbying climates and contexts are very different. Lobbyists are registered in the United States and work in a context which does not include the domination of the legislative branch by the executive as we have in Canada. Washington lobbyists are much better accepted as a legitimate part of the legislative process, while in Canada the media tend to be rather naive about them, and have wrongly given the word "lobbyist" an aura which borders on the pejorative. Professor Stanbury has unfortunately quoted as authorities some general news writers who have not seriously studied lobbying. For example, the writer of a single magazine article on the subject, who, I was informed, spent no more than a week or so researching it, is quoted with as much respect as "authorities" in the field who have invested months or even years in research. A lot of fanciful nonsense has been written about lobbying, and unfortunately some of it is quoted in Professor Stanbury's paper, quite uncritically as with the Blunn observation: "The fact is, most senior civil servants welcome lobbyists with open arms."

No statistical information or any other empirical verification is suggested to support the statement. It is certainly a gross overstatement, at least in my experience. In his paper, Professor Stanbury tells us:

> In any event, there appears to be substantial agreement that Cabinet ministers (particularly the minister(s) sponsoring new legislation or regulations) and civil servants who act as policy advisers are the most important targets.

Since it is the function of most civil servants at one time or another to function as policy advisers, almost the entire civil service falls into this category. I am not sure who was surveyed to determine that there was "substantial agreement," but most of the people I have talked to would feel that Cabinet ministers should only be approached if it is unlikely that the lobbyist can get what he wants from the department without approaching the minister, or, the department having accepted the proposition, if the minister himself is likely to oppose it — that is, as a last resort. Moreover, if the lobbyist's proposal has any technical content, the chances are that the minister will not understand it and will simply defer to the advice of his personal staff or senior officials. Accordingly, the key persons to approach are usually the particular special assistant of the minister who is assigned to advise him on that subject (or his executive assistant) and the similar special assistant of the deputy minister.

The Executive and the Legislature

I should like now to raise some issues which I consider important, but about which there has been very little written in the papers I have seen in this conference. We have heard a great deal of loose discussion about the executive branch in Canada dominating the legislative branch, and how much better off we might be as a country if this domination were reduced. Unless and until this happens, for the student of lobbying, an examination of two further areas would be fruitful. What do we mean by the executive; and if the executive dominates the legislature, does anyone dominate the executive? I do not have the time here to explore these issues in detail, but I would like to raise a series of questions that might be pertinent to further inquiry.

What do we mean by "the executive", — not in 1776, when the Americans made the term so fashionable in discussing the allocation of powers between the executive, the legislature and the judiciary, but today? Is the executive branch, in the *Canadian* context, the Cabinet? The bureaucracy? Or all, or parts of both? For example, is the Privy Council Office properly included within the executive branch or the legislative branch, or as some cynics might suggest, as part of the court which surrounds the monarch known as the Canadian Prime Minister? In looking at the executive, is power distributed evenly, or is it all at the top? Or does the distribution vary, depending on the task the executive is performing, for example, enforcing regulations versus drafting them?

Looking at the second set of issues, if the executive branch dominates the legislative branch, does anyone dominate the executive, or is it fair to apply the words at the end of the children's nursery rhyme, The Farmer in the Dell, that "the cheese stands alone"? Does the big cheese stand alone, or is the executive dominated by others outside government in all or some of its activities? If, as some observers suggest, the executive is dominated by so-called "special interests," what are the linkages through which control is exercised?

My own simple answer might be that in some (but by no means all) of the areas of public policy, the full resources of the government and legislature are no match for the very powerful national and multinational corporations, especially now, when economic times are tough. The government knows that it cannot deliver jobs, or oil, or shoes, or milk, or even the mail. The government can redistribute money and make rules, but only the private sector can deliver the goods. This leads me to ask whether our Minister of Energy really tells the oil industry what to do, or is it more probably that they tell him what they are willing to do? Who really drew the line and decided how far to go in the voluntary automobile rust code which Canadian car companies recently adopted — the federal-provincial Conference of Consumer Ministers or the automobile industry?

Model of Lobbying

These kinds of questions lead me to ask you to reconsider the basic model of the legislative process as we all seem to have been describing it, in light of the lobbying phenomenon and the realities of power relationships. The model we have been following is linear, progressive, and delivery-oriented. Let me explain:

(a) *Linear:* The process is described as going from gathering information to devising a policy, to drafting legislation, to legislative debate, to passage of the legislation, to passage of necessary regulations, to implementation or enforcement of the Act and the regulations. In this context, Mr. Stanfield's concept of legislative overload means that we cannot match our output of laws to the demand for new legislation.

(b) *Progressive:* Each step just described builds on the former, and represents increased refinement.

(c) *Delivery-Oriented:* The purpose is to deliver to the public — the voter or the taxpayer — the legislative goods he needs.

In this model, the lobbyist is seen as having some informational and persuasive input. The earlier in the process his input, the better the lobbyist. But consider whether this model is realistic. It is mechanistic, as it tends to see the governmental process as confined principally to a series of discrete legislative events. It fails to distinguish between activity and accomplishment. Given the enormous volume of legislation today, much of it to amend existing statutes or regulations, and quasi-legislation such as tax interpretation bulletins, we have to see the process as on-going, as a seamless web. Viewed this way, the role of the lobbyist — if the group he represents is powerful enough — may be to create new legislation, or whole new policies, or even new departments of government. The objective may be to defuse present or potential criticism of his client, to protect market positions, or to redistribute income or wealth in one's favour. On the other hand, the goal of the lobbyist may be very modest: to delay proclamation of a statute or of regulations requiring compliance with an Act (the *Packaging and Labelling Act* is a good example) for a few months or years. Such a delay may be worth millions of dollars. Alternatively, the lobbyist's task may be to request exemption from an Act or its regulations, or simply to obtain an informal understanding that the Act would not be enforced against the lobbyist or his client.

Who Are the Lobbyists?

Who are lobbyists? Nobody knows for sure, but they can probably be found in one of the following six categories (listed in no particular order of importance):

(1) law firms and lawyers

(2) party bagmen

(3) senators and M.P.'s

(4) professional full-time lobbying firms who represent clients

(5) employees of major firms, who have been assigned the task of lobbying on a part-time or full-time basis, like Bell Canada's Vice-President of Governmental Relations

(6) associations, some of which are broadly representative, others merely a facade for one or two large corporations.

What makes one lobbyist effective and another ineffective? In addition to general intelligence and the all-important social skills, I would suggest discretion and good contacts. The lobbyists are so discreet, so secretive that you have probably never heard of them. Indeed, some lobbyists I know who depend for their success on close relationships with a small group of public service mandarins would probably sue me if I even suggested that they were lobbyists, as any publicity of their activities could damage their credibility. This small elite denies the label "lobbyist" because they do not themselves make presentations to government officials. They gather information from the bureaucracy as to what sorts of things they would like to see in a presentation, then write the script for the clients, who deliver the presentation themselves.

The second important attribute is the ability to develop and maintain close contacts, both with the political party in power and with the bureaucracy, and of course, with the industry who is the client. The Ottawa lobbyist has to know who in government actually does what, and who really runs or decides what, and where. It is not enough to know titles and names, as in many cases large departments will have a small number of key individuals, not necessarily at the top, who, because of length of tenure, personal skills, or contacts of their own are the principal influence in the making of a particular decision.

What Do Lobbyists Offer?

Professor Cheffins in a panel discussion yesterday underlined the importance of lobbyists, but hastened to spell out that he did not believe that they offered government officials large amounts of money in brown paper bags. But he left open the question, what do they offer? Why are some lobbyists so persuasive?

In my experience, a very important factor is the information they convey, much of it gossip. This is often vitally important to the civil servant, who wants to know, for example, which deputy minister is presently dissatisfied with his assistant deputy minister, or what job opportunities there might be for him in and out of government. As Ottawa is a rather closed, cliquish little town, several of the better lobbyists also act as informal welcoming committees to Ottawa, helping to integrate key new members of Parliament and bureaucrats into the Ottawa social scene. One must also underline the importance of the district of Ottawa in which the lobbyist lives, his expense account, and his social skills.

Another benefit the lobbyist has to offer is a precise viewpoint on legislation. Sometimes the government, by its sheer size or drafting ineptitude, may propose a law which would inadvertently cripple or injure an industry and it is important for the lobbyist to communicate these problems. However, such gross errors, once communicated, are easily corrected or exemptions provided, and do not require inordinate lobbying skills. What does require skill is to persuade the government to make a positive decision, whether legislative or discretionary, in favour of one's client, even when it is rather clear that it is not necessarily in the interests of the broad general public, and may be opposed by certain other not inconsiderable specialized interests. This is the real test for the lobbyist's skill and power.

Lobbying in Canada vs U.S.

I would like now to turn my attention to a couple of significant differences between Canada and the United States. Lobbying in Canada is much more centralized, and less open. If you can now persuade Michael Pitfield or Jim Coutts (or whoever the key person might be in that policy area) to your point of view, often that will be the end of the matter. You need not talk to literally hundreds of Senators and backbenchers, in an elaborate process of wheeling and dealing. Conversely, if one of two key persons in whom power is concentrated turn you down, your chances of getting what you want by talking to others is virtually nil. That is why in Canada it is so important to start lobbying at the bottom, not at the top. If you start at the bottom and they turn you down, you can always go higher, but if you are refused at the top you have no place to go. The political scientist interested in studying the distribution of power in government, rather than constructing elaborate charts showing different branches, levels and departments of government and their supposed interactions, might focus his attention on whom the lobbyists lobby. Their appointment books will tell you where the power resides in the Capital.

Let me share with you the innermost secret of lobbying, by letting you in on a little known fact I discovered a few years ago: *the Government of Canada is secretly being run by persons earning no more than $20,000 a year.* Anyone who has worked for a minister can tell you that it is a rare minister who runs his department, or even knows what is going on in it. He spends a great deal of his time attending Cabinet meetings and handling onerous political responsibilities for his region of the country, his constituency and the party. The Cabinet minister has become an institution, whose time is planned on flow charts by his staff, whose correspondence is written for him, and whose information is carefully filtered and selected by those around him. Given these facts, not only might you have to wait several weeks to get an appointment with a minister, the chances are you will be given no more than fifteen minutes to half an hour, following which audience, the matter will be turned over to his staff for follow-up and decision. While the minister undoubtedly has a veto, he really cannot do much more than prevent others from doing something he considers foolish, since he does not himself have the time to move levers to get things done the way he might want them done.

The deputy minister himself spends a great deal of time at Cabinet meetings, accompanying the minister, and the rest of his energies must be devoted to administering the department and smoothing out relations with other departments so as to ensure that his own department's power base, budgets and importance are not eroded. The assistant deputy minister, on a smaller scale and with a more particular focus, has much the same functions as the deputy. This leaves the directors general and directors — the equivalents perhaps of lieutenants and sergeants in the armed forces — to run matters on a day-to-day basis. They rely, for most of their initiatives, on employees with a myriad of classifications who might be considered the privates or corporals. Such a person might characteristically be under thirty years old, a few years out of university, and a generalist with five years' experience spread across two or three departments of government, but with no specialized knowledge in any particular field. In preparing any policy, such a person would survey some of the literature, do a bit of thinking and talking around the office, bounce his ideas off a few of the affected groups, and prepare a draft Cabinet document. Even with this hasty and somewhat superficial basis for policy formulation, the originator of the "cab doc" would have a great advantage over anyone above him in the departmental hierarchy. He would now be the department's authority on the subject, and for reasons of organizational solidarity, his superiors would feel compelled to defend his views against "outsiders" once the "cab doc" has gone up the ladder. It is absolutely crucial for those who wish to influence the governmental process on an on-going basis to identify the policymaking privates and corporals and to present their ideas and needs to them at an early stage. Then, the effective lobbyist will maintain contact with the project as it goes up through the department, making sure that he talks to every rung on the ladder. If you forget to talk to someone, he or she may be offended, and may influence the policy to your detriment.

If we step back mentally, and look at the entire process again, it is clear that only the privates, with a bit of assistance from the sergeants, can *initiate* anything. The others are busy approving, altering, or vetoing proposals, when not preoccupied with protecting their departmental or interdepartmental status. I have been told on more than one occasion by someone at the "private" level that they were amazed or frightened at the ease with which their policy proposals (often in important areas in which they had no special knowledge or expertise, had only a little time to prepare, and did very superficial research) sailed through to the Cabinet level virtually unaltered. On the other hand, I have heard complaints from a few frustrated but fairly senior and knowledgeable persons at this lower level, that their proposals were stalled or sent back down by persons higher in the hierarchy who might recently have been transferred from another department, simply because the new director, ADM or DM was too unsure of himself in his new policy field to let the matter run up to the next level. The support or opposition of key lobbyists can have considerable influence in moving policy proposals in either direction.

What does all this tell us, as students of lobbying, about the important question we have all been grappling with throughout this conference: "Who really runs the Government of Canada?" From what I have said so far, it should be clear that there is no answer because the question itself is absurd. It is obvious that no one really runs the Government of Canada. The Government of Canada is not a machine, which can be run, but a series of discrete, random events: a happening. Most people can arrange their affairs so as to be present at, or influence a few of the events, some of the time. But there are so many levels in the hierarchy, and so many events interacting with one another, that the government is beyond the effective control of anyone at any particular point in time.

Public Interest Groups

I will now try to deal with one last topic: the problems of public interest groups in attempting to lobby. The most effective lobbyists are those who represent fairly narrow, but highly concentrated economic interests. In our political process, broad public interests are usually sacrificed to the narrower ones. Why are groups representing such broad public interests usually unsuccessful when they do try to lobby?

So far I have been discussing the factors that make a lobbyist effective, and it should be pretty clear that most public interest groups do not have members with these characteristics. Additionally, however, they have some special problems:

(a) Their lobbying activity is often restricted because of their charitable status. In order to be given a charitable number by the Department of National Revenue (without which one cannot provide receipts to render contributions tax deductible) one cannot be actively involved in lobbying. Hence if a public interest group becomes involved too overtly in the lobbying process, there is a danger that it would lose its charitable number. This policy tends to discriminate in favour of the covert (and usually effective) lobbyist, and against the overt (and usually less powerful) group. Presthus (whose book is cited in Professor Stanbury's paper) has commented on the tactics of these groups as follows:

> Protest rallies, however currently fashionable, are obviously exceptional and confined mainly to labour and ethnic groups. Their use of such tactics lends support to the conclusions about the marginal socio-political status of such groups, which forces them, in effect to go outside the system to work toward ends which their resources do not always enable them to achieve within it. . . . It is clear that political elites generally regard such tactics as illegitimate; indeed, a common rule among experienced lobbyists is never to apply pressure in such patent ways.

(b) Citizens' groups normally have very small budgets. They often have no full-time staff, or if they do, no lobbying staff. There is usually also no access to significant amounts of the time of accountants, economists, public relations experts and others necessary to put together an organized, sophisticated presentation. They are often forced to use information from government sources, and the usually very aggregated statistics provided by Statistics Canada.

(c) Public interest groups have no real political clout because they cannot deliver campaign contributions or votes. They do not have any real grass-roots networks. The ability to cite "large memberships" is often unconvincing. For example, the Consumers' Association of Canada claims to have 100,000 members but any knowledgeable person to whom it makes this representation knows well that this is merely the total of the number of subscribers to its magazine, all of whom are automatically given "membership" in the organization. This includes doctors and dentists offices, libraries of all sorts, and persons who may have ordered the magazine as part of a package deal with Consumers' Union's promotion for its very popular magazine, *Consumer Reports*. CAC could no more deliver a significant portion of the votes of its 100,000 members to any political party than the Canadian Labour Congress could deliver the votes of its several million members to the New Democratic Party. If Consumers' Union stopped promoting jointly with CAC, one wonders what might happen to CAC "membership"?

Yet CAC is Canada's largest consumer group. Unlike the United States, with a large and active citizens' group movement, a small public interest bar, and a new corps of full-time Washington public interest lobbyists, the small number of serious consumer activists (as distinguished from merely subscribers) in Canada precludes these groups from having any serious political clout.

(d) The contribution that citizens' groups can make is often negative, that is, to obstruct or to modify a change they oppose. They rarely have the power to promote new legislation. In a speech delivered by the Honourable Warren Allmand, Minister of Consumer and Corporate Affairs, to a conference of consumer groups in Montreal, the Minister mentioned that his Cabinet colleagues rarely had their arms grabbed by passers-by as they walked down the streets demanding ''where is that new competition legislation.'' For that reason, he said, he was frequently being asked in Cabinet, ''where is the support for this legislation, if any?'' As have the five previous ministers who have held the Consumer Affairs portfolio in the past seven years, Mr. Allmand asked, almost despairingly, for consumer groups to support the proposed competition legislation.

JOHANNA DEN HERTOG*

I would like to present an alternative perspective on lobbying — one not covered in Dr. Stanbury's analysis. Dr. Stanbury has analysed what I would call ''professional'' lobbying. He has not considered in his paper the lobbying of all descriptions that is carried out in Canada and in British Columbia by those groups who do not have the money or the organizational structure to pay lobbyists. It is to this kind of lobbying that I wish to address my remarks today.

I would like to relate some of my lobbying experiences as someone who has worked for a few years in various feminist organizations and in the labour movement. I hope to demonstrate how ineffective our present legislative system is and how many misconceptions governments have of the groups that come to see them. I hope I can demonstrate also how difficult governments consistently make it for individuals and groups to even approach them, and how vast are the changes that are needed before this situation will ever be improved.

Women's Rally for Action[1]

In the fall of 1975, I was working as an Ombudswoman for the Status of Women in Vancouver. In December 1975, the provincial government changed. A month later, the Office of the Provincial Coordinator on the Status of Women had been abolished, the Special Adviser to the Minister of Education had been dismissed and the government declared that it would cut off funds for many of the organizations sponsored by the Status of Women.

We decided to lobby. We undertook a massive campaign — we enlisted large numbers of volunteers, created a thorough organizing committee, wrote a

---

* Director of Research and Legislation, British Columbia Federation of Labour, 1977- ; previously Ombudswoman, Vancouver Status of Women and Director, Rape Relief, Vancouver.
[1] See *The Rally Story* (Vancouver: Women Rally for Action, 1976).

comprehensive brief, sent letters to every M.L.A., spoke to the media at every opportunity, and most importantly, organized our rally to be held in Victoria.

How were we received at the rally? First, the brief was not read by the overwhelming majority of the M.L.A.'s, and particularly not by the government members in spite of the fact that it had been sent in ample time. Secondly, M.L.A.'s consistently avoided making appointments with us. In some cases constitutency party organizations had to be drawn in before an M.L.A. would even speak to anyone on the phone or arrange for a meeting. Finally, most of the M.L.A.'s showed not only ignorance of the issues but in many cases were rude and insulting to the people they met.

The effects of this undertaking were significant, both internally and externally. Internally, it sapped our strength to organize anything major for over another year. In addition, it resulted in a large number of the participants becoming either cynical or apathetic about the legislative process. Externally, by March 1977 over two-thirds of the women's centres and other organizations supported by the Status of Women had been closed due to lack of funds. But apart from an increase in Hansard comments on women's issues and one Act (the *Change of Name Act,* which does not cost a penny) not much had improved; indeed, most things had become worse.

On the basis of this experience, I would now like to make a few more general remarks concerning the lobbying process.

The Lobbying Context: A Class Perspective vs. a Pluralist Perspective

I believe that lobbying in our present Canadian society should not be viewed primarily from a pluralist perspective — that is, looking at models of competition and bargaining among various power groups. Dr. Stanbury briefly acknowledged that the pluralist model is not an altogether adequate model since many groups do not have an organizational voice. Although that is an obvious fact, I believe that legislators, civil servants and other interest groups or lobbyists in practice forget that fact. They act as if the comparative silence of some group interests is an indication that the views of that group are not important and may therefore be ignored.

The success of lobbying is measured by comparing your results with those of other pressure groups. From my experience, most legislators and civil servants apply the same measuring stick to everyone who approaches them — individuals, constituents, labour delegations, business delegations. The yardstick of success is not defined anywhere, but measures include things like:

(1) the amount of established presence a group has with the media
(2) the number of people who are visibly supporting your position
(3) the comprehensiveness of your brief or other presentation
(4) your knowledge of the structure of government
(5) your politeness and style
(6) the size of your organization

(7) your vote affecting potential and

(8) whether your political ideologies and prejudices mesh with those of the legislator you are lobbying.

The application of these criteria by legislators and civil servants consistently results in women's groups, labour groups, minority groups, and the unemployed getting fair or bad marks for their lobbying efforts. On the other hand, high marks are accorded to the legal and medical professions, large corporate concerns, the oil lobby, and other large financial interests.

According to that pervasive measuring stick that legislators use, we (women, workers, minorities) never seem to be able to "perform" in a manner which most effectively presents our case. Our supporters are not visible like Alcan in the pages of the *Financial Post,* our material is often lacking in comprehensiveness, we often are not timely in presenting our demands to governments, and the media does not seem to cover us.

The result of the application by legislators and civil servants of this "success" yardstick is that, at most, the interests of only 10 percent of our twenty-three million people are well-represented before the lawmakers of the country. The other 90 percent of the people are virtually unrepresented by any effective organization. The consequences of this state of affairs are disastrous — we have a vast amount of legislation that benefits the entrenched professions, the oil companies, and other corporate interests and very little legislation that assists the vast majority of people in our society — women, the unemployed, workers and racial and ethnic minorities.

ALASDAIR J. MCKICHAN*

The lobbying function does exist in Canada even though that label is sometimes imbued with sinister overtones which, I suggest, it does not usually merit. In any legislative process, organized sectors in society have an interest in making their views known and, if the legislative process is to work with maximum efficiency, they probably have an obligation to do so in any event.

Characteristics of a Successful Lobby Group

What then are the characteristics of a successful lobby group? My own assessment would be as follows.

(1)   The members of the organization lobbying are numerous, vocal and identify themselves strongly with the lobbying organization. When it comes to the crunch, the decision makers are likely to take into account the number of individual votes at stake and it helps, of course, if they are concentrated in a geographical, and hence, political, sense.

---

* President of the Retail Council of Canada, Toronto.

(2) If the organization has an association with farming, fishing or labour, that certainly is an advantage.

(3) If the ends of the organization can be met, totally or in part, without direct expenditure of government funds, that helps as well.

(4) If employment is at stake, especially where there is a multiplier effect in the nature of the employment, that is a cogent argument.

(5) Regionality may be of interest according to the political sensitivity of the times.

(6) If the lobbying organization can command technical or trade information, unavailable to the legislators otherwise, that may help its position.

(7) If the lobbyists' objectives are fashionable, that helps. It also helps if they are relatively few and readily understandable.

(8) The lobbyists will be better-received if they have reached an accommodation with the other interested protagonists — be they labour, other industries, consumer groups, etc. If the lobbyists can show positive overall economic effects to bolster their cause, this also will help. This is the usual basis of argument for business groups.

(9) The skill of the professional lobbyist used — whether he or she be union leader, business association manager, farm leader — plays a part, as does the commitment of the organization's membership. Timing and positioning are, of course, also important and these factors may or may not be in the control of the lobbyist.

It is often assumed that the larger, better-financed and more experienced the organization, the more likely are its chances of success in a lobbying mode. My experience is that it ain't necessarily so! Think of the difficulties the metal mining industry has had in recent years with the tax policies of federal and provincial governments. Think of the lack of success of the automobile manufacturers in achieving a code on rust prevention which met with their approval. Think of the fact that it was not the Canadian Bankers' Association but the reluctance of the provinces that stalled the passage of the *Borrowers and Depositors Protection Act*.

Functions of Lobbying

I must say that I agree with the main thrust of Professor Stanbury's conclusions in relation to the definition of the lobbying function. In my view, the most constructive aspect of a lobby is the educational work which it does. Most reasonably sophisticated organizations now present their arguments backed by research rather than simply making assertions. Sometimes, the research is even jointly conducted between the lobbying organization and government, and its conclusions endorsed by both of them. Often, the information which the lobby provides is not readily available from another source. Often, the results of the research make the conclusion sought by the lobbying group self-evident.

So large and pervasive are governments in all walks of life these days that any individual in any business is liable to be sideswiped simply by inadvertence. Recently, the federal government introduced quotas on the import of clothing. The quotas were primarily designed, of course, to inhibit the flow of low-cost imports from the low-wage countries of the Far East, South America and the government-controlled economies of Eastern Europe. Because of international trading obligations, the quotas had to be applied globally and in the result, some hundreds of importers and retailers of high-fashion/high-cost merchandise were almost driven out of business. It took a vigorous lobby on behalf of the affected companies to provide them with special dispensation.

As Professor Stanbury suggests, it is difficult for legislators to sort out the variety of noises they hear from a particular interest group. An organization can help to sort out the sometimes conflicting views within that group. One of the most useful features of any organization is to deliver a clear message, or at least to identify the viewpoints extant within the group.

Sometimes the existence of a lobby is treated as an implied criticism of the ability of elected representatives to perform an adequate job in representing all their constituents. Perhaps this is an unfair criticism. First, it is an inefficient use of a politician's necessarily limited time to attempt to represent his constituents down to the very last detail of their singular needs. It makes sense for the politician to concentrate on the broader issues and allow a lobbying group to deal with the technical aspects of the problem. To use a concrete example, if a plant manufacturing railway boxcars is threatened with closure and the loss of two thousand jobs, that would be an appropriate area of concern for the local Member of Parliament. If the management of that same plant had a problem with the Department of Transport on the safety aspects of the design of a journal box, that would be more appropriate for solution by that company's management or the industry's trade association.

It is true that in a pluralist process, all interests may not be equally represented and more influence may go to the better organized. However, in Canadian society, it seems to me there are very few groups which have not recognized the need for organization and representation. Almost every special interest group be they the disabled, the poor, the native people, have formed their own pressure groups. Recent events have shown that legislators and civil servants pay at least as much attention to these groups as to the older, established lobbies of business and labour.

Professor Stanbury suggests that sometimes an organization will have difficulty maintaining its own internal pluralism and in the interests of solidarity, may abandon an important minority viewpoint. The risk is real. However, to an extent, there are internal disciplines. If any organization offends a faction within it too severely, it runs the risk of seeing a breakaway organization established.

Professor Stanbury cites the effectiveness of the business lobby in relation to three particular pieces of legislation — the *Competition Act,* the Patent Law revisions of some years ago, and the *Borrowers and Depositors Protection Act.*

It seems to me these particular pieces of legislation could have been equally well chosen as examples of the *ineffectiveness* of the business lobby. Stage I of the amendments to the *Combines Investigation Act* still retains within it the capricious misleading advertising sections, while Stage II although billed as a surrender to business actually perpetuates all the more serious of the flaws which gave the first version of the bill such deservedly bad press. The Patent Law revisions did, I believe, receive only the criticism which they deserved. The threat of passage of that legislation actively discouraged the carrying on of research and development within Canada and even caused the transfer of more existing research functions to other countries by the multinationals. The *Borrowers and Depositors Protection Act,* as I suggested, has been held up more by the justified doubts of the provinces than the activities of the businesses primarily affected. But that bill, also as first introduced, was really in regrettable shape as evidenced by the pages and pages of amendments brought in by the former minister. Considerable work remains to be done on it before it can be said to help anybody.

Guide to Successful Lobbying

How should a successful lobbyist go about his work? I am not claiming to fall in the successful category, but I suggest that successful practitioners in the business adopt some or all of the following strategies.

(1) Be aware of society's trends and attempt to anticipate them. In lobbying, as in any other occupation, it is hard to swim against the stream. Any lobbyist will discredit himself and his organization if he attempts to achieve objectives which are clearly at variance with the mood of the times. Those businesses which recognized that consumerist issues were receiving support from a substantial, if passive, proportion of the population, and indeed, often made good marketing sense in their own right, came out ahead in customer-oriented markets over the last decade.

(2) Where appropriate, take prophylactic action. The lobbyist should see his role not merely as influencing governments or other controlling bodies, he should also see that he has an obligation to bring messages back to his members and attempt to win their support for rational behaviour within their own organizations.

(3) Consider programs of self-regulation where these are appropriate.

(4) Appreciate that society and the legislative process have fads just as idiosyncratic as the world of fashion. Today, it is economic stability; yesterday, it was national identity; tomorrow, it will be the conserver society. Each of these has relevance in its time, but each of them tends to get downplayed as a new preoccupation surfaces. The lobbying group must be sensitive to these issues, but on the other hand, it must not get overwhelmed with the current preoccupation at the expense of all others.

(5) Beware of crying 'wolf! wolf!' The lobbyist always risks destroying his credibility both with his constituency and with his audience if he reacts to too many issues or issues which prove to be insubstantial.

(6) Appreciate that in Canada, perhaps contrary to public opinion we have, generally speaking, high standards of public morality, where an extremely high percentage of lobbying is open and above-board. Most of it is carried on not in the shadowed recesses of the Rideau Club but in the offices of the ministers and much more in terms of volume, in the offices of civil servants. The civil servants concerned are only rarely the deputy ministers or other high-visibility officers, but most frequently the individuals who have the technical knowledge and the power of recommendation. It is only realistic to appreciate that the minister, a harried victim of his parliamentary and departmental timetable, can only hope to deal with the broadest of issues while he must constantly be preoccupied with the realities of re-election, of a likely short period in office in any one department, and with making a contribution to the broader issues of the day which monopolize Cabinet time, be they the state of the economy, national unity or whatever.

(7) The martialling of public support through the media is sometimes the right receipe for tackling a particular issue, but not often. Only the most simplistic of issues is likely to be well understood by the public. A special interest cause, no matter how soundly based in reason, is likely to be regarded as special pleading by those sectors of society not immediately affected. The reactions of the media cannot readily be anticipated; sometimes they may make much of an obscure cause and on other occasions they will lose interest quickly in a seemingly burning issue. Apart from these considerations, strong media support may have an impact quite contrary to that anticipated. A minister may feel that he gains most marks for his department or his government by adopting a ''tough'' posture in defiance of what he will paint as misinformed opinion.

What Could Government Do?

Just let me conclude by setting down a few suggestions for ways in which it seems to me government could facilitate better public input to the legislative process.

(1) Allow realistic time for public consideration of new legislation. It is not uncommon for dramatically new legislation to be introduced to an astonished world and then speeded through the legislative process before there is time for informed study or comment.

(2) Reduce the sheer volume of legislation. The weight of legislation arriving in the office of any national organization, which has concerns both federally and in the ten provinces, boggles the mind. The last ten years have produced such a weight of legislation that a great deal of it is not well understood, much of it is not even known to those whom it purports to regulate. All this is apart from the drag, in an economic sense, that over-abundant

legislation produces on the economy. For all these reasons we need a slowdown in the eagerness of the legislators.

(3) Governments are increasingly making intelligent use of pre-legislative inquiries, informal discussions, production of white papers, green papers, or position papers. All this pre-legislative inquiry is to be commended.

(4) Make intelligent use of parliamentary committees. This means that the committees must have sufficient time to familiarize themselves with the subject at hand, they should have appropriate staff backing and a means should be found of encouraging specialization among members.

(5) The existing strong capability existing among Senators should be utilized to the full. Full benefit from the Senate can probably only be achieved after it attains more public credibility by a reform of the method of appointment and an improvement of its representative character.

(6) To the extent possible, the first set of regulations to be applied under an Act should be tabled with the bill. It is often difficult to determine the actual reach and impact of legislation when the bill itself only contains the vaguest enabling powers.

(7) The federal Parliament and provincial legislatures should develop a vehicle within the parliamentary process for the hearing of available evidence on the state of the respective economies involved. It might be appropriate to establish such a mechanism as a regular feature of parliamentary debate in advance of the tabling of the Budget. After all, the assumptions on which a Minister of Finance formulates his Budget are not themselves secret. They should, in fact, be open to the widest comment and an effort should be made to seek that comment from the best available economic experts.

Conclusion

In conclusion, let me simply say that business has taken some steps in rationalizing the input it makes to federal and provincial parliamentary processes. The establishment of the Business Council on National Issues and the renaissance of the Canadian Chamber of Commerce are both helpful signs. All parties are still faced with the conundrum of achieving a useful mechanism for the discussion in the least partisan way of the big issues facing the economy. In my view, no amount of effort devoted to solution of that question can be regarded as excessive.

A BASIC BIBLIOGRAPHY

LOBBYING AND INTEREST GROUP REPRESENTATION IN THE LEGISLATIVE PROCESS IN CANADA

Anderson, J.E. "Pressure Groups and the Canadian Bureaucracy." In Kenneth Kernaghan, ed., *Public Administration Canada: Selected Readings*, 3rd ed., pp. 292-302. Toronto: Methuen, 1977.

Baxter, Clive. "Lobbying — Ottawa's Fast-Growing Business." In Paul W. Fox, ed., *Politics: Canada*, 4th ed., pp. 206-10. Toronto: McGraw-Hill Ryerson, 1977. (Originally in the *Financial Post*, July 12 1975, p. 6 as "Familiars in the Corridors of Power: Plainman's guide to the lobbyists, who are now legion in the nation's capital.")

Berry, Glyn R. "The Oil Lobby and the Energy Crisis." *Canadian Public Administration* 17 (Winter 1974): 600-635.

Clement, Wallace. *The Canadian Corporate Elite: An Analysis of Economic Power*. Carleton Library No. 89. Toronto: McClelland and Stewart, 1975.

Doern, G. Bruce. "Pressure Groups and the Canadian Bureaucracy: Scientists and Science Policy Machinery." In W.D.K. Kernaghan, ed., *Bureaucracy in Canadian Government: Selected Readings*, pp. 112-19. Toronto: Methuen, 1969.

Kwavnick, David. *Organized Labour and Pressure Politics*. Montreal: McGill-Queen's University Press, 1972.

Kwavnick, David. "Pressure Group Demands and the Struggle for Organizational Status: The Case of Organized Labour." *Canadian Journal of Political Science* 3 (March 1970): 56-72.

Lewis, Robert. "The Hidden Persuaders: Guns Don't Make Laws, But Gun Lobbies Damn Well Do." *Maclean's* June 13, 1977, pp. 40b, c, h, i.

Litvak, I.A. and Maule, C.J. "Interest-Group Tactics and the Politics of Foreign Investment: The Time-Reader's Digest Case Study." *Canadian Journal of Political Science* 7 (December 1974): 616-29.

McGillivray, Don. "How the Media Can Affect the Message." *Canadian Business Review* (Spring 1978): 4-6.

McGillivray, Don. "Lobbying at Ottawa." In Paul Fox, ed., *Politics: Canada*, 3rd ed., pp. 163-72. Toronto: McGraw-Hill, 1970. (Originally published by Southam News Services, April 9-15, 1964.)

Milbrath, Lester. *The Washington Lobbyists*. Chicago: Rand McNally, 1963.

Neilson, W.A.W. "Improving the Interaction between Marketers and Governments: A Former Government Official's View." In Mel S. Moyer, ed., *Marketers and Their Publics: A Dialogue*, pp. 204-37. Toronto: York University, Faculty of Administrative Studies.

Newman, Peter C. *The Canadian Establishment, Vol. 1*. Toronto: McClelland and Stewart, 1975.

Pratt, Larry. *The Tar Sands: Syncrude and the Politics of Oil*. Edmonton: Hurtig, 1976.

Presthus, Robert. *Elite Accommodation in Canadian Politics*. Toronto: Macmillan, 1973.

Presthus, Robert. *Elites in the Policy Process*. London: Cambridge University Press, 1974.

Presthus, Robert. "Interest Group Lobbying: Canada and the United States." *The Annals of the American Academy of Political and Social Science* 413 (May 1974): 44-57.

Presthus, Robert. "Interest Groups and the Canadian Parliament: Activities, Interaction, Legitimacy and Influence." *Canadian Journal of Political Science* 4 (December 1971): 444-60.

Pross, A. Paul. "Canadian Pressure Groups in the 1970's: Their Role and Their Relations with the Public Service." *Canadian Public Administration* 18 (Spring 1975): 121-35.

Pross, A. Paul, ed. *Pressure Group Behaviour in Canadian Politics*. Toronto: McGraw-Hill Ryerson, 1975.

Rowley, J.W. and Stanbury, W.T., eds. *Competition Policy in Canada: Stage II, Bill C-13*. Montreal: Institute for Research on Public Policy, 1978.

Schultze, Charles L. *The Public Use of Private Interest*. Washington, D.C.: Brookings Institution, 1977.

Stanbury, W.T. *Business Interests and the Reform of Canadian Competition Policy, 1971-1975*. Toronto: Carswell/Methuen, 1977.

Thorburn, H.G. "Pressure Groups in Canadian Politics: Recent Revisions to the Anti-Combines Legislation." *Canadian Journal of Economics and Political Science* 30 (May 1964): 157-74.

Van Loon, R.J. and Whittington, M.S. "Interest Groups in Canada." In *The Canadian Political System*, 2nd ed., pp. 286-309. Toronto: McGraw-Hill, 1976.

Chapter Seven

The Influence and Responsibilities of the Media in the Legislative Process

by
*Geoffrey Stevens**

The Need for Self Examination

"All I know is just what I read in the papers." (Will Rogers)

Most reporting, on TV or in the papers, is done by men and women who appear innocent of serious knowledge in the fields they describe . . . Attacks on the media from politicians are not *only* the result of wounded feelings or frightened defensiveness. They emerge also from the perception of veteran politicians that, when they deal with the media, they are dealing with people who have less experience than they should have and know a great deal less than they should know. Trudeau's contempt for the press is only in part a function of his personality. It is also in part a realistic appraisal of a situation that should deeply concern every publisher, broadcast executive, editor and reporter in the country. (Robert Fulford (*Saturday Night,* October 1977))

Journalists are a strange and disturbing breed. We pride ourselves on being alert to the motivation and rationalization of others, especially politicians. Yet we are singularly incurious about our own motivation and unaware of our own rationalizations. We eschew introspection, perhaps because we fear it. We are quick to criticize, but we recoil from criticism of our own efforts. Attacks on our work, on our understanding, or on our role are translated, in our minds, into an assault on the freedom of the press. We are quick to defend the freedom of the press: we are slow to examine what that freedom means and the responsibilities it entails.

Romance and Realism

The need for self-examination and self-criticism has never been greater. Journalism, to my mind, has always been a craft struggling to be accepted as a profession. Today — thanks, in part, to Watergate — journalism is not only recognized by young people as a profession, but a glamorous one at that. The old "Front Page" image of the hard-drinking reporters and hard-bitten editors has

* Associate Editor, *The Globe and Mail,* Ottawa.

been replaced by an image equally unrealistic of journalism as something approaching a noble calling. Everyone wants to be a journalist. There are more students in journalism schools in the United States today than there are jobs on all the daily newspapers of the United States combined. In Canada, schools of journalism are bursting at the seams. New schools are opening; every community college, it seems, now offers courses in journalism.

Where all these students are going to go I do not know. If they do manage to find jobs on newspapers or in radio or television, their illusions will be shattered — as a good many already have been. They will find that while journalism may be more popular than it ever has been, it is subject to greater criticism than ever before. They will also, if they are honest with themselves, recognize that the criticism is more deserved than the popularity.

A small incident that happened in 1965, shortly after I was assigned to the Ottawa Bureau of *The Globe and Mail,* sticks in my mind. Walter Gordon, then Minister of Finance, had presented his budget and, when he finished reading the Budget Speech, he retired to the press gallery lounge to brief reporters on the contents. When he finished his explanation of fiscal and monetary policy, one of my radio colleagues put a question: "Mr. Gordon, could you tell us — just what *is* a deficit?" At the time, I was amused. Everyone else in the room (I hope) knew what a deficit was, although some of us (myself included) might have been hard-pressed to explain the difference between a budget deficit and a current accounts deficit. If it happened now, I suppose I would be outraged. But I would not be particularly surprised.

The Education of Reporters

To return to the two quotations at the start of this paper, it is a sobering thought that, as Will Rogers put it, all that people do know about what goes in Ottawa, and in the legislative process, in general, comes from what they read in the papers (or hear on radio or television). Robert Fulford is quite right in observing that journalists have less experience and knowledge than they should have. In fact, I would go further than Fulford. Most of the people who report on the legislative process are poorly trained (if they are trained at all), lack comprehension of many of the subjects that they must report on, and (as a general indictment) not only know less than the civil servants who develop policy, and the politicians who announce it, but in many cases the journalist knows less than his readers (or listeners). For example, out of perhaps two hundred and twenty members of the parliamentary press gallery in Ottawa, I cannot think of more than a dozen who really understand how the legislative process works, and why it works the way it does.

In fairness, the level of competence in the press gallery in Ottawa is, in my experience, a good deal higher than the level found in press galleries in provincial legislatures. The degree of competence has also increased quite dramatically in the past ten or fifteen years (notwithstanding the fact that a posting to Ottawa is no longer considered to be the summit of a reporting career). There may be fewer giants — great generalists such as Blair Fraser — but there are more specialists in an age in which government becomes increasingly specialized and complex. Most major news organizations now have, in Ottawa, their specialist on finance and economic affairs, on social policy, on federal-provincial relations, and so on (including, these days, on the RCMP). This trend to specialization has reached the point where one member of the Ottawa Bureau of *The Globe and Mail* recently received the ultimate accolade — a letter of apology from Senator Eugene Forsey admitting that he had been wrong, and the reporter right, on a constitutional question. Finally, a case can be made that the reporting which comes out of Ottawa is as competent as the advice which comes into Ottawa from business and labour groups — and perhaps even as relevant as the welter of conflicting views which the academic community tries to persuade federal politicians to accept.

Having said all this, the fact remains that the media stand indicted for superficiality, for concentrating on trivia and ignoring substance, for focusing on the drama and losing sight of the serious functioning and equally serious malfunctioning of the process. The indictment is difficult to refute, and I plead as guilty as the next person.

Parliament and the Press

I have been asked to address myself to the influence and responsibilities of the media in relation to the legislative process. Having inflicted on you my personal views and biases about the competence of the media, I will turn to the task at hand. I do so, however, with the caveat that the legislative process represents only one part, and a relatively small part at that, of the work of the political reporter or commentator. Much of my time, at least, is taken up with matters beyond the immediate context of Parliament. Activities of political parties. Bureaucrats. International subjects which seldom come before Parliament, including the Law of the Sea and relations between the administrations in Ottawa and Washington. The work of regulatory agencies and tribunals. The Supreme Court of Canada. Federal-provincial negotiations. Public opinion analyses. And, not least, elections, real or apprehended. To say that the working of the legislative process is but one aspect of a rather large job is not to excuse any neglect of the legislature. Rather, it is an attempt at an explanation.

Reading the press (or listening to radio or television), one comes away with the impression that the legislative process is, at best, inconsequential, and, at worst, irrelevant. But before we shoot the messenger, we should consider the attitudes which create the impression. What is Pierre Trudeau's attitude toward the legislative process? The Prime Minister's contempt for the press, I suggest, is rivalled only by his dislike of election campaigns and his indifference, if not disdain, for Parliament. How can the public, or the press, be expected to take the House of Commons seriously when the Prime Minister of Canada dismisses

Opposition M.P.'s as "nobodies," when he devotes considerably more effort to preparing for his weekly press conference than he does for the daily Question Period? How can we be expected to treat debates in the House as important events when the Prime Minister seldom (not more than two or three times a year) participates in those debates? (In fact, unlike Lester Pearson, he rarely stays in the Chamber long enough even to listen to debates.) Or, to refer in passing to the Other Place, how can we be expected to regard the Senate as a legitimate legislative assembly when the government populates that chamber with men and women whose contribution to the public weal has been the raising of money for the government party or organizing a campaign in one part of the country or another?

How can anyone be expected to view Opposition members as legislators when a man of the stature of John Diefenbaker (otherwise a great defender of Parliament, when it suits his purpose) defines the function of the Opposition (as he did in 1964, and has repeated many times since) in these words: "The duty of the Opposition is to turn out the Government"?

The best examination of the legislative process in Canada that I have come across is John Stewart's book, *The Canadian House of Commons*. In it, Dr. Stewart, himself a former Liberal M.P., makes this observation:

> They (Opposition) strive to wear the ministers down by attrition. In this attitude they are almost certain to be supported by the newsmen, who feel deprived when there are no parliamentary skirmishes to report.

Of course, newsmen feel deprived when there are no skirmishes to report. Of course, they look to Parliament for the theatre it provides. Members of Parliament have precisely the same attitude. M.P.'s are forever complaining that the press gallery empties after Question Period each day, leaving a solitary Canadian Press reporter (and maybe two or three others) to observe the rest of the day's deliberations. The complaint is justified. It is also justified, however, to note that the only seats which empty more quickly than the press seats following Question Period are the seats of the members. M.P.'s enjoy the confrontation and occasional drama of the Question Period; they are as bored as anyone else with the tedium of debates on legislation. (It can be argued that members would pay more attention to debates if the press paid more attention. It can also be argued that the press would pay more attention if M.P.'s paid more attention. It is a circular argument which leads nowhere.)

"The House of Commons," writes Dr. Stewart, "is the ordinary scene of the battle. It is the great public stage at the centre of the national amphitheatre." Leaving aside the skirmishes of the Question Period, the trouble with John Stewart's statement is that it is very rarely borne out in practice. The Pipeline Debate of the 1950s and the Flag Debate of the 1960s stand out because they were atypical. Great debates seldom occur in Parliament (witness the 1974 debate over wage and price controls or the debate, since November 15, 1976, over the future of the Canadian federation: both debates were waged, or are being waged, outside Parliament and the legislative process). Parliament no longer, if it ever did, exerts a major influence on public policy. Parliament does not control government expenditures. Parliament's role as a legislative body is limited to ratifying legislation and, occasionally, amending it, usually in minor ways. Every day, Parliament is confronted with decisions made elsewhere — by (a) the Cabinet, (b) an increasingly powerful civil service, and (c) the institution of the federal-provincial conference. It is no wonder members of Parliament feel frustrated. It is no wonder that the press looks elsewhere.

Influence of the Media: A Look at Some Cases

The odd thing is, the fact that Parliament is under-reported and under-appreciated by the media does not lessen the media's influence on the legislative process. If anything, the reverse seems to be true. So rarely does the press concentrate its full attention on the legislative system that, when it does, the effect is quite pronounced. For example, in 1973, the Liberals, then clinging to a shaky minority government, introduced the *Protection of Privacy Act*. In committee, the Opposition parties succeeded in inserting a provision requiring the police to notify the subjects of electronic surveillance that they had been under surveillance if, ninety days after the bug or wiretap was removed, charges had not been laid. Otto Lang, then the Minister of Justice, tried unsuccessfully to have this notification provision eliminated when the bill returned to the Commons for the report stage debate. The bill then went to the Senate, which did strike out the provision and sent the amended legislation back to the Commons. With virtual unanimity (itself a rarity), the media insisted that the notification procedure be re-inserted, and the Commons did so. Given that many Conservatives were unhappy about the notification procedure because of the constraint it imposed on the powers of the police, I do not think the provision would have been inserted in the first place, or re-inserted, had it not been for the pressure or influence of the media. More recently, of course, this provision was stripped out of the law. This can be explained in part by the return of a majority government. But it is also partly due to the fact that the media — which has an extremely short attention span — did not rally to the cause the second time around.

The *Privacy Act* espisode was an exception to a general rule. This rule is that the media's influence tends to be marginal once legislation has been introduced in Parliament. The media can draw the attention of the government and of Parliament to flaws in legislation, but once a bill has been introduced by the government, the media are as impotent as the Opposition to force the Cabinet to change the major principles and provisions. As with the Opposition, the media are unable to do much more than to cause the government to delay passage of a particular bill or to reconsider some of its details.

The greatest influence the media have on the legislative process is at the very beginning, before the process formally begins. Pressure from the media can persuade the government to proceed with legislation on a certain subject and it can help to create a public climate favourable to the legislation. The media's influence, however, does not extend to causing the government to follow a course that it does not want to follow or that it feels the public is not ready for it to follow.

A few examples. In 1968, at his first press conference after being elected leader of the Liberal Party, Pierre Trudeau said legislation to limit election spending by parties and candidates and to force disclosure of the sources of political funds would have top priority with his new administration. The press certainly supported the introduction of such a law. Yet it took five years and three general elections before the Trudeau Government came forward with the *Election Expenses Act*. The reason: the government was not ready to proceed and it did not think the public cared.

Capital punishment is an issue on which the media helped to persuade the government to proceed with a measure which the government wanted to introduce, but was afraid of the consequences. Although, according to the polls, around four out of five Canadians favoured the retention of the death penalty (at least for the murderers of police officers and prison guards), by and large the media supported abolition. At least the most influential elements of the media did. Without reasonably strong support from the media, I do not think the government would have introduced the legislation and I do not think Parliament, on its free vote, would have passed it. The political consequences of abolition were too great to risk flying in the face of concerted media opposition, had that opposition existed.

As a final example, the experience with legislation to "decriminalize" marijuana (to take it out of the *Narcotic Control Act* and bring it under the *Food and Drug Act*) illustrates, I believe, the limits on media influence. The government made up its mind, following publication of the interim report of the LeDain Commission in 1970, to introduce legislation. Understandably, it was nervous about this course and a bill did not appear until after the 1974 election. Generally speaking, the media, in the early 1970s, were sympathetic to decriminalization. And so, it appeared, was a substantial segment of the general public. Bill S-19 was introduced in the Senate. Hearings were held and the Senate, with misgivings, eventually passed the bill. The government, however, did not call the bill for debate in the Commons. When the last session of Parliament was prorogued, Bill S-19 died on the Commons order paper. It has not been re-introduced in the current session, and it will not be revived until after the election, if then. What happened was public attitudes changed. The media, sensing this hardening of the public mood, fell silent on the marijuana issue. The government, finding no encouragement from the media and precious little support from the public, quietly gave up on Bill S-19. It is possible that, had the press kept up the pressure, the government would, regardless of the public attitude, have screwed up its courage and carried on with the legislation, as it did on capital punishment.

So far, we have been dealing with the influence of the media in situations where the media play a role on one side of an issue or the other, through editorial pages or political columns or through the slant of news reports. There is, however, another influence, through the process of selection. Even if perfectly balanced in their treatment, the media can — and do — exercise a degree of influence when they decide which subjects, which bills, will be reported and which will not. Media coverage can cause Parliament to take a more careful look at legislation. The result may be better legislation; it may also mean slower passage.

Television in the Commons

Finally, no discussion of the influence of the media would be complete without reference to the televising of Parliament. Television in the House, which started in the fall of 1977, is too recent a phenomenon to permit more than the most tentative appraisal. To my mind, however, television has had three effects. First, it has heightened the profile of the Leader of the Opposition. Prior to television in the House, Joe Clark seemed to occupy a notch a slot below and a slot behind the Prime Minister. Now, however, he is seen every day to be sharing the same stage with Trudeau. He is on his feet, questioning the Prime Minister as an equal, rather than as an inferior to a superior. Television, I suspect, has made Clark appear to be more an alternative to Trudeau than he appeared before. To a lesser degree, the same is true of Ed Broadbent, the leader of the New Democratic Party. Second, television has increased the credibility of Opposition M.P.'s in general, and of the major Opposition critics, in particular. Canadians have a fairly good idea of who federal ministers are and they have an impression as to their ability. Outside their own regions, however, most Opposition members are an unknown quantity. Television has introduced the country to a new cast of parliamentary performers — M.P.'s such as Flora MacDonald, Sinclair Stevens, Elmer MacKay, Bill Jarvis, John Fraser, Jim Gillies, Lincoln Alexander, Walter Baker, among many others. Viewers have an opportunity to see and to judge the alternative government — which may be helpful, or harmful, to the Opposition, depending on the opinion the public forms of them.

Third, television in the House has forced every newsman on Parliament Hill to be more careful, more scrupulous, in his own reporting. Now that the people can see what actually goes on in Parliament, journalists have to make sure that their own work is a fair, accurate reflection of that activity. This effect is totally to the good.

Responsibility of the Media

Let us turn now to the other side of the topic — the responsibility of the media in the legislative process. I confess that I always feel uncomfortable in a discussion of media responsibility. It is a subject without an adequate definition. Responsibility to whom? To oneself? To one's editors, publishers, or news directors? To one's readers or listeners? To the subjects of one's news stories, columns or editorials? Responsibility for what? For being honest and fair? For being candid, even if one's views are unpopular? For being comprehensive, for reporting every event, no matter how trivial? For the exercise of one's own independent judgment, no matter how imperfect that judgment may be?

Journalists know, more or less, when they are being responsible and when they are not. But if you were to ask ten of them what they mean by responsibility or irresponsibility, you would get ten quite different answers.

Part of the problem is that freedom of the press is defined essentially in negative terms. There are laws which state that the press shall *not* commit libel or slander, that it shall *not* publish material which would jeopardize the security of the state, that it shall *not* advocate genocide or disseminate any other material which falls under the heading of hate propaganda. There are rules or standards of conduct within the media which oblige the press *not* to print lies, *not* to deliberately mislead, *not* to hold a public figure up to the unwarranted contempt of his peers. Overwhelmingly, these laws and rules are honoured.

There are no laws or rules, however, to say what a free press *must or should* publish or broadcast. Publishers, editors and broadcasters may print or broadcast whatever they choose on any subject, or nothing at all on a subject. No one can force me to write about a subject, or to express a certain view on a particular subject that I do write about. This is the way it must be in a democracy, although it makes for an untidy system and it imposes a very considerable responsibility on writers, editors and broadcasters to exercise their discretion with extreme care.

I feel this responsibility every day. Every day, there are things I am tempted to say in print. I do not say them because I feel that somehow it would be irresponsible. In most cases, if I stopped to examine my reaction, I probably would not know why I feel it would not be responsible. In a personal sense, therefore, responsibility is more intuitive than institutionalized.

I do feel that the press has a responsibility to try to be as objective as humanly possible in its news coverage. Complete objectivity is impossible; the act of selecting what one will report (and it is not possible to report everything), precludes total objectivity. In the absence of perfect objectivity, the press, I think, has a responsibility to be honest in its treatment and presentation of news and opinion. It has a responsibility to be fair. In my case, as a political columnist, honesty and fairness mean that, before I embrace a specific cause, position or argument, I should make very sure that I am thoroughly acquainted with the competing causes, positions or arguments. The press should, in my view, have as full an understanding of the ideas it rejects as it has of the ideas it endorses.

The Globe and Mail is — and this must be a personal opinion, of course — the best newspaper in Canada. I also believe it is the most responsible. I have never, however, heard anyone at *The Globe and Mail* offer a definition of responsibility. Perhaps I could suggest one: responsibility means respect for one's audience. A responsible journalist does not talk down to his readers or listeners. He does not insult their intelligence. He does not give them information or opinion which they know, from their own experience, is false or ridiculous. He does not treat complex subjects in a superficial manner. He does not treat insignificant matters as though they were insignificant. He may well seek to entertain his audience, but first he will seek to inform it.

We all recognize irresponsible journalism when we encounter it. In the last analysis, the most effective remedy is to stop buying the newspaper or listening to the radio or television station. The influence and responsibility of the media is a complicated subject and, in closing, I might offer two observations. In his book, *CP: The Story of The Canadian Press,* published in 1948, M.E. Nichols quoted an observation made by a man named W.B. Lanigan, who was the freight traffic manager of the CPR (and the brother of the versifier, George T. Lanigan). W.B. Lanigan said this: "The press, more than the pulpit, more even than Parliament or the people, is really (the) guide to the destinies of Canada." The second observation is from an American, Zechariah Chaffee, Jr., in *The Press Under Pressure* (Nieman Reports, April, 1948): "The press is a sort of wild animal in our midst — restless, gigantic, always seeking new ways to use its strength. . . . The sovereign press for the most part acknowledges accountability to no one except its owners and publishers."

The two observations, I submit, are equally absurd. The truth lies somewhere in between. The press is not a saviour or a devil. It is not a hero or a villain. It is not a house pet or a wild animal. It may not be as competent as it should be. It may too often be lazy. It may too infrequently be a source of inspiration. But there is one thing it always is. Good or bad, loved or hated, the press is inevitable.

COMMENTS

WALTER D. YOUNG*

It is important to make a distinction at the outset between the several media of communication for it is clear that not all have the same impact on the legislative process. We know that the general public are now more dependent on television for information about the political process, while the Members of Parliament and legislative assemblies continue to rely heavily on newspapers both for information of a general sort and about government in particular. The most cursory glance through Hansard will demonstrate the remarkable impact of the press on Parliament: most members sooner or later during a session will use as the basis for questions, speeches and interjections, material gleaned from the press. Each member depends upon the press for information from his riding.

For the politician the press sets the agenda. As Mr. Stevens indicated in his remarks, this means that in a subtle way, the agenda in Ottawa is influenced by the *New York Times* in that the choice of major stories by that paper exerts some influence on editorial choice in Toronto, Ottawa and Vancouver. The decision to feature some news and "bury" other news impinges directly on the political process by providing the rank ordering of significance of items that will confront the politician as he begins his daily search for current issues.

Quality of Reporters

No one would argue then with the proposition that newspapers remain a key element in the political equation in Canada, particularly so where Parliament is concerned. It is disturbing then to read in Stevens' paper that of the two hundred and twenty journalists accredited to the press gallery, no more than a dozen have, in Mr. Stevens' judgment, any thorough knowledge of the process they report. Those of us familiar with the denizens of the press gallery in Victoria will not find this assertion difficult to accept; it is nonetheless disturbing.

We are some distance away from the "good old days" described recently by F.S. Manor of the *Winnipeg Free Press*. Then, he asserted, the great newspapers in London and Paris drew their editorial staff from amongst the top graduates of the great universities, put them out to learn the trade in the provincial dailies, and then brought them in to apply their intelligence as correspondents or leader writers for the *London Times* or *Le Monde*. It would seem that such a determined search for quality is no longer conducted.

Having charged his colleagues with incompetence, Mr. Stevens does seek to exonerate some of them by arguing that many are specialists on matters such as finance, energy and the like. This is a thin excuse since it assumes that

---

* Professor and Chairman of the Department of Political Science, University of Victoria

parliamentary reporting can be handled piecemeal when the process itself is anything but piecemeal.

As a further excuse Mr. Stevens cites the contempt of Mr. Trudeau for Parliament as justification for the gallery reporters' apparent ignorance of the institution. He further suggests that the view of John Diefenbaker that the function of the Opposition is a purely negative one is further justification for the ignorance of the press gallery. Neither of these arguments are supportable.

In the first case if the reporters understood Parliament they would have contempt for the Prime Minister's attitude. It would seem that Mr. Stevens is suggesting that the reporters are so blinded by the glare of the Trudeau intellect that they can only mimic his cynicism. In the second case it seems curious to blame John Diefenbaker. While there is much for which that man must bear responsibility, I would suggest that the quality of the parliamentary press gallery is not one of his mistakes.

Question Period and Press Releases

Mr. Stevens suggests that reporters, like M.P.'s, flee the chamber once Question Period is over because they know that the speeches will not only be tedious, they will also be pointless. There is some point in this argument, but it is less than Mr. Stevens makes of it. Most reporters rush back to their desks to engage in the delicate task of re-writing the press releases government and parties provide them, for that is a much simpler task than actually reporting debates. Government departments do not supply such awesome quantities of potted news on the off chance that it might be used. They know it is used. Moreover it seems quite likely that, if the major dailies started reporting members' speeches, the speeches would begin to assume somewhat more importance than they do at present.

The concentration of press and parliamentarian alike on the Question Period reflects not only the drama of that procedure, but the fact that it is covered. The relationship is circular: because it is covered, it is well attended and dramatic; and because it is well attended and dramatic, it is covered. As Mr. Stevens points out, the press does have power. By concentrating on an issue it can, as the prime agenda setter, keep it before the house. It follows that what the press chooses to cover becomes more important. The impact of television on the House of Commons is instructive in this regard for the heightened coverage has, it seems, changed attendance patterns.

Reference is often made in discussing the role of the press to the power of the corporations that own newspapers. It is often argued that, if Brigadier Malone sneezes, every editor in the F.P. chain catches cold. This is one of the oldest chestnuts in the business for the truth is that the degree of independence in each newspaper is remarkable. In fact, there is little attempt made to maximize the benefits of concentration of ownership.

Trivia and Parochialism

Readers of the daily press in Victoria will be familiar with the strange penchant of our papers to ignore the better columns and stories printed in the larger papers in the chain in favour of inconsequential and often misleading filler from Canadian and American wire services. The *Colonist* decided today that its readers would be wiser with the knowledge that "Gallstones [are] the Leading Canadian Abnormality," and the following five inches of story, rather than a column by F.P.'s own Geoffrey Stevens or Allan Fotheringham, or a story from such reporters on the Vancouver *Sun* as Neale Adams or Jess Odam.

If there is a besetting sin of the newspaper business, it is the fascination with trivia and the deeply imbedded belief in the importance of the parochial over the provincial or national. The outlook of the readership is too parochial to begin with. It seems remarkable that at a time when a major concern is the state of confederation our papers provide so little information to their readers from outside the borders of their province or city. This is particularly remarkable when a chain like F.P. has papers in every major city.

For the legislators who rely upon the press, the trivialization and parochialism of the press is a major disservice. Dependent as they are upon the press to facilitate the educative function of the legislative process — a process which educates the legislator and the constituent — it is surely not a great deal to ask that the press accept its responsibility and ensure that both the quality of its reporters and the quality of its reports rise a good deal higher than the present standard in most Canadian cities.

Geoffrey Stevens considers that the *Globe and Mail* is the best newspaper in Canada. Few would deny that statement. It is much more difficult to single out the worst; there are so many vying for that title. If the press is inevitable, must it be inevitably mediocre? Dominated on the one hand by excessive parochial concerns, and on the other by a political executive that controls it by judicious use of press releases and leaks, the press has surrendered much of its freedom, and in so doing has forsaken its once signal role as the fourth estate. Given the condition of the third estate, that is a sad circumstance indeed.

BRUCE HUTCHISON*

Mr. Stevens, an insider of politics, and a respected authority on Canadian affairs, has given us such a perceptive analysis of the so-called media that I can add only an outsider's dubious comment, a long way from the centre of things.

As an old newspaperman, I know little about the other media but I can assure you that in the printed press no single happy medium will be found. Every newspaper worth its salt is always dissatisfied with its performance and so it should be. The same is true of all human institutions in an age when nothing seems to work very well any more.

---

* Editorial Director, Vancouver Sun, political commentator and author.

More Influence or Less?

Now, according to the conventional wisdom, which is often wrong, the influence of the press has declined in modern times, but influence is too subtle for easy measurement. With the prejudice of my trade, I would argue, on the contrary, that the influence of the press is as strong today as it ever was. It is perhaps even stronger, though exercised in a changing fashion.

At least it is strong enough to provoke the frequent anger of the men and women most concerned with it — I mean the politicians. And they have good reason for their discontent. One can understand the frustration of an elected person when he spends days or weeks of research and makes a considered parliamentary speech of real substance only to find some unimportant paragraph headlined because it is titillating, whimsical or scandalous, while the meat is buried in the tomb of Hansard. G.K. Chesteron, the leading journalist of his time, once wrote that there were only three ways to deal with a speech — to report it in complete text, to summarize its arguments fairly or, in charity, to ignore it altogether — and the last way, he thought, was usually the best.

When I began in this business, the newspapers had space for almost full texts and their parliamentary reports were so long that nobody would read them if they were printed now in a different society, a society overwhelmed by the daily blizzard of news, bewildered by indigestible information, punchdrunk with sensation and always looking for quick, easy answers, when there are none. If the public really wants the detailed records of politics that we used to write, it can find them, at nominal cost, in Hansard, but its circulation is less than that of the most obscure weekly newspapers. The public as a whole wants livelier reading. It has a fixed addiction to trivia.

One result of these contemporary attitudes and the new techniques that report them is the decline of Parliament, the increasing power of the executive and the erosion of the democratic process. Or so most elected persons warn us. However that may be — a subject too complex for this particular discussion — how can we measure the actual influence of the press? And how can we judge whether it is good or bad?

In some respects that influence has certainly deteriorated since earlier pioneer days when newspaper editorials were holy writ for the politically devout. But if the modern readers wisely refuse to take their views and principles from some anonymous source, the editorial columns still influence public thought like water dripping on a stone and gradually altering its shape for better or worse. Repetition is a powerful weapon.

Anyhow, the decisive influence on events cannot be reckoned by a scientific Gallup poll because, in all societies, a minority, perhaps only about ten percent, is the effective moulder of opinion. The political party, the man or woman, the attractive doctrine and even the newspaper that can sway this group will generally sway the community. Revolutions, and indeed all great social changes, are the work of small numbers with large ideas. In such work the influence of the press must be considered as a whole, including not only the newspaper's own opinions but its treatment of the news, its feature stories, its use of syndicated material, Canadian and foreign, its photographs and cartoons, the views of its columnists, and, above all, its selection and emphasis.

The Press vs T.V. and Radio

The impact of this bulging and contradictory package is, so to say, osmotic and subconscious. It percolates into a public mind almost unaware of its effect. The effect is profound all the same. Whether it is as influential as the effect of the competing electronic media no one can yet say but the competition, I believe, is healthy. The print medium, which takes hours to prepare and market its product, cannot compete with television and radio for scoops, and therefore must depend on its wider coverage, its accuracy and a depth of analysis impossible in the brief capsules offered by its rivals with their instant news, capsules that are often more dramatic than significant. So, in general, are the one-minute television appearances of elected persons who must try to explain some complex and insoluble problem in a few sentences, a hopeless task but the only way they can reach the national audience within the rigid electronic framework. This makes for good theatre but poor argument.

Here we encounter a curious phenomenon never mentioned in the deliberations of the Task Force on National Unity or in this erudite assembly. Politicians, even if they are unilingual, have to speak in two separate languages. In Parliament they use a kind of professional shop talk, citing facts and figures well known to their peers but not to the public. When they address a lay audience, directly or by television, they use a much simpler and overcondensed idiom if they are to be understood at all.

In the same way newspapers also use two idioms, the serious in depth argument of the editorials — or so we like to think — and the intimate, colloquial, folksy lingo of the feature story, the sport page, the entertainment world and the signed column.

It is all very well for learned critics to deplore the extra-parliamentary language, or televised wisecracks, of the politicians and to sniff at the literary style of the press. But in both cases the public must be reached in a language that it can understand. The multitude cannot be moved by the arcane jargon of the experts and its attention cannot be held for long by a recital of abstractions or statistics.

If the politicians and the press have a similar and joint communication problem, they live in an adversary relationship whatever their personal feelings may be and, as a rule, the latter are friendly. The politicians must use the press to reach the public. To do its job, the press must study, analyse, suspect or approve the utterances and acts of the politicians. Such is the essential machinery and balance wheel of the democratic process. Without honest politicians and honest media, in mutual tension, there can be no free society.

Responsibilities of the Press

This ancient platitude brings me to the second item on the agenda, the responsibilities of the press. There is no time to discuss them properly but I would venture to suggest that the newspapers, despite their many flaws, are far more responsible now than they were in the past. With their improved technology and economic resources, they bring to the reader every day a worldwide diet of information, comment, entertainment and conflicting ideas unknown and unobtainable only a few decades ago. Anyone who cares to read the old newspaper files will see a remarkable improvement both of scope and quality. He will also see that the better modern newspapers, unlike their predecessors, are not unquestioning advocates and appendages of political parties, and their factual news reports, however inadequate, are no longer deliberately slanted as they were in a previous generation. When slant creeps in it is the result of human error, the prejudice or, more likely, the incompetence of the reporter, not of policy in any respectable paper. On the other hand, slant, or personal opinion, is the essence of editorial comment and of the signed column and so long as it is clearly labelled as such the reader can accept or reject it and is not misled.

Another change in the press, generally for the better, should be noted. The newspapers permit their columnists a freedom of expression unimaginable in the past. The views of the columnists, more often than not, are in direct conflict with those of the publishers and editors. As never in earlier days the newspaper has become what it should be — a forum where ideas, no matter how controversial or perhaps crazy, are published for the consideration of the readers who can judge their worth. When today's political heresy may be tommorow's orthodoxy, which is quite probable, the honest newspaper is bound to print it, even while disagreeing with it.

But contrary to the beliefs of some journalists, the responsibility of the press does not include the right to govern the nation. Others, who should be better equipped, are elected for that purpose. Responsibility does include, however, the right to report, investigate and expose the public business — also to offer advice, usually ignored by government and opposition alike. Whether the advice currently offered is wise or foolish, only future events will reveal. But it may be noted in passing that many of the economic judgments now being solemnly pronounced on all sides of politics as blazing new discoveries were printed, years ago, in most newspapers and rejected at the time, as preposterous.

And yet, ending where I began these speculations, it is still true that the press, like every social institution, lags far behind the needs of humanity at a time not only to try men's souls but to question the survival of any free society and, in the age of nuclear weapons and poisons, the endurance of our species. Of such things all our politicians are aware, though in politics they are too often shunted aside because smaller concerns appear more urgent, particularly in an election year. Hence the final responsibility of the media, as was well said by a forgotten Senate committee, is to prepare the public for a future very different from the present and, I would suspect, much less comfortable.

CATHERINE BERGMAN*

I have no quarrel with what has been said this morning about the responsibility of the press although I would like to add a comment here: I suggest that this responsibility is not quite the same for francophone and anglophone journalists. I have to be careful not to be misunderstood, so I first will tell you what I do not mean.

Almost a year ago the Quebec Minister of Communications suggested that Quebec broadcasters have a social responsibility towards the creation of a national collective conscience. More recently, the Lévesque government has revived the old argument that freedom of information and comment is of public interest; therefore, it should be protected by the authorities. This theory has been clearly rejected by the Fédération professionnelle des Journalistes du Québec which declared that the role of government should be restricted to keeping an eye on the concentration of ownership. The Fédération rejected the suggestion that the press has a special role to play in the particular context of Quebec.

Interpreting the Quebec View

That is not to say, however, that the notion is totally irrelevant, and here I come to the point of management. Francophone journalists have to work in a world which is largely English, not only in its language, but also its interests, perceptions and its sensitivities. Claude Ryan, in a presentation to the Special Senate Committee on Mass Media in 1970 pointed out that the francophone media suffer from a smaller source of news than their anglophone counterpart. The Canadian Press, which is our bread and butter, moves twice as much material in English as in French. The francophone media, therefore, have to make do with material gathered for an anglophone audience. You can immediately see where that puts us when it comes to the selection of news, which Geoffrey Stevens identified as our main responsibility. The power of the press is a power of selection, but the francophone press does not have that power. For example, the front page of the *Globe and Mail* determines not only the line-up of the CBC news, and the front pages of many English-Canadian newspapers; it influences the line-up of the French news as well. This process would not be so bad if there was some cross-pollination. But, unfortunately there is little, if any, reciprocity. And in these times where differences in perception are particularly crucial, where words like national unity do not mean the same thing in Quebec as in the rest of Canada, it is particularly unfortunate. Add to this the fact that, by a series of circumstances, the Quebec public has been deprived of three of its main

* National radio correspondent, Société Radio-Canada, Ottawa

newspapers during the operationally crucial period of the life of the Lévesque government, and that Radio-Canada has been so intimidated as to exert a self-censorship of unprecedented proportions, and you will understand the concern of an editorialist who wrote recently that there is no media at the present time to reflect exclusively the Quebec view of things, let alone a Quebec view of things Canadian. In my opinion, this is one of the most serious problems in Canada today.

PIERRE O'NEIL*

Geoffrey Stevens has alluded to the context in which the legislative process takes place and in that connection I would like to make two comments.

First, it is a very sorry lot of journalists that is called nowadays to cover the process of legislation through the committees and the House of Commons. In the evolution of government as theatre and politics as entertainment, the essence of the play is not what has reporters running and readers reading. The big stuff is the actor, his manner of dress, his looks on television, his wife, his talent, his fortune, and his hobbies — and not necessarily in that order! Performance, and not the play itself, is what counts. The divisions of caucus, the pronouncements of stars, their travels, their encounters with other actors of the drama supercede the long and most often tedious work of the House and committees.

Remoteness & Isolation

My second comment has to do with the remoteness of the legislative process and political reporting from day-to-day realities. This I suppose is affected by the fact that things happen in Vancouver that are legislated upon in Victoria. They happen in Calgary, Montreal and St. John but are legislated upon in Edmonton, Quebec City and Fredericton. It is well known that nothing ever happens in Ottawa but that is the place from which all legislative wisdom flows. In addition, not only are some of our capital cities remote from the real action, but within these capitals, legislatures are small worlds unto themselves where you can spend days or weeks without too much contact with the outside world.

Another factor of isolation lies in the fact that in some of these legislatures the real opposition is not always in the House. There have been times since 1970 when opposition to the Quebec government was not in the legislature but in the streets, pressure groups, labour unions and political parties underrepresented in the legislature. Perhaps the opposition to Mr. Lévesque is not now in the National Assembly. There have been periods in the past twenty years when one could have the same feeling in Ottawa. That situation adds a touch of unreality to the legislative process.

---

* Director of Television News, Société Radio-Canada, Montreal

In that context of isolation, the vanguard of our political press, the parliamentary correspondent, is dependent on the so-called Tuesday to Thursday club. One is in the hands of his editor when it comes to feedback which is one of the reasons why so many parliamentary correspondents write for their editor-in-chief. And right there the possibilities for distortion are enormous. Finally, the context of isolation is also marginally more evident in the press gallery from the fact that a number of parliamentary correspondents could not, at least in my days, read *Le Devoir* for instance.

The aura of isolation is further heightened by the fact that the members of the House of Commons and those who cover it live in a huge national fish bowl. Generally speaking, our political press is made up of people who live in the fish bowl, the political correspondents, and people who look at the fish bowl, the editorial writers. The first group perceive reality from the fish bowl's point of view. The second may be more familiar with the number of problems but are less familiar with life in fish bowls and therefore are a little more prone to faux pas and do not always exert the influence they might wish they had.

Influencing Politicians

The parliamentary correspondents are in a slightly better position than the editorial writers. They know or should know the legislative process very well but their perception of problems being legislated upon often leaves much to be desired. Nevertheless, because of their proximity to power, they certainly affect the behaviour, if not the thinking, of the M.P.'s. Senator Lamontagne has written of this phenomenon:

> Most politicians are 'news worms'. They are as fond of rumours, scoops and personal stories as most reporters. Both groups live in the same isolated world although they usually despise each other. This cohabitation produces strange results. In most cases the politician is almost unconsciously mystified by the reporter. Thus, while the mass media have little impact on the public, they have a great deal of influence on the politician. Therein lies the rising power of the press.

But I ask you, what is the influence on the legislative process of a press whose influence is rising but only in relation to a politician who is becoming more and more impotent? Because I think we agree here that for a multitude of reasons the politician is experiencing a dramatic reduction of his own influence on legislation. On the whole, it is my contention that we are not very influential on either the politician or our audience. I say this in a totally impressionistic way and I am talking less in terms of the media at large than in terms of political and interpretive reporting.

As Mr. Stevens mentioned, there is a need for more competence, much harder work and research before we may expect better reporting of the multi-faceted process of legislation. There is also a need for more straightforward and complete reporting at large, and for concentration on the real problems, not necessarily those that through the institutionalization of information we have a tendency to report. I am unable to resist mentioning the perhaps well-known views of a former editor of the *Miami News* who said that if Jesus Christ reappeared and walked down the Miami streets proclaiming the second coming he would probably not get space in the papers unless he hired a press agent and had his publicity man call a press conference to proclaim the glad tiding. And to get the story out of Miami and onto the wire services it would be necessary for one of the Miami papers to get a special angle so it could copyright its story and thus make the wire service take notice of it as something extraordinary to which the former editor's friend commented: "That is a hell of a way to have to get access to a press which claims to reflect the community it serves."

A journalist is nothing less than a professional witness. The job calls for a keen appreciation of the relevant facts and true sense of self-discipline. Well done it is a most useful, honourable and rewarding craft — for I agree with Geoffrey Stevens, sometimes I dare not say profession.

FRANCES RUSSELL*

I would like to develop another dimension to the question of the influence and responsibilities of the media in the legislative process — one with which I have had experience in two provinces — and that is the impact of polarized politics on the media and vice versa.

Political Polarization

Political polarization — the existence of only two parties, sharply divided on the lines of clearly opposed social and economic ideologies — heightens and intensifies every aspect of the political process, from elections, through the role of public opinion, the conduct of the legislature and, most particularly, the responsibilities of the media.

I think you are all aware of what I mean by the term polarization. It is used to define the situation which exists when politics becomes a contest, not between competing consensus-seeking political parties, but between the ideology of socialism and the ideology of free enterprise.

We in the press pride ourselves on objectivity. Obviously, none of us can be completely objective, because as living, breathing people, who have chosen political journalism as a career, we do have opinions, views, even biases. So what I mean by objectivity is the ability to stand aside personally and assess both sides critically and to avoid partisan identification.

While that is sometimes difficult to achieve, most journalists agree that is the primary goal which we seek. Political columnists, who are paid to have opinions, wish to avoid taking a partisan political stance because we believe, and

---

* Political Columnist, Winnipeg Tribune.

rightly, that the greater our objectivity, the greater the impact we will have on the politicians, the legislative process and the public.

Such non-partisan objectivity is relatively easily maintained in non-polarized political situations. As particular issues cross party lines in non-polarized legislatures, so can a journalist champion one cause or another without jeopardizing his non-partisan position.

However, in polarized political climates, such as the one in British Columbia, in my native province of Manitoba, in Saskatchewan and now, on a different level, in Quebec, there is no more middle, no more neutral or floating ground. Issues are black and white, they are always stated in highly simplistic terms, they do not cut across party lines, the public is for or against, and the press, no matter what it does and whether it is willing or unwilling, objective or non-objective, fair or unfair, gets labelled.

Objective Reporting

It is, for a journalist nurtured on the professional ideal of as great an objectivity as is humanly possible, a shattering experience. Put simply, no matter how fair or objective you think you are, you simply will not be seen that way. Like nature abhors a vacuum, polarity abhors non-ideology. In fact, it really abhors objectivity. It will label you, willy-nilly.

If objectivity is no longer a realistic goal for a journalist, for what, then, can he or she strive? I would like to return to Geoffrey Stevens' two points here — the first being fairness and the second, understanding what ideas you reject as clearly as the ideas you embrace.

But above and beyond that, the journalist, I think, must step back and decide what he believes in philosophically, not on an *ad hoc* basis but quite systematically. He can choose one side or the other, of course. Or, and this is the route I personally favour, because it is the closest to the ideal of fairness, he can formulate his own personal stance, articulate it, and then, be consistent and above all, maintain his own personal integrity.

In polarity, a credible media is more crucial than ever. A credible media can ameliorate or blunt the excesses of the polarized political or legislative process. It can help the public maintain its own balance against the efforts of either side to stampede citizens one way or another. And it can be a voice for moderation and common sense against the forces of what could be termed the "true believers."

A BASIC BIBLIOGRAPHY

THE INFLUENCE AND RESPONSIBILITIES OF THE MEDIA IN THE LEGISLATIVE PROCESS

Adam, G. Stuart, ed. *Journalism, Communication and the Law*. Scarborough: Prentice-Hall, 1976.

Carter, Douglas. *The Fourth Branch of Government*. Boston: Houghton Mifflin, 1959.

Chaffee, Zechariah. *The Press Under Pressure* (Nieman Reports, April 1978).

Fletcher, F.J. "Between Two Schools: News Coverage of Provincial Politics in Ontario." In D. MacDonald, ed., *Government and Politics of Ontario*. Toronto: Macmillan, 1975.

Hamlin, D.L.B., ed. *The Press and the Public*. Toronto: University of Toronto Press, 1962.

Kesterton, W.H. *The Law and the Press in Canada*. Toronto: McClelland and Stewart, 1976.

Lyons, L.M., ed. *Reporting the News*. Cambridge, Mass.: Belknap Press of Harvard University Press, 1965.

Nichols, M.E. *CP, The Story of the Canadian Press*. Toronto: Ryerson Press, 1948.

Rutherford, Paul. *The Making of the Canadian Media*. Toronto: McGraw-Hill Ryerson, 1978.

Seymour-Ure, C. *The Press, Politics and the Public*. London: Methuen, 1968.

Warnock, John. "All the News It Pays to Print." In Ian Lumsden, ed., *Close to the 49th Parallel, etc.*, pp. 117-34. Toronto: University of Toronto Press, 1970.

Williams, Francis E. *Dangerous Estate, The Anatomy of Newspapers*, London: Longmans Green, 1957.

Zolf, Larry. *Dance of the Dialectic*. Toronto: J. Lewis and Samuel, 1973.

Chapter Eight

Procedural Reform in the Legislative Process

by
C. E. S. Franks *

"Procedure is all the constitution the poor Englishman has," a British parliamentarian said a few years ago. This may be true in England, but it is not in Canada. In England, Parliament is, in a very real way, still supreme; executive and legislative power are centralized in Cabinet and Parliament; elections frequently lead to changes of government; and parliamentary discussion and arguments influence the outcome of elections. In Britain, parliamentary procedure establishes the ground rules for political struggles. Canada isdifferent. Executive and legislative power are divided between the central government and ten provinces, and diplomatic relations and treaty making between these levels of government are a major, if not the most important, part of political decision making; only two of the last thirteen elections — during forty-five years — have produced changes of government; and argument in Parliament seems to do little except slow down and cause inconvenience to the dominant Liberal government. We have a huge body of constitutional law, a written constitution, and sophisticated and extensive discussion of constitutional reform, in which parliamentary procedure does not figure. And in view of the threats to national unity, doubtless to many people worrying about parliamentary procedure is something like arguing over wine lists on the Titanic. The recent record of the House of Commons[1] shows that procedural reform has not had a very high priority: the Standing Committee on Procedure and Organization has not met since 1976, and its useful suggestions for reform made in the first session of the present, Thirtieth, Parliament have led to no further action. There is not likely to be action before the next election and, if it produces a minority government, procedural reform might be further deferred.

All this sounds negative, and suggests that procedural reform is not going to do much to ameliorate the basic political problems now facing Canada. But the same is true of many aspects of political reform. Procedural reform is only a

---

* Professor of Political Science, Queen's University.
[1] This paper will exclusively consider procedure and procedural reform in the House of Commons, neglecting the Senate.

small part of Canadian politics, and can only produce minor changes to the political processes. But perhaps, in the long run, the sum of many small improvements is more significant than grand designs that get lost in the sand.

Reform to parliamentary procedure is important and possible. Few people would question that Parliament works better now than it did in the sixties, or that it has become more useful and more important, and it is largely because of procedural reforms, such as improvements to the committee system, the reduction of obstructionism, an enhanced position of Speaker, and so on, that Parliament has regained its lost esteem. There is a great deal more than can be done, and this paper will look at a few of the possibilities. Procedure might seem dry and remote from the urgent political problems of the day, but two points should be borne in mind. First, improvement to procedure means improvement to political discussion in general: a better hearing for the variety of opinions in the country; a more sensitive and responsive government; better policies, laws, and administration. This in turn diminishes the sense of crisis and catastrophe which pervades all too much discussion of issues in Canada. Secondly, Parliament is the most important national forum in Canada, and the only national forum where directly elected representatives of all people confront a government face-to-face on issues of national policy; and for this reason alone it and reform to it are important and worthwhile.

Improvement does not mean the same thing to all people. To the government, improvement means more certainty of getting its financial and legislative programme through the House in reasonable time; to the opposition, improvement means more opportunities and tools for finding the weak spots in the government, and bringing these weaknesses to the voters' attention. The public has a third interest beyond that of any party: that parliamentary processes should enable different viewpoints to be reflected in government, and that parliamentary processes enable the public to understand and support, rather than acquiesce or submit to, government. Much of the difficulty in achieving reforms comes from conflict between these competing interests: the obvious one between opposition and government; and the less obvious but more important one between the role of Parliament as the central focus of intense partisan conflict, and the role of Parliament as the national forum which legislates and inquires on behalf of all the diverse people, regions and interests of Canada, rather than those represented in one, two, or more political parties. In the following sections, I shall examine some of the main areas in which reform is needed, and examine the possible reforms in light of how they affect these diverse and often conflicting functions of Parliament.

CONTROL OVER TIME

Time is one of the most important commodities in parliamentary politics. The number of days the House of Commons can sit in a year is limited. In recent years it has often sat on more than 180 days, reaching a high of 214 in 1964. The

Committee on Procedure and Organization in 1976[2] considered that 150 sitting days in a year was enough, and would ensure that there would be, in additon to the existing Christmas, Easter, and summer recesses, six further week-long breaks during the yearly session, in which members could visit their constituencies and renew their necessary contacts with the people they represent. This proposal of 150 sitting days is about the minimum that has been suggested for a full-time Parliament (in addition to 15 working days for committee work), and a more realistic goal would be, somewhere between 160 and 170 days, which is still a reduction of over one month from the present. Subtracting from this total of 160 days, 8 days for the Address Debate, 6 days for the Budget Debate, 25 allotted days (opposition days on Supply, which we shall come back to later), and perhaps 3 days for debates on matters of urgent public importance, a session would leave the government about 118 days in which to get its legislative programme approved. (It should be noted in passing that the reduction of the Throne Speech and Budget Debates, and Supply, to this total represents one of the main achievements in recent procedural reform, for much of the most tedious and obnoxious obstruction used to take place on these occasions.) One hundred and eighteen days would appear adequate for a government's yearly programme of about 50 bills to be discussed: about half the bills in each session are routine and should pass with brief discussion, while many more require only a total of a day's sitting, and only a few are so contentious as to demand several days of debate. But recent sessions have been excessively long — extending for periods of nearly two years, and often containing over 250 sitting days (the longest, the first session of the Thirtieth Parliament, began on 30 September, 1974, ended on 12 October, 1976, and included 343 sittings). Much of this time has been taken up with unnecessarily long debates on government legislation, especially on Second Reading.

Reforms to procedure on bills will be looked at more closely in the next section; here I only want to make the point that far too much time is now taken on legislation. Ideally, a parliamentary session should begin and end in a year. A year is the period of the budget cycle, of the pattern of recesses and sittings, and it should also be the framework within which bills are processed through Parliament. Controlling and limiting the time spent on legislation is the key to achieving a return to the good practice of annual sessions.

The burden of limiting debate on legislation must fall on the government. The opposition has little interest in it and, quite the opposite, superficially appears to have a great deal to gain through obstructing and delaying bills, picking as many holes as possible in the government's programme, and attempting to wear the government down so that it is shown to be incompetent. Canadian oppositions since 1960 have been obstructionist. A deeper look,

---

[2] Canada, House of Commons, Standing Committee on Procedure and Organization, *Minutes*, 30 Sept. 1976, 20:54.

however, suggests that opposition parties have probably been harming themselves through excessive time spent on debates. A recent survey has shown that newspaper reporting of Question Period exceeds reporting of debates on government motions by a ratio of 35:1, even though far more time is spent by the House on the debates than on questions.[3] The exodus of members, visitors, and press gallery from the chamber and its galleries after Question Period, which leaves them almost deserted, illustrates the same lack of interest in debates. Mr. Ged Baldwin, a senior opposition member, has stated that: ''debate has got out of hand in this House. And there are reasons for it: it is too long, it is too repetitive, it is too virulent, it does not do the job.''[4] If the opposition's purpose in prolonging debate is to persuade the public, it is obviously failing because it is ignored; if its purpose is to prevent the government from governing, it is also failing because ultimately the government gets its legislation through; and if its purpose is to lead to the government's defeat at the polls, the record shows a singular lack of success: one defeat in the six elections since 1960. To go even further, a good case can be made for the argument that the opposition loses more than it gains by prolonging debate: its effective points get drowned in a sea of verbiage; excessively long debates conceal the sparseness of government legislation on the order paper; too much freedom leads the opposition to sloppiness and a weakened inclination to separate what is of fundamental importance from what ought to be supported or only opposed on minor points and let through without delay; and the opposition gets caught up in a bad habit of mindless and irresponsible opposition to virtually every piece of government business without being forced to consider whether, if it were in power, it would be doing the same thing. This ''opposition mentality'' — of being against everything and in favour of nothing — reduces the opposition's credibility as an alternative government. The government also ought to be disturbed that its explanations of legislative proposals are so poorly conveyed to the voters. There are also grounds for suspecting that the government sometimes by-passes Parliament to avoid delays, which weakens Parliament as a whole. The use of broad enabling legislation, and reliance on regulations through Orders-in-Council, are two such by-passing techniques.

An effective method of timetabling might be a bitter pill, but it would help the government, opposition, and Parliament. It would require two sorts of change: first, an effective method of closure which does not, like the present one, add a day to the debate and require at least two days of debate at each stage; and secondly, a means by which the government can timetable all stages of one, two, or three bills in advance, replacing the cumbersome and little used Standing Orders 75(A), 75(B) and 75(C).

---

[3] *Ibid.*, 20 Nov. 1975, 9:10.
[4] *Ibid.*, 9:11.

The trauma of the pipeline debate of 1956 still has its legacy in Conservative hostility to, and Liberal caution about, these sorts of timetabling devices. But many other things have changed in the past twenty years. The position of the Speaker has improved to the point where both sides, as in Britain, ought to be prepared to trust his decision on whether a closure motion should be accepted or not, without debate, and the problems of an overburdened Parliament are by now so obvious to all members that they must feel relief, in secret at any rate, at the thought of a reasonably shortened, planned and orderly parliamentary timetable. Nothing in reforms should prevent the opposition from picking the subjects it wants to oppose vigorously and devoting substantial parliamentary time to them, but reforms must permit annual sessions in which the government can get a reasonable legislative programme through Parliament. A sense of purpose and direction in debate would likely make it more interesting to reporters. Reductions in the length of normal speeches from forty to twenty minutes, and a more effective means of extending sessions beyond 10:00 P.M. would also contribute to better use of time, but better closure and guillotine are the key reforms.

THE HANDLING OF GOVERNMENT BILLS

The handling of government bills must be improved and better control over time will do a lot to help. The kind of stalemate Parliament has got itself into shows up in Professor John Stewart's figures: in 1969-1970, 34 of 65 government bills, or 52 percent, took less than two hours at second reading; by 1974, this had dropped to 3 out of 15, or only 20 percent, and it has not significantly improved since.[5] Between 1950 and 1955, the House passed one public bill for every 1.8 sittings, by 1970-1974 this had dropped to one for every 3.3 sittings. The House is obviously wasting time on bills, and drowning meaning in a sea of verbiage. Enough has been said about closure and the guillotine already; here, what must be examined are the purposes which this verbiage is supposed to serve, and what procedural reforms could better achieve these ends.

Debate on legislation has two purposes. One is to help the battle between parties and, as has been argued above, the present system probably harms both sides. The second is to aid in the overall processes of government, irrespective of which party is in power, and to encourage good relationships between governed and governors. The present parliamentary practices in handling public bills do not do much to help achieve this second purpose, and this is one of the most serious faults in parliamentary procedure. All too often it seems as though government prepares its legislation in secret, submits it to the House of Commons, where it undergoes a prolonged and unintelligible, badly reported and

---

[5] From his admirable book, *The Canadian House of Commons: Procedure and Reform* (Montreal: McGill-Queen's University Press, 1977), p. 270.

uninterpreted process of meandering discussion, and then becomes law, with few among the interested and intelligent public even being aware of what has happened, let alone having had an opportunity to influence the decisions through participation in interest groups or other contact with Members of Parliament. The gap that this creates between government and citizen is manifested in increasing disenchantment with and scepticism of government, and by the increasing divisiveness of issues and increasing difficulty in discovering a common national consensus or opinion in support of policy. Parliament is in danger of failing to accomplish its function of mobilizing consent, through serving as the link between those in authority, and those to whom they are accountable, the electorate.

More concise, relevant, and carefully prepared debates on legislation would help to recreate this link, as would a government with more respect for Parliament, and a more knowledgeable press gallery. But there are also other changes in the processes of handling legislation which can help. These are extension of the present white paper and green paper techniques, and mean more involvement by Parliament before government policy has become congealed into a bill to which the government is committed and is reluctant to have changed by Parliament. A white paper is a statement of the government's intentions and proposals for legislation; a green paper represents an earlier stage, indicates interest in a policy area, and outlines various possible approaches without indicating that the government favours one over the other. The use of both of these devices, especially when the white or green papers are considered by a parliamentary committee where witnesses can be heard and research staff engaged, does much to further communication and build up support for change. Similarly, Parliament ought to experiment with having the committee stage before Second Reading, and make it possible to amend legislation at this early stage. If parliamentary discussion and decisions could have a direct impact on legislation, Parliament would immediately become more relevant, and draw more attention.

One of the worries about this sort of more intense involvement by Parliament in formulating legislation is that Parliament is more representative of the advantaged and "have" sectors of society than of the disadvantaged "have-nots." Pressure groups are also oriented towards the powerful and the advantaged and, to make matters worse, our politics and economy are marked by the absence of working class participation in the former, and weak, partial working class organization in the latter. The skewing of political decisions in favour of the influential minority is always a risk in the Canadian power structure but, in spite of examples like taxation reform, I have yet to be convinced that this danger is greater when Parliament makes the decisions than when the executive makes them. The problem with the pluralistic heaven, as Schattschneider has remarked, is that the choir sings with a marked upper class accent.

An approach that has been tried in Sweden is to assign the development of legislative proposals to groups with broader membership than the standing committees of Parliament. Perhaps too few citizens are adequately represented by interest groups in Canada to make this feasible here, but maybe we should be thinking along these lines, and experiment with legislative committees which would include representatives from labour and business, as well as politicians. These could function much like royal commissions, but with the added advantage that their activities would build into both sides of Parliament knowledge about issues and would give Parliament the power that knowledge creates.

As the functions of government have increased over the past century, Canada perhaps more than any other western country has seen policy making concentrated into the executive side of government. In the United States, Congress is the forum where compromises are hammered out, and the final hard choices made. In Sweden, royal commissions like the legislative commissions proposed above are the main formulators of legislative proposals. In England, the political parties and a complex network of powerful interest groups representing all sectors of society participate in policy forming. But in Canada, where parliaments have traditionally been weak, and interest groups, elitist and either rudimentary or regional or both, and where political parties are not marked by widespread participation or mass membership, an overburdened executive has increasingly made policy, defended it, and implemented it, being in effect the only influential body with a national perspective and a concern for the nation as a whole. If the proposals suggested above would take some of this burden away from the executive and give it to Parliament and other bodies, then that is good for it is far more important that the nation consent to and understand policy than that policy please the Cabinet and senior civil servants; and a broadening of effective participation in decision making, not more public relations, is the road to more general citizen commitment and support. If the policies that emerged were often inconsistent and even contradictory, this would be no bad thing: the Canadian electorate is diverse and needs many contradictory things. Government is not there only to serve those with logical and consistent minds.

One of the biggest dangers to Parliament over the next few years will, I suspect, be its being put into the shade as federal-provincial relations, and possibly the working out of a new constitution take the limelight. Federal-provincial negotiations so far have been almost exclusively on an executive to executive level, without participation by the federal or provincial parliaments. Executives have their own interests, however, which in federal-provincial relations often involve more of a competition for legitimacy and power than a concern for the effect of policies and decisions on the citizens. It would be a healthy corrective to this imbalance if white or green papers on federal-provincial relations were examined by Parliament before negotiations take place, in a manner so that Parliament can consult broadly and publicly. At present the outcomes of federal-provincial diplomacy are laid before Parliament as *faits accomplis*, treaties which must be ratified but cannot be changed. This diminishes Parliament and handicaps the responsiveness of government.

COMMITTEES

The reformed committee system has proven its worth, but more needs to be done to correct lingering defects. There are two major problems. First, the allocation of tasks, government bills, estimates, and other inquiries, gives the committees two sorts of functions, one on the bills, of handling the government's programme during which the government must control the committees, and secondly, one on more general parliamentary inquiries in which government control ought to be absent so that the committees can act as independent forums for non-partisan investigation. The need for government control for the first function creates problems to independence and non-partisanship for the other. The second problem is that the present system puts too great a burden on Members of Parliament. There are too many committees, they are too big, and they are expected to do too much.[6]

The remedies for the second sort of problem are obvious: the number of committees should be reduced to eighteen or fewer from twenty-four; and their membership should be reduced to fourteen or so from the present twenty. The increase in seats in the House to two hundred and eighty-two, and more in future, will also help slightly to ease this problem.

The second problem requires a different remedy, but one which will also help solve the first. The task of handling the committee stage of most government legislation (unless it comes before Second Reading) should be taken away from the standing committees and given to special legislative committees. These should have thirty to fifty members, should be chaired by an independent chairman who would preside much as the Speaker does in the house, and should clearly divide on party lines. Their format should be that of a mini-parliament, with government and opposition facing each other, and there should be no question that the government controls the outcomes. Government control could then be eliminated from the present standing committees, and they would also have a lighter workload: at present nearly 30 percent of their time is taken up with legislation. The chairman for both the legislative and standing committees could be chosen from either side of the House because chairmen would no longer need to be one of the instruments of government control, any more than are at present the Speaker or the chairman of Committee of the Whole (often an opposition member) or the chairman of the Public Accounts Committee (also an opposition member). These innovations to the committee system would clarify the now ambiguous relationship of government to committee, there being no doubt of government control in the legislative committees, and no doubt of its absence in the standing committees. More members would also have an

---

[6] A good discussion of reforms to the committee system can be found in the *Minutes* of the Standing Committee on Procedure and Organization, 20 Sept. 1976 (No. 15), Appendix I, "Draft Report of the Sub-Committee on Committee Procedure," and 30 Oct. 1976 (No. 20), Appendix L, "Sub-Committee on Committee Procedure." Nearly all the changes proposed in this section can be found in these two documents.

opportunity to fill the influential position of chairman, and the legislative committees in particular would become excellent training grounds for future speakers.

PRIVATE MEMBERS' TIME

The present arrangements for private members' time of hour-long periods on different days during a session are unsatisfactory. Debate lacks continuity, motions and bills do not come to votes, and on many occasions the House has difficulty even in maintaining a quorum of twenty. Yet private members' time can be extremely influential. The original monopolies legislation in Canada was a private member's bill, and divorce reform and the abolition of capital punishment both were set in motion through private members' activities. The House should set aside one day a week for private members' time (this would easily be possible if time wasted on government legislation were reduced), and there should be provision for ensuring than many bills and motions come to a vote. Closure is essential on private members' business.

Many worthwhile policy reforms would not demand increased expenditure, and hence could be introduced and passed as private members' bills. These include such things as: amelioration of our extremely harsh and punitive Criminal Code; family law, rights of native women; much of labour law, and so on. There is no good reason, for example, why parliamentary consideration of decriminalization of marijuana possession should have to await the pleasure and convenience of the Prime Minister. A bill making this change ought to be just as easily introduced by a private member, and voted upon by Parliament to become the law of the land.

FINANCIAL PROCEDURES

The reforms of the late sixties reduced the time spent by the House on financial business (which exceeded seventy days in the obstructionist session of 1960-1961, and eighty days in the equally bad session of 1964-1965), and placed the main emphasis on twenty-five "allotted days" for which the opposition chooses the topic for debate. The reduction in time has been all to the good, but the intervening years have shown that it is difficult for the opposition to mount twenty-five substantial debates on supply items during a year, and the supply days consequently often lack interest. The opposition has repeatedly requested that items from the estimates be considered in Committee of the Whole on some of these days, and this was tried as an experiment in the first session of the present Parliament. It seemed to work reasonably well then, and provided a chance for more give-and-take, and questioning of ministers in the House, where press coverage is better than in the committees. This change ought to be made permanent.

I have less sympathy with the proposal to establish a standing committee on expenditures. We already have too many standing committees, and they are supposed to consider the estimates. So far they have not been very adventurous in examining estimates, but I would rather see them encouraged to do more here, in their new non-partisan structuring, with some opposition chairmen, than see the addition of more committees performing an overlapping function.

Lastly, I would like to consider one aspect of the most newsworthy of all committees: the Standing Committee on Public Accounts. This committee ought to meet *in camera*, with press coverage delayed until the end of its investigation, when a full verbatim transcript would be published along with the committee's report. At present, with press coverage of all proceedings, members grandstand too much, investigation lacks direction as each member attempts to appeal to the press rather than continue an orderly inquiry, and the committee is far too partisan. The Saskatchewan Public Accounts Committee meets *in camera*, and this procedure is one of the main reasons for its success. This reform, I realize, is not likely to be welcomed either by the press or by members of the committee, both of whom find the sensational aspects of its work appealing, but many years of observation have convinced me that the sort of premature and lurid exposure the committee now receives impedes intensive and productive investigation and, in the final analysis, handicaps Parliament's ability to control the public purse.

TOWARD MAKING REFORMS

The proposals for procedural reform I have outlined might seem idealistic pie in the sky, but apart from the suggestions of legislative commissions and *in camera* meetings of the Public Accounts Committee, they are very similar to the proposals made in the Procedures Committee in 1976. But reform has not gone any further in this Parliament. The committee has not met since 1976, and although its proposals were considered by caucuses, they have not been debated by the House and are now in limbo. Even the temporary changes which were experimented with in the first session have lapsed. Change will have to wait until after the next election and if a minority government then emerges, partisan warfare might make the prospect of real reform even more remote. The introduction of one hundred and fifty or so new members to the House, and the loss of some of the most valuable of the experienced and sensible reformers will mean that the new Parliament will have to go through a difficult educational process before reforms can be made. Nevertheless, procedural reform is important to the effectiveness and influence of the House, its committees, and its individual members. The past fifteen years have seen as much reform as in any other period in the House's history: the House can only maintain its vitality if it evolves to meet new conditions, and in the difficult time ahead it is all the more important for the House not to neglect procedural reform. It is to be hoped that the intransigence produced by intense partisanship is not so great in the next Parliament that members from both sides will be unwilling both to give a little and take a little in making reform possible.

Before closing, there are two further aspects of reform I would like to mention. The first is television, and as far as I can see its introduction has been all to the good and has helped link Parliament and the citizen. Nevertheless, one has only to compare the presentation of Parliament on the French and English networks to be forced to realize that simply televising Parliament has done little to break down our two solitudes. Secondly, I have not dealt directly with the vexing problem of the accountability of government to Parliament. Committees must be the main instrument for detailed accountability, and the reforms to discourage partisanship and government control are crucial here.

At the beginning of this paper, I suggested that many people might feel that procedural reform was not important in this period of crisis. But I wonder. We can list some of the basic problems: federal-provincial and French-English relations; the dominance of the Liberal party; the seeming lack of will and energy of the government; the difficulty the House has in holding ministers accountable; the increasing perception of all political problems in regional rather than national terms; the dominance of Parliament by the executive; and within Parliament the virulent partisanship that colours most activities and handicaps many of them; the lack of philosophical clarity in the position on issues taken by the parties; the excessive discussion of administrative detail rather than general direction and policy; and the superficial coverage of debates and committees by the press. At first glance these problems seem far removed from reform of procedure. But there are few of them that have not been mentioned in this paper, and are not affected by the reforms that have been discussed. Procedural reform is more important than it appears, and in spite of its being a seemingly dry topic, the survival and well-being of our country in part depends on it.

COMMENT

JOHN A. HOLTBY*

Professor Franks has written at some length concerning the House of Commons of Canada. As one who serves a provincial House, I will comment on some of the aspects of procedure which have concerned the Legislative Assembly of Ontario and I will make a few observations directly concerning Professor Franks' paper. It is, of course, inappropriate for me to suggest reforms for the House of Commons and I will not do so, but it might be helpful to make some comparisons and venture some comments.

I would like to make two preliminary observations which I think are self evident. First, the British parliamentary system is not universally praised as the healthy supreme body which Professor Franks suggests it is. This is certainly the message which has come from this conference. I would suggest that a major similarity in Britain and Canada is a parliamentary and public frustration with what is perceived to be a non-responsive bureaucracy in a regulated society. Somewhat tongue in cheek I would suggest that this continued colonial outlook on the part of those who refer in hushed terms to the "Mother of Parliaments" is a failure to realize that in Canada, from 1867 onward, we have gone in different directions than have those at Westminster. Our two systems are ever increasing in divergence and it is more and more difficult to refer to "mother's example" as a justification for the way in which we do things in this country.

Technically, the British printed works such as Erskine May's *Treatise on Parliamentary Practice* while useful as historical documents, are not always appropriate in the Canadian context. Certainly there is no reason whatsoever why a Canadian Parliament should be bound by a precedent at Westminster which may have come into being to meet a specific British situation for which there is no parallel in the Canadian system, but many people feel because it is in "May" that it is transferable to the Canadian scene. I do not make these comments to be disrespectful of any House, but to comment on the attitude which many people genuinely feel, and which is reflected in Professor Franks' reference to the Supremacy of Parliament in Britain where he asserts that "parliamentary procedure [still] establishes the ground rules for political struggles."

The second remark concerns Professor Franks' reference to the "wine lists on the Titanic" to which procedure is compared. Perhaps a more accurate reference to procedure might be one which would refer to the life boats. Constitutional debate or change does not do away with the need for rules, and the procedurally aware member is in a better position to influence matters than is the member who has not mastered the vocabulary and technique of the parliamentary meeting. Unfortunately because of the pressures of constituent's social work and the other demands made very early in the career of a new member, few members

---

* First Clerk Assistant, Legislative Assembly of Ontario.

other than House leaders and chairman have the opportunity to become expert in the practice of the procedural art. The subject of procedure is not one which attracts a great deal of attention, but it should be remembered that it provides not only the ground rules for debate but also the safety valves on the boiler of political dispute.

Procedural Changes in Ontario

In 1972, Ontario's legislature, through an independent commission, began to explore how the role of a private member could be enhanced. This has resulted in a number of procedural changes which have given real initiating ability to members regardless of their place in the House. There are those at this conference who suggest that Parliament should be a more ''efficient or expedient'' place, and certainly this is the thrust of Professor Franks' paper.

In Ontario in 1973-74, the third session of the 29th Parliament sat for 122 days and passed 216 Acts. The first session of the 31st Parliament sat for 55 days and passed 96 Acts. Of the 216 bills referred to above, 178 were government bills and of the 96 bills passed in the first session of the 31st Parliament, 67 of these were government bills, the remainder being private applications for legislation. It may be argued that minority government had more to do with this than did procedural change. I will leave that decision to those more qualified to draw those conclusions, but there has been a marked decline in the amount of legislative initiation.

Numerologists will study with interest the Standing Orders of the Legislative Assembly of Ontario, because for some mysterious reason the number ''twenty'' has taken on an increased significance. Twenty members standing in their places after the Second Reading of a bill can require the referral of the bill to a standing or select committee of the House. A bill may not pass more than one stage in one day if it is opposed by twenty members standing in their place. On the petition of twenty members the annual report of any agency or ministry of government shall be sent for study to a Committee of the House, and on the petition of any twenty members the government is required to place on the Order Paper an order for debate of any report of a committee of the House whether or not the adoption of the report has been moved. (It has been suggested that the Party Whips maintain packages of inflatable replicas of members to be pressed into action at the mere mention of the number twenty.)

A major change has been the new initiatives given to private members for private members' public business. A ballot is conducted for the order of precedence and each Thursday afternoon two private members' bills or resolutions are debated. Provincial Order 36 is as follows:

36. The following procedures shall govern Private Members' Public Business:
   (a) each Thursday, from the completion of the Routine Proceedings until 6:00 p.m., shall be allocated for Private Members' Public Business;
   (b) the Parties shall take turns, sharing the time, with up to 90 minutes allowed for each item;

(c) there shall be no limit on the right of Members to introduce Private Members' Public Bills;

(d) there shall be a ballot in each caucus, conducted by the Clerk of the House, in which each Member may enter his name once, to draw the names of Members who will be able, in the order drawn, to have a Bill or Resolution of their choice put to the House for debate and vote;

(e) the ballots shall be held on July 4th, 1977, for this session and the results shall be posted;

(f) if objection to the Bill or Resolution being voted on is received either from one-third of the Members by written petition to Mr. Speaker at least 48 hours in advance of the debate; or from 20 Members standing in their places when the question is about to be put to a vote, then the item will not be voted on. Debate will, however, have been allowed on the item for up to 90 minutes;

(g) the names of objectors filing the petition against a vote on any item shall be recorded in Votes and Proceedings the next sitting day after the deadline for filing a petition of objection;

(h) no question will be put to the House before 5:50 p.m. The votes on all items not opposed at 5:50 p.m. shall be stacked and put forthwith. If a division is requested by five members, there will be a five-minute division bell, following which all questions shall be put forthwith;

(i) Private Members' Public Bills which receive second reading shall be carried on the Order Paper daily and will be called by the Government House Leader in the same manner as Government Orders;

(j) on any Thursday there shall be not more than two items scheduled unless otherwise agreed by the House Leaders after notice; and at least two weeks' notice of any item for any Thursday shall be provided and all Bills intended for debate shall be introduced, at latest, on the Tuesday of the second week previous to the week in which such Bill is to be debated; and notice of a motion intended to be debated shall be printed on the Tuesday of the second week previous to the week in which such motion is to be debated;

(k) there shall be no adjournment of the debate on any item of Private Members' Public Business from one Thursday to another;

(l) there shall be no limit to the number of Resolutions of which a Member may give notice.

Of the first twenty bills brought forward under this procedure, seven were blocked under 36(f), five were defeated at Second Reading, eight were given Second Reading and referred to Committee and one bill received Royal Assent. Three private members' resolutions were adopted by the House to express an opinion of the House.

The Ontario House in providing more time for and prominence to the private member has moved in the opposite direction advocated by Professor Franks who, realistically, I suspect, views the Commons as an instrument of the executive.

Reforming Supply Procedure

I turn now to a reform which has yet to be advocated in a strong way. In most Houses, the Supply procedure consumes a large amount of time which, in the minds of many observers, is questionable given the number of man hours devoted to the parliamentary scrutiny of public expenditures. Recent studies have shown that Parliament saves very little money in its scrutiny of Supply. There is, of course, the traditional procedure for members to raise grievances before the Crown is granted Supply, but for all practical purposes Parliament appears to have surrendered its ability to cut public expenditures. One need only suggest a reduction in a vote and the corridors of the legislature are buzzing with the rumors of questions of confidence and a general election, all because Parliament questions the expenditures of a few thousand dollars.

Other Reforms

If parliaments wish to regain control of the scrutiny of public expenditures, I suggest there is a need for a new means of scrutiny. In the case of the provinces, one might wish to try a small committee of perhaps seven members. To that committee one would commit the Estimates, the Public Accounts and the Auditor's Report. This committee would not perform the functions of the Public Accounts Committee which would need to continue its work. Critics of departments would not be eligible for membership and substitutions would not be permitted. The committee would be assisted by a small staff which, for the first year, should look only at increases in expenditure. For future sessions throughout the life of the Parliament the committee should give close scrutiny to departmental spending and the question of the need for continued departmental activities. The committee will need a real taste for blood and the government will need to encourage the committee to cut expenditures. In order that these cuts will not cause undue hardship or confusion the estimates should be tabled six to eight months before the beginning of each fiscal year.

New vehicles will need to be provided for the raising of grievances and the discussion of ministerial policy. To this end, I would suggest an increase in the number of debates to be held in the House on departmental policy. With these debates taking place in the House one would hope that more media attention would be focused on the debate. These debates along with the day-to-day use of the Question Period and the procedure already in place for emergency debates, would continue to give a day-to-day departmental and policy scrutiny which the Committee of Supply has at least in theory provided.

We have heard earlier in this conference about the relationship of Parliament to the public and the insensitivity of parliamentarians to the needs of communities far from the capital. It has been suggested by others and I would bring the proposal forward once again, that parliaments, national or provincial, should move about their jurisdictions. The problems of the fishermen on the west coast or the question of provincial status for the two territories would receive a different sort of attention if Parliament sat in Victoria, White Horse or Yellowknife for two or three weeks during a session. This type of perambulatory assembly was used early in the political life in Upper Canada and, I believe, served to unify the jurisdiction by creating an awareness of a national institution and cohesive identity as well as familiarizing the population with governmental institutions.

It might be argued that television has gone a long way to create a similar feeling, but I doubt this because of the one-way direction of television and the continued attachment of members to their office work load. In Ontario, tours of the northern part of the province have been arranged for members from time to time and these have increased the sensitivity of members to parts of the province remote from the capital. I expect that this proposal will meet with great objection because of inconvenience and expense, but I doubt that it would be difficult to entice the House of Commons to leave the snows of Ottawa for the arrival of spring in Victoria.

Many of the proposals in Professor Franks' paper give rise to questions about the nature of Parliament. Is the parliamentary form a useful one in an educated society? Historically, Parliament acted as a check. The opposition's functions are basically negative. Is it useful in a Canadian context to suppose that proposals coming from Mr. Speaker's left are less worthy of consideration than those coming from the Cabinet ranks? If one reflects on Mr. Stanfield's remarks, would it be useful to consider a separation of the executive and legislative branches, keeping in place the daily Question Period?

The Role of the M.P.

The major concern I have about Professor Franks' paper as I stated earlier is that he wishes to expedite the government's work in the House by cutting back on the abilities of members of the House to scrutinize the government's stewardship. The closure of debate and rigid timetabling will not lead to a healthier democracy, but instead will permit the governing party to escape the wrath of public opinion which requires time to be mobilized for the opposition and the media. The one weapon which the opposition has is prolonged debate.

I cannot agree with the proposal that the Public Accounts Committee meet *in camera*. Once again the argument is made that the British have followed this practice. They have in fact just recently begun to meet in public. Parliament's principal weapon against extravagance or maladministration on the part of the public service is publicity. *In camera* meetings and dry reports do not have the sense of theatre which attracts media attention for long periods of time. The issuance of a report from the Public Accounts Committee would generate, in my view, three days of press interest. The ongoing meeting of the Public Accounts Committee on major issues raised by the Auditor General focuses attention for a longer period of time on the issues at hand.

The issues raised here — the ability of a member to go about his parliamentary work in the chamber and in committees — might appear to be dry and rarified. But I agree with Professor Franks that unless procedural reform is pushed vigorously and intelligently our quest for better government will be hampered unduly. That is a risk that we can scarcely afford.

A BASIC BIBLIOGRAPHY

PROCEDURAL REFORM IN THE LEGISLATIVE PROCESS IN CANADA

Beauchesne, Arthur. *Rules and Forms of the House of Commons,* 4th ed. Toronto: Carswell, 1955.

Blair, Ronald. "What Happens to Parliament?" In Trevor Lloyd and Jack MacLeod, eds., *Agenda 1970,* pp. 217-40. Toronto: University of Toronto Press, 1968.

Boursnot, J.G. *Parliamentary Procedure and Practice in the Dominion of Canada,* 4th ed. Toronto: Canada Law Book, 1916.

Dawson, W.F. *Procedure in The Canadian House of Commons.* Toronto: University of Toronto Press, 1962.

Franks, C.E.S. "The Dilemma of the Standing Committee of The Canadian House of Commons." *Canadian Journal of Political Science* 4 (December 1971): 461-76.

Franks, C.E.S. "The Reform of Parliament." *Queen's Quarterly* 76 (Spring 1969): 113-17.

Jackson, Robert J. and Atkinson, Michael M. *The Canadian Legislative System.* Toronto: Macmillan, 1974.

Lloyd, Trevor. "The Reform of Parliamentary Proceedings." In Abraham Rotstein, ed., *The Prospect of Change: Proposals for Canada's Future,* pp. 23-29. Toronto: McGraw-Hill, 1965.

Lovink, J.A.A. "Parliamentary Reform and Governmental Effectiveness in Canada." *Canadian Public Administration* 16 (Spring 1973): 35-54.

Lovink, J.A.A. "Who Wants Parliamentary Reform?" *Queen's Quarterly* 79 (Winter 1972): 502-13.

MacDonald, Donald S. "Change in the House of Commons — New Rules." *Canadian Public Administration* 13 (Spring 1970): 30-39.

Mallory, J.R. and Smith, B.A. "The Legislative Role of Parliamentary Committees in Canada: The Case of the Joint Committee on the Public Service Bills." *Canadian Public Administration* 15 (Spring 1972): 1-23.

March, Roman R. *The Myth of Parliament.* Scarborough: Prentice-Hall, 1974.

Rush, Michael. "The Development of the Committee System in the Canadian House of Commons — Diagnosis and Revitalization." *The Parliamentarian* 55 (April 1974): 86-94.

Rush, Michael. "The Development of the Committee System in the Canadian House of Commons — Reassessment and Reform." *The Parliamentarian* 55 (July 1974): 149-58.

Stewart, John. *The Canadian House of Commons: Procedure and Reform.* Montreal: McGill-Queen's University Press, 1977.

Ward, Norman. *The Public Purse.* Toronto: University of Toronto Press, 1964.

Chapter Nine

Public Policy and Legislative Drafting

by
William H.R. Charles *

    I have been asked in this paper to consider the role played by the legislative drafter in the development of legislative policy. This may, at first glance, appear to be a rather futile chore since the usual conception of a draftsman is someone who puts things into legal language, generally in such a way as to confuse everyone. He, or she, is generally thought of as a packager or translator who takes decisions made by others and molds them into the proper legislative form and shape. His general concern is with the proper use of words and manner of expression, and it has been said of this poor soul that he must, of necessity, be "an intellectual eunuch" and "an emotional oyster."[1] Such phrases, by themselves, do little to clarify the functions performed by the drafter, but they do imply a rather neutral and static, if not almost moribund, state of activity. Descriptive expressions such as these hardly convey the impression of a dynamic participation in the policy-making process.

    But is this picture of the draftsman as some minor official performing a rather unexciting, mechanical chore a correct one? If not, what constitutes a proper description of the draftsman and his functions, particularly in relation to the formulation of legislative policy? One purpose of this paper is to delve into the mysteries of the drafting process and to determine whether the accepted concept of the draftsman as a word monger is justified, or whether it is an over-simplified view of his function. If our investigation indicates that the draftsman is, in fact, performing functions not generally attributed to him, including involvement with the policy-making process, then some consideration must be given to the question of the extent to which such participation is proper, from both a functional and legal or constitutional point of view.

---

* Professor of Law, Dalhousie University.

[1] The phrase "intellectual eunuch" has been attributed to the late Middleton Beaman, one time Legislative Counsel of the House of Representatives by Professor Reed Dickerson of Indiana University, formerly assistant Legislative Counsel, U.S. House of Representatives. Professor Dickerson used the term "emotional oyster" in an address delivered at the Legislation Institute, held at the University of Notre Dame, March 30, 1955. See "How to Write a Law," *Notre Dame Lawyer* 31 (1955): 14-27.

Hopefully, in the process of determining whether the draftsman is in fact a stenographer or a novelist, a short-order cook or a gourmet chef, a clearer appreciation of his role in the legislative process as a whole will emerge.

To obtain an accurate picture of the actual functions of Canadian draftsmen, I have sought the assistance of a number of people in legislative counsel offices across the country. It would obviously be impossible to contact every person engaged in the drafting process, and I have not attempted to do so. But I have contacted a group of approximately twenty and have asked them to respond to a series of questions about their drafting functions. The response has been generous, in spite of the usual heavy workload, and I am indebted to them. Without their kind co-operation, this paper could not have been written.

THE OFFICE OF THE LEGISLATIVE COUNSEL AND ITS RELATIONSHIP TO THE ATTORNEY GENERAL

At this point, it might be useful to draw a distinction between draftsmen who labour in the offices of the legislative counsel, whether at the provincial or federal level, and drafters who function within individual government departments.[2] Although both categories are involved with drafting legislation, personnel employed as legislative counsel perform, as we shall see, a wider range of functions and have different responsibilities. My remarks in this paper, therefore, will be directed primarily, but not exclusively, to draftsmen functioning within legislative counsel's office as either senior or assistant legislative counsel. Since this is the case, perhaps we should clarify the role of legislative counsel and explore more fully the duties and responsibilities of those occupying such a position.

It seems to be the accepted practice in all Canadian provinces, and within the federal government, to have all government legislation either drafted or reviewed and passed as to form by an official designated as the legislative counsel. In some provinces, this official is also involved in the drafting of private members' bills, which would include legislation sponsored by either members of the government in power or members of the opposition.[3] In other provinces, the drafting of non-governmental legislation is done by a law clerk who operates separately from legislative counsel's office. In the province of Newfoundland, for example, recent legislation provides that the senior legislative counsel, in addition to administering the office of the legislative counsel, is also the law clerk of the Assembly and performs the duties of the law clerk of the House of Assembly pursuant to the standing orders of the House.[4] In the province of

---

[2] This distinction was particularly emphasized in the reply received from R. Cosman, Legislative Counsel/Law Clerk, Government of the Yukon Territory.

[3] This seems to be the situation in Ontario, for example.

[4] See section 20 of Bill 116, 2nd Sess, 37th Gen. Assembly 25-26 Eliz. III, 1977, *An Act Respecting the Preparation and Revision of the Statutes and Subordinate Legislation of the Province*. The same situation prevails in the Yukon Territory.

Saskatchewan the office of legislative counsel and law clerk operates as an independent agency and, as part of its function, prepares legislation for opposition members of the legislature as well as the government.

Historically, the office of legislative counsel was first developed in England in 1798. Prior to that time bills were drafted, for the most part, by private members of Parliament, with certain important bills being a judicial product. There was no central drafting office. The first government draftsman, a Mr. William Harrison, is believed to have worked very hard in his initial years without a salary. By 1833 Harrison had both a salary and a title, that of Parliamentary Counsel to the Treasury. The post seems to have been vacant for a few years from 1837 on, and the government seems to have reverted to the earlier situation with legislation, even important bills, being introduced and carried by private members. The Home Secretary, assisted by a lawyer, did prepare some of the more important government bills.[5]

As the volume of government-sponsored legislation grew, other government departments by the 1860s found it was necessary to obtain legal assistance in drafting departmental measures. The system proved very unsatisfactory. The fees paid to barristers for piecework were high, a uniform style was impossible, statutes in conflict with each other were passed and the Treasury Department had no control over provisions and statutes authorizing expenditures. To resolve this unsatisfactory state of affairs, the Chancellor of the Exchequer in 1869 created, not by statute but by Treasury Minute, an office within the Treasury to draft all the government bills. With the passage of time, the functions of legislative counsel came to be more closely identified with the operations of the Attorney General's department.

In Canada, the office of the legislative counsel is usually a part of the Attorney General's department or ministry and works closely with it in matters of the government's business. This is not universally the case, however, and as has already been indicated, in Saskatchewan the office of the legislative counsel and law clerk is an independent agency and is not attached to the Attorney General's department. But, whether the office of legislative counsel operates as part of the Attorney General's office or as an independent agent, drafters who work in the department, including the senior legislative counsel, are usually employed as public civil servants. There are some exceptions to this rule as well. The legislative counsel in Newfoundland[6] and Nova Scotia,[7] for example, hold office during pleasure. Because legislative counsel function as part of the Attorney General's Office in a close relationship with that department, they tend to be governed by the same rules and traditions insofar as their professional responsibilities are concerned. I think it is important that we keep this fact in

---

[5] The historical evolution of the Office of Legislative Counsel is outlined by Arnold Kean in "Drafting a Bill in Britain." *Harvard Journal of Legislation* 5 (1968): 252-61.

[6] See section 22 of Bill 116 (Nfld.).

[7] See section 50 of the *House of Assembly Act*. R.S.N.S. 1967. C. 128.

mind because it seems to me to be relevant in determining the proper function of the legislative counsel, insofar as he may be involved in the formulation of legislative policy.

The Attorney General occupies a rather ambivalent position within the government in that he is expected to speak both as a lawyer and as a politician. He functions as legal adviser to both the Crown and the government of the day and, in addition, he is also a servant of the House of Commons. At the same time, however, the Attorney General is also a politician and is responsible together with the rest of the Cabinet for action that is taken. But in spite of what may appear to be a schizophrenic kind of existence, it remains the clearest rule that in the discharge of his legal discretionary duties, the Attorney General is completely divorced from party politics. As Professor John Edwards has explained, the Attorney General occupies a

> . . . slightly different position from the ordinary Minister . . . [W]hen a law officer participates in a Commons debate involving any questions of law, he is generally expected to assume an attitude of independence and to speak as a lawyer, not as a politician bent on defending the position adopted by the government.[8]

The Attorney General and members of his staff are expected to act as legal advisers for government departments. In a similar way, legislative counsel spends much time advising the government, ministers of the government and Cabinet on all matters concerning legislation, particularly during the period when the statute is being prepared and during its passage through the House. Like the Attorney General, legislative counsel are generally officers of the House and, as such, may have a variety of duties to perform, including being counsel to the Speaker and to all members in matters concerning bills, assisting opposition members in the preparation of their bills and amendments, attending in the House to assist on matters of law and drafting, and acting as counsel to committees of the House who are considering bills. These functions are not uniformly performed by legislative counsel in all provinces, however. In some jurisdictions, for example, legislative counsel does not attend in the House when bills are being considered to assist on matters of law and drafting, as is the case in Ontario. As we have already noted, in Newfoundland and some other provinces, senior legislative counsel also functions as law clerk of the House.

I think it is important to have some appreciation of the broad functions performed by legislative counsel so that his role in the drafting process can be more accurately assessed. The effect of being part of the Attorney General's department is reflected in the following response received from a senior legislative counsel:

> In our province legislative counsel are employed by the Attorney General and, in accordance with his traditional duties to advise the government objectively, unbiased by political motivations, and to enforce the laws and guard against unreasonable interference

---

[8] J.L.J. Edwards, *The Law Officers of the Crown* (London: Sweet and Maxwell, 1964).

with the rights of citizens, legislative counsel is expected to assist the Attorney General in carrying out his role.[9]

As I have already indicated, it is also necessary, I think, in a discussion of the drafter's influence upon policy development, to distinguish between the draftsman in his role as legislative counsel and the draftsman as a member of a government department. The latter, not being a part of the Attorney General's department, functions uninfluenced by the traditional ethics and responsibilities of the Law Officer's position. The departmental lawyer, being more closely aligned with the mission of his department, may be more involved in policy development than is legislative counsel and may adopt a more partisan attitude insofar as that policy is judged by standards of fairness or reasonableness of its effect upon civil rights. The departmental draftsman will not usually have the same breadth of experience or appreciation of government operations that is normally found in persons performing the function of legislative counsel. But, on the other hand, if the departmental draftsman is a legally trained person, then he should share a certain common ground with the legislative counsel. Both, for example, will work for others on a solicitor-client basis, which carries with it certain traditional duties and responsibilities. Both will also be conversant with the basic principle and tradition of the common law, a factor which may be very relevant when considering the rights of citizens. While recognizing that all drafting is not necessarily done in the offices of legislative counsel, my examination and discussion of the role of drafter will focus upon the activities of legislative counsel insofar as they involve development of legislative policy.

HOW A BILL IS BORN: POLICY IDEAS AND THEIR DEVELOPMENT

Before drafting in the narrow, popular sense of the word can begin, someone must have suggested the need for new legislation. The cry that "there ought to be a law" is frequently heard and the pressure for legislation can come from a number of different sources. It might be the result of an election promise, in the case of a newly elected government, or may have its source in the recommendations of a special parliamentary committee, the reports of law reform or Royal commissions or reports and proposals emanating from government departments. In some cases, a legislative proposal may flow from a minister's personal conviction on some matter of public policy. Many suggestions for important changes in the law originate with the practising Bar although these tend to be primarily of a legal nature and do not ordinarily have broad social and economic implications. Whatever their origin, the proposals usually reflect social pressures which, in turn, are a reflection of current social needs and problems.

Occasionally, the proposal for legislative enactment will take the form of a bare declaration that a problem exists, which may or may not be identified in

---

[9] This observation came from British Columbia.

detail in the proposal, without any suggestions as to how the problem should be resolved. In other words, a problem is presented by the sponsor but no solution is offered. In other cases, not only is the problem analysed and identified but possible ways of dealing with it are also outlined and a course of action is recommended. As Professor Driedger has explained,

> A statute is the formal and legal expression of a legislative policy, and it follows that before a statute can be drafted the policies thought to be implemented by it must be determined.[10]

Since the main object of this paper is to explore the extent to which drafters, and in particular legislative counsel, are involved with and influence the development of legislative policy, it might be wise to take a few moments to clarify what we mean by this term.

One explanation or definition of the term ''policy'' sees it as representing

> a response to some kind of problem, one acute enough to intrude on the well-being of a significant number of people and other organizations or on the well-being of the government itself, one conspicuous enough to draw the attention of at least some legislators.[11]

It has also been suggested that a policy involves ''a web of decisions and actions that allocate values.''[12] Policy making is the activity of arriving at significant decisions. ''They are the doing aspects of the political system.''[13] But policies are to be distinguished from decisions because ''they set the parameters of future decisions by developing a long term perspective in issue areas.''[14] Not every decision should be considered a policy. As one Canadian authority has explained,

> The decision to provide a particular Opportunity for Youth Grant or a Local Initiative Project to a particular group is a decision but not a policy. The decision to establish such programs was a policy decision.[15]

Obviously, the formulation of legislative policy is a politically important part of the legislative process. What can the draftsman contribute to such an exercise? Even if he can add something of value, should he be precluded on the basis of some constitutional or other principle? Professor Driedger has stated that,

---

[10] Elmer Driedger, ''The Preparation of Legislation,'' *Canadian Bar Review* 31 (1953) p. 36.

[11] W.J. Keefe and M.S. Ogul, *The American Legislative Process: Congress and the States,* 3rd ed. (New Jersey: Prentice-Hall, 1973), p. 14.

[12] David Easton, *The Political System: An Inquiry into the State of Political Science* (New York: Knopf, 1971), p. 130.

[13] Van de Slik, *American Legislative Processes* (New York: Crowell, 1977), p. 9.

[14] R.J. Jackson and M.M. Atkinson, *The Canadian Legislative System: Politicians and Policy Making* (Toronto: Macmillan, 1974), p. 65.

[15] *Ibid.*

> Under a parliamentary system of government modelled after the British legislature, policy is settled and determined, in the first instance, by the government and finally by Parliament.[16]

The government in this context presumably means the elected members of the Cabinet. If the process of drafting as a function is thought of solely as putting the developed plan or policy into appropriate legislative form and language, then it could easily be argued that to involve the draftsman in policy formulation is to extend him beyond his range of competence and functionally would be improper and a mistake. If, on the other hand, the process of drafting requires the draftsman to be involved in some way in the policy development activity, then the critical question concerns the extent of his involvement.

Reed Dickerson, well-known American legislative counsel and author of several texts on legislative drafting, argues for a more liberal view of the drafting process and urges that a distinction be made between drafting and writing, the latter being the last stage of the drafting process. In making this important distinction, Dickerson describes the drafting process by reference to the following descriptive analogy:

> *The Classic Analogy:* the analogy with architecture and engineering is becoming so commonplace that I hesitate to use it. At the same time the drafting process is so widely misunderstood that it would be unfair to the reader not to use the most apt parallel that exists.
>
> The notion of the draftsman of a statute as both its architect and its builder is not new, but the legal profession persists in acting as if its most important implications were false. Lest these implications be lost to the reader, let me review briefly what the architect does. He does not arrive at the last moment merely to ornate a building already completed. He is almost the first man, after the client, to be actively engaged in the project. At the very outset he must know what the client's objective is. What kind of a building does the client want? A single family dwelling, an electric substation? A college science laboratory? If a science laboratory, the architect must find out what the specific needs are. How many students are reasonably to be expected? Which sciences are to be taught, and to what extent? Where is the building to be located; which way is it to face? How far will it be from the other buildings? What are the lighting problems? What library, office and storage facilities will be needed? What will be the fire hazard? How much money and time are available?
>
> One important factor will be the relation of the new building to those already built. The architect will need to study the materials, construction and form of the related buildings so that the new building will adequately dovetail both the needs it serves and the architectural style to which the institution is already committed.
>
> He will also need to relate these things to what is legally permissible in that area. What does the Building Code permit or require? Will the new building involve zoning limitations or restrictive convenants? What permits will be needed?
>
> Next, and hardest, is the problem of organizing the elements into a concrete whole that will give the client the greatest service with the least expense, inconvenience and compromise.

---

[16] Driedger, *op. cit.*, p. 36.

The final architectural steps are to fit the whole into an appropriate artistic pattern and to add those stylistic configurations that will make the building an acceptable aesthetic experience to those who work in it or have to look at it from the outside.

In some way the legal architect is more deeply involved than the superficialities of style would indicate. He must participate in exploring the objectives, sketch the structural framework, fill in the broad surfaces, work out the significant details, and add the aesthetic touches.

What most people (including most lawyers) think of as "drafting" is really the last stage of drafting. "Drafting" and "writing" are not synonymous. The writing stage is simply that at which the legal architect takes on the added functions of builder, construction engineer, plasterer, plumber, painter and landscape gardener.

Contrast with this approach the conventional view that says, "Now that we have worked out the plan, let's call in a lawyer to put it in legal language". In other words, now that we've put up the building let's get an architect to decorate it for us![17]

If this is an accurate description of the drafting process, it is a far cry from the limited function of being a legal stenographer or translator that is usually credited to the draftsman.

To determine with some degree of accuracy what the draftsman does, we should perhaps examine in more detail the process that is followed in Canada once a suggestion for legislative action is made. In the course of this examination we will keep a sharp eye on the draftsman to see what role he plays.

The Persuasion Stage: Getting the Policy Accepted

Whatever the initial source of the proposed legislation may be, a minister of the government must decide at some point to sponsor the proposal and try to have it accepted as part of the legislative programme by his colleagues in Cabinet. But the minister's acceptance of a policy idea is only the beginning of what can be an involved process during which the policy of the proposed enactment is discussed and debated. All of this precedes the actual drafting of the bill. The process followed in Ontario, although not necessarily identical in all respects with that of other provinces, provides a good illustration of what is involved at the pre-drafting stage. It is discussed here as general background for the ensuing discussion of the draftman's role in the development of policy. An outline of the federal procedure is also included for general information and comparison purposes.

The Pre-writing Process in Ontario[18]

Once the minister has approved of the need for new legislation, the idea is written up as a policy submission. The submission includes a discussion of the problem that has given rise to the need for legislation, background analysis,

---

[17] R. Dickerson, *Legislative Drafting* (Boston: Little, Brown, 1954), pp. 11-12.

[18] I am indebted to Arthur M. Stone, Q.C., Senior Legislative Counsel, Province of Ontario for much of the information contained in this section. Mr. Stone's views and an account of his experience as a draftsman are included in a presentation he made as part of the Law Society's Continuing Education Program.

alternative causes of action and recommendations. The same document is often used by the legislative draftsman as the basic reference source upon which he relies for guidance when drafting the bill. The policy submission is also frequently tabled in the House as background information for members when the bill is introduced.

From the sponsoring department, the policy submission makes its way to the ''policy field.'' This is basically a committee of ministers heading departments whose operations are in some way related to the proposed legislation. If approved by the Policy Field Committee, the policy memorandum is sent to the draftsman and to the Policy and Priorities Board of the Cabinet. This latter group reviews the proposal in light of broad policy matters including public policy, political considerations, and financial priorities.

The draft bill, once completed, is sent to the Legislation Committee composed of four or five ministers. Here it is subjected to a detailed clause by clause study and analysis. The draftsman and ministry officials attend the committee meetings and explain the bill in detail. From the Legislation Committee the bill passes to the full Cabinet where any contentious points that may have arisen are debated once more. If the Cabinet approves the bill, the minister is then free to inform the caucus of government members of his intention to introduce the bill in the House.

The Pre-writing Procedures of the Federal Legislative Process[19]

Like Ontario, the federal procedures involve a lengthy pre-drafting phase that deserves some explanation as well. Approximately one year before the legislative programme is to be presented to Parliament, the Privy Council Office requests government departments to submit lists of topics for possible legislative action. The responses are collated and developed into a master list humorously referred to as the ''shopping list.'' The ''shopping list'' is then reviewed with ministers of the government, either individually or as a group, to identify measures that seem to accord with the policy themes the government plans to develop. From the large master list a smaller priority list is established, with non-priority items placed on a secondary, or backup list. During the course of the year an item may be moved back and forth between the priority list and the secondary list depending upon circumstances. An item designated as a ''priority proposal'' is then sent back to the department for further study and elaboration. Sometimes, depending upon the field of activity covered by the proposed legislation, an interdepartmental study group will be established. The objective is to produce a policy memorandum or ''Memorandum to Cabinet'' as it is called. The memorandum covers basically the same points already referred to in the

---

[19] The outline of the federal process is based upon information supplied by Fred E. Gibson, Chief Legislative Counsel, Department of Justice, Ottawa.

discussion of the Ontario policy submission. If it is acceptable to the minister, he signs it and it is sent to the Cabinet.

The volume of new legislative proposals flowing to Cabinet necessitates some division of labour within that body. To handle the flow, the Cabinet has established approximately eight subject-matter committees, such as the Economic Policy Committee, to name one. Each subject-matter committee, composed of selected ministers and assisted by government experts who are invited to attend, discusses the policy memorandum presented to them and makes recommendations to Cabinet. If the Cabinet approves, instructions are issued to the Legislation Section of the Department of Justice to draft the necessary bill. Once drafted, the bill is sent to the minister responsible, and if accepted by him, it is passed on to the Committee on Legislation and House Planning. This committee subjects the bill to a clause by clause examination to ensure that it conforms to the policy memorandum. If the bill passes the close scrutiny of the Committee on Legislation and House Planning, it is sent on to the Cabinet for Cabinet approval and caucus discussion. If the proposal manages to survive reasonably intact, it is finally introduced into the House or Senate.

The Draftsman and Development of the Policy Proposals

Elmer Driedger, dean of Canadian draftsmen, has stated that,

> It is not the function of a draftsman either to originate or determine legislative policy. But the dividing line between policy and law, between form and substance, is not a sharp one and the draftsman cannot always escape being involved in policy discussions.[20]

On the basis of information received from legislative counsel across Canada, it appears that in jurisdictions with large, well-staffed government departments, such as the federal government, Ontario and a few others, legislative counsel is not usually involved in the policy discussion stage of the birth of a bill.[21] In smaller jurisdictions, however, it seems to be the accepted practice to include legislative counsel in the process of policy formulation.

Theoretically, legislative counsel might be involved in a number of different ways. He might, for example, be invited to attend the policy discussions merely as an observer, whose purpose is to familiarize himself with the background of the legislation he will ultimately have to draft. Such background information should make his drafting job easier and help to insure that he has accurately captured the intention of the sponsors. There is a practical problem here, of course, in that there are usually a limited number of legislative counsel available and the volume of legislation increases each year. It is not possible for legislative counsel to actually sit in at an early stage while each piece of new legislation is being discussed. The general opinion among draftsmen seems to be that it is

---

[20] Driedger, *op. cit.,* pp. 36-37.

[21] As Kerek A. Seiger, Legislative Counsel for the Government of the Yukon Territory observed, "It is perhaps a truism that the greater the degree of sophistication in government the narrower is the role of the draftsman."

theoretically a good idea for this procedure to be followed, but time and workload constraints do not always make it possible to do so.

From this minimum level of participation, it is conceivable that legislative counsel might be invited to attend policy discussions in an advisory capacity for the purpose of answering any questions the sponsors might wish to put to him. The queries could range all the way from a strictly legal opinion as to the constitutionality of the new enactment, or whether it would be inconsistent with other statutes already in the statute books, to more general non-legal questions such as whether there is a social need for the new legislation or whether it is fair and reasonable.

As one might expect, information provided by legislative counsel confirms the fact that sponsors do turn to them at an early stage for legal advice. More surprisingly, perhaps, the responses also indicate that the proponents of legislation do seek the opinion of legislative counsel as to the social need for the new legislation, as well as their opinion concerning its fairness or reasonableness. Admittedly, the occasions upon which such advice is requested are relatively infrequent. However, most legislative counsel acknowledged they were prepared to give a personal opinion if asked. It may be questioned whether the opinions given by the draftsmen in these circumstances would be useful or not. In a particular situation the draftsman may not have sufficient experience or background in relation to the particular subject matter of the proposed bill to make his comments valuable. But if he is an experienced legislative draftsman with a special experience in the area being dealt with by the proposed legislation, his views could be quite relevant and useful.

Some legislative counsel take the view that they are not competent to comment upon the social need for legislation and that this is not the proper function of the draftsman.[22] In their view, policy proposals should be instituted by the minister and senior departmental officials. Quite clearly, legislative counsel who are asked for their opinions and who accede to the request run the risk that their opinions may be in conflict with official government policy.[23] In such an event they might find themselves in a rather awkward position. Perhaps it is this factor, among others, that inclines them to the view that the draftsman should not be asked such questions.

If invited to attend policy development sessions, should the draftsman offer his views concerning the legal and social value and implication of the new legislation if he is not asked to do so? Here again, much depends on the experience of the draftsman and the type of legislation being considered. If legislative counsel takes the view that he has been asked to participate as an adviser in the solicitor-client sense of the term, he may also conclude that it is his

---

[22] Opinion on this point was quite divided with a slight majority expressing the view that the draftsman should be consulted but pointing out that this was not done very often.

[23] Only one response specifically referred to this difficulty but it may have been an underlying factor in others as well.

professional responsibility to advise his client on matters falling within his competence whether asked to do so or not. As one legislative counsel put it,

> It is the essence of the lawyer's professional responsibility to enhance the client's capacity to make effective decisions in the client's own self-interest by (1) advising him of further options, and (2) warning him of unforeseen dangers where these may not have previously been adequately considered by the client. This responsibility cannot adequately be discharged where the lawyer restricts his responses to specific inquiries and remains silent when the client consulting him does not specifically inquire on the point.[24]

Whether the author of this statement intended it to apply to legislative counsel who is asked to participate in the policy development discussions or whether he intended it to apply only at the later writing stage is not clear, but it seems to me it is equally applicable at both. The position expressed in this statement is supported by that of another legislative counsel who expressed the view that,

> [I]f a client needs help to develop policy he is entitled to every bit of experience, knowledge and resources you have available and are able to give within the time available to you.[25]

Occasionally, when the sponsors have only the vaguest of ideas of what they want and the policy discussions do not seem to be making headway, they will ask legislative counsel to put together a "discussion draft." With this as a starting point, the sponsors will then begin to develop and refine their own concepts of what they want. Obviously this procedure requires legislative counsel to make certain policy decisions himself in order to prepare the draft bill. Professional draftsmen know the dangers of this approach to legislation, but, apparently, many do it on occasion to assist the government. The draftsman in this situation consoles himself with the knowledge that the client still has the opportunity to review the draft, eliminate undesirable aspects and eventually reach a policy he thinks is what he wants and will do what he desires.

Objections to Participation by the Draftsman

One objection taken by some legislative counsel and previously referred to, is that legislative policy should only be formulated by the politicians who are elected to the legislature and that it is not within the competence of draftsmen to suggest or help develop policy. Professor Driedger has voiced the opinion that the draftsman is not needed until there is something to draft.[26] It is true that the minister initially, and the legislature ultimately, have to make decisions about legislative policy, but the initiators of policy are quite often civil servants in various government departments or other private citizens or interest groups.

---

[24] R.D. Adamson, Assistant Legislative Counsel, Province of British Columbia.

[25] James W. Ryan, Legislative Counsel, Province of Newfoundland and Labrador.

[26] E. Driedger, "Public Administrators and Legislation," *Canadian Public Administration* 1 (June 1958), p. 14.

These people are not elected representatives. It is true that government administrators usually may have more experience and knowledge of the subject area covered by the legislation than would legislative counsel, but, like him, they are also non-elected officials. If political responsibility to the electorate is the key factor in determining whether legislative counsel should or should not be involved in the development of legislative policy, it does not appear to be a strong argument. The question of the competence of the draftsman will depend to a large extent upon the particular experience of the particular draftsman and his familiarity of the subject matter of the individual legislation with which he is involved at any particular time.

The constitution of the Legislative Counsel's Office in California states that legislative counsel must neither oppose nor propose legislation. This statement could be construed as an absolute prohibition against any involvement in the development of policy or it could merely mean, as one senior legislative counsel has suggested, that the draftsmen's personal views should not be the basis for the legislation, "where to do so would affect one's objectivity."[27] If the proposed legislation happens to involve an issue that is emotionally charged with strong religious, economic or political beliefs, such as abortion, capital punishment, or wage and price controls, legislative counsel, in his strategic position, may be tempted to insert his own personal beliefs into the policy discussions, if he is permitted to be involved. As a participant in policy discussions, the draftsman must somehow reflect a neutral stance in the sense of not taking sides or being biased in any way. The expectations of some clients are reflected in the following statement by an American legislator:

> In all the time he [draftsman] has been associated with us, I have never heard him intimate directly or indirectly the least opinion about policy, whether this or that policy should become part of the bill, whether it was right or wrong, wise or unwise policy or proposition. He and these other gentlemen [Associate Counsel] have been absolutely neutral on the question of right or wrong, wisdom or unwisdom of any affirmative legislation. Their work or duty is to put the legislative intention or object of the committee or congress into clear, concise, unambiguous terms in the bill or act.[28]

Other American draftsmen do not necessarily adopt the same strictly neutral position. As Theodore Ellenbogen, a member of the American Bar Advisory Committee, once commented,

> I remember that I used to sit on a task force where you just don't sit around the table and keep your mouth shut. You are asked, "What do you think?" or "Can you be helpful in solving such and such a problem?" I always try to be helpful. This doesn't mean I decided policy but, if there were alternatives that I could see I would present them. . . . I even volunteered a possible compromise and said, "Well, here is something you might want to

---

[27] This interpretation was suggested by Jim Ryan, *op. cit.*

[28] Chairman of the House Committee on Ways and Means, as quoted in J.P. Chamberlain, *Legislative Processes, National and State* (New York: Appleton-Century, 1936), p. 263.

consider'' — they rephrased it. Now I don't think this does any damage to the professional standing of the draftsman or impairs his integrity.[29]

Whatever the theoretical objections to the involvement of legislative counsel at the policy development stage might be, there is one important practical problem that has quite an important limiting effect on the extent to which legislative counsel are in fact able to participate in the policy development of legislation at the early stages. The difficulty has been referred to earlier but might be emphasized once more. I am referring to the huge volume of legislation that must be prepared for each legislative session by the draftsmen. There are just not enough legislative counsel available at any one time to have them sit in on the policy sessions connected with each individual legislative proposal that has been put forward for enactment. Admittedly, some legislative provisions are merely amending provisions, but even so the volume is still great.

In those circumstances where the draftsman is asked to prepare a draft bill as the focal point for policy discussions, either because he is considered to be well versed in the subject matter of the proposed act or because the sponsors are unable to clarify their own thoughts and something must be done, the policy input by the draftsman is considerable. Although it is a practice to be avoided, if possible, in the opinion of one draftsman, at least, '' . . . there is nothing in the role of legislative counsel that should preclude him from accepting instructions to prepare policy proposals for legislation.''[30] No doubt most draftsmen would prefer not to have government officials leave economic, financial and social engineering problems to the draftsman to resolve, but this does in fact occur, although not on a regular basis. There are dangers here. One possibility to be guarded against is that the parties asking for advice will try to exploit the office of legislative counsel '' . . . to enhance their own position in public debate on the policy they eventually decide upon.''[31] This is obviously a factor that legislative counsel will have to take into account and avoid as much as possible. Another danger is that the government, in order to flesh out a legislative program, will take up such a discussion draft and put it in the House or Assembly for first reading purposes only, in an effort to elicit public response. The intention is not to have the bill go beyond first reading. But if the bill is not closely monitored, it could be accidentally enacted, as apparently did happen once.[32]

Although it does not appear to be a widespread practice, legislative counsel are involved in varying degrees in the pre-writing policy formulation process. Depending upon their experience and the inexperience of the sponsors, they can have a significant input into the policy that is eventually developed. From the

---

[29] Quoted in R. Dickerson, *Professional Legislative Drafting: The Federal Experience* (Chicago: American Bar Association, 1973), p. 136.

[30] This view was expressed by one of the draftsmen from the Province of British Columbia.

[31] R.D. Adamson, Assistant Legislative Counsel, Province of British Columbia.

[32] James Ryan, *op. cit.*, recalls an occasion in Newfoundland when a "discussion draft" in an area more legal than social or administrative was enacted by oversight. Although thoroughly disliked by lawyers, judges and legislators, it survived for a decade.

draftsman's point of view, being able to sit in on the policy discussions should make his drafting job easier and the finished product, the draft bill, a truer reflection of the policy decisions upon which it is based. Given his own preferences, the legislative draftsman probably would not wish to take on the added burden of choosing between competing policies in order to solve economic, social or other kinds of problems and would prefer to leave this difficult function to others. However, the realities of the situation seem to compel his involvement, in this way, in some cases, particularly in the smaller provinces. As long as the sponsor has the final word or decision, there does not appear to be anything fundamentally wrong with the draftsman helping out by providing a discussion draft or otherwise involving himself in the development of policy by making suggestions, if he is asked to do so.

Preparing the Draft Bill: The Writing Stage

Once the legislative policy has been formulated and agreed upon by the minister responsible and Cabinet, it is sent to legislative counsel in the form of instructions. If he has not been involved in the policy discussions, the drafting instructions, whatever form they take, will be the draftsman's only guide to drafting the new legislation. As might be expected, drafting instructions vary in comprehensiveness and detail, but it is probably safe to suggest that in most cases they suffer from underdevelopment rather than overdevelopment.

The first basic task of the draftsman is to gain a thorough and complete understanding of what he is being asked to do. If the subject matter of the proposal is very technical, he will have to familiarize himself with the area by consulting with experts, either within the government service or external to it. To put it slightly differently, the draftsman must first submit the instructions to a critical analysis in which he attempts to obtain a thorough understanding of the true nature and the ramifications of the policy objectives and how they are to be achieved.

One of the first questions legislative counsel will have to answer, in his role as legal adviser, is whether the policy objectives can be achieved in legislation. As Professor Driedger has remarked, "Not all social ills can be cured by legislation and he [the draftsman] must critically examine the policy he has been asked to express in legislative language, not so much in his capacity as draftsman but as lawyer."[33] If the draftsman has been involved in the policy development stage he might have had an opportunity to raise the question of implementation at that point. Obviously, if he sees difficulties, in the sense that the statute may be difficult or impossible to enforce, it is his duty as a legal adviser to bring this fact to the attention of the sponsors of the legislation. How tactfully this is done will determine whether he is looked upon as an obstructionist or wise counsel by those who are trying to get the legislation drafted.

---

[33] Driedger, *op. cit.*, p. 37.

THE LEGISLATIVE SCHEME

In Canada, legislative counsel is responsible for providing the legislative scheme required to carry out the policy objectives.[34] The policy memorandum he receives may, or may not, outline the method for implementing that policy.[35] In cases where the sponsors have given some thought to policy implementation and provided for this, the draftsman will be required to assess such provision in light of his general experience. On occasion, a draftsman is able to suggest a way of giving effect to a proposal that is quite different from the one originally proposed by the government sponsors but which achieves the intended objective by a process that is simpler or less Draconian or more politically acceptable.[36] Not only is this a permissible function but one that the government expects the draftsman to fulfill. It must be remembered, however, that the draftsman is merely making recommendations for change at this point. He does not make final decisions. But his recommendations, depending upon his personal status and experience, can have a significant influence upon the final decisions that are made in connection with policy.

In situations where the instructions do not go so far as to include implementation directions, the draftsman must prepare a legislative plan or method by which the legislative policy will be achieved. If he has previously been consulted at the policy development stage, he may have been asked for advice as to how to implement the legislation. His experience with a large volume of legislation quite clearly enables him to contribute valuable guidance on this important issue. Drawing up the legislative scheme may also reveal some subsidiary issues that may require a policy decision. Questions involving the type of sanction, if any, to be used, procedural questions involving the onus of proof, for example, or the use of privitive clauses may arise and have to be answered. Clients or sponsors will usually leave such decisions to the draftsman because they involve primarily legal considerations. But there can be danger here for the draftsman. One legislative counsel has recounted his experience with a so-called "boiler plate clause" involving seizure provisions. These provisions, which provide for the seizure of equipment used in the carrying on of unlawful activities, were employed extensively in the *Fisheries Act* and subsequently were extended to other legislation more or less automatically. They were used routinely until a member of the legislature, who appreciated the economic significance of them as sanctions, objected to their being inserted so casually into

---

[34] Arthur Stone makes this point clearly in his address to the Law Society's Continuing Education program. See Note 18. Development of the legislative plan or scheme as a prime function of the draftsman has also been emphasized by Professor Driedger. Although this appears to be accepted in Canada, it is not necessarily true of other countries. See Curtis and Kotts, "The Role of the Government Lawyer in the Protection of Citizens Rights," *Australian Law Journal* 49 (1975), p. 341.

[35] The responses received from draftsmen were almost unanimous in pointing out that they were consulted as to the best way to achieve the policy objectives of the legislation. This is particularly so where the drafting service is well established and experienced.

[36] Curtis and Kotts, *op. cit.*, p. 340.

other legislation. Legislative counsel explained that he and his fellow drafters had been concerned for some time but could not do much about the situation until the matter became public and the political pressure developed. It is not clear from this anecdote why legislative counsel could not convince the administrators or sponsors of subsequent legislation that indiscriminate use of this type of sanction was unwise. Apparently they were unable to convince the minister of the political dangers involved. The story does raise the issue, which will be discussed shortly, of the position of legislative counsel in cases where his advice about the proposed legislation is offered and ignored.

In the process of critically analysing and examining the instructions or working up the legislative scheme, gaps may appear in the policy framework requiring additional decisions to be made. These may involve social rather than legal issues. In most cases the draftsman feels obliged to consult with the sponsoring agency and, by a series of conferences with the administrators and other experts, will attempt to have decisions made. At these conferences legislative counsel will have an opportunity to influence policy by expressing his own views. If he has strong views about the legislation generally, he may express them, but most draftsmen will be rather circumspect in this regard and will not wish to be too openly critical of government policy. The fact remains, however, that there is an opportunity to influence policy considerations, even on subsidiary matters, and decision in detail can sometimes be as important as decisions regarding the main policy principles. Certainly the philosophy of some senior administrators has been, ''You can have the main policy, leave the details to me.''

On the basis of views expressed by Canadian legislative counsel, it seems quite clear that there is considerable scope for the draftsman to have an effect on policy at the drafting stage. Whether by the process of filling in gaps by the addition of needed legal provisions, the questioning of policies already decided upon, or by pointing out the need for additional policy decisions on subsidiary issues, legislative counsel occupies a unique position. If well respected and experienced, his opinion will be sought and heeded. As active members of the drafting section or civil law section of the Uniform Law Conference of Canada, legislative counsel frequently have occasion to recommend the adoption of uniform legislation. In addition, legislation such as the *Interpretation Act,* a statute that concerns itself with the rules of statutory interpretation, or legislation dealing with the internal structure of legislation, particularly falls within the special expertise of the Legislative Counsel's Office and thus the office itself becomes the sponsor.

THE DRAFTSMAN AS PROTECTOR OF CITIZENS' RIGHTS

But, apart from those situations in which legislative Counsel's Office is the sponsoring agency, to what extent should the draftsman seize the opportunities presented and deliberately try to change policy that has already been agreed upon by other sponsors or clients. Quite often administrators and other experts, with the best of intentions, in an effort to achieve their policy objectives, will resort to overkill. Provisions become over-regulatory and the citizens' civil rights can often be severely affected as the result. Privitive clauses limiting appeals to the courts or provisions allowing rights to be determined without a hearing or a notice of a hearing can all seriously affect such rights. What should and can the draftsman do in these circumstances? One senior legislative counsel for the province of Ontario has publicly explained,

> It is also especially the responsibility of the draftsman to supply common sense to the practical application of the policy intent. The draftsman has to look at the proposal from the point of view of the lawyer and the politician as well as of the administrator and lawyer.
>
> The Ministers depend on the drafting process to eliminate the bombs and hold down the excesses or overkill to which administrators and experts, with the best of intentions, are prone.[37]

Many of the provisions inserted by overzealous administrators conflict with basic traditional concepts of the common law which are known to and fully appreciated by the draftsman as a lawyer. In these cases, Canadian legislative counsel seem to have no hesitation in objecting to them and pointing out their effect. As they explain, quite often the sponsors did not appreciate the effect of the provisions upon traditional legal concepts, many of which have been developed to protect the citizen from the power of the state. When the conflict is pointed out to them, in most cases, the sponsors will quickly accede to the suggestions for change. If the sponsor refuses to make the change, legislative counsel can, and do, supply an explanatory memoranda to the draft bill outlining the objections to the provisions and leaving it to the minister responsible and the Attorney General to settle the issue.

Although the majority of Canadian draftsmen do not see themselves as official guardians of civil rights, they do acknowledge a duty to warn of encroachments upon individual rights. In provinces with civil or human rights legislation or, in the case of federal legislation, such as the *Canadian Bill of Rights,* the draftsman is more formally directed to the protection of citizens' rights. In the provinces of British Columbia and Ontario, the general principles governing the drafting of legislation have been institutionalized to a greater extent than elsewhere. Draftsmen operating within these jurisdictions have precise guidelines to follow. Copies of the guidelines are included in Appendices 1 and 2. In the event the sponsor refuses to change a provision which violates these guiding principles, the matter is taken up with the Attorney General and the minister of the sponsoring department.

The draftsman has a further influence at the actual writing stage. One of his major functions is to communicate as clearly as possible the policy ideas that

---

[37] Arthur Stone, Province of Ontario.

have been agreed upon. Occasionally, for political reasons, he is asked to be a little less precise than he could be so that the intention behind the provisions does not emerge quite so starkly. This same dilemma occurs even in connection with the explanatory note that accompanies the legislative text. Quite often the sponsors seem more concerned with the wording of the explanatory note than with anything else. Should the draftsman draft in a deliberately vague way so that the full policy effect may not be appointed? This poses an ethical and professional problem for the draftsman, as does the request for a statute that is not really needed, at least not in legislative form, but is needed for political purposes. Most draftsmen do not feel so strongly that they will resign if their advice is not followed, although that is one possible course of action.

The draftsmen, by unanimous agreement, also have sole control of drafting policy. This means they determine how the legislative policy is to be expressed. Using this power the draftsman can also control to some extent the impact that the legislative policy will have on the minds of the legislators, the public and the judiciary.

REGULATIONS

Although the statute is expected to and usually does reflect the major policy decisions that have been made, much of the supporting or supplementary detail is dealt with in subordinate legislation and commonly referred to as regulations. Who drafts the regulations? If it is the Legislative Counsel's Office, is the same procedure followed as in the case of statutes? Does he receive instructions concerning the content of the regulations or is he left on his own?

At the federal government level, regulations are drafted usually by officials of the department, in consultation with the legal officer of the department who acts as draftsman. The first draft is submitted to the Privy Council Office for review to ensure that it complies with the *Canadian Bill of Rights* and the *Regulations Act*. Regulations are examined to make certain that their substance falls within the authority conferred by the parent statute. The Privy Council Office may raise questions of policy but rarely does. Although the Department of Justice is expected to review regulations and is entitled to raise questions of form and substance, a shortage of legally trained draftsmen may limit the Justice Department's review to matters of drafting form only.

It would seem, then, that the draftsman and the department officials together decide upon the substance of the regulations. One former federal minister of Justice has expressed the view that it is preferable to let departmental draftsmen draft regulations because the regulations tend to be quite technical and to relate more to policy than to law. In his opinion, because of their technical content, it makes more sense to have the drafting done in departments by lawyers who are familiar with the administrative procedures and policies of the department.[38]

Quite clearly, the expectation is that the draftsman will have a significant role to play in developing the substantive content of the regulations, much more than is the case with the drafting of statutes. With the Privy Council Office and the Department of Justice subjecting the regulations to only a cursory examination in relation to policy and substance, decisions made at the departmental level will probably go unquestioned. There is, however, some effort made to see that proper procedures regarding the provision of hearings are maintained and that discriminatory provisions are removed.

Provincially, the role of legislative counsel varies somewhat in relation to regulations. In Saskatchewan and Nova Scotia, legislative counsel does not draft regulations while in most of the other provinces he does. Opinion was evenly split on the question whether the drafter had more scope for policy input when drafting regulations. Those who thought there was more opportunity to help develop policy expressed opinion in different ways. Observations ranged from recognition of the ease with which unreasonable regulations could be drafted and the temptation to fill in gaps to the acknowledgement that

> because of the regulations by department, the draftsman often finds himself much more on his own in making suggestions that are basically of a policy nature rather than receiving directions as to policies from the sponsor.[39]

I would be surprised if the draftsman, and here we may be talking to a greater extent about the departmental draftsman rather than legislative counsel, did not engage more fully in the development of the substance of regulations than he would if he were drafting statutes. Considering the great quantity of subordinate legislation that is enacted annually, the contribution of draftsmen to the policy contained therein could be very substantial.

CONCLUSION

On the basis of information, observations and opinion provided by legislative counsel and draftsmen from different parts of Canada, it is clear to me that ''intellectual eunuch'' is hardly an accurate or apt description of the actual role performed by these officials in the legislative process. To think of the draftsman as solely concerned and occupied with the translation of policy directives into proper legislative language is highly erroneous. The draftsman does more than this. He plays a key role in the process of legislative enactment and, in so doing, performs at least three major functions.

As legal adviser he is looked to for guidance, particularly in relation to legal matters. Whether it involves problems of constitutionality, procedure that that

---

[38] The Hon. John Turner in *Proceedings of the Special Committee on Statutory Instruments,* (Ottawa: Queen's Printer, 1969), pp. 236-37.

[39] The observations of Mr. Beverly G. Smith of New Brunswick are shared by several other Legislative Counsel.

accords with the rules of natural justice, or a choice of sanctions, his influence is felt. As one close to the power source with the broad overview, he may even be consulted as to the social impact of the proposed legislation. If he is not consulted specifically, he has at least the opportunity to voice his own opinions in this regard; an opportunity that is apparently taken. As architect of the legislative scheme, his ability to develop or mold the vehicle that will give effect to the legislative policy cannot be underestimated. As writer or composer, his selection of the language used and his positioning of the various parts of the statute can also affect the extent to which the policy is actually reflected and made known to the audience for which it is intended, whether this be the politician, the citizen, the Bar or the Judiciary.

Reed Dickerson has warned,

> Legal drafting is not for children, amateurs or dabblers. It is a highly technical discipline, the most rigourous form of writing outside of mathematics. Few lawyers have the special combination of skills, aptitudes and temperament necessary for a competent draftsman. This is partly due to inadequate training. More fundamental is the widespread misunderstanding of what adequate draftsmanship involves.
>
> I meet few [lawyers, government officials and law professors] who do not consider themselves well trained and even expert draftsmen. That the average lawyer or law professor senses little inadequacy either in himself or among Bar members generally may explain the condescension they often show.[40]

Drafting is not just writing, although this is an important part of the job.

In the process of carrying out his functions as legislative counsel, the draftsman quite clearly is in a position to influence the development of legislative policy. He does not make final decisions, however, and acts throughout as a consultant only. But his influence is considerable. Is there anything theoretically objectionable to the draftsman being anything more than a legal stenographer? I would say NO. The benefits to be gained by having someone with legal knowledge and a broad perspective of government and legislative processes involved in the development of legislative policy at all stages seems to me to far outweigh any possible adverse consequences of such participation. To accurately reflect the sponsors' intentions in the draft bill, the draftsman must have a thorough and complete understanding of what the sponsor wants. As unofficial watchdog and protector of individual rights, the draftsman renders a valuable service.

But with power goes responsibility. Fortunately for Canadians, the personnel employed in the Office of Legislative Counsel seem to have a well-developed sense of personal and professional integrity. Some sense of this attitude as well as the essence of what it means to be a draftsman is found in the following comment by one Canadian legislative counsel who has spent more than a quarter of a century drafting legislation.

---

[40] Dickerson, *op. cit.*, p. 3.

The experienced professional has nearly always been hooked by the attractive features of the role: creativity, closeness to power, last minute deadlines, watching politicians at work, completing something useful and, above all, being on occasion the only one to help the government solve a problem. It is the problem-solving feature that I find most exhilarating in drafting.[41]

---

[41] James W. Ryan, Senior Legislative Counsel in Alberta (1952-1960), Trinidad and Tobago and concurrently, the Federal Government of the West Indies (1960-62), the Government of Canada (1962-75) and the Government of Newfoundland (1976-1978).

APPENDIX 1.

GENERAL PRINCIPLES GOVERNING THE DRAFTING OF LEGISLATION IN BRITISH COLUMBIA

1. No deviation from the *Canadian Bill of Rights* or the *Human Rights Code*.
2. No unreasonable restrictions on the liberty of the person, or undue powers of arrest or search.
3. No unreasonable restrictions on freedom of speech or expression.
4. No unreasonable restrictions on freedom of assembly or political activity.
5. In hearings before administrative tribunals, no unreasonable restrictions on
   (a) the right to a public hearing;
   (b) the right to give evidence and cross-examine;
   (c) the right to natural justice.
6. Provision for a right of appeal from administrative decisions.
7. No unreasonable interference with property rights and no expropriation without compensation.
8. Trial of criminal offences not to be withdrawn from the courts.
9. No abrogation of the requirement of mens rea in statutory offences.
10. No ouster of the jurisdiction of the courts and no privative clauses.
11. No retrospective operation of statutes.
12. No restriction on section 13 of the *Interpretation Act* binding the Crown.
13. No *Henry VIII* clause whereby Acts can be amended by Order-in-Council.
14. No unlimited spending authority.
15. No interference with other ministers' legislation without their consent or Cabinet decision.

Office of Legislative Counsel

APPENDIX 2.

THE DRAFTSMAN'S FUNCTION IN ONTARIO

The draftsman's first and most important function is a legal one: to analyse the policy objective and decide what changes in the law are required to permit the policy to be implemented. This requires probing to understand the true nature of the policy objective, testing its relationship to the existing law, characterizing the problems in law and settling on the necessary changes in the law, but no more than is necessary.

In producing a draft, the draftsman is responsible:

(1) for supplying common sense in the practical application of the policy intent;

(2) for the design of the procedures necessary to carry out the policy intent;

(3) for the preservation of civil rights and standards of justice in the content of the draft;

(4) for the impact of the provisions as drafted on the administration of justice;

(5) in the case of a regulation, for ensuring that the regulation is within the delegated authority and in the case of statutes, for identifying the extent to which the Bill would be *ultra vires;*

(6) for the wording, arrangement and accuracy of the draft.

Where difficulties are unresolved, the draftsman should consult with Senior Legislative Counsel or, in the case of regulations, the Registrar of Regulations.

The task of producing a draft requires care in organizing details and their interrelationships and a grasp of the proper use of English. The draft must be simple and concise. This can only be accomplished by intensive analysis of the subject and words used. The amount of detail or generality must be calculated to strike a balance between the right to certainty in the law and the flexibility a court must have to obtain justice in particular cases.

The draftsman must control the draft. He should maintain one master copy which only he may change to reflect discussion. He will find it easier, where possible, to use meetings for discussion and development of the thinking and to carry out the result by formulating the wording privately.

The draftsman's relationship with those from whom he receives his instructions is that of solicitor and client. This principally means that all matters of intent are confidential. Any indication of this must come from the Ministry or Member involved. However, in the case of a government Bill it is the draftsman's duty to see that any other Ministry affected is aware of the content of the Bill.

Private Members' Bills are totally confidential as against everyone except the Member.

While a Bill is before the House, the draftsman is counsel to the House and should be present on all occasions when the Bill is under consideration. He may be called upon for advice. His advice should be confined to objective professional statements on drafting practices and the law.

Office of Legislative Counsel

COMMENTS

DOUGLAS LAMBERT*

While there may be some disagreement on the extent to which legislative counsel should be involved in "public policy" or "policy" questions, there is likely to be unanimous agreement that they are expected to be proficient in, and to advise on, matters of

(a) law,
(b) parliamentary procedure and practice,
(c) literary style, composition and grammar,
(d) practices and techniques for carrying statutory schemes into effect through public and private administration, and
(e) practices and procedures for settling the content of enactments.

Matters of Law

Advising on matters of law is only one area of the competence of legislative counsel. It is the only area that is encompassed within the definition of the "practice of law" in the *Legal Professions Act* of British Columbia. The fact that a significant part of the practice of the calling of legislative counsel is not the practice of law does not distinguish them from other lawyers. A large part of the work that is done by solicitors is not the practice of law. In particular, the negotiating of the terms of agreements in writing does not come within the definition of the "practice of law" in the *Legal Professions Act*.

Indeed, it is very difficult to be sure of the whereabouts of the edges of the practice of law. Even the usual test, that if it is work actually done by chartered accountants then it is the practice of law, is not completely universal!

The point I wish to make is that, like most other lawyers, legislative counsel cannot distinguish between matters on which they ought to be giving advice and matters on which they ought not to be giving advice merely from an analysis of whether the matter in question constitutes the practice of law. Clients demand much more from their solicitors than advice on legal problems and if they do not get such advice, couched in a suitable way, then they are likely in the course of time to consult another lawyer who will give them advice.

Policy Questions

If legislative counsel then are expected to advise in matters that are not purely "the practice of law" why should they shrink from involving themselves in seeking solutions to matters of "policy," or "public policy"? The answer

---

* The Honourable Mr. Justice Douglas Lambert, Court of Appeal of British Columbia; at the time of writing, Chairman of the Law Reform Commission of British Columbia.

must be that either legislative counsel are not expected to be knowledgeable or wise and do not expect of themselves that they will be knowledgeable or wise in relation to the decision that must be made; or, alternatively, that legislative counsel, in spite of having useful knowledge or wisdom should, for some other reason, not give advice.

There are clearly areas where the question is one of "policy" and where legislative counsel are expected to be knowledgeable or wise and should expect of themselves that they be knowledgeable or wise.

One example of such a policy area is where the policy question involves a thorough understanding of the common law. In such an area, legislative counsel should be expected to be at least as competent as any other lawyer in giving the policy advice and resolving or helping in the resolution of the policy question. Such a policy question might be: "Should a landowner be liable to a trespasser who is injured on the landowner's land by a careless invitee?" Appendix 1 to Professor Charles' paper, British Columbia's *General Principles Governing the Drafting of Legislation* is pregnant with policy questions on which legislative counsel should have a major involvement because the policy question is, essentially, a matter of legal policy.

There is a second area of policy where legislative counsel are particularly knowledgeable or wise and where, clearly, they are expected to be involved in seeking the solution to policy questions. That area of policy is the area where the accumulated experience of a legislative counsel has built up an extensive expertise on questions relating to the administration of statutory schemes. Such a policy question might be: "Can a fund for paying the unpaid wages of workmen whose employer does not pay them be established and administered from land registry fees on the registration of land zoned for business pruposes, through payments into and out of the Consolidated Revenue Fund?"

The example of legal policy questions and the example of accumulated expertise policy questions are not exhaustive of the areas where legislative counsel have traditionally been involved in the solution to policy questions.

On the other hand, there are other areas where the policy question is one where the legislative counsel is not expected to have any expertise and where his views are of no more relevance than the views of any other single person, and clearly of much less significance than those of the minister responsible for the legislation in question, or for the field in which legislation is contemplated.

Clearly, the legislative counsel should not venture uninvited into an area of policy where he is not expected to have any particular expertise. Even in the case of a specific request for his advice on such a question, he should be most cautious before offering that advice.

Limits of Advice

It is a persistent danger to which all lawyers are exposed that they will become so closely involved in solving the problems put to them by their clients, and the problems raised by those problems, and so intent upon the solutions they themselves devise, that they will lose the objectivity and judgment which can only come from a detachment from the consequences flowing from the alternative solutions to the problem. This difficulty faces legislative counsel in exactly the same way as it faces any other lawyer.

Like any other lawyer, the legislative counsel should not stand aside and permit his client to make errors through a failure to appreciate the law and the legal and administrative consequences of his acts, merely on the ground that the client did not ask for advice on the particular question.

Again, like any other lawyer, the legislative counsel will be asked for advice on matters that are not strictly legal. In deciding whether to give advice, and the nature of the advice that should be given, he should balance the same factors that any other lawyer would balance. Before giving the advice he should be sure that the client understands that he is not getting legal advice. He should also be sure that the client understands the nature of the experience that makes it sensible for the client to persist in seeking that advice from the lawyer and for the lawyer to give it. If the advice is sought in an area where the lawyer does not feel that he has particular competence by reason of relevant experience then he should warn the client of the risk that the value of the lawyer's legal advice may be debased if the lawyer becomes involved in the policy solutions of non-legal matters. If the client persists in his request for advice, at this stage, then it seems to be the usual practice for lawyers to give it, though, after enough warnings and disclaimers by the lawyer, it must be fairly frequent for the client to disregard the advice, once given.

In my experience it would be very rare for a legislative counsel to find that his basic approach to involvement in the solution of policy questions must become different from that of other lawyers, by reason of the fact that the legislative counsel is likely to be a member of the public service. Whether the legislative counsel is responsible to the Attorney General or to the legislature, the importance of the maintenance of his independent judgment is likely to be clearly recognized so that his approach need be no different from that which should govern any other solicitor/client relationship.

Conclusion

In conclusion, I would say that, in my view, skilled legislative counsel combine the ability to become deeply involved in pushing policy questions to a solution, making whatever contribution of their own they think is appropriate, with the ability to retain a detached judgment so that they can probe for and cure any deficiencies which that policy solution might pose in the total legislative package.

RICHARD F. DOLE, JR.*

Few professional bill drafters in the United States are accorded the influence in the legislative process which Professor Charles attributes to Canadian legislative counsel. His description of the nature of this office in Canada is most enlightening to a person from south of the Canadian border.

Influence in Canada and the United States

In Canada, for example, legislative counsel apparently are required to be lawyers and perceive their role in advising legislators as involving the solicitor-client relationship. This perception naturally has no application to the substantial number of professional bill drafters in the United States who are not lawyers. It also may be inaccurate with respect to those who are attorneys. The difficulty with conceptualizing a professional bill drafter who is a lawyer as having an attorney-client relationship with a legislator who seeks drafting advice is that it may imply that a professional bill drafter owes a greater obligation to that legislator than to other members of the legislature. Yet a professional bill drafter ordinarily is employed by one or both houses of an American legislature to provide non-partisan drafting service to all members of the employing body. It would seem more accurate to consider that all professional bill drafters, whether or not they are lawyers, are employees who owe the same obligations to all members of the employing legislative body, one of which is maintenance of the secrecy of all confidential communications. This perception surely reflects the manner in which a bill drafter's professional obligations are enforced in both Canada and the United States. It is the employing legislative bodies rather than the Canadian Law Societies or American Bar Associations and courts that ordinarily impose sanctions for misconduct.

Different Systems: Different Roles

However the obligations of a professional bill drafter are characterized, the differences between the Canadian and American legislative systems significantly affect his or her functional role. In contrast to the Canadian parliamentary system in which the government is selected by the legislature from among its membership, American chief executives are elected independently by voters in electoral districts that are substantially larger than those in which members of a legislature are elected. This not infrequently results in one party controlling the office of chief executive and the other party controlling one or both houses of the legislature. Even if the same party controls the office of chief executive and the legislature, the differing constituencies and independent elections of a chief executive and a legislature foster independent legislative initiatives.

---

* Professor, Bates College of Law, University of Houston; Professor, University of Iowa at the time of writing.

Legislatures in the United States tend to develop their own policies, sometimes in direct conflict with those of a chief executive. In American legislatures, like the federal Congress, in which committee membership is immunized by a seniority rule from manipulation by legislative leadership, legislative committees are independent power centres within each house of a legislature with often decisive control over the fate of proposed legislation.

Because legislative policy in the United States is formulated in multiple fora, the involvement of professional bill drafters in the initial development of policy often is far more limited than in the Canadian parliamentary system. The executive branch of government tends to formulate its legislative proposals behind closed doors. In American legislatures with substantial staffing, like the federal Congress, professional and personal staff play a dominant role in the initial development of legislation. It frequently is not until a bill is considered ready for formal introduction that professional bill drafters are consulted concerning bill form and wording. Indeed, in many states professional bill drafters are required to give pre-introductory approval to the form and wording of all bills.[1]

This consultation, however, ordinarily is more limited than that contemplated by the British Columbia and Ontario drafting principles set forth in the Appendices to Professor Charles' paper. Primary considerations are compliance with state constitutional bill form requirements, like the single subject title rule,[2] and the enacting clause rule,[3] as well as other formal requirements imposed by statutes and legislative rules. A representative state bill drafting manual, for example, provides:

> Determining the policy and objectives of legislation is the prerogative of the legislator. The drafter's function is to determine the present laws affected, make proper amendments, devise actual statutory language, and place the bill draft in proper form. The drafter may not express his or her personal ideas but must remain an impartial technician.
>
> Upon the request of a legislator that a bill be drafted which is of doubtful constitutionality, the drafter should inform the legislator of the constitutional problems and, if possible, devise a method of accomplishing the purpose of the bill which is constitutional. If the legislator nevertheless wishes to introduce the bill after the drafter has suggested the constitutional difficulties, the drafter should draft the bill in accordance with the legislator's instructions.[4]

This state bill drafting manual contrasts sharply with the British Columbia Drafting Principles in stating that a professional bill drafter must allow questions of substantive, as opposed to formal, unconstitutionality to be resolved by a legislator. Notwithstanding the existence of material questions of substantive constitutionality, if a legislator wishes to introduce a bill, a professional drafter is

---

[1] E.g., Iowa Senate Rule 26, Iowa House of Representatives Rule 30 (67th General Assembly, 1977-78).
[2] E.g., Texas Constitution of 1876, Art III S35.
[3] E.g., Texas Constitution of 1876, Art III S29.
[4] 1977 Iowa Bill Drafting Guide, at p. 31.

to write it as instructed. In Canada, however, Professor Charles indicates that legislative counsel may pursue constitutional objections discounted by a legislator with the minister concerned and with the Attorney General.

One reason that legislators in the United States may be less concerned with substantive constitutional objections than Canadian legislators is their constitutional independence from the executive branch of government, including the Attorney General. American legislative attitudes toward substantive constitutional objections to proposed legislation also are influenced by the power of the American judiciary to invalidate unconstitutional laws. American legislators not infrequently have chosen to leave determinations concerning the substantive unconstitutionality of statutes to the courts.

Professional bill drafters have various institutional affiliations in the United States, but few are assigned to the Attorney General's Office as is common in Canada. The typical arrangement is affiliation with a legislative office or agency. The United States Senate and House of Representatives each have an office of Legislative Counsel. Many states have legislative service or research bureaus that provide professional drafting services to both houses of a state legislature.[5] Although appointments to these legislative offices and agencies can involve partisan considerations, appointees traditionally have been expected to provide non-partisan professional services to all members.

To the extent that a professional bill drafter in the United States has less involvement in policy development than many Canadian legislative counsel, does it follow that the "intellectual eunuchs" and "emotional oysters" referred to by Professor Charles exist primarily south of the Canadian border? I do not think so, and neither, I believe, does Professor Charles. In his concluding observations he portrays a professional bill drafter as potentially performing three principal functions: that of legal adviser, that of architect of the legislative scheme, and that of composer.

Meaning of the Words

The talismanic significance that the English, Commonwealth, and American courts have given the every jot and title of statutory verbiage is well-known. A.P. Herbert once attributed to a presumably fictitious Lord Justice Mildew the statement that, "if Parliament does not mean what it says, it must say so." Actual judges have expressed similar sentiments under what is known as the plain meaning rule of statutory construction. The United States Supreme Court once commented: "[W]here the language of an enactment is clear and construction according to its terms does not lead to absurd or impracticable consequences, the words employed are to be taken as the final expression of the meaning intended."[6]

---

[5] E.g., Iowa Code SS 2.58-.66 (1977) (Legislative Service Bureau).
[6] *United States* v. *Missouri Pacific R.R. Co.*, 278 U.S. 269, 278 (1929).

The United States Supreme Court subsequently has disavowed the plain meaning rule,[7] yet it persists in a number of states,[8] and reappears from time to time in the decisions of lower federal courts as well. The 1974 decision of the Tenth Circuit Court of Appeals in *Colorado Public Interest Research Group, Inc. v. Train*,[9] is a case in point. The federal court of appeals in *Colorado* considered that what was to the court the plain and obvious meaning of a federal statute made irrelevant the administrative construction of the statute which was solidly based upon a United States House of Representatives committee report, specific statements by floor managers of the bill in both the United States House and Senate, and the floor statement of a United States House conferee concerning the meaning of the Conference Committee Report. In construing federal statutes the United States federal courts ordinarily give substantial weight to this type of legislative history. It has been said facetiously that legislative history must be unclear before the United States federal courts will consider the wording of a statute. In the *Colorado* case, however, the federal court of appeals dismissed as "inconclusive"[10] the uniform interpretation of the federal statute articulated by its principal legislative proponents. In point of fact, the principal conflict was with a floor statement by a single opponent of the bill in the House of Representatives.[11]

It is not surprising that the United States Supreme Court reversed the federal court of appeals decision in the *Colorado* case.[12] Yet, as recently as 1976 it was necessary to obtain a decision from the United States Supreme Court reaffirming its rejection of the plain meaning rule in the construction of federal statutes. Moreover, in other instances federal legislative history truly is conflicting or inconclusive, and in many states there is little or no accessible legislative history.

Deference to the constitutional prerogatives of the legislative branch of government requires courts in the United States to respect constitutional expressions of legislative purpose. To the extent that legislative history exists, a professional bill drafter must familiarize himself or herself with it. Professor Charles' implication that bill writing is a demanding form of literary composition is apt. Mr. Justice Frankfurter once observed:

> The problem derives from the very nature of words. They are symbols of meaning. But unlike mathematical symbols, the phrasing of a document, especially a complicated enactment, seldom attains more than approximate precision. If individual words are inexact symbols, with shifting variables, their configuration can hardly achieve invariant meaning or assured definiteness.[13]

---

[7] *United States* v. *American Trucking Association, Inc.*, 310 U.S. 534 (1940).
[8] E.g., *In Re Camden Shipbuilding Co.*, 227 F. Supp. 751 (D. Me 1964), applying state law.
[9] 507 F. 2d 743 (10th Cir. 1974).
[10] *Ibid.*, p. 748.
[11] Arthur W. Murphy, "Old Maxims Never Die," *Columbia Law Review* 75 (1975), p. 1309.
[12] *Train* v. *Colorado Public Interest Research Group, Inc.*, 426 U.S. 1 (1976).
[13] F. Frankfurther, "Some Reflections on the Reading of Statutes," *Columbia Law Review* 47 (1947), p. 528.

The high art that all professional bill drafters are expected to practise is selection of symbols of meaning that approximate policies which may have been formulated without their assistance or concurrence. Substantial power inheres in the practice of this art. Yet, the power over the law that a professional bill drafter derives from selection of statutory wording is his or her least legitimate power. In my opinion, it would be desirable to enact legislation which permits the courts to consider objective legislative history as an extrinsic aid to statutory construction regardless of the facial ambiguity of statutory text. Additional legislation should ensure the accessibility of basic legislative history by at least requiring the preparation and retention of committee reports concerning enacted bills. The legislative branch of government is too important for the effectuation of its policies to depend upon the words selected by a professional bill drafter.

DISCUSSION

Question 1

Why has there been such a movement away from the use of preambles? Are not preambles useful as explanations of the purposes underlying the actual sections of a statute?

Answer:

Each speaker, led by *Mr. G. Alan Higenbottam,* Chairman of the session and Legislative Counsel for British Columbia, stated that it was not desirable to include a preamble in a statute. The words of the sections of a statute should speak for themselves. All panelists agreed with *Professor Dole's* pithy summary of the discussion of this issue: "At best a preamble merely duplicates the sections of a statute; at worst it conflicts with those sections which can lead to great confusion." *Mr. Lambert* agreed that, from a legislative drafting perspective, preambles should not be utilized. He did point out, however, that in some recent cases the insertion of a preamble might have helped the courts decide in favour of the constitutionality of a statute. He cited the *Anti-Inflation Act Reference* as such a case.

Question 2

What, if anything, should a legislative drafter do if he disagrees with the policy contained in a statute he is drafting or if he does not like the actual wording of his final draft?

Answer:

Mr. Higenbottam suggested that the unhappy drafter could attach a memorandum to the final draft in which he would outline his concerns. Then Cabinet ministers and other civil servants who examined the proposed statute would see his memorandum and become aware of the draftsman's doubts. Neither *Mr. Lambert* nor *Professor Charles* expressed any concern with this course of action. *Professor Dole* said that this could never happen in the United States. He referred back to the main theme of his earlier comments — the policy role of the legislative draftsman in the United States is much less than that outlined for the Canadian draftsman in *Professor Charles'* paper. The fact that a Canadian draftsman could attach a memorandum of dissent to his draft statute was just one more example of this important difference.

Question 3

Should Canadian courts make more use of legislative history in interpreting statutes?

Answer:

Professor Dole cautioned against a too facile adoption of the American practice. He suggested that, although legislative history can be very useful, the pendulum may have swung too far in the direction of utilization of legislative history at the expense of judicial focus on the actual words of the statute. He cited *Mr. Justice Frankfurter's* famous protest against this trend to the effect that "only when the legislative history was ambiguous, would American courts look at the actual words of the statute."

A BASIC BIBLIOGRAPHY

PUBLIC POLICY AND LEGISLATIVE DRAFTING

Bakshi, P.M. *An Introduction to Legislative Drafting.* Bombay: Tripathi, 1972.

Coode, George. *Legislative Expression on the Language of The Written Law,* 2nd ed. London: James Ridgway, 1852.

Cook, Robert. *Legal Drafting.* New York: Foundation Press, 1951.

Dale, Sir William. *Legislative Drafting: A New Approach.* London: Butterworths, 1977.

Dick, R.C. *Legal Drafting.* Toronto: Carswell, 1972.

Dickerson, Reed. *The Fundamentals of Legal Drafting.* Boston: Little, Brown, 1965.

Dickerson, Reed. *Legislative Drafting.* Boston: Little, Brown, 1954.

Dickerson, Reed. *Professional Legislative Drafting: The Federal Experience.* Chicago: American Bar Association, 1973.

Driedger, Elmer. *The Composition of Legislation,* 2nd ed. Ottawa: Department of Justice, 1976.

Driedger, Elmer. "Legislative Drafting." *Canadian Bar Review* 27 (1949): 291-317.

Frankfurter, F. "Some Reflections on the Reading of Statutes." *Columbia Law Review* 47 (1947): 527-46.

Chapter Ten

The Future of Representative Parliamentary Democracy

by
*John P. Mackintosh**

I originally thought when I was invited here, it was "to make a dinner speech," so I packed my dinner jacket, thought up a few blue stories and came along. I did not quite expect to give a lecture on the future of parliamentary democracy, a rather portentous title; but, what I will try to do is say something about what we have gone through in this conference, in every sense, and try to pull together what has occurred to me on the topic at hand in the hope that it will be of some small value to you.

I think it has been a useful, stimulating conference and if I may say so, a hard working conference. I calculated ten and one quarter hours solid last night which was very good for people like myself. I came wanting to be immersed in Canadian politics and it has happened and I have benefited enormously from it.

Mr. Stanfield's Pessimism

I thought that we started off well with the speech by Mr. Robert Stanfield, a speech which struck a rather pessimistic note. He said, if you remember, that you could not, in his view, combine the present all-pervasive role of government with parliamentary democracy. He said the two were incompatible.

For Mr. Stanfield there were two possibilities. Either it was necessary to reduce government or it was necessary to improve the efficacy of democratic control. It is quite clear to me that for him, the preferred choice was to reduce the size of his government. But I do not think anyone has really taken this up. I do not think many of us believe it would be possible to cut back, in any very large sense, the degree of government intervention and government activity and government expenditure that has developed since the last war.

---

* Member of Parliament and Head, Department of Politics, University of Edinburgh. Dr. Mackintosh's remarks were delivered at the closing session and are reproduced here as transcribed, subject to minor editing. An ebullient and independent man, Dr. Mackintosh brought to the Conference his wealth of parliamentary experience and scholarship, his exuberance for fresh inquiry and his very singular candor. His many Canadian friends and admirers were shocked and saddened by his death on July 30, 1978.

We have seen governments from time to time in the western world attempt this task and try to go back to an earlier situation. After a great deal of anguish and tremendous financial axe swinging, they have ended up by reducing expenditure by 2 percent or 3 percent and by the end of a full term of office, expenditure has usually gone up by a further 5 or 6 percent, so that I do not think anyone seriously imagines that this can be done on any major scale. Therefore the only alternative is to turn and look at methods of increasing the effectiveness of parliamentary government. But before leaving Mr. Stanfield's proposition, I would just like to point out that there is a great deal of truth in what he said and it does seem to me that we have got to take his point seriously.

19th Century Parliamentary Government

Remember that parliamentary government — I do not say democracy necessarily, but parliamentary government — in its hey day was a nineteenth century creation. Then it worked really well and it was effective. It had in its early stages a limited franchise but it worked well at that period largely because, as Mr. Stanfield observed, the issues were limited. Government operated in a narrow, restricted sector, shut in by people's attitudes as to what government could legitimately do or legitimately tackle. This is why the propositions of parliamentary democracy, the classic propositions, were accurate at that time.

In the first place, there was no problem of enforceability. Governments enacted simple regulations, police-type regulations; the kind of regulations that had moral backing for each individual. The citizen could see why the government was asking him or her to do this or that. In Britain, there were occasional policy decisions like possibly giving home rule to the Irish, or compulsorily educating people — they came to the same thing, I suppose, in some ways. Irish jokes are rather the thing at home just now! Nevertheless, it was clear that the government was undertaking a specific limited degree of activity whose rationale was clear. The legislative assembly could understand the issues at stake because they were fairly clear cut. They could debate them and change them on the floor of the House if necessary. The concept of parliamentary responsibility was clear. There was a small civil service in Britain at that time of some seventy-five thousand people and all the major ministers were really on top of their jobs and could honestly say that they had personally seen or taken every major policy decision that occurred in their department. Lord Palmerston said that he wrote every foreign office dispatch of any consequence that went out of the foreign office in his period and there is no denying the accuracy of this statement.

Under these circumstances, to talk of responsibility to an assembly made sense. The assembly could feel that it was participating in decision making and of course in this situation the whole doctrine of parliamentary sovereignty had meaning. It had meaning because Parliament could set out to do something. It could put its hand to a task and if it decided to enforce a law of this kind, there was no problem. It could go through and then be enforced.

So you can understand in this situation why the old doctrines of parliamentary responsibility, of sovereignty and of legislative supremacy, all had some reality. But it is the same set of doctrines which we are still trying to use in a vastly different situation. What is needed now is to see whether these principles still fit the current realities and whether it is feasible now to revitalize or to keep in place parliamentary institutions in a very different situation. I accept Mr. Stanfield's point that part of our trouble has been that parliaments today, or the governments over whom these parliaments watch, have tried to do so many more difficult and different things.

Doing Many and More Difficult Things

In the first place they have tried to do some things where success is not clear. They have tried to achieve growth targets; they have tried to improve the environment and they have tried to end pollution. They have tried to achieve all sorts of objectives where it is not quite clear whether the goal is attainable. These are often ambitious targets which cannot all be achieved at once but the consequence of failure is that nothing damages one's concept of sovereignty so much as to take a shot at something and miss. I often think that for individuals as well as for communities, success lies in having a target which you can achieve. You feel so much better than setting yourself a more difficult target and falling short of it, and yet parliament after parliament, government after government, has done precisely this, and I think that is a major reason why we are doubtful about parliaments today.

Governments, certainly in the United Kingdom, have set themselves targets and failed and then, because Parliament is associated with government, the failure has rubbed off on Parliament. It is not particularly helpful then for parliamentarians to go back to their constituencies and say "Sorry — we just should not have tried that. It was beyond our grasp. We could not make it. We said 4 percent growth but we could only make 1 percent or 2 percent — we are sorry, that is all the machine could do. We were, in fact, seeking the impossible." People then say, "well why did you tell us you could do it? — and do not come back and try that one again." Then an air of depression settles on the whole situation.

Revitalizing Parliament

So now we turn to the question, is it feasible? Is it possible to revitalize Parliament and restore its former efficacy or at least give back some of the strength of control over governments which parliaments enjoyed in the period when the institution was in its position of maximum confidence, in its most satisfactory state?

How could this be done? How does one revitalize Parliament? I think there are two ways that have been discussed at this conference. One that came out strongly from Professor Smiley's paper was the view that one cannot have an effective Parliament if the major decisions are taken outside it and Parliament is left to work on peripheral questions. So one whole area under consideration has been whether it is possible to get the major decisions back inside Parliament or inside the system in some way. The second major approach was whether it is possible to increase the effectiveness of Parliament in dealing with the executive. That means preponderately increasing backbench and opposition control over the government of the day.

The Big Decisions

I want to take these two questions in turn and to deal first with the problem of how it might be possible to get the big decisions, some of which have gone outside Parliament, back within the purview of the legislature. Please do not imagine this is a problem which is special to Canada. Professor Smiley put it in the Canadian context, pointing out that your major decisions all have a territorial dimension. As far as I can see, most of your politics, and certainly those concentrating on the provincial-federal problems, have increasingly tended to be settled by a machinery which he called "executive federalism," a system outside Parliament in the sense that the legislatures have had relatively little effect on the outcome. As I say, I do not think this is a problem by any means confined to Canada. If you look at other countries, there was great worry in the United States not many years ago, that many of the key decisions over the whole involvement in Viet Nam and Southeast Asia were taken without the knowledge of Congress or without its participation. In the case of the United Kingdom, there is a great deal of worry that the major decisions about resource distribution (with us, these are not territorial questions but social class and ideological issues) are being taken at meetings between the Trades Union Congress, the Confederation of British Industry and the government, with Parliament simply left to endorse them.

One gets some very vivid pictures of this in our House of Commons. I remember an occasion when the Miners' Union executive was meeting on a critical question of whether it would try to break the Conservative government's pay policy and whether there would be a major strike (which eventually led to the downfall of the Heath government). I ran into Roy Mason who was the miners' leading M.P., and an ex-officio member of the executive of the National Union of Mine Workers. I said, "I thought your chaps were meeting to decide this important question." He said, "Yes, they're meeting now and look at this." He produced a telegram with some disgruntlement, which said, "Crucial Miners Meeting — Please Instruct Miners' M.P.'s to Say Nothing and Keep Quiet." This shows that when critical decisions are being taken, M.P.'s and Parliament are frequently excluded even though in this case, the miners themselves had specific Members of Parliament associated with their union. This problem of exclusion from major decision making thus affects many legislatures. Can anything be done about this?

In the first place, I would like to push aside two of the customary answers to this question.

Taking Parliament for Granted

One answer is for people to say, "The major decisions have always taken place outside Parliament. Do not imagine that it has ever been any different." Of course, in a sense this is true. One never got prime ministers or ministers coming to Parliament and saying, "Look chaps, there's a crisis on. What are we going to do?" They never came down and said, "Any ideas?" They came down with a policy and put it to Parliament expecting that it would, perhaps with some amendments or changes of emphasis, be endorsed.

Notice that what really matters is that Parliament's power to reject a settlement or to affect a settlement even after it had been taken meant that Parliament's views were subsumed in the decision. Ministers would be careful how they acted so long as they knew that there was this check. It is not necessary to have constant demonstrations of force in order to achieve the fact of control, provided the power is there. I noticed, in this respect, the effectiveness of the Bundestag when Mr. Brandt was negotiating the Ost-politique. He was looking over his shoulder at the Bundestag the whole time when he had a paper-thin majority and a number of supporters were clearly dependent on refugee votes for whom the whole East-West question was absolutely red hot. As a result, although he was negotiating with the Soviet Union, rather than negotiating with the Bundestag, he nevertheless knew that he had to carry his party in Parliament with him, bit by bit. Similarly, I would have thought that any American president, even without legislative checks, now would be very hesitatant about involving American troops in a foreign war on a foreign territory without being very sure that he could carry Congress with him every inch of the way.

Again, if you take the U.K. Parliament, it was quite different in the nineteenth century and right up to the 1920s. The key figures in industrial disputes were in the House of Commons. If one studies Parliament in the 1920s, when there was a rash of very serious strikes just after the First World War, the fascinating thing is that Sir Alfred Mond, the leader of the CBI, or the then Employers' Federation, and the leaders of the TUC were all members of the House of Commons because it was then still, in a sense, the forum of the nation — the people who mattered were there. When they got up to speak in disputes of this kind they were not merely the member for X or the member for Y, they were also the member representing these tremendously powerful pressure groups. Such figures are no longer there. The key unions do not send their best men. Industry does not send its up-and-coming men into Parliament. These people may well feel that it would be foolish to take seats in the House of Commons because it would diminish their standing. They would then be bound to some extent by party loyalty, by party regulations. Operating outside the House as the leaders of major pressure groups, they have far more influence. Indeed, in a recent poll held in Britain, 54 percent of the respondents said they thought Mr.

Jack Jones, General Secretary of the Transport & General Workers' Union had more power than the Prime Minister. This verdict did not enthuse Mr. Callaghan, but there is a point to be taken and there may well be something in it.

So, do not let us fall for the argument that there was a period at the height of parliamentary democracy when it was not important to carry the House and that ministers could ever assume, in dealing with outside forces in key matters, that Parliament could be taken for granted.

Muddling Through?

Then again, there is the other answer to this question which says, "do not worry — the present position is a typical one. You know that Britain has muddled along for years so let us just muddle along a bit further. What has sufficed for centuries will last a few more decades." I find these arguments very tedious. A good example of it occurred the other day when I was having dinner (somewhat against my wishes) at an Oxford college. For the sake of after-dinner conversation, I was talking to the Master of the College about what I regarded as the unfortunate plight of the British universities at the moment in terms of finance (and, you know what I was thinking about!). After I had gone on for some time, the Bursar of the College was clearly getting more and more fed up with this. He got very fidgety, turned to me and said, "Mr. Mackintosh, you must understand that the last century has been a most exceptional period in the history of university finance." I feel like Lord Keynes about this long-run and short-run thing. In the long run, we are all dead, and as far as I am concerned, this centrury is good enough for me!

I do not think we can accept either of these arguments for tolerating the present position. I would have thought it was self-evident that if one sets out to have parliaments and if one assumes that they are going to represent the people in questioning and reviewing major decisions of government, it makes no sense if the key decisions are not clearly referred to them. So what should one do about this problem put before us very starkly by Professor Smiley?

Voting Systems and the Representation of Interests

Professor Smiley produced a voting system which was designed to see that Canadian parties become national in the sense that there were not sections of the country unrepresented in the major parties and that, therefore, the parties returned to your House of Commons could, in a sense, arbitrate these territorial problems which affect Canada so strongly at the moment. I think he, to a lesser extent than Miss Flora MacDonald, made the point that the Senate could be used for this purpose if Canadians were prepared to consider the American pattern of electing senators for a limited period from each of the provinces.

It does seem to me that it is wrong to limit ourselves to the idea that the only kind of parliament possible is on the basis of a one-person, one-vote electoral system. We must recognize the fact that there are power blocks in our society as well as individuals and that in order to run any modern country, you must carry the big power blocks or at least some of them with you because if such power blocks (whether they be Quebec or the Transport & General Workers Union) are going to resist you, then the task of government is made more difficult, if not impossible.

I often wonder why people do not think a little bit more about some of the medieval parliaments in this way. After all, if one asks why the House of Lords ever existed, it was for precisely this reason. The reason why medieval English kings bothered with the House of Lords was simply that they could not govern the country with a large number of barons marauding around and paying no attention to what they were being told to do. The kings found, and it is the situation that we face in Britain today, that the government or monarch could not take the barons one by one because that put the Crown and the Duke of Northumberland on the same footing and on that particular year, perhaps, the Duke of Northumberland had more footsoldiers than the Crown. So this was not a very happy situation and thus the Crown forced them all to come together into one chamber. Why? For the simple reason that then if Duke X wanted to make trouble and said he was not going to pay the taxes to fight the French that year, he was not having a dispute with the Crown alone; he was explaining why the other dukes were going to have to pay more or contribute more to cover for his deficiencies. So it was not the king alone that put pressure on these reluctant barons, it was the other noblemen who said, ''Why should Duke X get away with less?''

In Britain, this was repeated recently when Mr. Callaghan tried to insist on an incomes policy despite the opposition of Mr. Hugh Scanlon of the Amalgamated Engineers Union. The Prime Minister could not win him over by direct negotiation but, when Mr. Scanlon went down to the TUC and said, ''I don't know about your lot, but we're not going to settle for this amount,'' it was the other Trade Unions that said, ''oh yes, you jolly well are; otherwise, we will have to get less out of the situation.'' Because of this bargaining advantage, it makes sense, to my mind, to try and get all the power blocks institutionalized because then they have to make what is essentially a special case for themselves in front of their peers, their *equals* — that's what the word ''peer'' means in the old sense — and that is why we had a House of Lords. It was brought into existence for hard, practical reasons and perhaps we pay too little attention, certainly in British political science, to these separate chambers. They may be found in the European Community, France, Belgium and the Netherlands and are usually called Economic and Social Chambers. Officially recognized, they house the big power blocks who are brought in particularly for planning, for forecasting purposes, for the allocation of resources and for seeing that all the major groups understand and accept the political and economic targets for the nation.

As I say, I think that if such a second chamber is the price for bringing these groups into an institutional milieu and for making people explain their case in public — then this is what a parliament is about; explaining, and being "hansardized," that is, being able to be held "on record" as taking certain positions, then I would have thought one ought to be prepared to consider it. Remember that power blocks can be territorial as well as economic and the problem is exactly the same, in that sense, as representing Canadian provinces in a Senate or upper House of some kind.

Increasing the Power of Backbenchers

I have discussed the possibility or problem of bringing the major decisions within parliamentary institutions. I want now to turn to the other aspect — the possibility of increasing the power of backbenchers over the executive. This was raised in our first session by Mr. Gordon Gibson and Mr. Richard Guay who said, more or less, that what was wanted was a situation where the executive was not totally dependent on the chamber; where it was possible in fact to defeat the government without destroying it. Thus, it would be possible to control and constrain the executive without being constantly accused of aiding one's political opponents. It was in that sense that some speakers and certainly Professor Smiley cast, if not longing eyes, certainly appreciative eyes, at the system in the United States with their separately elected and normally irremovable President and a Congress which is really a genuine legislature in the sense that it has real bite.

I think there are problems. It has been pointed out again and again in this conference that we must be very careful in picking up other people's institutional ideas and grafting them onto our own system. I was surprised to find some people thinking that there were some ideas still available in the House of Commons. Mr. Holtby said he thought that Canadians had a colonial complex. Well, if Canada has a colonial complex, Britain may be safely accused of having an aged menopausal complex. I do not want to be unduly denigratory of our situation but I think we can learn from other countries and we have to ask if we are careful in gauging the appropriateness of their answers to our institutional and social conditions.

My only point about the United States as a model in this particular situation is that I do not think we looked at some of their difficulties. I think the Congress often has honeymoon periods with the President when it goes along with the President and does not, in fact, act as a very effective check. Then there are other periods when Congress decides to act as a check and absolutely nothing happens at all. These periods may last for five or ten years; so I think there are difficulties of deadlock and executive blockage which do occur in the American model.

The other model that we have of a presidential system with the parliament separate is the French model and I think it is helpful because it shows that this model does not always increase the power of the legislature. In the case of France, it has produced a weak National Assembly dominated by the President though what happens when the Assembly gets a different majority from the President, we shall never know. Or at least we will not know until the next election, and given M. Marchais we will never know. Which is a pity! Those of us who are political scientists would ask the French to do something about this so that we could at least find out how their system would work if it went through a normal alternation of parties. The French case causes me to be cautious about the presidential model.

If we turn to the parliamentary model in Canada and in the United Kingdom, I do not think there is any great difficulty about increasing the power of the backbenchers in a technical sense. I think everyone would accept that you cannot now increase the power of a modern legislature by working on the floor of the House in any kind of mass meeting or debating situation. The only way a modern parliament can become multi-faceted, capable of looking at a government in all its activities and keeping a check on it is by developing an effective communications system; and, again, I see no basic problem about designing such a committee system. For instance, one could say that a minister had to go back to the old nineteenth century procedure, then prevalent in Britain, where it was necessary first to get leave to introduce a measure and the minister or member had to convince either the House or a committee of the House that there was a case for legislation before the bill was framed. This allows Parliament to get in at the pre-legislative stage and talk about the principles before they have hardened. The government can also concede points if it senses opposition and can adjust its position before it has committed itself and thus lose face. When the committee or the House has agreed to the principles, the bill would then be drafted and have a second reading with a full debate on these principles. The bill would then return to the same committee which could not only consider each clause in detail but would also have powers to investigate and to hear evidence on the pros and cons surrounding the measure.

Studying the Problem

We have been studying this problem in Britain. For my sins I worked for seven years on the Select Committee on Procedure in the 1960s where we produced proposals for a select committee system of this kind. Like many other good proposals, they were turned down. They were turned down despite the advocacy of that great performer Richard Crossman, though one must admit that his support did not always help with the other members of the Cabinet. The reforms became classified as another of "Dick's ideas." One of our other problems was that the prospect of any reform was too much for Mr. Selwyn Lloyd, the Conservative spokesman on procedure and a charming man who always used to say, "is this a change?" When we admitted rather shame-facedly that it was, he said, "But you know, I am against all change." We soon became more adroit and would answer — "It's going backwards, sir, to what used to be the procedure in the last century" — and then he would cheer up, but only slightly. So, we never got very far with these proposals and they were in fact defeated. But what I want to put to you is that the problem was not one of technique, it was one of political will.

You will be interested to know that our latest Select Committee on Procedure will in fact recommend these reforms once again, [*Ed. note — reported on August 3, 1978 as House of Commons Paper 588-10*] buttressed by their findings during a visit to Ottawa to check on the results of your 1968 committee reforms. I must say, however, on the basis of my discussions here over the past two days, that I fear my parliamentary colleagues do not fully understand the Canadian reforms. My impression is that they may not have appreciated that your chairmen of the committees are selected by the government, that in fact committees can only deal with things that are actually referred to them by the chamber and that there are various points where government pressure is exercised on these committees. I am indebted to Professor Franks for enlightening me on these things which I will no doubt try to explain to the House of Commons when our Committee does report. [*Ed. note — Dr. Mackintosh passed away on July 30th, four days before the Committee reported to the House of Commons.*]

My point is not to denegrate what the Canadian House of Commons has done but to emphasize once again that I do not think the problem with this question of strengthening backbench control over the executive is a problem of finding or devising the appropriate institutions. It is a problem of political attitude, of political philosophy and of political will on the part of the government and on the part of the people concerned. The chief problem is whether such reforms fit in with the ethos of the political parties, and with their view of how the political system should work. What made it impossible for us to get these reforms adopted by the House of Commons in the 1960s was that our parties genuinely believe that it is the task of the backbencher to *support* the government, not to criticize it. I used to have this explained to me regularly by the chief whip and in very simple language — pointing to the division lobby and making derogatory remarks about my conscience, he used to pry and propel me (being a rather large man) in that direction. But, nevertheless, as I say, it is the ethos of the party structure that makes it difficult for people, as John Reid described so ably this morning, to take advantage of all the opportunities which even the existing procedure grants to backbenchers to exercise an effective hold over the executive.

Criticizing One's Own Party

Now, what can be done to break this? What can be done to get the view through to our politicians and to the public on whom they rely for votes, that it is legitimate and proper for Members of Parliament to be Conservative or Labour or Liberal and *also* be prepared from time to time on a committee to expose a mistake by their own government, to criticize it, to put it in an embarassing position and occasionally, at times, to defeat it?

You may not have noticed here because it is a trivial internal matter in Britain but we do have one Select Committee whose members have been doing this recently. This phenomenon was set up a long time ago as a Select Committee on the nationalized industries. A subcommittee looked at the steel industry and pointed out that the minister was not exactly telling the truth and that this year the Steel Corporation is going to lose about   500 million. I was very interested in the reaction of the minister. It was not, ''My God, what about the   500 million''; nor was it, ''How interesting!'', or anything of that kind. His reaction was to scold the Labour members of the Committee and to say, ''You are playing the Tories' game; you are playing the other side's game; you should not do this sort of thing,'' and pressure was brought to bring the government members into line.

How can we get it accepted that this investigatory function, this holding of statutory bodies responsible for their policy and expenditure is a legitimate activity for legislators in a parliamentary system and properly ranks ahead of a reactive and automatic ethos of supporting your party; that your task as a member representing your constituents has a broader responsibility and that within the task of supporting your party there is the sub-task, if you like, of criticism and control? Without imagination and courage and a sense of higher mission, we are simply seen as disloyal for not completely supporting the government and criticizing it. One is always open to the argument from the government — ''You are breaking us — you are destroying us — this is election year — stop it! — you are only giving comfort to the other side.'' How can one get away from it? As I say, institutionally there is no problem. The answer rests in an effective committee system, in which membership is secure and in which the members choose their own chairman, have adequate staff and have accurate adequate information. The problem is whether M.P.'s, parties and parliaments will be bold enough to create and use such techniques.

Representative Democracy or Direct Democracy

I think that the stumbling block, certainly in Britain, is that we are in a fundamental muddle about whether we want representative government or direct democracy. I am referring, of course, to a problem as old as Burke's *Letter to the Electors of Bristol,* as to whether an M.P.'s task is to put his own views and judgment at risk and then tell his constituents and accept their verdict or whether the M.P.'s task is to do in some sense what the party or the public are alleged to have imposed upon him. If blame for this muddle is to be allocated, I think the main fault lies with my profession of political theorists; we are the people who have not been clear on what democracy means. As a result, we are left with this real clash between representative democracy and direct democracy.

I think many people, certainly some of those teaching politics as well as among those practising it, believe that in some sense, representative democracy is a poor substitute for direct democracy. It would be better, they think, if you could actually consult the people — all of them, all over the country. One regularly hears this argument that proper democracy existed in Athens where the people all sat under a tree and governed the city state. Admittedly, the slaves were not there and the women were not there, but all the proper people were there. It is like settling business at the annual meeting of your club. In that situation the people are perfectly satisfied. That was direct democracy and as a result, representative democracy is an inferior alternative according to this view, simply because in a modern state it is not possible to get everybody together. They cannot all be consulted. Clearly, according to this argument, it would be better if Members of Parliament, once they had a whiff, an inkling of what the masses outside want, would then shut up and do exactly what the people want.

This whole approach is spreading in Britain and it is corroding our capacity to run a representative system. It weakens any possibility of having an effective capacity for accountability in the House because that relies upon the judgment and the action of the individual M.P. The search for parliamentary reform must never lose sight of this fact.

The worst example of this trend in my period in the House of Commons, was when it was openly said, first by Ted Heath in rather guarded language, and then later by the Labour party, that Britain could not join the Common Market simply on the vote of the House of Commons. We had a 2 to 1 majority on principle that Britain should join the European Community and Mr. Heath said that this was not satisfactory — we should not go in without "the full-hearted consent of the British people." The Labour party took it one stage further and insisted on conducting a referendum which, interesting enough, produced a 2 to 1 majority for entry, exactly the same proportion as there had been in the House of Commons. But only after the referendum had taken place was the decision held to be proper and binding. The dreadful implication of this drift to my mind (I am being very smug about this because I was the only person in my party to vote against the principle of having a referendum) is that it categorizes decisions of Parliament into two groups — the trivial ones or the less important ones which Parliament is entitled to take and the critical ones which have to be taken by the electorate — the people to whom the M.P.'s must approximate if they can. This idea of shifting the responsibility to the public is very catching. Those of us who pointed out that the device would be used again were proved right when the next difficult issue arose — devolution for Scotland and Wales. In order to get a few more M.P.'s to vote for the bill, the government said that by bringing in referenda in each case, M.P.'s who were unhappy about devolution could vote for the bill on the grounds that by doing so, they gave the sovereign people a chance to express their opinion and thus settle the matter. Some months later, Mrs. Thatcher said that if she had to face a crucial industrial dispute she would not attempt to settle it by coming to the House of Commons. She will have a referendum.

I hope that I have illustrated the difficulties caused by this confusion between direct and representative government. I hasten to point out that I am not talking about referendas being given a special place in a written constitution in order to entrench certain clauses. I concede that is a different matter. What I am examining is the proposition that referenda are a substitute for representative government. The disastrous implications of this tangent are now becoming only too clear in Britain and we will pay dearly for the course that we have embarked upon.

I have colleagues who voted for the Devolution Bill, who are now happily trotting around Scotland and England explaining why they are bitterly opposed to devolution. They think it would be a disaster. But they voted for it! One of them says he voted for it because it was in the Labour Party Manifesto and the public endorsed that list of promises by returning the Labour party to power. Labour got 39 percent of the popular vote which was just enough to give them a majority at the October 1974 election. The other M.P. says that he dislikes devolution but he voted for it in order to give the public a chance to turn it down properly at the subsequent referendum. Is it any wonder that the public might be mildly confused by this performance?

Limits of Consultation

The present situation is patently unsatisfactory and we must squarely face the core problem. If it were possible for us to consult everybody, to have real direct democracy — would that be preferable to representative democracy through an elected assembly? Do not think that this is such a crazy idea because Mr. Wedgewood Benn thinks it is technically feasible. He was once Minister of Technology and became fascinated with modern techniques and gadgets. He also fancied himself as a great populist and has toured the country saying, in effect, that a great day is coming when you will be able to do without these M.P.'s, these aristocratic sugar-daddies who sit in Parliament satisfied that they know what's best for you — there will come a day when after the close of the Coronation Street serial and before the 9:00 news, there will be your fifteen minutes for legislating the nation's affairs. The screen will feature Mr. "X" who will explain why certain amendments to the current bill being enacted ought to be rejected, to be followed by Mr. "Y" who will explain why these amendments should be carried. Then the public will have a few minutes to think before pressing the red button on your set for the ayes or the blue button for the nays. The big computer will whirl and the figures will be tabulated in Whitehall to show the national will.

Now, if you could in fact use modern technology this way to consult everybody and thus get back to one assembly of the kind that took place under the tree in the middle of Athens, would it be a better setup? I think we have not thought our way through this and my own view is that it would not be beneficial. I think that it would be a disaster to go out among the public to ask for support on a whole series of questions and get positive answers to the lot. Who would say "no" to more growth, full employment, stable prices, the general revival of prosperity and all such desirable things?

The problem about politics is that the system must put choices before people and these are usually complex choices. The answer to each choice situation involves a whole series of policies and programmes that are interrelated and must come out of a limited fund of resources. It is impossible to boil them all down to a set off between red buttons and blue buttons. That is nonsensical. Instead, we need to have party leaders come before the electorate with a coherent programme, with an attitude and an approach to these matters and a readiness to take responsibility for their overall judgments. Then the voters know whom to sack or reward at the next election.

I think we have failed to make the case for representative government, not as a poor alternative to direct democracy, but as the proper way of conducting democracy in any modern society. If we could do that, I think we would be in a much stronger position to try to get the sort of atmosphere into our political life which would allow our parties and our backbenchers in Parliament to make use of the techniques that are already available in order to get adequate control over the executive.

Theory of the Mixed Economy

Mr. Chairman, one further argument before I conclude and that is on the theory side. I do think that there is a point in going back to what Mr. Stanfield said at the beginning. We have not only failed as producers of democratic political theory. I think we have also failed on the economic side. We simply must produce a theory of the mixed economy which, without engaging in senseless curtailments of government activity, clearly draws the line at those aspects of private rights and economic activity which are not suitable for the state to regulate. I think without a chart that maps out the area for legitimate government activity that we will constantly be in the position of reacting to continual demands for action which in turn spawn political promises that set unattainable goals. In time, the whole process discredits the entire parliamentary system.

Anyone who has stood for election knows you get asked everything. I remember the last election — some fellow said to me, "What are you going to do about the divorce rate in Scotland?" I said, rather pathetically, "It was not my fault" (which he regarded as a frivolous answer). You are asked these fatuous questions (and politicians are prepared to answer them sometimes) because too many politicians are prone to accept some responsibility over areas of social conduct where only political fools ought to tread.

Summing Up

Please allow me to recapitulate. First, we must bring the larger or major issues back into the parliamentary arena. Secondly, efforts must be made to convince the public that representative government, as opposed to direct democracy, has real virtue. Thirdly, we must produce a definition of the area of competence of Parliament and, fourthly, by adopting and improving the techniques I have described, we must entrench the power of backbenchers to allow for proper control of the executive.

If all this were to happen, then we would find the pressure groups coming back to Parliament instead of going to the executive. They would come to Parliament because, in that very graphic phrase of Professor Stanbury's, "That's where the money is." The people who want to steal money go where it is — the people who want pressure groups to be effective go where they can affect decisions. If, in fact, Parliament began from time to time to affect the decisions of government, then the pressure groups would begin once again to channel some of their activities through Parliament. Parliament once again would become the forum of the nation, the place to which people turned and looked for some expression of democratic control over the government.

If we pursue the course suggested, we will have done something to bring Parliament more up to date, to bring it into line with current needs and to revitalize our democracy.

Looking at the alternatives, I do not think they are horrific. I am not a doom merchant, I do not think they are frightful. What would happen if nothing were changed, leaving Parliament to bumble along in its present state? The answer is clear. Quite simply, we would continue to be run largely by the bureaucracy. I do not use this word in a nasty sort of sense. If we come to the Scottish bureaucracy, I am so old that I have taught most of them now and they really are an admirable bunch of fellows — they are honest, decent, hard-working, but there is much that they cannot do.

What worries me is that there are many people in Britain who would prefer to be ruled by the civil service. This may sound odd to you but I have encountered tremendous opposition to the idea of an elected Parliament in Scotland coming from people who basically prefer rule by civil servants who are people like themselves, people to whom they can talk, with whom they can deal, where there will be no nasty elected element appealing over their heads to the public at large. This is what bothers me — the weakness of going on as we are doing, which is government largely by the civil service with occasional blowups when the party in power is defeated and a new party comes in; then there is a slight change of emphasis or direction, the odd referendum, the odd plebiscite, the odd expression of public opinion in a much publicized by-election, the odd activity of this kind as it were, taking the bureaucracy and giving them a jolt to the left or to the right. That is the sort of government that we will get if we do not do something to revive our parliamentary system. Now, as I say, it would not be a disaster, it is much of what happens at present, but I do not think it is satisfactory. I do not think it is satisfactory because it means that the gap between the government and the governed will continue to widen. The unelected will govern.

I do not wish to trespass on your own problems in the Quebec situation but we do have somewhat similar issues in the United Kingdom. However, I suspect that part of the public's response to the existing situation arises from this feeling that there are remote mandarins governing both Quebec and Scotland. No one knows where they are. In Scotland, it is said that they are in London (in fact they are in Edinburgh) but because they are unknown and cannot explain their policies to the public, they are not clearly held responsible. This sense of anonymous government has done much to fuel a political drive which I think, if it dismembered the United Kingdom, would be unfortunate. It would be unfortunate because it would only be an opting-out policy and would not solve the underlying problems. It would simply leave us with a Scottish Parliament equally ill-equipped to bridge the gap and the current lack of rapport between government and governed would remain. Devolution would not have solved anything since the basic problem would remain unscathed.

Then again, I am old-fashioned, Mr. Chairman, in that I believe democracy is a good thing because it asks people to consider the well-being of the whole. Democracy asks pressure groups and individuals to contemplate the wider consequences of their actions. If we continue to move in the direction of government by this partnership of the executive and bureaucrats, the real danger is that the public will think increasingly of government as ''them''; and then each group will cease to think of the whole community. Each bloc or faction will think only of what they can extract from ''them,'' of what they can get from the people running the show.

As a politician I spend more and more of my time going from one demonstration meeting or protest meeting to the next — from meetings advocating pressures, strikes, or active resistance of some kind or other. When I say, ''But look, what good will it do you to get this — other people will at once demand equal treatment. In any case, your methods if adopted by everybody, would reduce our community to chaos,'' the answer is always the same: ''This is the only way of getting anything out of 'them' — pressure is the only thing they understand.'' People who believe this tack will ignore their Member of Parliament. They will take direct action. I do not think this sort of talk and occasional action will produce a disaster. But it does undermine the values, the morality, the whole legitimacy with which we have invested representative parliamentary democracy.

I do not think there is any alternative to improving our Parliaments. There is still a tremendous fund of support for them. What I have noticed is that when anybody wants to set up a new state, when we want to set up a devolved Scottish government, when we want to set up a European community, people immediately say, ''Neither will be adequate until there is a European Parliament and a Scottish Assembly to exercise democratic control.'' I think it is now our task to explain how this control could be made truly effective and satisfactory so that the values of democracy, which I do not think we talk about adequately or promulgate properly, can be maintained.

Ladies and gentlemen, I am grateful to you for inviting me to this conference. I have gained an enormous amount out of it. It always helps to have to rethink one's position, even if late on a Saturday evening, and I thank you for bearing with me on this occasion.

QUESTIONS AND ANSWERS WITH DR. MACKINTOSH

Question 1

Dr. Mackintosh gave me the impression that he is optimistic that the role of Parliament in decision making can be strengthened. Given the complexity of our present day society and the fact that so many areas of decision making seem to be removed from public discussion, is it reasonable to expect that any Parliament can ever again really regain control? For example, the very fact of joining the Common Market meant for Great Britain that some decision making was automatically removed from the control of the British parliament.

At the international level, I recall your support in a separate forum for an international Parliament, with effective powers to monitor the very crucial decisions which affect the well-being of every individual. It was suggested that we need this kind of Parliament on the principle that, otherwise, we would have "destruction without representation." These are major areas of decision making that go beyond popular control and yet I do not see how we can retrieve any influence in the making of decisions even at the national level. Have we not, in fact, gone beyond the point of being able to regain any meaningful control by Parliament?

Answer

I am not suggesting that all such decision-making powers could be restored, but I think we could improve matters and halt the present drift in the other direction if Parliament were prepared to increase its effectiveness. Incidentally, could I just make one point about the loss of decision-making powers to the European community? This was a very interesting exercise because one of the things that besets Parliament, the British Parliament in particular, is living on its past reputation — a feeling that things are only as good as they used to be or better than they really are. This came out very strongly in the whole discussion of British membership in the Community because the anti-marketeers kept saying, "We in this Parliament consider and scrutinize every bill — we amend and revise and force concessions on all sorts of bills. This whole range of democratic activity will be lost to Brussels. We are forfeiting this time-honoured duty in joining the EEC."

Then we joined the Community and as proposals for legislation came from the Commission, they were laid before a Select Committee of the House of Commons for comment going to the Council of Ministers for the final step. In other words, the House of Commons is invited to comment before the matter is decided. It was suddenly realized that the House of Commons did not have the machinery capable of this kind of work. The Commons does not have the committee structure necessary to meet this responsibility. M.P.'s were living in a day-dream world of the past because, in fact, they were passing bills on the nod or through standing committees without scrutiny. Now they were being forced to assume legislative responsibilities for European proposals on a scale unknown within living memory with respect to British legislation. In that curious way, joining the Community has forced the British Parliament to pull itself together and to realize that if it is going to live up to what it thought it was doing, it must reform not merely its handling of European delegated legislation, but its handling of British internal legislation. In that sense, the experience has had a salutary effect.

That is just a slight sidepoint to show you how the realities have changed. Incidentally, every time one proposes a change in Britain there is this curious reflection of the past. One gets people saying that it would be atrocious to let Scotland run its own educational system because then Scottish M.P.'s at Westminster would be legislating for education in Bradford but not in Glasgow, for housing in Liverpool but not in Perth, and so on. Again, the mistake of this argument is that M.P.'s do not act in this way whatever part of the United Kingdom is affected. Those on the government side accept government policy in these matters, the opposition opposes and this picture of legislation being devised and rewritten on the floor of the House is once again pretending that something exists which does not.

If you are asking how could we get backbenchers involved in international decisions, I think if it were clear that in certain circumstances members could defeat or cause great difficulty to the government, then the government would have to explain and carry the Parliament with them.

For instance, we in Britain have no defence committee and what happens is that the government plays its part in NATO but tells Parliament as little as possible in the hope that they can get by without any serious dispute. In the long run, I am sure that this will be a disastrous mistake. In the first place, if politicians want the public to support a defence treaty under which citizens may have to fight one day, it is essential to keep on telling them, generation after generation, why this defence arrangement is necessary. The leaders must make the case. Secondly, voters want to know what the government is spending their money on! British voters are largely in the dark and this is because Parliament has no effective method of inquiry. We need the establishment of a defence committee with the power to vote funds so that the government could not get its Estimates on defence until it had convinced the committee and Parliament that the whole NATO exercise was worthwhile. This would be both a valuable and educational political process.

I think it could be done. We have got very close to it, because when the Chiefs of Staff went to see the government and said our defences were in danger, a number of us refused to vote for the Estimates. That is the only way of teaching ministers. Pressure is the only thing they understand. I think it could be done but only with a significant change of attitude on the part of the backbenchers.

Question 2

You have raised some interesting opportunities for intervention in a parliamentary sense, but it seems to me that the problem is that the backbencher challenges the government in that way. In this day and age that means that the M.P. is challenging the party leaders. He is challenging the people who control the party machine. How do we get backbenchers in a Parliament to make the challenge, not just to the government in order to have that kind of control that you are talking about, but to the party itself when the M.P.'s need the party machine? They need the party more than the party needs them. How do you reconcile party government and the strength of party organization with this idea of backbenchers having some real authority?

Answer

I do not wish to be patronizing but you have put your finger on a very important point and I would only slightly rephrase it. I do not think the problem is this tremendous "party machine" that one hears about.

I remember asking somebody, what was the average Eskimo family and they said to me, "A husband, a wife, two children and a social anthropologist." Now if you say to me, "What is the average Labour constituency party or 'riding' party," the answer would be that it is an old-age pensioner, a 1968 vintage leftist and an American Ph.D. student watching them! In many places, constituency parties are very small nowadays. The real problem, I think, is twofold. First, and this is very serious, is that the ambitious and effective politician wants to keep in with the leaders of his party because he feels that he has never been a success unless he has made it into the Cabinet. This was a section of my speech that I left out for time reasons, but I do think that one of the ways in which we must change the atmosphere in politics is to reach a situation where being a backbench Member of Parliament, combined with sundry other activities, is a satisfying job in its own right. There are two members of my party at the moment who go around and everybody looks at them with slight awe because they are the only two ever known to have declined a Cabinet posting. They actually were called in by the Prime Minister who said, "X, we need your help." The answer was a polite, "no." On these occasions you are expected to swoon and to have to be revived, but if there were more of these situations, if, for example, one preferred being Chairman of the Defence Committee to being Under Secretary for Tomatoes, this would be an absolutely splendid step forward in the direction of more parliamentary influence. So, one whole problem that has to be coped with is the fact that decline, like success, builds on itself! If Parliament is ineffective and the only people who are effective are ministers, then the legitimate aspiration of a backbencher is to become a minister, the best may well be appointed and so the situation reinforces itself. If, on the other hand, Parliament becomes more effective, then being an active committee man can become a satisfying job and the best people will seek such jobs and the Prime Minister's patronage will seem less important.

At one time, in the late nineteenth and early twentiest centuries the Prime Minister was *primus inter pares*. His leading colleagues in the House of Commons had their own money, social prestige and position so that being minister of this or that was nothing but a chore. They would accept a Cabinet invitation as a favour, but they were not falling over themselves to get a place. That is one side of the coin in controlling M.P.'s. The other side is the nomination in the constituency (not what the local machine will do as a vote-getter because the national campaigns are now fought on television). The real thing that matters is the nomination. Provided that the M.P. can control that process in his own area, he is all right. There is a real problem in the United Kingdom in trying to run without a party ticket because so much voting is habitual in Britain. Again, we have made some slight steps forward in this. For instance, because of his view towards membership in the European Community, Dick Taverne was refused nomination by his local party. He persevered and ran again and has twice been re-elected. Mr. S.O. Davies was also sacked, ran again and was re-elected. But even with this improvement in the record of independent candidates, few have held on long at that particular game. The M.P. must get another ticket if he gives up his previous ticket in order to stay in politics. The rebel M.P. must deal with these two ends of the spectrum, patronage from above and nomination at the local level. You are quite right — the M.P. must become liberated from both influences.

Question 3

Surely, the problem is that the public expect their M.P. to do well and to become a minister. If he is always acting as a critic he confuses party supporters while opponents would rather have someone else as their M.P. in any case. The real difficulty — and can you tell me how to get over it — is how to get one's voters to accept that the role of a long-term critic, especially if he is on the government side, is a worthwhile and proper one?

Answer

I do not know how one does it. There is no easy answer, but clearly one must try. There is a public attitude, certainly in Britain — I do not know if it is true in Canada — which makes it harder, and that is the idea that the M.P. could combine being a politician with something else. I say this with mild feeling because it is very hard to break through that particular barrier — to keep another job and be a politician which gives you satisfaction — which allows you to maintain this kind of independence.

I find that the public's attitude is that having been a Member of Parliament is like having had a nasty disease. Or, to use another analogy, one feels that if you want to join another occupation again, you must suffer through a "cleansing process."

The British public are a little confused in their attitudes to politicians. If it is their own M.P. and they have met him and he has done something for them, that is different. Then he becomes a person. He is on their side. If he is seen just as a politician in general, then it is a very unfortunate and difficult situation because one takes the blame but has none of the positive opportunities that come from being in the government. How we are going to break down this attitude? I do not know but, again, I would hope that it happens. One sees small signs of improvement certainly in Britain about this problem. There was a time when people used to say to me, "How sad that Mr. Wilson did not put you in his government," and now they say, "We understand why you did not want to join Mr. Wilson." I am sorry I did not produce a more adequate answer on this question because I cannot think of one — we simply must change these attitudes.

Question 4

I am delighted to accept your rejection of the need always to move up the ladder of preferment, but could you give us a reaction to the compulsory voting as they have in Australia?

Answer

In my basic view, it is a rather simplistic one. I am against compulsory voting because I think the right to yawn and turn away and to something else is a democratic right to be cherished. It can be a very positive gesture to say that I want nothing to do with any of you. I think the voter should be entitled to do this.

Question 5

In the first part of your speech you talked about using our upper chambers more effectively in the context of the royal reasons for bringing the nobility together. I believe you even used the phrase "corporate state." But, in the second part of your speech, you emphasized how we could better fashion the existing system to give backbenchers more responsibility over policy formation. Are you saying that we could reconcile party government sufficiently with our representative functions as M.P.'s so that we would not need an upper house?

Answer

No, I am not saying that. I think you will always have these pressure groups and interest groups so long as the government is doing so much which affects people and I do not think it is possible to go back on that. People will organize to deal with the government. I would like to see pressure groups coming to the

House of Commons more often because decisions could be affected by what happens there and in that sense one catches them both ways. One has them as interest groups and one has them making submissions to M.P.'s as decision makers.

Please do not think that I am also suggesting that there should be a new level of consultation with pressure groups. What one has to face is that this consultation goes on now. But at the moment it goes on largely in Britain between the bureaucracy and the pressure groups and they strike bargains and agreements between them. Then this is reported to the legislature or it forms the basis of bills which one must accept or reject as *faits accomplis*.

It would be a healthier democracy if those decisions were made, (a) where the public can see the full nature of the negotiations in terms of what was given away and, (b) if this were done in front of other pressure groups so that one knew exactly what was happening and had people on the public record.

Membership in the EEC, I am happy to report, has brought lobbying and pressure group activities more into the open because the Common Market practises open government. Therefore British pressure groups going to Brussels cannot behave as they behave in London where there is a convention of secrecy. If you represent a pressure group in London and you see a British administrator, strike a bargain and then tell your members, you are struck from the negotiation list because one of the assumptions on which negotiation takes place is that you never tell anybody — it is all done in private. What happens now is that these negotiators or the leaders of pressure groups (if it is farm prices, for instance) are only able to make their case in Brussels in public with the Commission, the press and anyone who will listen. They have to make their points and say, "We are wanting this for wheat and we are wanting that for mutton and we are wanting so much for potatoes," and then the Common Market Commission comments. Then the British government has to say, "Either we back our own farmers or we do not. We must decide whether we go half way with them or a quarter of the way with them." But, one thing they cannot do is to come back to Britain and say, "We cannot disclose what we said," because their statements are all over the newspapers! So, in that sense, there has been what you might call a 'creeping back' of open government from Brussels and again it is a trend that I thoroughly welcome.

APPENDIX

PROGRAM OF THE NATIONAL CONFERENCE ON THE LEGISLATIVE PROCESS, UNIVERSITY OF VICTORIA, March 31-April 1, 1978

Friday, March 31, 1978
9:00 a.m.

Greetings:

The Hon. William R. Bennett,
Premier of British Columbia

Dr. Howard E. Petch,
President,
University of Victoria

Dr. Michael J.L. Kirby,
President,
Institute for Research on Public Policy,
Montreal

Prof. William A.W. Neilson,
Conference Chairman,
Faculty of Law,
University of Victoria

Dean F. Murray Fraser,
Faculty of Law,
University of Victoria

9:35 a.m.
THE PRESENT STATE OF THE LEGIS-
LATIVE PROCESS IN CANADA:
MYTHS AND REALITIES
The Hon. Robert L. Stanfield, P.C., Q.C.,
Member of Parliament — Halifax

10:15 a.m.
Coffee

10:45 a.m.

Panel Discussion:

Chairman:
Dr. Walter Young,
Department of Political Science,
University of Victoria

Prof. Ronald I. Cheffins,
Faculty of Law
University of Victoria

Mr. Gordon F. Gibson,
Member of the Legislative Assembly —
B.C. (North Vancouver — Capilano)

Mr. Richard Guay
Member of the National Assembly —
Quebec (Taschereau)

12:30 p.m.
Lunch break

2:00 p.m.
THE CONDUCT OF FEDERAL-
PROVINCIAL RELATIONS IN A
PARLIAMENTARY SYSTEM

Prof. Donald V. Smiley,
Department of Political Science,
York University

2:45 p.m.
Coffee

3:15 p.m.

Panel Discussion:

Chairman:
The Hon. K. Rafe Mair,
Minister of Consumer and Corporate Affairs
Chairman, Cabinet Committee on Confed-
eration, B.C.

The Hon. Lou Hyndman,
Minister of Federal and Intergovernmental
Affairs and Government House Leader,
Alberta

Miss Flora MacDonald,
Member of Parliament,
(Kingston and The Islands)

Dr. Norman Ruff,
Department of Political Science,
University of Victoria

Mr. Arthur Tremblay,
Deputy Minister of Intergovernamental Affairs, (1971-77) — Quebec

4:45 p.m.
Adjournment

8:00 p.m.
COMPARATIVE ASPECTS OF THE
LEGISLATIVE PROCESS:
MODELS FOR CHANGE

Dr. Samuel C. Patterson,
Professor of Political Science
University of Iowa

8:45 p.m.

Panel Discussion:

Chairwoman:
Dr. Kathleen Archibald,
School of Public Administration,
University of Victoria

Prof. Ronald M. Burns,
School of Public Administration,
University of Victoria

Dr. John P. Mackintosh, M.P.,
Head, Department of Politics,
University of Edinburgh

The Hon. Robert L. Stanfield, P.C., Q.C.,
Member of Parliament — Halifax

Saturday, April 1st, 1978
9:00 a.m.
THE BACKBENCHER AND THE
DISCHARGE OF LEGISLATIVE
RESPONSIBILITIES

Mr. John M. Reid,
Member of Parliament
(Kenora — Rainy River)

9:45 a.m.
LOBBYING AND INTEREST
GROUP REPRESENTATION

Dr. William Stanbury,
Faculty of Commerce and Business
Administration,
University of British Columbia

10:30 a.m.
Coffee

11:00 a.m.
THE INFLUENCE AND RESPONSIBILITIES OF THE MEDIA

Mr. Geoffrey Stevens,
Associate Editor,
Globe and Mail, Ottawa Bureau

11:45 a.m.
Luncheon

1:15 p.m. — 3:00 p.m.

Three concurrent discussions:
**1. The Backbencher and the Discharge
of Legislative Responsibilities**

Chairman:
Mr. C. Stephen Rogers,
Member of the Legislative Assembly —
B.C. (Vancouver — South)

Mr. John A. Fraser,
Member of Parliament
(Vancouver — South)

Mr. Donald C. MacDonald,
Member of the Provincial Parliament —
Ontario (York — South)

Prof. Paul Thomas,
Department of Political Science,
University of Manitoba

**2. Lobbying and Interest Group
Representation**

Chairman:
Dr. K. George Pedersen,
Vice-President,
University of Victoria

Ms. Johanna den Hertog,
Director, Legislation and Research
B.C. Federation of Labour

Mr. Alasdair J. McKichan,
President,
Retail Council of Canada
Toronto

Mr. Andrew Roman
Executive Director & General Counsel,
Public Interest Advocacy Centre, Ottawa

3. The Influence and Responsibilities of the Media

Chairman:
Mr. David Vickers, Victoria
Barrister and Solicitor,
former Deputy-Attorney General of British
    Columbia

Ms. Catherine Bergman,
National Correspondent,
Société Radio-Canada
Ottawa

Mr. Bruce Hutchison,
Editorial Director,
Vancouver Sun

Mr. Pierre O'Neil,
Director of Société Radio-Canada TV News
Montreal

Ms. Frances Russell Murdoch,
Winnipeg Tribune

Dr. Walter D. Young,
Department of Political Science,
University of Victoria

3:00 p.m.
Coffee

3:30 p.m.
Concurrent Sessions:

1. PROCEDURAL REFORM IN THE LEGISLATIVE PROCESS

Prof. C.E. Franks,
Department of Political Studies,
Queen's University

4:15 p.m.

Panel Discussion:

Chairman:
Mr. Ian M. Horne,
Clerk,
Legislative Assembly,
British Columbia

Mr. John A. Holtby,
First Clerk Assistant,
Legislative Assembly,
Ontario

Mr. Jerald D. Yanover,
Legislative Assistant,
Office of the President,
Privy Council, Ottawa

3:30 p.m.
2. PUBLIC POLICY AND LEGISLATIVE DRAFTING

Prof. William Charles,
Faculty of Law,
Dalhousie University,
Halifax

4:15 p.m.

Panel Discussion:

Chairman:
Mr. G. Alan Higenbottam,
Legislative Counsel, British Columbia

Mr. Douglas Lambert,
Chairman,
Law Reform Commission of
    British Columbia

Prof. Richard Dole, Jr.,
University of Iowa,
Member, National Conference of Commissioners on Uniform State Laws

5:30 p.m.
Reception for registrants
University Centre

7:30 p.m.
THE FUTURE OF PARLIAMENTARY
DEMOCRACY

Dr. John P. Mackintosh, M.P.,
Head, Department of Politics,
University of Edinburgh

8:30 p.m.
Conference Conclusion

ORGANIZING COMMITTEE

For the University of Victoria:

- Professor William A.W. Neilson, Faculty of Law, Chairman
- Professor James MacPherson, Faculty of Law, Assistant Chairman
- Dean F. Murray Fraser, Faculty of Law
- Lorne Borody, Administrative Assistant, Faculty of Law
- Dr. James Cutt, Acting Director, School of Public Administration
- Dr. Larry Devlin, Director of Continuing Education
- Helen Fletcher, Continuing Education
- Lynne MacFarlane, Manager of Information Services
- Dr. Walter D. Young, Chairman, Department of Political Science

For the Institute for Research on Public Policy:

- Dr. Michael J. L. Kirby, President
- Dr. Louis Vagianos, Conferences Director